John Beilein at Michigan

John Beilein at Michigan
A Basketball Revival
Tim Rooney

McFarland & Company, Inc., Publishers
Jefferson, North Carolina

This book has undergone peer review.

Library of Congress Cataloguing-in-Publication Data

Names: Rooney, Tim, 1981– author.
Title: John Beilein at Michigan : a basketball revival / Tim Rooney.
Description: Jefferson, North Carolina : McFarland & Company, Inc., Publishers, 2020. | Includes bibliographical references and index.
Identifiers: LCCN 2020000922 | ISBN 9781476679211 (paperback : acid free paper) ∞
ISBN 9781476639154 (ebook)
Subjects: LCSH: Beilein, John, 1953– | Basketball coaches—Michigan—Ann Arbor—Biography. | University of Michigan—Basketball—History. | Michigan Wolverines (Basketball team)—History.
Classification: LCC GV884.B444 R66 2020 | DDC 796.323092/277435 [B]—dc23
LC record available at https://lccn.loc.gov/2020000922

ISBN (print) 978-1-4766-7921-1
ISBN (ebook) 978-1-4766-3915-4

British Library cataloguing data are available

© 2020 Tim Rooney. All rights reserved

No part of this book may be reproduced or transmitted in any form or by any means, electronic or mechanical, including photocopying or recording, or by any information storage and retrieval system, without permission in writing from the publisher.

Front cover image: John Beilein stoically observes his team during Michigan's exciting early season victory over North Carolina on November 28, 2018 (photograph by Marc-Grégor Campredon)

Printed in the United States of America

McFarland & Company, Inc., Publishers
  Box 611, Jefferson, North Carolina 28640
  www.mcfarlandpub.com

To CHASE and TAYLOR.
May you spend your days living the values described on these pages.

With a deep appreciation for the greatest editor,
website designer, wife, and mother all in one.
Thank you, LINDSEY!

Contents

Preface	1
1. The Right Man for the Job	5
2. Michigan's Basketball Past	13
3. Building the Foundation	17
4. Recruiting the Undervalued	23
5. The Fresh Five	28
6. The Continuous Cycle of Development	35
7. Not Just a Shooter	40
8. The Rebuild	48
9. Attacking a Weakness	60
10. Off-Season Adjustments	70
11. Remodeling	77
12. Broken Ankles	87
13. Defensive Growth	93
14. Finishing Strong	99
15. Taking Over the Big Apple	103
16. Late Nights in Wichita	112
17. Party in Los Angeles	117
18. Sending Cinderella Home	124
19. One Final Game	129
20. Thank You, Michigan	134
21. Underrated Once Again	141

22. A Contrast in Tempos	146
23. A Freshman in Name Only	153
24. The Calendar Turns	158
25. Culture Is the Only Way	165
26. The Pride of Lima, Ohio	169
27. Constant Adaptation	173
28. Spartan Battles	179
29. The Green River	187
30. A Trip to Des Moines	192
31. Going Back to Cali	201
32. The End of the Beilein Era	207
Chapter Notes	211
Bibliography	231
Index	245

Preface

When John Beilein recruited basketball prospects to play for Michigan, they would sometimes ask the head coach if he would stay for their entire career. "I plan to," Beilein would answer, but he always added the caveat "Plans sometimes change."[1]

On May 13, 2019, it was revealed that plans had indeed changed. ESPN's Adrian Wojnarowski tweeted, "Michigan's John Beilein has agreed to a five-year deal to become coach of the Cleveland Cavaliers." Unbeknownst to all but a select few, Beilein had secretly interviewed with the NBA team. The lifelong coach had engaged in similar discussions with the Detroit Pistons the previous year, but most had assumed that Beilein would finish his illustrious career in Ann Arbor.

Naturally, his exodus saddened the Michigan faithful. The 66-year-old embodied the platonic ideal of a coach. He was an incredible developer of talent who operated with a strong code of ethics. He was also the winningest coach in Michigan history. Beilein had inherited a program with a decade absence from the Big Dance and left it in the upper echelon of the college basketball universe.

Beilein's incredible legacy at my alma mater inspired me to examine the foundation of his success. I grew up in a basketball-crazed house, so the sport was an early obsession of mine. My father played at Boston College for Bob Cousy and continued to embrace the sport by coaching many of the youth teams that my brothers and I joined. We grew up down the street from B.C. and, as season-ticket holders, attended every game we could. Annual March excursions to the Big East Tournament at Madison Square Garden were formative experiences featuring Ray Allen, Allen Iverson, Alonzo Mourning, and many other future stars. Rumeal Robinson attended a rival high school in the Boston area; I still recall watching him sink the winning free throws in the national championship for Michigan—a school I was only beginning to learn about. Two years after that championship, I became captivated by the arrival of five fabulous freshmen wearing black socks and baggy shorts. Boston College's best team in my lifetime soon followed with a run to the Elite Eight, led by current Michigan assistant Howard Eisley. I was officially hooked on college basketball at a young age.

That early passion has continued unabated my entire life. When I arrived in Ann Arbor as an incoming freshman in 1999, I envisioned highly ranked classmates LaVell Blanchard and Jamal Crawford leading Michigan's next great team. A high scoring, closely contested loss to Duke just seven games into the season seemed to confirm the possibility. But the wheels quickly fell off, and my four years of basketball spectating in Ann Arbor were remarkable only for their utter mediocrity. When John Beilein was hired in 2007, my interest was noticeably piqued. I was well aware of his post-season success featuring aesthetically pleasing offenses. As a fellow upstate New York native, my dad appreciated Beilein's coaching journey—a stamp of approval that strengthened the new head coach's credentials in my eyes. It took a few years to fully establish himself, but by the time Tim Hardaway, Jr., and Trey Burke arrived, it seemed clear that Beilein's tenure running the program would be a success. When they were joined by a talented freshman class in 2012-13, that team's run to the national championship revealed to the entire country just how skilled Beilein was in talent evaluation and player development.

While Beilein was molding the Michigan basketball program, I was building my career in Major League Baseball. The 2019 season marks my 15th year working in scouting and development. I have a passion for learning how the best succeed in this field, which intersects nicely with some of Beilein's greatest talents. My interest in writing this book was a quest to better understand how Beilein was able to separate himself from the competition. His ability to project on players' capacity to grow and his aptitude for building a developmental program to promote that growth has served as an endless source of fascination for me. By the time Michigan's 2017-18 team had ripped off nine straight wins and was celebrating a second straight Big Ten Tournament Championship, I was inspired to begin work on this book. Beilein's obsession with "doing the next right thing" and his emphasis on adopting a growth mindset were particularly relevant for me because I was raising young children for much of his time with the Wolverines. I wanted my kids to learn the values that he instilled in the Michigan program. This book is my attempt to capture his unique blueprint for achieving success in an ethical way.

Fortunately, it was a story whose details I was already intimately familiar with, having observed from afar at an almost obsessive level. My professional background colored my understanding of many of Beilein's techniques and strategies. Once I made the decision to begin writing in March of 2018, I started carefully curating all the media I could find about Beilein and the Michigan program. It was a richly rewarding experience to craft the story while enjoying their incredible run to the national championship in 2018, followed by the successive team's season-opening 17-game winning streak.

This work examines Beilein's entire tenure at Michigan in granular detail with a particular emphasis on understanding *how* he went about achieving such success. The greatest focus is placed on his last two seasons, which I view as the ultimate culmination of his careful program building combining with his more recent evolution as a coach and person. I've tried to include a variety of viewpoints to offer the most complete picture possible.

I'm incredibly indebted to the work of those in the media; this book does not exist without their efforts. I lack a press pass and now live far from Ann Arbor, so the tremendous work of many local journalists shapes much of this book. The Michigan fanbase is lucky to have such talented writers capturing the spirit of the team. Brendan Quinn and the staff at *The Athletic*, Nick Baumgardner of the *Detroit Free Press*, Steve Kornacki at Mgoblue.com, Andrew Kahn of MLive.com, James Hawkins of *The Detroit News*, and the entire *Michigan Daily* staff have all unearthed countless interesting stories about the players and staff, providing a deeper understanding of the forces that shaped the program. National writers, podcasts, and videos have added additional perspective. Press conference quotes courtesy of transcripts available at Asapsports.com and video recordings posted on YouTube provide many of Beilein and his players' thoughts and opinions. Additionally, the writing and analysis provided by Umhoops.com and Mgoblog.com has been invaluable to gain a deeper quantitative and qualitative understanding of the team's development and to enjoy the shared experiences of fellow fans.

Statistical information from Kenpom.com (started and run by Ken Pomeroy) and Barttorvik.com (started and run by Bart Torvik) helped add analytical color to the team's accomplishments and style of play. These sites examine the game utilizing a per possession basis, to allow for better comparisons across playing styles. One of the simplest and yet most descriptive such statistics that the book will frequently refer to is points per possession (PPP). Just as it suggests, it measures how many points a team scored divided by the total number of possessions. As a rough guidepost, one point per possession is generally about average; this corresponds to shooting around 50 percent on two-point field goals and 33 percent on three-pointers. Both Pomeroy and Torvik then make further tweaks and adjustments to account for competition in their Adjusted Offensive Efficiency and Adjusted Defensive Efficiency metrics. These values allow for the best method of comparison between teams across the country. Individual player's Offensive Ratings are explained by Pomeroy as "the personal version of team offensive efficiency." Win probability is also referenced at times, courtesy of Bart Torvik's site; it describes a team's percentage chances of winning given a specific score and time remaining. A deeper understanding of their metrics is not necessary for the enjoyment of this book, but I encourage any curious reader to explore their sites to learn more. Additionally, all recruiting rankings listed throughout the book are from 247sports.com—arguably the most reliable national recruiting website and home to the work of Sam Webb, Zach Shaw, and others.

I've relied heavily on all of the above-mentioned sources to analyze John Beilein's tenure at Michigan and to explain how he built the program. My hope is that by offering an in-depth look at Beilein's techniques, readers will understand exactly what made his Michigan teams so incredibly enjoyable to follow.

Chapter 1

The Right Man for the Job

On March 8, 2017, a plane carrying Michigan's basketball team suddenly abandoned its takeoff plan at the Willow Run Airport. As Moe Wagner recalled, "Evacuation! Evacuation!" was shouted as the Boeing dropped its speed, careened off the runway, and smashed through a fence. "Are they worried this thing is going to explode?"[1] Wagner wondered. Once the emergency doors were opened, the passengers exited via inflatable slides flapping in the wind and sprinted away from the troubled aircraft.

Head coach John Beilein recalls, "I still remember vividly the motor running so loud in my ear, and the fumes from the gas still being all there." Before fleeing, Michigan's coaches and some of the players stayed to make sure everyone got off the plane. "I was so impressed by our kids," Beilein said. "We had Mark Donnal throwing the exit door out the window, getting the cheerleaders and the band off. Our guys were stepping aside and getting people off."[2] A post-crash report later issued by the National Transportation Safety Board discovered damage to the plane's right elevator. The pilot had noticed the effects of this when the plane failed to respond to his control as normal. A huge windstorm had rattled Detroit that day, possibly jamming the elevator. Although the plane was traveling at a speed considered unsafe to abort—and the copilot advised against it—the pilot chose to end the flight anyway. His decision probably saved some of the lives of the 116 people on board.

Physically, the only injury to the Michigan team was a cut on Derrick Walton's leg that needed stitches. Mentally, however, the players were limping. Senior player Zak Irvin made a teary call to his mother. The team's intended destination—the Big Ten Tournament in Washington, D.C.—no longer seemed urgent. The players considered sitting out the contest—and who could blame them following this near brush with catastrophe? Yet the Wolverines decided to press on. Accepting an offer to use the Detroit Pistons' plane, Michigan loaded up early the next morning. Moe Wagner remembers the fear that he felt on takeoff: "Getting on a plane again, so soon after our crash—I feel scared out of my mind. I think we all do."[3] He was temporarily cheered when point guard Zavier Simpson messaged a prayer emoji to the team group chat. Wagner, and several others, responded by reciprocating the sign. The plane landed safely in the Capitol and the players donned practice jerseys to take on their first-round opponent, Illinois. Due to the on-going investigation of the crash site, the basketball team was unable to retrieve its uniforms from the ill-fated Boeing.

Anxiety, lack of sleep, no uniforms ... it could have been enough to derail the Wolverines. Yet these factors seemed to have the opposite effect, gelling the team on the court. Eighth-seeded Michigan rolled over Illinois, Purdue, Minnesota, and Wisconsin to capture the conference championship. The team would continue its late season bloom and made it all the way to Sweet 16 in the NCAA Tourney.

The perseverance Michigan showed by getting back on a plane and winning the Big Ten Tournament was a trait that John Beilein had spent several years infusing into his program. So was the calmness and selflessness the coaches and players displayed when helping passengers exit a plane that could have exploded. John Beilein doesn't just live his own life by this moral code—he also makes sure that it defines his players. Team above self, constant incremental improvement, and doing the next right thing are all hallmarks of the Beilein era at Michigan. Of course, to appreciate the success that Beilein was able to achieve at the university, you have to first understand the culture that shaped him.

Beilein's upbringing in western New York instilled in him the values that he has spent a lifetime trying to ingrain in young men. As one of nine children in a blue-collar family in a blue-collar town, he came to learn the importance of work ethic and self-reliance. "We had nothing growing up, I mean nothing, but the family,"[4] Beilein said, looking back. His parents naturally served as an important influence in establishing his values. Speaking about his father Art, Beilein said, "I learned a lot from him. I learned that you've got to grind. There are no shortcuts. Just go to work every day."[5] He had similar respect for his mother Josephine, who was one of 13. "She competed for food on the table, who was going to eat. There were three or four in a room, three in a double bed. They were Irish/French families who came to dig the canal. Yeah, she was a tough cookie,"[6] Beilein said.

Service to family, the community, the church, and the country were all focal points in the future coach's upbringing. Josephine Niland Beilein served as an election inspector and town board member. She was also first cousin to the Niland brothers whose incredible story was the inspiration for the movie *Saving Private Ryan*. Bobby and Preston Niland died on D-Day storming the beaches of Normandy. Ed Niland was shot down in the Pacific and kept in a Japanese POW camp. Their fourth brother, Fritz, was sent home from France so that their family would not have to suffer any more losses. The sacrifices made by his family before his birth gifted Beilein with perspective and appreciation. "They had so much tragedy in their life. They were so resilient—we didn't talk about it. Now it hits me how unique that was and what great stock we all come from."[7]

A high school in Newfane, New York, gave Beilein his first chance to carry on his family's legacy of service. He became a high school history teacher and eventually the varsity basketball coach. Having played basketball for four years at Wheeling College in West Virginia (now Wheeling Jesuit University), Beilein was a natural pick for the job. However, his friends were surprised when he soon left his teaching job to become head coach at Erie Community College in Buffalo, New York. When Bob Narrish, Beilein's former teammate at Wheeling College, was asked if he had thought Beilein would become such a successful coach, he answered, "Nah, probably not. Probably a teacher."[8] Yet, after decades of coaching, "teacher" still seems the best word to encapsulate the man. In his time at Michigan, Beilein consistently demonstrated the ability to develop his players—in both their individual skill level and in their cohesion as a team. He sets high expectations and, with a patient yet exacting approach, helps his students reach them. He is known for literally teaching players how to properly pass and catch a basketball on the first day of practice—bringing to mind the great John Wooden's approach of teaching players how to correctly tie their shoes on day one. Beilein goes all the way back to the beginning and starts building the foundation properly, even if it means taking a few steps backwards.

This doesn't go unnoticed by his players. "He teaches us in a family environment, and is looking out for us. When you have that, you're willing to buy into anything,"[9] Muhammad Ali Abdur-Rahkman said.

Tim Hardaway agreed: "One thing that makes Coach Beilein really special is he's a teacher of the game."[10]

"He approaches everything like a professor,"[11] said Beilein's son, Patrick, who played for his father at West Virginia.

This is exactly how John Beilein prefers to be identified. "That's who I want to be known as, as a teacher and mentor, not the coach,"[12] he said at the 2018 Final Four.

Part of Beilein's success may be attributed to the fact that he never missed a rung as he ascended the coaching ladder. As was frequently mentioned during Michigan basketball broadcasts, he stands out from his peers by having never served as an assistant coach. His head coaching journey slowly and steadily stopped at every level of basketball. He ascended from high school coach, to junior college, to NAIA, to Division 2, to lower-level Division 1 jobs, to the University of Michigan, and finally the NBA. It's an unprecedented, step-by-step rise to some of the marquee coaching jobs in the world. And Beilein has earned every promotion by making an impression with his incredible basketball acumen, as well as his integrity, his ability to teach and develop, and the respect that he shows for others.

After joining the collegiate ranks at Erie Community College for four seasons, Beilein moved to Nazareth, an NAIA school, for a single season. Despite such a short stay, he remembers it well. At a 2013 Final Four press conference, thirty years afterwards, he fondly recalled, "My first game at Nazareth was at Brockport State (NY). Jeff Van Gundy was the starting point guard at Brockport State and his father was the head coach. Both teams showed up with gold uniforms. The Brockport State guys had to go back to their rooms to get their new uniforms."[13]

That incredible attention to detail has helped Beilein post winning records for every coaching job. Tommy Niland, Jr.—John Beilein's uncle and the athletic director at Division 2 Le Moyne—recognized his nephew's gift and offered him the head job at the small school in Syracuse. Beilein's son Patrick would later enjoy his own success as Le Moyne's head coach. During his time at Le Moyne, Beilein attended the 1989 Final Four when Michigan won its only national championship. One unique memory stands out. "I do remember this very vividly: I heard "The Victors"—I heard the best fight song in the world. Kathleen and I looked at each other and said, 'That is the best fight song I have ever heard.' That's why it's so eerie when I hear it today, that it ended up being my destination."[14] After nine successful seasons with the Dolphins, the senior Beilein received his first Division 1 head coaching job at Canisius. In 1996, he took the Golden Griffins to their first NCAA Tournament in 39 years. After the 1997 season, it was finally time to leave western New York for a bigger opportunity at Richmond. There he became the fastest coach to reach 100 wins in school history.

That record helped him land his next job at West Virginia. Beilein garnered national attention in Morgantown by taking the Mountaineers to the Elite Eight in 2005 and the Sweet 16 in 2006. His star player Kevin Pittsnogle was named to the 2006 John Wooden All-America team, and point guard Mike Gansey was a finalist for the Oscar Robertson Award. Beilein also had the opportunity to coach his son Patrick at West Virginia, where he scored over 1000 points. This was quite a turnaround from the dysfunctional program that Beilein was handed in 2002. His predecessor, Dan Dakich, lasted only one week on the job before leaving, fearful of potential NCAA sanctions. The Mountaineers did pretty well for themselves with their second-choice coach.

After nine long years without an NCAA Tournament bid, the Wolverines came calling for Beilein in 2007. He was so hungry for the position that he personally handled the substantial buyout on his contract at West Virginia. Former Michigan player Tim McCormick was on the university's search committee. He shared the excitement he felt at the time: "Michigan has had good recruiters and good coaches, but Beilein is the best basketball coach Michigan has ever had. His offense is creative and exciting, he mixes zone and man-to-man defenses, and he's won wherever he's been."[15]

Beilein made his intentions in coming to Michigan clear at his introductory press conference, saying, "We have one great opportunity here to put the University of Michigan basketball program back on a national stage and be national contenders." He certainly accomplished that, reaching the national championship game twice, and becoming the winningest coach in school history. From 2013 to 2019, no program won more NCAA Tournament games than Michigan, and Beilein helped develop eight first-round NBA draft picks.

A big driver behind this former teacher's success is that he understands the long game. There are no corners cut with Beilein. He carefully avoided the murky underbelly of basketball recruiting. While there was some occasional frustration among Michigan fans that the program didn't secure higher ranked recruiting classes, the great majority came to take pride in the values and standards that Coach Beilein upheld.

Beilein's integrity has also won him the reputation of a "coaches' coach"—a man who is deeply respected by his peers but doesn't garner the press clippings or the short-term success that could have been achieved by compromising his values. In 2017 his peers recognized him as the "cleanest" coach in Division 1 by a large margin because he always plays by the rules. That is also the reason why he served as the head of the NCAA's Division 1 Men's Basketball Ethics Coalition. University of Michigan president Mark Schlissel certainly appreciated the head coach's character, saying in 2018, "It's nice to have one less thing to worry about in the world, and having a guy like Coach Beilein responsible for such a high-profile thing at our University gives me great reassurance. He's a great mentor, classy guy, high integrity—he's the best."[16]

"Time is a friend of truth" is a quote that Beilein favors and it can easily be applied to his basketball reputation. With time, the larger basketball world came to recognize the skills that Beilein's peers appreciated. In 2018, he was named CBS Sports' Coach of the Year.

The offensive success of Beilein's teams was one of the factors that undoubtedly drew national attention to Beilein's talents. "Offensively, he's a savant,"[17] said New Orleans Pelicans GM David Griffin. As Michigan fans know, when a John Beilein offense is clicking, it is truly beautiful to behold. The Texas A&M Sweet 16 matchup in 2018 serves as a recent example, but there have been many others over the years: Nik Stauskas raining threes over Florida in the 2013 NCAA tournament and the team's explosive first half against Texas in the 2014 tournament come to mind. Three of Beilein's Michigan teams finished in the top five in the country in KenPom's Adjusted Offensive Efficiency—a metric that evaluates offensive success while adjusting for tempo and opponent.

Creativity is one of Beilein's most important offensive weapons. "I think necessity is the mother of invention," he said. "When I was a Division 2 coach some 35, 30 years ago, the three-point shot line came in. We weren't blessed with great athletes, but we had to find another way to win. I had four children to feed and had to find other ways to win. So I began to really watch the NBA, the Princeton style, the different things. Then I said, if ever I can get a job like Michigan, a place where I have better athletes, we're still going to run the same type of system because it will work. I think you've seen it with many of the pro teams and I think we were one of the first ones."[18]

That system is based on simple principles that have stood the test of time. His teams emphasize limiting turnovers as an important part of their offensive identity. Protecting the basketball is essential to receiving playing time. "We love to be able to get a shot every time up the floor. You can shoot a lower percentage and have a bad night, but if you get a shot every time, it's really a game of possessions," Beilein believes. "We also preach it every day. People don't want to turn the ball over in our practice, and people don't want to turn the ball over in games, because they know valuing possessions is a huge philosophy that we have."[19] That emphasis led to Michigan finishing in the top 20 in the nation in fewest turnovers per possession in each of Beilein's last seven years. In five of those seasons, they finished in the top eight, including the fewest turnovers per possession in the country in 2012-13.

Along with ball protection, Beilein promotes sharing the basketball with crisp passing. "We really value the assist as much as the shot. We talk as much about that. The other thing, to get assists, the pass has to be on time and on target," Beilein said. "So we've had pretty good teams that take care of the ball, but also value making the extra pass."[20]

Over time, with an adherence to those principles, he has honed his offensive system to get to his ideal five-out design that relies on consistent motion and the ability to read and react to what the defense gives. Michigan's 2013 and 2014 offenses were two of the best in history as measured by Kenpom—all thanks to Coach Beilein serving as brilliant composer to the sweet, sweet music. He was way ahead of his time when he built an offense based on tenets and principals that have since been promoted in the modern game and embraced by the analytical movement. "You're watching the NBA playoffs, and they're running stuff that we run. Now I don't know if they watched us, or I watched them,"[21] Beilein said in the 2018 offseason. Basically, John Beilein has been setting up open threes with creative spacing and limiting turnovers way before all the cool kids in Golden State were doing it.

As great an offensive mind as Beilein has, he's still been open to change and has searched out ways to improve his system. As the quality of athletes he's gotten to mentor has increased, the alley-oop became an acceptable replacement to the backdoor layup. Once he recognized that elite ball-handlers and decision makers could exploit mismatches, he liberally incorporated the ball screen into the offense. "The only reason I'm coaching now 43 years after I started is because I've always embraced change."[22] Beilein spends his free time trying to glean knowledge from others to make himself and his teams better. After visiting a number of NBA teams in the 2015 offseason, he said, "You pick up so many different thoughts. I come back not with 30 things, but with five or six things that I'm going to implement immediately."[23]

He's come around more and more to embrace analytical data that can help his team gain an edge. As strength coach Jon Sanderson said, "When I first presented him with data back then, Coach didn't receive it very well.... Now in 2018, he uses the data I present to him to 100 percent to make decisions such as how hard to practice. He has evolved as a coach."[24]

Arguably more impactful than any of these adjustments, is that Beilein ceded stewardship of his defense—first to Billy Donlon in 2016-17 and then to Luke Yaklich the following year. "I know what I don't know,"[25] Beilein said. Through that demonstration of humility, he was rewarded with consecutive top-three finishes nationally in Kenpom's Adjusted Defensive Efficiency in 2017-18 and 2018-19. After years of offensively oriented teams, defense became the backbone to Michigan's success in Beilein's last few years.

Coach Beilein has given young men guidance, but also the room to grow into adults. He has served as a father figure and mentor that understands life is bigger than basketball. He emphasizes that he loves "those moments where I think you see all your work has paid off. That young man has become a better man or a better basketball player, hopefully both."[26]

New Orleans Pelicans GM David Griffin said, "the level of admiration, and frankly, fatherly affection that his former players have for him is unmatched in my experience in basketball. I've never been around a player of his that said anything other than incredibly powerfully heartwarming things about Coach [Beilein]. He's like a fabric of their lives even after they leave him."[27]

The accolades and appreciation have come from all corners of the basketball world. An NBA scout told *The Athletic* that he believes Beilein "would do well at the next level because of his creativity and attention to detail."[28]

Boston Celtics head coach Brad Stevens said, "He's done an incredible job. No doubt, he's one of the best coaches at any level in the world."[29]

Detroit Free Press writer Nick Baumgardner said, "He's the most unique coach in the country I think. He's probably the best teacher in the country, he's the cleanest coach in the country, he does everything that you say you want done almost perfectly."[30]

It's for all these reasons that many have come to deeply admire and hope to emulate John Beilein. The best part is that he would have no idea why. He's too busy trying to do the next right thing, and he just assumes everyone else is too. But they're not. He's the rare successful public figure that we can tell our children to model themselves after—not just for the success, but because of all the virtues that have allowed the success. Athletic director Warde Manuel agrees. "He's a person I want my son around. His integrity is unquestioned—the way he is and the way he's operated for all these years."[31] And Manuel means that—his son worked as a student manager under Beilein.

The Michigan fan-base has come to love Beilein for all of these admirable traits. It's why he is the winningest coach in program history. And it's for all these reasons that, one day, we will be fortunate enough to see his plaque at the Naismith Memorial Basketball Hall of Fame in Springfield, Massachusetts.

Chapter 2

Michigan's Basketball Past

When John Beilein was hired in 2007, the basketball program's history of success was but a faint memory. The program's extended stagnation was particularly vexing to those who proudly remembered the glory years past. A rich tradition of great players and great teams colored the university's record books dating back to Cazzie Russell's arrival on campus in 1963. Head coach Dave Strack recruited Russell out of Chicago and Bill Buntin out of Detroit. With Strack's leadership, that talented pair won the Big Ten and reached the Final Four in their first season together. Russell and Buntin combined to average an incredible 48 points and 21 rebounds per game. The following year they repeated those achievements and reached the NCAA Championship game before losing to UCLA and John Wooden in the title game. That 1964-65 team finished 24-4, including 13-1 in the Big Ten—accomplishments that earned Coach Strack the United Press International Coach of the Year award. Russell and Buntin were both named All-Americans after the season. Buntin left to play for his hometown Pistons, while Russell returned and posted a remarkable senior season. The Wolverines won the Big Ten yet again as Russell averaged over 30 points per game and won the Associated Press College Basketball Player of the Year award. Before the New York Knicks drafted Russell as the #1 overall pick in 1966, Michigan's greatest star spent that final year of his college career at Yost Field House, drawing such large crowds that the university was compelled to build a new arena. The Crisler Center opened the following year and was nicknamed "The House That Cazzie Built," thanks to the renewed energy he had created in the program. Russell's number 33 hangs in its rafters to this day, the only number to be retired in program history.

Strack went on to land Michigan one more future superstar in Rudy Tomjanovich. He coached the Michigan's native's first varsity season before passing the head coaching reins to his assistant Johnny Orr. Tomjanovich made himself at home in Cazzie's house, ultimately being named an All-American himself in his senior season after he averaged more than 30 points and 13 rebounds per game. After Tomjanovich moved on, Orr's teams continued to steadily improve, culminating with a national championship appearance against the undefeated Indiana Hoosiers in 1976. Despite losing the game, Orr was awarded the National Association of Basketball Coaches' Coach of the Year award. When he decided to take the Iowa State head coaching job in 1980, Orr exited Michigan as the program's all-time winningest coach. It would not be the last time a Michigan coach moved on to a school with less tradition under unusual circumstances.

The surprising move to the lesser program meant his assistant Bill Frieder would move into the head coaching role. Legend has it that Iowa State had actually called Orr to inquire about Frieder's services, but once the head coach found out how much they were willing to pay he suggested himself instead. When Michigan faced Iowa State in the second round of the 1986 NCAA Tournament, Orr's Cyclones upset Frieder's fifth-ranked Wolverines. Orr would go on to retire as Iowa State's all-time winningest coach as well.

Frieder, meanwhile, finally got his team to the second weekend of the NCAA Tournament two years later in 1988. But it was the following season for which Bill Frieder would be most remembered—though ultimately just as a footnote to an historic achievement.

The Wolverines started the 1988-89 season with high expectations, ranking third nationally in the pre-season AP poll. Led by star Glen Rice, the team was stacked with talent including four future first-round draft picks. In addition to Rice, Rumeal Robinson, Terry Mills, and Loy Vaught were all selected among the top 16 picks in their respective drafts. The group won their first 11 games before losing to Alaska-Anchorage in one of the most shocking upsets in school history. After recovering to win their next three, the team scuffled along to a mid-season 5–5 slump through the heart of the Big Ten schedule. One can only speculate whether Frieder's attention was fully focused during that rough patch. It was soon exposed that he was negotiating to take over as the head coach at Arizona State. Frustrated by a difference of opinion with Michigan football coaching legend and all-powerful athletic director Bo Schembechler, Frieder had explored other options. Before the NCAA Tournament began, he announced he was taking the Arizona State job but would finish the season with the Wolverines. Schembechler's famous response was that "a Michigan man is going to coach Michigan," and he sent Frieder on his way, handing the keys to assistant coach Steve Fisher.

Schembechler then addressed the team with one of his memorable fire and brimstone addresses. "Bo Schembechler gave us the most unbelievable motivational speech, to this day, of my life," Glen Rice said. "He made us believe that we could climb the highest mountain, he made us believe we could run through the thickest wall." He targeted each individual and emphasized their role on the team, and demanded they play for the name on the front of their jersey not the one on the back. "We just heard from the mightiest Michigan person ever," Rice said. "How are we going to let him down? How are we going to let ourselves down?"[1] Sparked by the adversity of their coach bailing, the true talent level of the team rose to the surface and carried the players through the NCAA bracket. Four wins later, they found themselves in the Final Four facing their Big Ten rival Illinois for the third time in the season. The Illini were the only team to beat the Wolverines by double digits all year; and they had done it twice—including a blowout win at the Crisler Center to close the regular season. This time, a Sean Higgins put back with seconds remaining gave the Maize and Blue an 83–81 hard-fought victory and sent them to the national championship game. Even more drama waited there in one of the most unforgettable finals in tournament history. When Michigan and Seton Hall went to overtime, Rumeal Robinson was fouled on a somewhat questionable call with just three seconds remaining and the Wolverines down 79–78. The point guard then hit both free throws to clinch Michigan's only national title. Rice was named the tournament's Most Outstanding Player after scoring 31 against Seton Hall as part of a total 184 points scored throughout the tournament—a national record that still stands to this day.

Steve Fisher naturally had the interim tag removed from his head coaching title and was responsible in 1991 for recruiting the most famous freshman class in the history of college basketball. Chris Webber, Jalen Rose, Juwan Howard, Jimmy King, and Ray Jackson were dubbed the Fab Five and quickly took the nation by storm. Their star-level talent was matched by their brash confidence, which led to a cultural impact that has lasted to this day. They were recognized by their long, baggy shorts and black socks, which modernized the game with an urban flavor. By the time February 1992 rolled around, all five freshmen were in the starting lineup—an NCAA first. They finished that season in Michigan's fourth national championship game, where they faced a more experienced Duke team led by Christian Laettner, Bobby Hurley, and Grant Hill. The Wolverines lost that game by a disappointing score of 71–51. However, the team got a second shot at a national title the following year when they met North Carolina in the final game. That contest was most memorable for Chris Webber's mistaken timeout call. Trailing by two with 18 seconds left, Webber secured a rebound and hesitated—likely getting away with a travel. He then rushed up the court, picked up his dribble, and signaled for a timeout. Unfortunately, Michigan had already exhausted their allotted timeouts and was punished with a technical foul. Webber's error robbed Michigan of a final chance to either tie or win the game, and North Carolina walked away with a 77–71 victory.

Although the Fab Five failed to produce a national title, they remain one of the most iconic college basketball teams of all time. When ESPN aired its film *The Fab Five* on March 13, 2011, it was the network's most-watched documentary of all time. However, the group's reputation took a serious hit in 1996 when Michigan's athletic department became aware of reports that some players had accepted illegal payments. Their investigation revealed that numerous players had a connection to Ed Martin, a Detroit native who had known Webber and Rose when they grew up, as well as many other talented players in the city. Martin ran an illegal numbers gambling game at the Ford plant where he worked. Webber and others—well aware that they were shut out from the huge profit Michigan was making off their popularity—accepted the financial help that Martin offered, courtesy of his gambling gains. Notably, current Michigan head coach Juwan Howard was never accused of any wrongdoing.

Even after the dynamic group moved on, Martin continued to aid Michigan players with housing costs, as well as purchasing hotel and airline tickets so family members could watch their kids play. It's a tale as old as time in college basketball that continues into the present. In 2017, details of an FBI investigation were released, exposing a laundry list of programs with athletes that had been illegally paid. Such developments have triggered a national debate about whether colleges should pay their revenue-earning athletes.

Upon conclusion of Michigan's investigation, Fisher was dismissed for his involvement in 1997, and replaced by his assistant Brian Ellerbe. Michigan basketball then effectively disappeared from relevance for the next decade. Ellerbe's teams scuffled along, never finishing better than seventh in the conference. In 2001, shortly after Tommy Amaker was hired to replace Ellerbe, the school chose to self-impose harsh sanctions on itself for the Fab Five era and vacated many of the wins earned on the court during Fisher's and Ellerbe's tenure. Eager to recover from the long, drawn-out scandal, the university had hired Amaker as much for his squeaky-clean record as his basketball acumen. While Amaker succeeded in getting the program back on ethically solid ground, on-court success was harder to come by. After failing to reach the NCAA Tournament in six seasons at the helm, Amaker was let go in March 2007.

Once again, Michigan basketball was in search of a new leader. The lack of on-court success had been painful—especially when combined with the seemingly never-ending way the university self-flagellated itself for actions that were run-of-the-mill operations at most basketball powerhouses. The next coach was going to have his work cut out for him to renew excitement in the floundering program. It was into that void that John Beilein stepped.

Chapter 3

Building the Foundation

Never one to look for quick fixes, Beilein knew that Michigan basketball required a total overhaul. To strengthen the foundation, he started with Zack Novak and Stu Douglass—two young men from Indiana who were overlooked by most of the college basketball world. "We just wanted two solid kids that we could count on. Kids that ran through the doors at Michigan because they wanted to play in the Big Ten,"[1] Beilein said. This was an approach he had been successful with in the past.

As Michael Rothstein wrote, "He'd done it everywhere he had been with players not many programs wanted, from Darrell Barley at Canisius to Scott Ungerer at Richmond to Johannes Herber and Kevin Pittsnogle at West Virginia."[2] And at Michigan he did it with Zack Novak and Stu Douglass. By prioritizing fit over talent, this Michigan program was going to be built slowly and correctly. Douglass and Novak's successful careers at Michigan laid the groundwork for the program's more recent achievements.

Novak said that Beilein preached his rebuilding plan to him all through the recruiting process. "He was insistent on one thing: he had the plan to turn Michigan Basketball around. He had turned around every program he had been at before and he was sure he would do it again. He just needed guys who believed in him and his vision. Time and time again, he spoke about wanting 'good guys' who would do things 'the right way.' There would be no cutting corners and it would be a process. At the time, I honestly had zero idea how I fit into the equation, but I couldn't help but believe in his plan."[3] Novak and Douglass' careers started off positively with the two no-name recruits contributing significant minutes as freshmen and blending in with the more talented Manny Harris and DeShawn Sims. The 2008-09 squad beat UCLA and Duke early in the season, when each opponent was ranked fourth in the country at the time. They made the NCAA tournament and won their first-round matchup against Clemson before falling to Blake Griffin and Oklahoma.

The following season brought the arrival of John Beilein's first top-100 recruit at Michigan in Darius Morris. Barely noticed in that recruiting class was an overlooked big man from Detroit named Jordan Morgan, who would wind up redshirting his freshman season before eventually leaving his own mark on the program. Morgan had similar memories as Novak regarding his recruitment. He would go on to provide a similar degree of leadership as Novak through his time at Michigan. "I'm not sure I really knew what 'rebuild the program' meant," Morgan said. "But from the minute that I met [Beilein], he used to talk to me about rebuilding. Rebuilding a program. Building something special. Being a part of rebuilding that. And that was what made me want to go to Michigan in the first place."[4]

Despite those added reinforcements, the 2009-10 season was a disappointment, ending with a 15–17 record. In the summer of 2010, John Beilein and staff took their team to Europe to play four professional teams, while also providing cultural and historical perspective for their student-athletes. Perhaps most importantly, the journey served as an important team bonding experience. The coaching staff, in particular, was hard at work determining the values they wanted to define Michigan basketball. Although they had begun to find the right type of players to center their program around, Coach Beilein and his staff felt they needed to take the next step. "When I got to Michigan we were struggling in those first three years, and I realized I couldn't just lead by example," Beilein said. "I had to make an intentional effort to shape the culture of the team. So I sat down and I asked, 'What are the five things you value the most?'"[5]

Assistants Lavall Jordan, Bacari Alexander, and Jeff Meyer joined Beilein to script out those five things they valued most. Josh Bartelstein, a member of that team, wrote, "The reason Michigan Basketball is now an elite program has a lot to do with the culture defined in that conference room in Belgium."[6] The five core values they selected would come to define Michigan basketball: Unity, Passion, Appreciation, Integrity, and Diligence.

But one essential element was still missing. "Then we added accountability, because we felt that our team held themselves accountable as individuals, but that didn't extend to others around them," Coach Beilein said. "Our players were so nice that they wouldn't step outside of their comfort zone to tell a teammate, 'You need to talk more in practice, you're too quiet.' Or, 'You have a relationship that is toxic to you, and you have to end it.' We were not good at that, so we added it."[7]

Listen carefully, and you'll have heard those values consistently preached by the players and staff in their comments. Perhaps you've noticed the acronym UPAID on their warm-up shirts, serving as a reminder to all who surround the team. Those core values became the connective tissue of the program, linking players from different teams that never spent a day on campus together, and defining what it meant to be a University of Michigan basketball player in the John Beilein era. "We talk about one or the other every day. Every day there's something about one of those things, and that's helped us build our team culture,"[8] Beilein emphasized. That following year, Michigan would need a strong culture to handle the challenges they would face.

Following the summer trip to Europe, the basketball season got off to a good start thanks to a soft non-conference slate. Novak and Douglass were joined on the court by talented freshman Tim Hardaway, Jr., the son of the NBA great of the same name. But once Big Ten play began, conference opponents started to knock the Wolverines around. That is when the team had to draw on its newly created core values. On January 27, 2011, Michigan, with a lowly 1–6 record in the conference, headed to the Breslin Center in East Lansing—a venue they hadn't won in since 1997. This challenge initially seemed to invigorate the Maize and Blue and they led by as many as 10 in the first half before heading into the break ahead 33–27.

They maintained their lead into the second half, stretching it to as many as 13 on a Zack Novak three-pointer with seven minutes remaining. The Draymond Green–led Spartans stormed back with a late 13–2 run to narrow the lead to two with 1:47 remaining. Novak's passion to win was never more evident than during a timeout that halted the run. Fists clenched and veins popping, he implored his team to give absolutely everything they had. Brian Cook at Mgoblog appropriately termed it the "aneurysm of leadership" and described it as "the grittiest, twitchy, alarming fit anyone's ever had."[9]

To this day, Novak is amused by the attempts to identify his words. "My favorite is when everyone is trying to guess what I was saying. I've seen articles where they [wrote] he was saying 'we need to focus,' or 'everyone give your best.' That's not what I was saying. I don't think anyone can print what I was saying. And we'll leave it at that,"[10] Novak told Nick Baumgardner a year later. Backing up his twitchy outburst, Novak drained six three-pointers that day. But his co-captain Stu Douglass still hadn't made a single one when the Wolverines' lead had dwindled down to two with under a minute left to play. With 33 seconds remaining, Douglass inbounded the ball at half court to point guard Darius Morris. Morris eventually penetrated into the lane, drew some defenders and dished it to Douglass at the three-point line. As future NBA Defensive Player of the Year Draymond Green closed out on him, Douglass quickly and calmly drained it over Green's outstretched hand to seal the victory.

Looking back, that win on Sparty's home court stands out as one of the major turning points in the program's history. "If you write up a book on what changed Michigan basketball, it might be Stu Douglass' shot from that right corner three-point line,"[11] said teammate Josh Bartelstein.

John Beilein agreed. "The rest is history, our record since that game has been phenomenal."[12] Indeed, Michigan has won over 70 percent of their games since that turning point. That win completely changed the trajectory of an initially lagging Michigan team. The Wolverines went on to qualify for the NCAA Tournament and blew out Tennessee 75–45. In the second round, they were a last-second Darius Morris missed floater away from taking #1 seed Duke to overtime. Following the season, Morris decided he would not return for his junior year. He became the first of many John Beilein recruits that, thanks to Michigan's player development expertise, left early for the NBA draft.

Morris' replacement was an undersized three-star recruit from Columbus, Ohio, who the hometown Buckeyes didn't consider worthy of a scholarship offer. Trey Burke, son of a high school basketball coach and close friend of Ohio State star Jared Sullinger, would go on to have as memorable a two-year run as just about anyone in Michigan basketball history. The 2011-2012 team was a unique blend of the culture-setter types like Novak and Douglass that John Beilein recruited earlier to Michigan, mixed with a few higher-level talents like Burke and Hardaway. This team would push Michigan one step closer to reclaiming its role as a traditional power.

It didn't take Trey Burke long to demonstrate that the industry recruiting rankings, along with Ohio State, had completely underestimated his ability. He scored in double figures in four of his first five games, including dropping 17 against Duke in an early season tournament in Maui. Then during a victory over Michigan State in January, Burke led all scorers with 20. He would go on to reach double figures in every game but four on the season. Later in Burke's career, Beilein reflected on the impression the young point guard made on him. "What we saw with Trey coming in, we really loved his talent, and I could see it, especially in high school. I could see it in AAU. I saw a winner in high school," he said. "After that Maui Invitational, I had no doubt he was going to fill in beautifully, and he has ever since."[13]

His teammate Tim Hardaway, Jr., matched his scoring exploits to create a dynamic backcourt that was a challenge for opponents to defend. He averaged 14.6 points per game on the season to Burke's 14.8. In addition to the offensive firepower that Burke and Hardaway provided, this Wolverine team had a certain grittiness to it. With talent to keep them in most games, the senior co-captains Novak and Douglass made sure they were mentally tough enough to win many of the close ones. But those qualities were not enough to beat either of their primary rivals on the road. Overall, four of their five conference defeats came away from Crisler. Fortunately, Michigan was yet to lose on their home floor heading into a crucial Saturday night matchup against Ohio State.

There was a logjam at the top of the Big Ten standings come late February 2012. The Michigan-Ohio State contest would have major implications

Trey Burke, who would go on to sweep every National Player of the Year award in 2013, was the most accomplished Michigan player in John Beilein's tenure (photograph by Bryan Fuller).

for the conference title. Given the gravity of the game, it was slotted for a primetime start on national television. The ESPN GameDay crew was in attendance and promoted the game all afternoon on their network. During the introduction of the starting lineups, public address announcer Bobb Vergiels subtly reminded everyone that Ohio State had passed on Burke. "Starting at point guard, the PRIDE OF COLUMBUS, Trey Burke." In a hard-fought, low-scoring affair that Michigan led throughout, drama arose at the finish. Ohio State closed to within one score at 54–51 with under a minute remaining. Michigan had possession and milked some clock before putting the ball in the hands of its best player. Burke drove toward the hoop aggressively before pulling up and arcing a high bank shot over Jared Sullinger, his childhood friend and two-time All-American. Burke's shot found the bottom of the net and sealed one of their most memorable wins of the season.

That 2011-12 team won six of their last seven conference games to earn a share of the Big Ten regular season title, their first in 26 years. Hardaway and Burke combined for 50 points in an overtime win over Minnesota in the Big Ten Tournament. Unfortunately, that would be the last victory of the season for Michigan—their post-season aspirations fell short with a first-round loss in the NCAA Tournament to Ohio University. Ultimately that team suffered from two related flaws. They lacked depth on the roster—they struggled to find reliable contributors outside their starting five, and they were overly reliant on their two best players—52.4 percent of Michigan's offensive possessions ended in either Hardaway or Burke's hands. Michigan has not had a pair of players with a combined usage rate that high since.

However, by winning a Big Ten title that team claimed an important step forward for the Michigan basketball program in the John Beilein era. Douglass and Novak had fulfilled the vision John Beilein outlined when he recruited them. Douglass never missed a game in his Michigan career, playing in 136 of them and briefly becoming the school's all-time leader in games played. He was a steady three-point shooter and could be trusted to make the right read in Beilein's complicated offensive system. Novak played in 134 career games, frequently playing out of position at the four and battling much larger players in the post. He totaled over 1000 points and 500 rebounds for his career.

But the impact the two players had on the Michigan program went well beyond the stat sheet. They provided leadership and accountability in a program that had been lacking those traits. Their influence on the program was appreciated by some of the school's all-time greats. "The solid glue of the team was those two guys," said Rudy Tomjanovich. "There's going to be stars and bigger names and guys who score more, but the guys down in the trenches, they are so important to the team."[14]

Cazzie Russell shared a telling exchange with Novak: "I looked at him and told him if I were going into an alley to fight, he would be the first guy I would grab."[15]

They clearly left the program in a better place and, for that, John Beilein was delighted to demonstrate one of his program's core values—appreciation. "This was their dream job. They were going to be at Michigan for four years, they were going to make it work," he said. "The more guys you get with those things, who understand what it means to be a Michigan grad and how you get to be a good player, it's invaluable. They brought the two things together."[16]

Chapter 4

Recruiting the Undervalued

Beilein and crew established an impeccable culture at Michigan. But the secret sauce to the basketball program was Coach Beilein's ability to evaluate and develop players at a level few can match. It takes talent *and* the ability to develop talent to achieve the way his programs have. As impressive as Beilein's offensive acumen is, it takes time to properly teach his system. When his players struggle to understand the offense that he wants to run, then it can look pretty ugly out there. We've all seen it—early in the season, his offenses looked stagnant at times. The players were hesitant and unsure, like a bunch of freshmen taking an AP course—it just hadn't clicked yet. Fortunately, one of Beilein's key tenets of development is that his teams consistently improved throughout the year with a well-timed crescendo come tournament time. The culture he established promoted continuous improvement. His players got better throughout the season and over their careers.

Successful development hinged on Michigan recruiting the right type of players. To achieve that, they pursued a different strategy than most schools. Many successful college basketball coaches are content to defer to their assistants who recruit as many highly ranked players as possible. Their schools dole out scholarship offers willingly, viewing it as a way to get in the conversation of a player's recruitment. Whether that offer is actually "commitable" or not is an entirely different conversation. There's a strong argument to be made that this method attracts exactly the wrong type of person. That's not how Michigan operated.

Instead, John Beilein endorsed a different approach: "Offer scholarships very rarely, very rarely. We're offering only to those that we really feel fit our program and that they really like Michigan as well."[1] Michigan would not offer a player until he visited Ann Arbor and met with the basketball staff. Beilein considered that campus visit essential to confirm that a player fit with the culture the staff worked so hard to create. "We're looking for the right kids. The

Michigan fit—the young man that's embraced academics along the way and also has a passion to be a great teammate and be a great player,"[2] he said.

In some cases, this approach limited Michigan's ability to attract the highest ranked players, much to the chagrin of some segments of the fanbase. But former player Jordan Morgan believes that Coach Beilein would "rather fail putting together teams like that than to succeed and sacrifice on his integrity."[3]

Beilein frequently referred to advice he received from Rudy Tomjanovich, who told him, "You're building a team, you're not amassing talent."[4] Throughout his college coaching career, he sought out coachable players with high basketball IQs that would thrive in his intensive development program. "It's a thing that we try to recruit from a standpoint by talking with them, watching them play. In AAU it's tough to see that sometimes. That's why we like to see practices, we like to know their coach a little bit. Have they been coached before? Thankfully most of our guys have really good high school coaches, and that helps us determine what they can handle from us."[5]

While some critiqued him for not going after "one-and-done" talent, he insisted that is not the case. "I would never turn down a kid that's a projected one-and-done if he understands that it's Michigan and he should unpack his bag for four years. But [if] after one year, he's got great options, we'll drive him to the airport," Beilein said. "We've just got to make sure that guys are playing college basketball for the right reasons. It's a destination. It's an experience in your life you'll never have again."[6]

Because of the requirements to play in Beilein's offense, Michigan prioritized skilled players over raw athletic specimens. "We want everybody to be able to shoot and pass. Speed and quickness and all these other things are intangibles. But shooting is usually a prerequisite. We feel you can make bad shooters good. You can make good shooters great. But you probably can't make too many bad shooters be able to space the floor the way we'd like to," Beilein said. "I know our teams will always have shooters."[7]

Another aspect that set the Michigan basketball staff apart was its ability to project into the future. They were not concerned what players looked like as high school juniors and seniors; instead they projected how these players would look with age and development. The third party and "industry" rankings were pretty much irrelevant to them. As Beilein says, "We try to project whether a player is on the rise or if he's already where he's going to be. A lot of the [analysts'] early projections on players, I think, are made because the players' bodies are ahead of everybody else's bodies."[8] Perhaps that's why 59 different college basketball programs signed a McDonald's All-American during Beilein's tenure, yet Michigan was not one of them.

Beilein made a career out of identifying talented players that were undervalued by others. He aggressively pursued Klay Thompson, Kawhi Leonard,

Caris Levert, one of John Beilein's many development success stories, skies to the hoop against Delaware State on December 12, 2015 (photograph by Bryan Fuller).

and Gordon Hayward years before anyone predicted they'd become the NBA stars they are today.[9] His ability to evaluate was an essential component to the success of the 2012-13 team that went all the way to the national championship game. Tim Hardaway, Jr. (ranked 161st in the country on the 247 composite list) and Trey Burke (ranked 93rd in the country) had already proven their recruiting rankings to be especially poor predictors of their talent level. Jordan Morgan was an afterthought to most in the recruiting world. Those three were joined by an incoming class in the fall of 2012 that would leave its mark on Michigan basketball history.

Glenn Robinson III, Mitch McGary, Nik Stauskas, Caris Levert, and Spike Albrecht would all make important contributions their freshman year. As a group, they were graded the eighth-best recruiting class in the country—an unusually high rank for a Beilein-assembled crew. However, with the exception of Mitch McGary, they weren't necessarily highly valued at the time Beilein secured their commitments. Glenn Robinson, for example, got a significant bump as he blossomed after an early commitment to Michigan before his junior year of high school. Looking back on that recruiting class, Beilein said, "Mitch McGary was the only one that was highly acclaimed. It was the good old grinding class that we normally get. We just really hit the jackpot in judging their capability to develop."[10]

Glenn Robinson became the third player on Michigan's team with NBA bloodlines, joining Hardaway and Jon Horford. No doubt John Beilein appreciated what those bloodlines and having a positive role model suggested for Robinson's development, just as he had with Hardaway and Horford. It also speaks to Beilein's reputation as a coach that men who had played at the highest level were happy to entrust their sons with him.

Michigan's focus on projection was a key factor in convincing Caris Levert to come to Ann Arbor. That focus led Beilein to look closely at players' birth dates and incorporate that into the evaluation process. Given Levert's immature frame, many programs hadn't paid him attention and he originally committed to Ohio University. In a fascinating twist of fate, Michigan's tournament loss to Ohio the year before helped Ohio's head coach John Groce receive and accept an offer to take over at the University of Illinois. That left Levert without a coach and Michigan was happy to fill the void. "We watched Caris, and the biggest thing is that he has an August birthday," John Beilein said. "We don't care about what year a player is. We want to know his birthday. When was he born? And Caris has an August birthday. He came to college at 17.... So we looked at Caris [when he was a senior] and said, 'What would he be like if he were a junior right now? Would we be recruiting him? Absolutely.' So that was a no-brainer for us, actually."[11] That's the same Caris Levert that showed up on campus as a gangly, young and under-recruited three-star recruit and wound up playing in the national championship game at 18 years old and was a first-round draft pick three years later.

Interestingly, they also used age as an important factor in the opposite direction as well. Mitch McGary and Spike Albrecht both spent a year at prep school and played their freshman seasons at Michigan as 20-year-olds. They were brought in under the expectation that they could help immediately with advanced games that required less development. McGary chose Michigan over Duke in what was framed as John Beilein's first high-profile recruiting win. His talent and size were apparent to all. But what appealed just as much to Beilein was McGary's mindset. "Mitch wanted this team chemistry. He didn't want to just be a star."[12] Spike Albrecht, on the other hand, hewed a bit closer to the Zack Novak and Stu Douglass mold of prospect. Even Beilein was unsure if he should trust his instincts in that case, saying, "Spike Albrecht went to a prep school, and had no scholarship offers. I've never watched so much video of a young man in my life. I told our AD, you're either going to fire me for this or it'll make us look pretty good, but I'm going to give this kid a scholarship."[13] Spike would, in fact, go on to make him look pretty good.

Nik Stauskas was listed as the 110th best prospect in the recruiting cycle, but Michigan fans quickly became enamored by the YouTube videos he and his father posted of Nik draining endless threes in their driveway in Canada.

That shooting stroke quickly translated, but it wasn't all he was capable of. Television announcers developed such a habit his freshman year of insisting that he was "not just a shooter" that segments of the Michigan fan-base soon developed a drinking game around the utterance of the phrase. That freshman class proved incredibly precocious and gelled surprisingly quickly with the returning players. They started off the season with an incredible 16 straight wins and 20 of their first 21.

Chapter 5

The Fresh Five

It wasn't the first time Michigan basketball had experienced success with five freshmen. This group differed a great deal from the Fab Five in style and temperament, but the obvious parallel was frequently drawn by the media. Eager to carve out their own legacy, the 2012-13 freshmen began casually referring to themselves as "The Fresh Five." Along with their more veteran teammates, they drew attention strictly for their success on the court.

After the incredible 20–1 start, this new group of underclassmen earned the coveted #1 ranking in the country. They carried the weight of those expectations to Bloomington, Indiana, to face the #3 ranked Hoosiers. The two played in primetime on a Saturday night in an exciting game that showcased both teams' deep and talented rosters. Despite Trey Burke's 25 points, the Wolverines fell short 81–73. Although they recovered to beat Ohio State 76–74 in overtime in their next game, the Indiana loss started a 1–3 stretch including a blowout loss to Michigan State.

When they lost to a weak Penn State team on February 27, it seemed as though maybe this talented group had hit their stride too early, and that their dynamic freshmen had hit the proverbial wall. At that point, Beilein and the team benefited from the cultural leadership that had been put in place. "We had what I called the investment committee. It was four or five seniors that were not playing much," Beilein shared. "They're the ones that called a big meeting after a tough loss at Penn State to say 'Guys, I know we're not playing, but here's what we're seeing.' And that sort of changed the mindset of the team that was probably being a little bit too much me at the time, and not enough us."[1]

In their final regular season game of the year, they had one last chance to both avenge their earlier loss to Indiana and to force a four-way tie for the conference title. Behind 10 first-half points from Nik Stauskas, Michigan led by three at halftime. It was a game that saw seven lead changes, and the two teams spent a majority of the second half within one possession of each other. Indiana's Cody Zeller led all scorers with 25 points, including the decisive bucket with 13 seconds remaining. Michigan had one last chance, but after a Trey Burke miss, Jordan Morgan tipped the rebound back up on the rim. It sat there on the cylinder, ostensibly defying physics, as the basketball gods seemingly debated who had earned the victory. And then it finally rolled off as the clock expired.

That fresh heartbreak combined with a lackluster showing in the Big Ten Tournament, didn't seem to put momentum on the Wolverines' side as they headed into the NCAA Tournament. Fortunately, talent and desire were. The disappointment of a #4 seed for a team that had earlier been ranked first in the country was mitigated by the opportunity to stay nearby, with their first two games played in Auburn Hills. After dispatching South Dakota State in the first round, Michigan faced VCU in the second round. Led by head coach Shaka Smart and their famed "Havoc" defense that featured constant full-court pressure and trapping, the Rams had made a Cinderella run to the Final Four just two years prior. Despite just a single day of practice, Michigan cruised, looking like they had been preparing to face this defense all year.

"The way they played today, that was terrific," Beilein said. "They reacted and played against pressure like they've worked so hard to be able to do."[2] Rare to celebrate, Beilein allowed himself a chance to enjoy the moment with family that weekend. To the delight of many, he described exactly how he let loose to Nick Baumgardner. "We had subs. It was crazy. The whole thing was a knock down, drag out party."[3]

After that "wild" feast, it was on to the Sweet 16 and a date with the #1 seed Kansas Jayhawks. An unforgettable game provided one of the most memorable moments in Michigan basketball history and officially made Trey Burke a legend. At the half, Michigan trailed 40–34 and Burke had yet to score a single point. He set about changing that quickly, knocking down a three-pointer in the first few minutes after the break. But Kansas maintained a comfortable lead for much of the second half and wound up ahead by eight with just 82 seconds remaining. A three-pointer from Burke and a Glenn Robinson layup chipped it down to 74–71. Two Kansas free throws pushed it back to five, and Burke came back with a quick layup to make it 76–73 with 14 seconds on the clock. The Wolverines were in need of a miracle, possessing just a 6.7 percent chance of winning the game at that point according to barttorvik.com.

Michigan immediately fouled Kansas and a single make would have effectively ended the game. Instead, Elijah Johnson missed the first end of a one-and-one and the Maize and Blue had one last chance. Hardaway rebounded the miss and passed to Burke and Michigan rushed up the floor. "Coach called a play for me, but it was really to try to get into the paint and get a quick layup,"[4] Burke shared later.

John Beilein stands in the center surrounded by (from left to right) Tim Hardaway, Jr., Trey Burke, Mitch McGary, and Nik Stauskas during the 2013 team's NCAA Tournament matchup against VCU (photograph taken by Bryan Fuller).

Hardaway set one screen on Burke's man and McGary set up behind him with his own devastating second screen. That created just enough space for Burke to rise up from ten feet beyond the three-point line and knock down one of the more cold-blooded shots in NCAA history. Even with those screens, 6'8" Kevin Young missed blocking the shot by just a fingertip. After the game, Beilein recounted his side of the message that had given his players. "We were saying there's time for two, but if you can get a three, an open three, we're going to take it. He was open, but it was about 28 feet from the basket."[5] The off-the-dribble three had become a reliable staple of Burke's game; he knocked down three unassisted three-pointers that day and finished with a season total of 39 that is yet to be surpassed at Michigan.

Even after the colossal shot, Michigan had only tied the game and would still need to finish the job in overtime. They were up to the task, with Burke and McGary combining for 9 of the team's 11 points as they closed out the 87–85 unforgettable victory. Burke posted a double-double with 23 points and 10 assists. McGary matched that with a monster performance of 25 points and 14 rebounds. He had begun to play his best basketball of the season right when they needed him most. McGary would finish the season 10th in the country in offensive rebounding percentage—a rarity under John Beilein whose teams eschewed offensive rebounds in favor of getting back in transition defense. McGary's active play drew the attention of college basketball fans across the nation that March and was an essential component to Michigan's tournament success.

The Wolverines had seemingly hit their stride at that point and gotten back to their early season confidence and swagger. They brought all of that with them into their game against Florida with a trip to the Final Four on the line. The game was pretty much over before it started. Michigan raced out to a 13-0 lead. If it were a boxing match, the referee would have stopped the fight. Florida would never get any closer, trailing by as many as 24 in the first half as Michigan knocked down 7 of 11 first half threes. "Not Just a Shooter" Nik Stauskas was primarily just a shooter in this one, but a darn good one, shooting 6-6 from distance. "Nik played one of his best games all season. We noticed that he was hot early on in the first half. We tried to continue to find ways to find him when he was open," Trey Burke said in the press conference afterwards.

Stauskas, sitting next to him, acknowledged appreciating the extra looks. "It's been a while since I had a game like this. My teammates did a real good job of finding me when I was open. My shot felt good. So I was just letting them fly."

The magical ride would continue on, to Atlanta for the Final Four and a faceoff with Syracuse. Beilein and Syracuse's head coach, Jim Boeheim, were intimately familiar with each other. During Beilein's coaching days at Le Moyne, Boeheim closely monitored the smaller school's success. Beilein clearly made an impression and was indebted for the help Boeheim later gave him, "He assisted me a great deal in actually getting my first Division 1 job at Canisius College. I believe he had something to do with me going to the Big East at West Virginia."[6] Those Mountaineer teams battled with Syracuse many times, though Beilein came up on the losing side in each one. But all that interaction left Michigan's coach well-versed in Boeheim's challenging 2-3 zone featuring long defenders at every position, and now he had more talent and five days to prepare his team for it.

One determining factor in the game would be whether Michigan could limit their turnovers against a unique defense designed to create them. It quickly became clear that Beilein had prepared Mitch McGary as the key to unlocking Syracuse's zone. McGary consistently flashed to the high post to receive an entry pass and then served as the decision maker for the offense. Years later, after employing the same strategy against a different opponent, Beilein revealed how they had creatively named the technique. "We call it shortstop. We call it Barry Larkin for the great Michigan shortstop who played with Cincinnati. So we hit Barry Larkin, and Barry Larkin made the plays."[7]

McGary proved an apt student at playing the role of Barry Larkin and stuffed the first half stat sheet with six points, seven rebounds, four assists, two blocks, and—most importantly—zero turnovers. Michigan led 36–25. "We knew that was an area that we might be able to exploit if we could pass out of there," Beilein told the media afterwards. "We did so many passing drills this year with Mitch pivoting. We say, catch, pivot, peek, make a pass. He did a great job. That six assists is a big number for him. He's a big target in there."

The Orange narrowed the lead for much of the second half as Michigan's offense struggled to convert. Syracuse closed within one on a three by James Southerland with 41 seconds left, but they would not score again as Michigan won a low-scoring affair 61–56. The key play down the stretch was a controversial offensive foul taken by Jordan Morgan as Brandon Triche drove to the lane. It was exactly the type of sacrifice of his body that Zack Novak would have been proud of. Ever since his last-second tip had fallen off the rim against Indiana, Morgan had rarely seen the court. McGary's emergence had limited the former rotation player to spot duty, playing only three minutes per game in the tournament to that point. His impact on the outcome provided sweet redemption for a hard-working player well-respected by his teammates. "We just told him, if we win this whole thing, you're going to have a moment," Michigan senior captain Josh Bartelstein said. "And that's going to be the reason we win. And sure enough, his moment came tonight. I'm just so happy for him."[8]

Some of the loudest cheers in the post-game locker room came as John Beilein hollered, "How about Jordan Morgan's charge?"[9] After those post-game celebrations, the team quickly got to work preparing to play for the national championship against Louisville two nights later.

Led by head coach Rick Pitino, the Louisville Cardinals entered the game as favorites. Pitino had had some discussion about taking over the Michigan program years ago before ultimately signing on with Louisville. With the benefit of hindsight, the University of Michigan is incredibly fortunate that things worked out that way. Russ Smith and Peyton Siva were Louisville's starting guards and leading scorers. They were quite often the two smallest players on the court, but also the two fastest. Gorgui Dieng was their seven-foot shot-blocking center. But it was two players that didn't feature prominently on anyone's scouting report that would be the story in the first half.

Trey Burke got the Wolverines off to a 5–0 start before the two teams battled to a draw over the first five minutes. Then Spike Albrecht checked in, the floppy-haired freshman who Beilein had once joked may cost him his job. In his very first season, Albrecht had already carved out a role on a team playing for the national championship. But as Trey Burke's backup, his minutes were limited. Coming into the game his previous highs were 15 minutes and 7 points. He would play 28 minutes against Louisville and score 17 points.

5. The Fresh Five

He checked into the ballgame with 15:34 on the clock in the first half. Thirty-five seconds later, he knocked down his first three-pointer to put Michigan up three. A minute and a half later, he hit another one to stretch the lead to six. One minute later, another. In two minutes, 54 seconds he had made more three-pointers in the national championship than he had in any other game all season. With six minutes left in the first half, he made his fourth three of the night. Then he added a layup to push the lead to 12. From the time he checked into the game until that layup with four minutes left in the half, Spike's clutch play increased Michigan's win probability by more than 38 percent.

About a minute later, Louisville forward Luke Hancock made his first three-pointer. Hancock only averaged 8.1 points per game, good for fifth on the team, but he was far and away their best three-point shooter. Twenty-four seconds later, Hancock made another. Forty-five seconds later, his third. Finally, he made his fourth three-pointer, all coming in just one minute and 59 seconds. In that sudden burst, Hancock negated Albrecht's work and single-handedly knocked Michigan's win probability back down almost 34 percent. Their matching marksmanship turned the first half into just about an even affair, as Michigan headed to the locker room winning 38–37.

In the second half, the two teams continued to stay within a few points of each other. Just after the under eight-minute timeout, Trey Burke sunk a free throw to complete a three-point play that closed Louisville's lead to two. The point guard, who would go on to win the Wooden Award as the best player in the country, demonstrated why that night in Atlanta. He scored 17 in the second half to give him 24 in the game. He made big play after big play. With just under six minutes remaining, he threw a beautiful alley-oop from behind half-court to a streaking Glenn Robinson, who finished with his elite athleticism. That made the score 67–64 Louisville.

Less than a minute later, Louisville guard Peyton Siva got loose on a fast break with only one defender near him. He received the ball at the three-point line with Trey Burke a half step behind him. Siva took the ball to the hoop and elevated to throw it down, but Burke measured him up and timed his own leap perfectly. Trey Burke's left hand met all ball at the rim, and then pinned it against the backboard. It was one of the cleanest blocks at the rim that you'll ever see, and it was beautiful. Except then the whistle blew—somehow a foul had been called on Burke. "I thought I had all ball and timed it up pretty good," Burke said at the post-game presser.

Siva made the two free throws and the Wolverines were fighting uphill the rest of the way. They did close it to four with 1:20 left. But on the next possession, Caris Levert rebounded a Louisville miss—only to come down with his toe on the out-of-bounds line. After that, the soon-to-be-named Most Outstanding Player of the Final Four, Luke Hancock knocked down two free throws that essentially put the game away. Final score 82–76. Hancock finished with a career-high 22 points. The country got treated to a high-level national championship, that, had any variety of breaks gone the other way, Michigan certainly could have won.

Despite the tough loss on the biggest of stages, Beilein still exercised his core value of appreciation in the aftermath: "We're the luckiest coaching staff in the world to be able to coach those guys…. What is really unique, not only they love the coaching staff, the coaching staff loves them, they love each other. The word 'love' was used over and over and over. Two 19-year-old guys said, I love you. That's pretty deep stuff."[10]

The players shared more details about their heartbroken locker room. "Everybody was crying not because of the result, but because this team would never be together again,"[11] said senior captain Josh Bartelstein.

"It hurts a lot because we came all this way. We really came together as brothers. I just love every single one of these guys,"[12] said Stauskas.

"We fought for 40 minutes. There was never a point in time that we gave up,"[13] said Burke.

Despite the disappointing finish, the 2012-13 team had reached levels that Michigan basketball hadn't seen in 20 years. They started the season as a roster overrun by talented yet inexperienced freshmen and finished as a unified band of brothers that fell just one game short of becoming national champs. Even without that final win, their season will be remembered forever. "We won't regret anything. I think I'll consider it a championship team forever even though we came this close,"[14] said Beilein.

Chapter 6

The Continuous Cycle of Development

The downside of having a talented young roster that overachieved was that some players may be ready to move on earlier than expected. While John Beilein had lost a few players early to the NBA in his time at Michigan, he faced the possibility of hemorrhaging as many as four players from the 2013 Final Four squad. It was a problem that would become a recurring challenge going forward.

The reason the Wolverines faced this situation was a direct result of their success evaluating and developing young players. Beilein's keen ability to project on body type and skill level, as well as his consideration of players' birth dates outpaced the industry as a whole. Of course, targeting young projectable players that fit the system and the culture was only the first step. Those players then needed to be developed the right way—another one of Beilein's specialties. "John is right up there with the best of the best from a player development standpoint. Kids get better playing for John,"[1] New Orleans Pelicans GM David Griffin told Adrian Wojnarowski on his podcast.

Recruiting analyst Brian Snow agrees. "You can just look [and see] guys have gotten better at Michigan. There's no two ways about that. Guys have developed and they've produced pros."[2] Development comes in a variety of forms. At Michigan, Beilein's ability to turn players into NBA talent was a by-product, not a goal. As a matter of fact, they rarely even discussed playing in the NBA in the recruiting process—even though it would have been quite the selling point.

"It's a little different here because they don't sell you on the NBA. But if you check the record, people go to the NBA,"[3] Charles Matthews shared. Indeed, from 2013 to 2019, only Duke and Kentucky produced more first-round picks than John Beilein's program.

Michigan did use that carrot once players arrived on campus to help convey the importance of development and buying in to a winning team-first culture. "One thing that we do have is that they all want to be NBA players," Beilein said. "We try to convince them that here's how you get to be an NBA player: you have got to develop your talents. What do NBA coaches like? People that win. What do GM's draft? People that win."[4]

Beilein's development plan was a holistic approach that incorporated body and mind. Obviously, a great deal of time was spent on improving players' skill level. That started by teaching fundamentals at the most basic level possible to ensure that players had the proper foundation. "You've got to walk before you run," Beilein said. "Everybody wants to run and everybody wants to get there in a hurry but it's so different than that in basketball, in football, everything. You can have the greatest offense in football, but if a dude can't block or if the quarterback can't throw on time and on target, it's not going to work. So you've got to spend hours on the fundamentals to make sure that when you progress you can do the little things right so that you don't have to think about it—you just do them."[5]

That meant investing time in learning every type of pivot and passing the ball properly. "Passing with spin, catching the ball on two feet, different pivots. And it has to be that way every single time, I hadn't heard coaches stress stuff like that in a long time,"[6] Jaaron Simmons said.

David Merritt still remembers Beilein's first practice at Michigan: "There's this attention to detail. I remember our first practice when [Beilein] came in, we all thought [he was] crazy because our first practice—the entire practice is catching the ball on two feet, making very routine passes, and doing scoop layups. After practice everyone was sitting around and we were like 'What did we just do? We play in college, why are we practicing [only] passing and layups?' That was the entire practice! But as we continued to get through the process, we learned those are the small steps that lead to not turning the ball over, that lead to running offense."[7]

ESPN analyst Dan Dakich, who spent his college career under Bob Knight and whose son Andrew played for Beilein, said, "He stays true to the fundamentals. Every practice, they work on certain things: passing, jump-stops, pivoting. He doesn't deviate from that or get in a panic if something goes wrong."[8]

There were detailed shooting drills and reworking of form—they even had a special ball branded "the Beilein Ball" that encouraged proper mechanics. "Lots of coaches work on shooting with players, but Beilein teaches guys how to shoot," an NBA executive told Gary Parrish. "He doesn't just *work* with them. He actually *teaches* them."[9]

Then there was the physical development plan individually tailored to each player and the vaunted strength and explosiveness summer training that

With John Beilein closely watching his footwork, Isaiah Livers practices his jump shot. Under Beilein's tutelage, Livers improved his three-point shooting percentage from 36 percent in his freshman season to 43 percent the following year (photograph by Marc-Gregor Campredon).

came to be known as Camp Sanderson. Led by strength coach Jon Sanderson, the results were easily seen in how much players such as Nik Stauskas, Caris Levert, and Moe Wagner transformed their bodies through hard work and dedication. Sanderson literally wrote the book on strength and conditioning in basketball (Jon Sanderson, *Basketball Strength and Conditioning: Above the Rim with Camp Sanderson*, Malloy Books, 2016). The players enjoyed working with him, especially once they saw the transformation. "Within the first couple weeks of really working with him, you start to see the results," said Stauskas. "Once you see the results, it just makes you want to go even more. It was after two or three weeks into the spring, I remember looking into the mirror and already starting to notice a difference."[10]

Sanderson's ability to develop players physically hasn't gone unnoticed by staff at the highest level of the game. An NBA scout told the *Detroit Free Press*, "You see them as freshmen and say, OK, they're talented, they've got some skill, they need to get stronger and work on their body. Then the next year you see them, the first practice and you're like, whoa. They're stronger, they're more explosive.... That's one thing I've noticed when I've gone around to teams [comparing]."[11]

This elite training program gave Beilein a competitive advantage when identifying talent. "[Beilein] knows in the back of his mind that he can recruit and offer a kid that is physically not fully developed, he knows in the back of his mind that area will be fully covered," Sanderson said. "If a kid isn't explosive enough, maybe he needs to gain a little weight. Maybe he lacks a little stability or had injury issues, we can really develop you."[12]

Watching players grow at Michigan and leave as significantly better players than when they arrived was one of the more enjoyable elements of Beilein's tenure. "I see plenty of basketball players around the state, around the country and everywhere who resemble the same player as a senior that they were as a freshman," former Michigan player and current college and NBA analyst Tim McCormick said. "I've seen so much growth from Michigan's players—not only the upperclassmen, but from the freshmen—from when they arrived on campus."[13]

And finally, Coach Beilein recognized the need for players to develop as human beings as well. He understood that his players have much more going on in their lives than basketball. He taught them how to handle and value the challenges that they face on and off the court. "We encourage our athletes to look at the big picture and embrace adversity. We encourage meditation and prioritize the important things in life. We recommend our student-athletes speak with our counselors," said Beilein. "We introduce our counseling staff to our players in one of our first team meetings of the year."[14]

The impact that he made sticks with his players for the rest of their lives. His son Patrick said, "I can't tell you the number of times guys at West Virginia would talk to my dad about their lives. Girl problems. School problems. He makes everybody feel comfortable."[15]

All of these forms of development coalesced and led to the tremendous on-court results that Beilein achieved. He established a consistent track record of Michigan teams improving throughout the course of the season. This didn't go unnoticed by University of Michigan president Mark Schlissel: "When you watch his teams, they get better during the season. And they get better at halftime. What's that? That's coaching."[16] Sometimes, the results came shockingly quickly. That is what happened in 2012-13 when Trey Burke, Tim Hardaway, Glenn Robinson, and Mitch McGary all ended the season with an NBA decision to make.

Burke had wrestled with the idea of leaving after his freshman season but decided to come back and strengthen his skills. Now, as a sophomore recipient of the Wooden Award, he seemed like an obvious bet to enter the draft. Tim Hardaway, Jr., had given Michigan three consecutive productive seasons. He had his most well-rounded and consistent season in his junior year and he also seemed poised to take the next step in his career.

Whether or not Glenn Robinson and Mitch McGary would choose to enter the draft became the real unknown after their outstanding tournament run. Robinson had shown off his athleticism and leaping ability to anybody watching all season, but he had also only played in a supporting role as a freshman. McGary got hot at the right time, stepping up for Michigan in the tournament when all eyes were watching. But he had also battled injuries and conditioning issues for much of the season leading up to that point. After the team returned from the Final Four, Beilein met with each of the four early-entry candidates and encouraged them to consult with the NBA advisory committee. "That was our advice. 'Let's find out from the real guys that know it.' They have been so accurate in the past few years with their advice, to our players and many players. I do trust it."[17]

Once there was an NBA decision to be made, the coaching staff supported and guided all their players through it despite the fact that Michigan basketball would have obviously benefited from a player's return. They followed a defined process and provided their players with the facts to make the best decision possible. Beilein added insight into that process. "We are very truthful with them. We come to them first, to be able to say, 'I believe you should be looking at the NBA right now. I'm not saying you should do it, but let's do some research.'"[18]

As expected, Hardaway and Burke decided it was time to move on, and both were selected in the first round of the draft. Beilein attended the draft to lend his support to his players, humbly cheering them on from the stands. His help in their journey was appreciated. "Coach Beilein and his coaching staff did a great job of preparing us for this moment,"[19] Hardaway said after the New York Knicks called his name.

Robinson and McGary decided to stick around for another year. The two had formed a close relationship and were excited about the opportunity to develop for another season under Beilein's tutelage. "I still have a lot of areas to develop in my game, and I am looking forward to doing that at Michigan with this coaching staff and my teammates,"[20] Robinson said in a press release.

John Beilein was thrilled to have another chance to coach the tandem. While he was honest with all his players about their NBA opportunity, he also knew there are benefits to returning for one more season. "We've had some guys go pro that I think yes, you should go because this is a great thing for you right now," Beilein said. "But others have stayed around, and the ones that stay around are usually very happy that they've stayed around."[21] But despite all the attention that Robinson and McGary received, it was another rising sophomore who would make the biggest leap developmentally to lead Michigan in 2013-14.

Chapter 7

Not Just a Shooter

Nik Stauskas had enjoyed a successful freshman campaign as a starter on the team that made it to the NCAA finals, but he had primarily played off the ball. His summer attendance at Camp Sanderson and his growing comfort playing with the ball in his hands allowed him to make the massive leap from "Not Just a Shooter" his freshman year to one of the best players in the country as a sophomore. He and the other returning players were joined by incoming freshmen Derrick Walton, Jr., and Zak Irvin. Walton was thrust into the starting lineup immediately while Irvin served as the team's sixth man. Both would be relied upon heavily in their first taste of college basketball, and for the most part, both acquitted themselves well. Despite the heavy reliance on two freshmen, expectations were high, as Michigan began the season ranked #7 in the country.

Mitch McGary's season got off to an inauspicious start as he suffered a lower back injury in August and missed the first few games. He returned for a road matchup in Ames, Iowa, as the Wolverines suffered their first loss of the season vs. Iowa State in a battle of Johnny Orr's two former teams. Next on the schedule was an early season tournament in Puerto Rico that culminated with a disappointing loss to UNC Charlotte. Michigan shot 31 percent from the field against the 49ers and turned the ball over 13 times. It was becoming clear that success would not come as easy to this group as it had for last season's squad.

A week later, a trip to one of college basketball's premier environments would result in another loss. At Duke's Cameron Indoor Stadium, the Maize and Blue lost 79–69 as McGary played what would be his most productive game of the season, scoring 15 points and grabbing 14 rebounds. Nik Stauskas, coming off of five straight 20-plus point performances, was limited to just four. Caris Levert picked up some of the slack, chipping in 24 points, but it wasn't enough.

Nik Stauskas (left) and Mitch McGary celebrate a basket against #1 ranked Arizona on December 14, 2013. Both players were first round NBA draft picks following the season (photograph by Bryan Fuller).

While the 2013-14 team had yet to play with much consistency early in the season, they had an opportunity to demonstrate what they were capable of when they hosted the #1 team in the country, Arizona, on Saturday, December 14. In front of a sold-out Crisler Center, Michigan outshot Arizona in the first half to head to the break ahead 37–28. That lead held firm through the under-eight-minute timeout in the second half when Nik Stauskas made two free throws to make it 58–50. On the next possession Arizona rebounded three consecutive misses before finally converting on an Aaron Gordon dunk. That was a theme that would continue for much of the game. The Wildcats' impressive height and length created problems for Michigan on the boards and allowed them to get back in the game. Led by seven-footer Kaleb Tarczewski, they wound up collecting 17 offensive rebounds in the game to just six for the Wolverines.

The teams traded baskets and the lead down the stretch. With just under two minutes left, Mitch McGary sunk two free throws to take a one-point lead. While nobody could have guessed it at the time, those were the last points he would ever score in a Maize and Blue uniform. Arizona took back the lead and made their free throws the rest of the way to win a close one 72–70. Although the loss was disappointing, the Wolverines had proven to themselves they could play with the best in the country. Unfortunately, McGary's back issue had flared up again, and he would eventually require season-ending surgery on January 7.

McGary's talent would be tough to replace, but Michigan had a fifth-year senior waiting on the bench who was up to the challenge. Similar to the end of last season, Jordan Morgan had lost his spot in the starting lineup this year. Although he was frustrated that he wasn't contributing more, he stayed positive for the good of the team. Morgan was rewarded for his patience in the Wolverines' next outing against Stanford, playing 24 minutes. The following game, he moved into the starting lineup, and remained there for the rest of his final season in Ann Arbor. His highly efficient offensive game, built around finishing his teammate's feeds at the rim, allowed him to post a robust Offensive Rating of 128.2, making him the 26th most efficient scorer in the country according to Kenpom's metrics.

Revived by Morgan's contributions and the team's newfound confidence, Michigan rattled off ten straight victories after the Arizona game. Eight of those wins were conference games, including two duels on the road against rivals who were ranked third in the country at the time of the games. On January 18, the Wolverines traveled to Madison and knocked off Wisconsin 77–70. Michigan took the lead two minutes into the game and held on throughout, pushing the lead as high as 15 in the second half. But the challenges of the Kohl Center road environment resurfaced long enough for the Badgers to close within one on a Ben Brust layup. Nik Stauskas answered with a beautiful step-back three with under a minute remaining to ice the victory. He scored Michigan's last 11 points of the game as part of a 23-point performance. Caris Levert added 20 of his own.

That duo was also lethal in East Lansing the following week, combining for 36 points. Freshman Derrick Walton scored 19, including calmly knocking down nine of ten free throws, to seal the 80–75 win. As they left the court afterwards, Nik Stauskas blew kisses to the Breslin Center crowd. Stauskas had stepped up when Michigan needed him, making five out of six three-pointers. "He hit some daggers that were tough shots with Gary [Harris] all over him," Beilein said. "It was a great matchup of two really good players, and that was a pretty efficient game by Nik."[1]

Ranked #10 in the country, the team was riding high until they suffered a mid-season slump, losing three out of five. But they quickly recovered with a second win over Michigan State, led by a combined 63 points from Stauskas, Levert, and Robinson. That victory kicked off a five-game winning streak to close out the regular season with a 15–3 conference record. The final win came against Indiana at home and featured a special pregame ceremony for Jordan Morgan. He had become a fan favorite for his hard work and grinder mentality. Morgan had been overlooked coming out of high school and he needed a redshirt year just to add enough physicality to compete in the Big Ten. His contributions often went beyond what showed up in the box score, and he served as a great teammate even when his playing time fluctuated. He passed Stu Douglass by the end of the season as the program's all-time leader in games played and also finished as the program's career leader in field-goal percentage at 63.1 percent. Morgan graduated with honors in engineering and was pursuing his master's degree during his redshirt senior year.

After the heartwarming ceremony, he gave the Crisler Center one last effort to remember. Morgan tied his career high with 15 points and posted his first double-double of the season with 10 rebounds, helping lead Michigan to an 84–80 victory. The win earned the program their second Big Ten champion-ship under John Beilein, and the Wolverines entered the conference tournament as the #1 seed for the first time in school history. They defeated Illinois and Ohio State in Indianapolis but couldn't take down Michigan State for a third time in the season, losing 69–55 in the tournament final.

John Beilein applauds in the background as Jordan Morgan triumphantly hoists the Big Ten Championship trophy in his final game at Crisler Center (photograph by Bryan Fuller).

The 2013-14 team's regular season was an unmitigated success. Nik Stauskas' evolution took his game to another level, and he was rewarded as Big Ten Player of the Year, averaging 17.5 points per game while shooting 44.2 percent from three. He had pulled off the impressive task of improving his offensive efficiency despite drawing greater attention from opposing defenses as Michigan's focal point. The offense frequently ran though the ball-screen with the ball in Stauskas' hands. When he passed out of it, the Wolverines' offense graded out in the 94th percentile in the country on those

Michigan football great Charles Woodson crouches in front of (left to right) Spike Albrecht, Cole McConnell, Brad Anlauf, Jon Horford, Caris Levert, Mark Donnal, Derrick Walton, Zak Irvin, Glenn Robinson, and Jordan Morgan after the team clinched the 2014 Big Ten Championship (photograph by Bryan Fuller).

possessions.[2] When he held onto the ball, he was one of the most efficient scorers anywhere. He had the ability to drive, stop on a dime and pull up, or he could step back in rhythm to drain a shot from anywhere on the court. He was most definitely not just a shooter.

Caris Levert also took a significant step forward after playing a small role his freshman year. He and Glenn Robinson served as Stauskas' sidekicks, both averaging about 13 points and four rebounds per game. Levert frequently guarded the opposition's best player, covering up for Stauskas' primary weakness and allowing him to conserve his energy for the offensive end. Walton and Irvin filled their roles, each knocking down over 40 percent of their three-pointers. Jordan Morgan was the reliable rock in the middle, while Jon Horford and Spike Albrecht rounded out the rotation. As a team they shot 40 percent from three-point land and had the third-best offense in the country according to Kenpom.

On Selection Sunday, the group received a #2 seed in the NCAA Tournament, putting them in good position to make a run. The first stop was Milwaukee to face the Wofford Terriers. On the opening Thursday of the tournament, the Wolverines took care of business and easily dispatched the

Terriers 57–40. In the second round against Texas and their coach Rick Barnes, viewers were treated to a John Beilein offense operating at peak performance. With consistent ball movement and spacing, Michigan found open shooters and knocked down 14 three-pointers. After one particularly hot stretch in the first half, the Longhorn Network twitter account was prompted to send out a shruggy emoji to acknowledge that Texas was essentially helpless against such a hot-shooting opponent. The Wolverines had opened up an 18-point lead that they would never relinquish, winning 79–65. That win was the 700th of John Beilein's career.

Humming along at a high level, Michigan and John Beilein had five days to prepare for the #7 seed University of Tennessee in a Sweet 16 matchup. Michigan quickly asserted itself in the early going, looking like the higher seed that they were. They controlled most of the first half, shooting 16 for 26 and taking a 45–34 lead into the locker room.

With just over two minutes left in the game, a Jordan Morgan dunk pushed the lead to eight and Michigan seemed comfortably in control. Tennessee's leading scorer in the game, Jordan McRae, quickly answered with a three-point play. And all of a sudden, the turnovers began. A program that had built much of its success on protecting the ball suddenly seemed unable to do so. Two turnovers and a missed shot were followed by a Tennessee basket to close it to three. Then Michigan received a temporary break as a foul was whistled when it appeared Caris Levert had lost the ball out of bounds. That good fortune was quickly for naught as Glenn Robinson immediately turned it over leading to a Jordan McRae hoop to make it a one-point game with 10 seconds left.

On the ensuing inbounds pass, Levert's foot stepped on the out-of-bounds line as he received the ball, giving it right back to the Volunteers. That made it four straight turnovers and there now seemed to be a legitimate chance Tennessee was going to win a game in which they had barely a 2 percent chance to win moments before. They took the ball out with nine seconds remaining underneath their own hoop, needing only one more bucket to knock Michigan out. Consecutive timeouts by both coaches afforded the Wolverines a bit of a reset, but they still needed somebody to step up and make a defensive stop. And who better for that job than a fifth-year senior that had struggled to find minutes earlier in the year?

Tennessee's plan was simple; they inbounded the ball to Jarnell Stokes so that he could post up on Jordan Morgan. Stokes took one dribble and put his shoulder down, only to have it meet the center of Morgan's chest, who had already beaten him to the spot. Just as he had done the year prior against Syracuse in a pivotal situation in the NCAA Tournament, and just as he had done countless other times throughout his career, there was Jordan Morgan willing to take a charge for the good of the team. The referee got a tough call right; charge on Tennessee, Michigan ball. A Stauskas free throw finished out the win 73–71.

Morgan personified all the great elements of the culture that Beilein and crew had carefully built. For him to once again have such an outsized impact on a crucial post-season win seemed quite apropos. Morgan's explanation in the press conference afterwards also felt true to form. "They set a screen for him to come open, so I knew that the play was going to be for him. And I just know he likes to play bully ball," he said. "I don't know. I just was there. It's just something I do. I take charges. That's what I do."

Beilein had been lauding his senior leader all season. "He's guarded some pretty good players. You see why last year he was named to the first team All-Defensive team," he said. "You can see his engineering degree all the time. He works angles that probably other opponents don't know he's working at."[3]

Michigan had been lucky to survive the late-game sloppiness they displayed in the Tennessee game. However, their next opponent was unlikely to be as forgiving. Kentucky was as talented as any team in the country even though their #8 seed didn't reflect it. John Calipari had made a habit of recruiting "one and done" freshmen at Kentucky and was having success with the strategy. His current roster featured seven players that were McDonald's All-Americans in high school. They had struggled in the regular season but seemed to be getting hot at the perfect time. Despite starting five freshmen, Kentucky had taken down an undefeated and #1 seeded Wichita State team in the second round.

For just the second time all season (the first having been against Texas), the young Wolverines were the more experienced team. That experience may have helped them race out to a 9–2 lead in the first few minutes. They maintained that lead much of the first half, lengthening it to as many as 10 with five minutes before the break. That spread was closed by a late Kentucky run and, after a well-played first half, the two teams had drawn even at 37. Nik Stauskas led Michigan with an impressive 18 of their 37.

The second half featured much of the same; two talented teams playing at peak form offensively. Every run that either team made seemed to lead to a big shot pulling the opposition right back into the contest. Kentucky took control early in the second half before Michigan battled back. Three consecutive dunks by Nik Stauskas, Glenn Robinson, and Jon Horford gave the Maize and Blue a 55–51 lead with 11:27 left to play. The Wildcats responded with an 11–0 run over the next five minutes.

Back and forth they went until Aaron Harrison hit his third three-pointer of the contest to give Kentucky a 72–67 lead with two minutes on the clock. Glenn Robinson responded with his own three and then Michigan's defense drew a shot clock violation to regain possession. Trailing by two, Derrick Walton brought the ball up court and handed off to Michigan's best player,

Nik Stauskas. Stauskas drove into the lane, spun, and got off a clean look from point blank range. It bounced off the back of the iron and rattled out to Caris Levert. The ball was quickly passed back to Stauskas for a fade-away three that also bounced off. Levert again corralled the offensive board, and some frantic ball movement worked its way to Walton who shot a three. One more miss led to one more offensive rebound and finally a tip-in, this time by Jordan Morgan. The score stood at 72–72 with 31 seconds left.

On the ensuing possession, Michigan took advantage of the foul they had to give and forced Kentucky to take the ball out with 10 seconds remaining. The Wildcat offense didn't attempt to run much action, but instead executed a simple dribble handoff to get the ball to Aaron Harrison. He created some space with a step-back and launched from NBA range. Caris Levert couldn't have defended the play any better, coming up just a fingertip short of the block. Much like Trey Burke's shot against Kansas one year before, Harrison's attempt found nothing but net.

"Tip your hat. It was a long ways away," Beilein told the media afterwards. "He hit big time shots for them." For the second consecutive year, Michigan fell a bit short to a similarly talented team from the state of Kentucky. This loss prevented the team from making a second straight Final Four appearance. Kentucky would go on to prove they were no fluke, advancing to the national championship game before falling to the Connecticut Huskies.

Chapter 8

The Rebuild

In what was becoming an annual tradition, NBA eligibility was a running theme through John Beilein's exit interviews with players following the 2014 NCAA Tournament. It had become a perplexing paradox; Michigan's greatest strengths of evaluating and developing had spawned their greatest challenge—managing a roster with frequent early departures. Nik Stauskas, with his Big Ten Player of the Year award in hand, was a fairly safe bet to be moving on to the NBA. Glenn Robinson, having once again played in a supporting role, still faced questions about his NBA readiness. Unlike Stauskas, the significant increase in his rate of possessions used had led to a less efficient offensive performance than the season prior.

The two players shared a press conference on April 15 to announce their intention to enter the NBA draft. They were appreciative of the coaching staff and made clear this wasn't an easy decision. "Imagining the kind success that we could have if we all decided to come back for a third year, you can't help but think what that would look like," Stauskas said. "That's what made it really tough for me is the relationships that I had with the players and the coaching staff here, and how much I'm going to miss them. But at the same time this is a once in a lifetime opportunity and I've been dreaming about this since I was seven or eight years old."

Robinson also detailed his gratitude: "As far as the coaching staff, they believed in myself [and the rest of the team] since the day we came in. A lot of people didn't necessarily believe in my talents as a player when I first came in to college or even recruit me. So for them to give me the time—I'm very grateful for it. Like Nik said, this is a once in a lifetime opportunity and I'm ready to take this step."

After missing the majority of the season, Mitch McGary appeared more likely to return but no decision had been announced. Then the choice was effectively made for him. Michigan learned that McGary had failed a drug test during the NCAA Tournament and would be facing a season-long ban the next year as a result. Rather than spending another year watching his teammates from the bench, McGary would be moving on as well.

Jon Horford surprised many by announcing he had decided to transfer to Florida for his fifth year and would not be back. And Jordan Morgan had completed his eligibility and would also depart Ann Arbor, leaving a memorable impact on the basketball program as well as in the lives of all those whose paths he crossed. Morgan made such an impression as a student-athlete at Michigan that he was singled out for his achievements by President Barack Obama in his speech at the university in 2014. "I want to congratulate Jordan for playing more games at Michigan than any other player in history [and] not only earning an undergraduate degree in engineering, [but] pursuing a graduate degree in engineering as well," Obama said. "That's the kind of student athlete we're talking about."[1]

As he had done the previous season, John Beilein attended the draft to support his former players. The Sacramento Kings called Nik Stauskas' name with the eighth pick—one slot higher than Trey Burke had gone the previous season. In somewhat of a surprise, the Oklahoma City Thunder selected Mitch McGary in the first round. And Glenn Robinson went 40th overall to the Minnesota Timberwolves. With all three of Michigan's likely draftees selected, John Beilein stayed in his seat. He was the last man still sitting in the "green room" where high draft picks are invited to sit and attend the draft. Although Jordan Morgan was not expected to be drafted, Beilein was holding out hope that as a player that represented everything it meant to be a Michigan Wolverine, Morgan would hear his name called as well. Eventually it was time to leave. "I tried to stay as long as I could with Jordan,"[2] Beilein said.

The Wolverines would be losing players that accounted for 53 percent of the minutes played from the previous season, and 57 percent of the points scored. While they had handled the departures of Burke and Hardaway, the continued attrition over two seasons would really test the program. Caris Levert had passed on his own opportunity to head to the NBA early, and expectations for him were high heading into the 2014-15 season.

When Levert was healthy during the 2014-15 season, he played well. But it quickly became clear that the new outfit would not enjoy the same success that the previous teams had enjoyed. A shocking early season loss to the New Jersey Institute of Technology was an obvious warning sign that things weren't quite right, and still stands out as the most embarrassing loss of the Beilein era. It was immediately followed by a loss to Eastern Michigan in which the Wolverines only notched 42 points. The struggles continued.

Levert saw his streak of 88 straight games played come to an abrupt end following a January 17 contest versus Northwestern. His foot had not healed properly from offseason surgery, and he needed to go back under the knife to correct it. Michigan limped through the rest of the 2014-15 season, finishing with a wholly forgettable 16–16 record. It was a stark contrast to what the program had become accustomed to, and the regression was painful.

Looking back on the few positives from that season, it was the first look at an unheralded guard from Allentown, Pennsylvania. Muhammad-Ali Abdur-Rahkman would eventually surpass Jordan Morgan as the all-time leader in games played and would serve as a crucial component on their next great teams. As an essentially forgotten recruit ranked the 434th player in his class, it took a fascinating series of events for the soft-spoken guard to even wind up at Michigan. John Beilein had gotten to know a coach by the name of Dave Rooney earlier in his career, back when Beilein was at Erie Community College and Rooney was coaching at Buffalo State. Though no longer coaching, Rooney had stayed close to the game monitoring the basketball action in Pennsylvania's Lehigh Valley, and was impressed by Rahkman's ability. "If you've been in this game long enough, you can tell who can play and who can't play,"[3] Rooney told Brendan Quinn. Although they hadn't spoken in a very long time, Rooney decided to reach out to Beilein on Abdur-Rahkman's behalf. The mutual respect between the two basketball lifers led Beilein to take the call seriously and look into Abdur-Rahkman. He liked what he saw. "I'm a Buffalo Braves fan from way back—I watched his athleticism and said, 'How many people know the name Randy Smith?' [He was] this elite athlete that just needed a jump shot, because he could take the ball to the basket," Beilein said. "[Rahkman] came from great DNA, and [I felt] that he could develop over time if he had the right attitude."[4]

Abdur-Rahkman came from a strong family background that suggested he would be a team player and make the most out of his abilities. His father Dawud served in the Army and had been a long-time college coach. He raised his son with strong values. "I'm lucky to be the son of a coach, especially a college coach," Abdur-Rahkman said. "He taught me the game and how to carry myself. He always said, 'You don't know who's watching you.' And I took that to heart and tried to be the best person I could at all times. That's helped me a lot."[5]

As for the unique name, for both father and son, it carries weight and expectations. "It's a tribute to [Muhammad] Ali. It's a tribute to my son," Dawud told Steve Kornacki. "It's a tribute to me and what I feel is important. He wasn't a perfect man by any means—none of us are. But his genuine concern for others and who he was stood up here (raising his hand above his head) at a time when people would not dare to say what he was saying."[6] As an older freshman that was physically ready to handle college basketball, and as the son of a coach that raised him with high expectations, Abdur-Rahkman was thrust into playing time in his first season. He wound up starting 13 games during that disappointing 2014-15 campaign.

8. The Rebuild

Watching Abdur-Rahkman from the bench was a shooting forward by the name of Duncan Robinson. Due to his redshirt status, he was unable to contribute that season. Robinson had attended Division 3 Williams College as a freshman and appears to be the first player to ever transfer from Division 3 to be on scholarship at Division 1. Unrecruited out of high school, he took a prep year at Phillips Exeter Academy in New Hampshire—after which, he still received no Division 1 interest. His coach at Williams, Mike Maker, said, "He fell through the cracks. That happens sometimes."[7] After a tremendous freshman season at Williams, Maker said, "We've got the best Division 3 player in the country."[8] But a head coaching opportunity at Marist opened up for Maker, and his past experience coaching under John Beilein at West Virginia led him to reach out to his former colleague on Robinson's behalf. Beilein liked what he saw and heard.

"I watched his film extensively. [He was] a freshman that led his team to the championship game in Division 3. I trusted what my [former assistant] was saying. I said, 'This makes sense for us.' He fills a void of a shooter—and also knowing our strength coach, Jon Sanderson, could develop that body over time with a redshirt year,"[9] Beilein said.

A simple glance at his highlight videos showed a lean 6'8" shooter with an incredibly pure three-point stroke that made fans dream about Nik Stauskas 2.0. But there is a reason no player before him had taken a similar leap. As Robinson put it, "I'm not sure I was a plus-athlete, even in Division 3. Up here, everybody is bigger, stronger ... and the game moves much faster."[10] His initial exposure to the higher level was a one-on-one round robin workout with Derrick Walton and Caris Levert when he arrived at Michigan in the fall. It did not go well at all. He called a friend at home and vented, "I might've made a huge mistake."[11] So he regrouped. He recognized that he had a full year to sit out and develop himself as completely as possible. He engaged fully in Camp Sanderson to add strength and twitch to his slender frame. He made the decision "to prioritize the intellectual side more and more,"[12] delving into psychology in search of a mental edge. And he had a full year of coaching from John Beilein and the Michigan staff. That year of all-encompassing development allowed him to overcome the challenges of transitioning to the Division 1 level and had him prepared to make significant contributions once he was eligible.

Austin Hatch played five more minutes than Robinson did in that 2014-15 season, but they were the only minutes he would ever play in a college basketball game. However, his impact on the program and the lives of others will be felt for the rest of his days. From the time John Beilein first watched Hatch play, he was smitten. "He was one of the best [high school] sophomores in the country. Without question." Beilein saw him score 30 and pull down 16 boards against future Indiana guard James Blackmon. Repeat: as a high school sophomore. Sometimes when we hear Austin Hatch's incredible story, that piece gets forgotten. John Beilein's assessment carries weight, for obvious reasons. "He reminded me of a young Wally Szczerbiak. He was tremendous. He'd just played a great team and dominated them,"[13] Beilein said. He still has a copy of the videotape. That came after the first plane crash Hatch's family endured.

In 2003, he lost his mother, sister, and brother in the type of accident that most of us would never recover from. Hatch and his father Stephen survived the crash, found strength in each other and somehow kept moving forward. Their relationship, forged even deeper by the devastating loss, reached a level rare even by father and son standards. "He was my best friend and we were as close as anyone. He probably would've been the best man in my wedding,"[14] Austin Hatch shared with Steve Kornacki in an outstanding profile on Michigan's website.

Stephen Hatch encouraged his son Austin to be an "uncommon man." He wanted him to live with integrity, to help others, and to push himself to achieve to the best of his abilities. His cousin, Kevin O'Donnell talked about the challenge Dr. Hatch faced after the first crash. "He had to live. He had to live for Austin. You talk about selflessness. That's probably the most selfless thing you can do—live for somebody else."[15] That selflessness left an impression on Austin that he will carry for the rest of his life.

To achieve the level of athletic success Austin did after such a debilitating loss is incredibly impressive in itself. That was certainly part of John Beilein's consideration when originally extending Austin Hatch a scholarship—his mental toughness already graded off the charts. Was this a kid that could handle adversity? He had already proven that in ways that hopefully others would never have to. Hatch was thrilled to accept John Beilein's scholarship offer; Michigan was his mother Julie's alma mater. "Michigan is in my blood. It was the dream to play here. When Michigan offered me the scholarship—that was it." Stephen Hatch was thrilled at the idea of Austin playing under such a great coach. "My dad fell in love with the man Coach Beilein was in addition to the school. He said, 'I know this is a place where my son will be coached hard, but he'll be loved.'"[16]

Then on June 24, 2011, just nine days after committing to play at Michigan, came the moment that would have finished most of us. After already losing his mother, sister, and brother eight years earlier, Austin lost his father and stepmother in another plane crash. Austin had incredibly survived once again but had to be airlifted to a nearby hospital, then transferred to another, and then finally airlifted to a rehab facility in Chicago. He suffered a severe head injury, from which 90 percent of victims never regain consciousness from. He was left in a coma for the next eight weeks. Hatch is fully aware that the odds suggest there is no way he should still be here. "Arnold Barnett, an MIT statistician, said the odds of surviving a plane crash with one fatality involved is one-in-3.4 million. So, I survived two of those, with multiple fatalities in both. So, the odds of surviving those two crashes is one-in-11 quadrillion and 560 trillion. That's a 14-digit number."[17] Having overcome that statistical absurdity, he set about the long and grueling rehabilitation process to simply learn to walk and talk again. He lost 50 pounds and struggled to even lift a basketball. In addition to the brain trauma, he had two broken collarbones, rib fractures, holes in his lungs, and fractures in his sternum and hip to recover from.

With the help of an extensive network of family and friends, he displayed an uncommon level of determination to get back to the best version of himself possible. He spent close to two years working his way back while living with his sister and guardian Maria in Fort Wayne. Then he spent his senior year of high school living with his uncle Michael in Pasadena and attending Loyola High School. There he played for coach Jamal Adams and the uphill climb continued. Coach Adams reached out to Rasheed Hazzard, a local basketball trainer and son of NBA great Walt Hazzard, to assist in Hatch's basketball rehab. Adams' request stuck in Hazzard's mind. "He literally asked me, 'Do you want to be part of a miracle?'"[18] Hazzard paired up with Austin for early morning workouts rebuilding all the pieces of the game that had previously come so naturally to him.

In what has become a theme in Hatch's life, the impact that he has had on those around him continues to be his legacy. Coach Adams said, "Austin's positivity, his faith, and always trying to get better is something I always admired. He was steadfast in improving. He had his moments of difficulty and frustration, and those moments would be awfully emotional. But he would come back and lift his head up."[19]

For Rasheed Hazzard, who had also recently lost his father, his time with Austin was life changing. "As much as people think I did for Austin's life, he did that much for me and maybe more. I tell him all the time, 'You don't really realize that you saved me in a lot of ways.'"[20] Hazzard also said, "He had this spirit about him that he could do anything, and he really believed it. And I believed it in him."[21]

After that year in Los Angeles, it was finally time to head to Ann Arbor, where John Beilein was still holding open Hatch's scholarship spot—regardless of his progression. Arriving on campus was a milestone that really resonated with Austin. "When I got out of the car here that first day, I went to see Coach Beilein and stuck out my hand for a handshake, and he gave me a big bear hug, and looked at me like, 'Man, you did it.' The mission hadn't been accomplished; the mission was just starting. But after all I'd been through, just coming here was a big deal and something to be proud of. It was a dream come true, and I was like, 'I'm finally here.' After being in the

Defended here by Rutgers' Shaquille Doorson, Austin Hatch displayed unusual perseverance to return to the court and play in five games during the 2014-15 season after two separate plane crashes (photograph by Bryan Fuller).

hospital for months, after learning how to walk again. It felt good being here because I knew I had to work for it. I was like, 'You earned this, man.'"[22]

He had made it this far when some of his doctors had questioned his ability to get out of bed for the rest of his life. He continued to push himself on the court, eventually getting spot duty in a few games. On December 22, 2014, against Coppin State, his recovery came full circle as he scored his first and only point in a Michigan uniform. Ever the driven competitor, Hatch still is frustrated that he missed a couple free throws. "I got fouled taking a three, and missed the first free throw, made the second and missed the third. I'm still mad about that. That's nothing to be proud of. But it is cool that I got to score one official point."[23] Following the season, Michigan made the difficult decision to transition Hatch to a medical scholarship, effectively ending his basketball playing career. He took advantage of the opportunity to stay heavily involved in the program as an undergraduate assistant coach and provided all those he encountered with a consistent and healthy dose of perspective.

One of those players that Austin Hatch would wind up spending a great deal of time around was a young man from Germany that John Beilein was heavily recruiting during that 2014-15 season. Beilein first saw Moe Wagner on a grainy video sent across the world that had gotten lost in his email box. Wagner had watched the 2013 Final Four and became intrigued by college basketball in general, but also a certain team in Maize and Blue in particular. When it was time to make a decision about staying in Germany as a professional or exploring opportunities in the States, Wagner had to rely on his own resourcefulness: "I cut my own [highlight] video together, put some corny background music in the back and made a very bad video and sent it out."[24]

A former contact of Beilein's in Germany named Yenal Kahraman passed the video along. On that film, Wagner stood 6'10" and showcased a variety of offensive moves. Included among them was a move that Michigan fans would become quite familiar with—one hard dribble to his right followed by a behind-the-back dribble drive left to the hoop. What did Beilein think about him after watching? "I looked at it and I said, you know what, this kid looks like a multidimensional player.... Tremendous upside."[25] Adding to that potential, Wagner was yet another Michigan recruit that was young for his class and would play his entire freshman season as an 18-year-old.

Beilein had experienced success with a German recruit in the past, having had Johannes Herber start every game in his West Virginia career. And he had been unsuccessfully searching for the elusive "Pittsnogle" in his time at Michigan. Kevin Pittsnogle was the inside-out big man that could knock down threes and opened up West Virginia's offense leading a run to the Elite Eight in 2005 and the Sweet 16 in 2006. After recognizing that upside and Wagner's potential to fill that elusive role, Beilein set off in typical fashion to do his detective work. "Beilein wanted to know everything, basically,"[26] Kahraman said. He reached out to Herber, to the German national team coach, to pro scouts—all to find out more.

Herber recognized the fit he had seen at West Virginia, "I knew from the way Coach used Kevin [Pittsnogle] that Moe could be a good fit in that offense."[27]

Armed with these endorsements, Coach Beilein hopped on a plane in the middle of that ill-fated season to fly to Germany. "So I just said, you know what? We can't, like, sit on this. I think this kid is going to be pretty good, but nobody's been over to see him," Beilein said. After that meeting, Michigan's coach was sold. "By the time I got out of the elevator, I said, 'If this kid's good at all, I'm going to give him a scholarship,' because he was so engaging. What you see right there is who he is."[28]

The next step was Wagner's official trip to Ann Arbor for the March 7 Rutgers game. He was allowed to practice with the team the day prior. There may no better testament to how much Wagner has since developed than to listen to Brendan Quinn share the results of that scrimmage: "He was terrible. No defense. No rebounding. Max Bielfeldt, Ricky Doyle and Mark Donnal stuffed Wagner in a body bag."[29]

But then there was "the move" again. This one didn't end with Nick Ward collapsing in a heap on the ground, but it was enough to earn a scholarship offer on the spot. The potential was clearly there, but plenty of hard work lay ahead to access it. Jon Sanderson outlined the physical development that Moe required. "We rank these guys in all these categories—power, speed, agility, vertical jump—and when [Wagner] got here, he was in the lowest percentiles in every category. He was 0-to-15 in every percentile among the Michigan players I've worked with in nine years," he said. "A real project. A classic case of let's get bigger and stronger."[30]

After that visit, Wagner committed to Michigan and arrived for a 2015-16 season in which the Wolverines hoped to return to their more successful ways. Wagner was the only incoming freshman on scholarship, but he would be joined by a newly eligible Duncan Robinson. The Wolverines were also relying on a return to health by Caris Levert along with added development and experience for the rest of the roster to lead the way. Derrick Walton and Zak Irvin were entering their junior seasons and expected to take on greater leadership roles.

Early season losses to Xavier, Connecticut, and SMU showed that success wasn't going to come easy to Michigan's latest iteration. With the exception of the SMU game, Levert came out playing well in his senior season and appeared to be the alpha dog that the team had so dearly missed since Trey Burke and Nik Stauskas had left for the NBA. Entering Big Ten play, the Wolverines stood 10-3 and seemed well-positioned to become another example of a John Beilein team that improves throughout the season and finishes strong. They traveled to Champaign, Illinois, for their first conference game just before the New Year to take on John Groce's team—the coach Caris Levert had originally expected to play for in college. Michigan won by 10 behind Levert's 22 points and a somewhat shocking 26 points from mild-mannered big man Mark Donnal. Despite the encouraging road win, it came with a dose of concern. Late in the contest, Levert twisted his ankle on an opponent's foot just as he dished to Donnal for one of his 11 buckets. Though it didn't look especially serious, Levert sat out the next game. And the next.

By the time he returned on February 13 to face Purdue, the Wolverines stood 8-4 in the conference, having withstood his absence well. With a healthy Levert returning to the lineup, things seemed hopeful for the 2015-16 Michigan team. But after playing just 11 minutes, it became clear that this team would not have a healthy Levert. The star senior didn't take the floor in the second half. His left foot had never fully recovered from his earlier operations and a few weeks later he was officially shut down for the season. His career at Michigan ended very differently than anyone had imagined. The mental toll of officially losing their senior leader caught the Wolverines off-balance. Following the Purdue game, Michigan lost four of their last five regular season games. Walton and Irvin had shown they weren't quite ready to step into Levert's shoes. Irvin rarely met a shot he didn't like but had struggled through a dismal shooting year, checking in at under 30 percent from three-point range while launching 161 of them. Walton flashed the ability to take over at times but was for the most part content to start the offense and defer to his teammates.

Duncan Robinson's first season at the Division 1 level was a success, as his pure stroke translated to an outstanding 45 percent three-point percentage and put him on track to average 11.2 points per game. His overall game was still limited as evidenced by the fact that he only made about one two-point field goal and one free throw per game, but it was a promising beginning.

No player benefited more from the playing time opened up by Levert's injury than Abdur-Rahkman. He had started the year quietly, only reaching double figures in two non-conference games. With increased opportunity came impressive development. Over the last nine games of the season, his scoring average climbed to 13.6 points per game as he showcased the ability to consistently get to the hoop and finish. Michigan would need to rely on Abdur-Rahkman's scoring ability to have a chance at post-season success. After the rough stretch to end the regular season, they entered the conference tournament on the bubble for the NCAA Tournament. Wins were required to solidify their invite and the Wolverines almost lost their first game.

In their first-round matchup in Indianapolis, Northwestern erased a 12-point second-half lead by Michigan to take their own one-point lead with 3:29 remaining. The Wolverines clawed back in front and two Duncan Robinson free throws gave them a two-point lead with 14 seconds left. After a Northwestern miss, the Wildcats' big man Alex Olah got the rebound and threw up a fade-away that found the bottom of the net as time expired to send the game to overtime.

Duncan Robinson knocked down two three-pointers in the extra period to give him a team-leading 21 points. Zak Irvin, never scared to take a final shot, curled around the top of the key to knock down one of his patented long two-pointers to give Michigan the win in his hometown. "We know our backs are against the wall right now. We know we have to make a dent in this tournament and win a couple of games," Irvin told the media afterwards. "The first step was beating Northwestern and we were able to do that today. We have to enjoy it but it's a quick turnaround until tomorrow."

That quick turnaround didn't leave Michigan much time to plan for #1 seed Indiana. Despite limited preparation time, the two teams appeared more evenly matched than the seeds suggested. The game featured nine lead changes and neither team ever led by more than six points. A Duncan Robinson three-pointer tied it up in the final minute, and the rarely used Kameron Chatman had his best moment in a Michigan uniform when he knocked down a game-winning three-pointer from the corner as the clock expired. Even he seemed a bit surprised afterwards in the post-game press conference: "I didn't think Derrick was going to pass it to me, and he ended up passing it to me. I hesitated a little bit, but then seeing how much time was on the clock, and then I just let it go. It felt good when it left my hands."

Despite a loss to Purdue in the next round, Michigan was going dancing in the NCAA Tournament. Sort of. They had to play as one of the First Four in Dayton, Ohio—needing to win their first game in order to advance to the conventional field of 64. To accomplish this, the Wolverines took advantage of an important contribution from their only freshman.

Moe Wagner didn't get significant playing time his freshman year but there were definitely flashes of his talent level. A 19-point performance in 16 minutes against Charlotte early in the season seemed to be a harbinger of things to come. However, his frequent early foul trouble and a tendency to become emotionally unhinged limited his impact for much of the year. He was also dealing with the usual adjustment challenges faced by freshmen— but his were amplified by being an overseas flight away from family and home. His roommate Brent Hibbitts saw it up close: "That was all tough for him, but he persevered."[31]

Wagner was an afterthought at the end of the regular season, only playing 14 total minutes in the last six games. But the post-season offered an opportunity to finish strong and Wagner seized it. Taking on Tulsa in the First Four game, Wagner was present for all phases that night. During his 22 minutes, he made both his shot attempts and added eight rebounds, four blocks, and a steal. After the game, Beilein spoke about the challenges Wagner had overcome: "I think he got his confidence back. You've got to remember he's 18 years old. He's still 18. He left Germany in July. And he hasn't been home. And this is a hard thing for him to go through, and he has just been such a pleasure to coach. But he really has some confidence right now. And you can see what we saw in him these last couple of games."[32]

Later in his career, Wagner pointed back at the game as a breakthrough for him mentally. "My favorite game was at Dayton, the play-in (NCAA First Four) game. It was my first game on the big stage, and I did things I hadn't done before. I thought, 'I can do this!' People actually struggled against me. That was the first time I felt that, and that was my favorite game here."[33] Duncan Robinson also chipped in a double-double with 13 points and a surprising 11 rebounds to help lead the Wolverines to a 67–62 victory and a trip to Brooklyn to take on Notre Dame.

Despite having just one day off to travel from Dayton to Brooklyn and prepare for their next opponent, Michigan started the game out strong. At halftime, they led by 12 courtesy of 50 percent three-point shooting. Regression to the mean soon brought the Wolverines back to earth as they slipped to 23 percent in the second half. Walton and Irvin combined to shoot 3 of 17 overall in the second half as Michigan slowly collapsed. Notre Dame took the lead for good with 3:43 left in the game and wound up outscoring Michigan by 19 over the last 20 minutes. The Wolverines' deficiencies had caught up to them once and for all. Lacking a reliable, efficient scorer, frontcourt toughness, and bench depth, the 2015-16 Michigan Wolverines had to knock down threes at a high percentage to win. Otherwise, they didn't have a road map to victory.

Injuries had certainly played a role, as Beilein attested after the game. "The depth that we had expected to have going into the season is sitting on the bench with Spike Albrecht and Caris Levert. We'll always wonder [what we could have done] with those two."

Derrick Walton pointed to the team's less than stingy defense as the primary cause of defeat. "Down the stretch we didn't collectively get enough stops in a row. And that was all the difference in the game basically. They were getting stops, and we weren't," Walton said. "That's pretty much what it boiled down to. We didn't make the necessary stops down the stretch that would hold them off."[34] While injuries and early entries to the NBA had created holes on the roster, it was undeniable that the team's defense hadn't been measuring up for a few years now. That offseason, Beilein set to work fixing the problem.

Chapter 9

Attacking a Weakness

Following the 2015-16 season, two of John Beilein's assistants received the opportunity to run their own programs. Lavall Jordan was hired as head coach by his alma mater Butler, while Bacari Alexander also became the head man at his alma mater, the University of Detroit Mercy. With two coaching vacancies to fill, Beilein considered his program's biggest weaknesses. One of the missing pieces during Beilein's tenure had been his teams' frequent inability to match the toughness and physicality that other programs possessed. His were offensive-oriented teams that were more skill and finesse based. While it had often been a winning formula, there remained significant room for improvement on the defensive side of the ball.

They had posted nationally elite offenses, but the highest their defense had ranked on Kenpom was 37th in the country during their 2012-13 run to the national championship. During the 2015-16 season, they had slid all the way down to 92nd. At that point, John Beilein realized he had to make an adjustment if the program was going to reach its full potential. So he did what the great ones do: he adapted and evolved. As he put it, he took a look around and didn't really like what he saw. "We had gotten to the NCAA Tournament, but our defense was not terrific," Beilein said. "We made it by outshooting people. That's when I said, 'You know what, I know what I know, and I know what I don't know. I want to hire somebody that thinks differently than me and prioritizes defense.'"[1]

It took serious humility for a man who had already taken Michigan to the Final Four to be willing to effectively cede half the game to an outsider. The program would have been on solid footing without that evolution, but all that mattered to Beilein was finding ways to get better. Sharing credit with another coach was the least of his concerns. The man for the job turned out to be former Wright State head coach Billy Donlon. He effectively became the team's defensive coordinator. Saddi Washington, from nearby Oakland

University, was hired as well—with a focus on working with the program's big men.

Michigan's roster also underwent some turnover that offseason. While most of the primary contributors at the end of the season would return, there was a great deal of shuffling farther down the bench. Transferring out were Aubrey Dawkins, Kam Chatman, and Ricky Doyle. Caris Levert was gone, having been selected 20th overall by the Brooklyn Nets. Spike Albrecht had moved on to Purdue for his graduate transfer season. Incoming freshmen Zavier Simpson, Jon Teske, and Ibi Watson would all see the court in 2016-17. Austin Davis would take a redshirt year, as would a talented incoming transfer from Kentucky named Charles Matthews.

Despite all the new faces, the success of the 2016-17 squad would ultimately need to be driven by their two senior leaders, Derrick Walton and Zak Irvin. The two captains hadn't quite been ready to front the team in Caris Levert's absence the year prior but felt better suited for the role as seniors. "Last year, we were just kind of thrust into it, and we weren't really prepared. Now, this is it. Both of us need to take our games to the next level,"[2] Walton said.

Early season wins against Marquette and SMU to win the 2K Classic in New York City were a promising start. DJ Wilson averaged 35 minutes in those games after averaging just six per game the season before. It was quickly becoming apparent that he was growing into his springy, pogo-stick frame and was on track to become yet another successful case-study in Beilein's development program. Derrick Walton was shut out against Marquette before re-asserting himself with 23 against SMU. His consistency was still lacking, but Michigan would require it to have a successful campaign. The positive vibes created on that trip to New York were quickly negated by a listless loss at South Carolina in which Michigan only scored 46 points, and then in a defeat at home to Virginia Tech.

A 2-4 start in conference play had many fans scratching their heads wondering if this was the new normal. The team got a motivational assist from Illinois forward Maverick Morgan when he essentially referred to Michigan as a soft team following an Illinois win during that rough stretch: "They are more of a white-collar team traditionally and at Illinois we're about toughness and [being] together."[3]

When Illinois visited the Crisler Center ten days later for the rematch, the Michigan coaching staff wrote "streetball fight" in permanent marker on the locker room wall before the game. Michigan came away with a hard-fought victory, and afterwards the players made clear that the statement had lit a fire under them. "I don't think we were the white collar team today,"[4] DJ Wilson said. The team carried that defensive tenacity with them for the rest of the season. The defensive improvement under Billy Donlon took some time, but starting with that Illinois game, there was a noticeable upgrade in the team's effort and toughness. Only one opponent would break 70 points scored against Michigan the rest of the regular season. Donlon made some analytically sound adjustments to the team's defensive approach that paid dividends. There was a concerted effort to deny the opposition three-point attempts that was particularly successful. Michigan finished ninth in the country in lowest percentage of three-point attempts allowed. Prior to that, they had never finished better than 107th nationally under Beilein. Donlon understood that while it is difficult for a defense to consistently impact the three-point shooting percentage of their opponent, it is well within their power to run their opposition off the three-point line and limit their attempts.

It was also around this time that Derrick Walton finally became comfortable as the team's alpha dog. He stopped deferring and started taking charge. He made the off-the-dribble three-pointer an important piece of the team's offense, particularly in late shot-clock scenarios. Following the Illinois win, Walton played at an All Big-Ten level the rest of the way. He upped his average to 18.3 points per game over the rest of the season. He also brought down an impressive 5.3 rebounds per game in that time, asserting himself as one of the best rebounders from the point guard position that you will see at the college level. His three-point percentage increased to 44 percent and he shot at a higher volume. It was a development that John Beilein had been hoping to see. "His evolution as a player has really spiked this year. Where you've seen the biggest spike is that he wanted to win so badly," Beilein said. "I think that Billy Donlon has had a great influence on him. Greg Harden, who has counseled the Tom Brady's and the Desmond Howard's of the world, has spoken a lot with him about him getting everything he can out of the blessings he's had."[5] Michigan was going to ride Walton's growth as a player as far as he could lead them. It continued as they ran Michigan State out of the Crisler Center 86-57, behind 20 from Walton and 19 from Moe Wagner on February 7. The team then proceeded to finish out the regular season 6-2 over their last eight games. Their late run was also aided by the development of their young big men.

Wagner stepped up his performance during his sophomore season to become an important contributor. He started to show flashes of the weaponized version of his game that would serve to change Michigan's offensive potential going forward. Having a 6'11" big man shoot threes at 40 percent, while being nimble enough to drive and work out of the post is a luxury few teams enjoy. That was the version of Wagner that Michigan was starting to see with more regularity. While inconsistency and foul trouble still plagued him, he also had some standout performances against the more traditional big men on the schedule. The footwork he developed as a young man playing soccer in Germany differentiated him from his competition. His diverse set of post moves, ability to shoot from distance, and the handle to put it on the floor, all combined to make him a challenging assignment for the opposition. Wagner teamed up with DJ Wilson to provide Michigan an athletic and offensively skilled tandem in their frontcourt. Wilson bought into Donlon's defensive scheme and blocked more shots over the course of the season than any Beilein recruit at Michigan ever had. Wilson wasn't always consistent, but frequently made the difficult look effortless. He became an important piece to the team with unlimited upside for the future.

With a 10–8 conference record, Michigan appeared destined for the NCAA Tournament but needed a few Big Ten Tournament wins to seal the deal. The team boarded their plane and prepared to head to Washington, D.C., on Wednesday, March 8, 2017. The plane began speeding down the runway at about 2:45 p.m., and just before liftoff, initiated a high-speed abort due to fierce winds. Having reached such a high velocity on the runway, the plane struggled to stop and wound up barreling through a fence and over a ditch. The passengers were safely evacuated but, needless to say, all were affected. They had a game early the next afternoon but weren't exactly eager to hop right on another plane. They held a team vote over what to do next and decided to go home that night and fly to Washington in the morning. "We have a 6 a.m. wake-up, at 6:30 we're going to leave the hotel in Ann Arbor and we've got a game at 12 and we're in our practice uniforms," outlined John Beilein. "Bo Schembechler called it 'sudden change' and you have one choice in life and that is to embrace it because life is about a lot of sudden change."[6] Early the next morning, the team took off successfully and enjoyed an uneventful flight. They arrived at the arena just hours before their game. Because their original plane had been cordoned off for investigation with all their uniforms aboard it, the team was stuck wearing their practice uniforms against Maverick Morgan and their old friends from Illinois.

Despite the harrowing 24 hours leading up to the game, Michigan rolled over the Illini once it started. They won easily 75–55. Walton, Irvin, and Abdur-Rahkman teamed up for 54 points between them. They seemed to play with the freedom of a group that knew this was just a basketball game. John Beilein explained it to the media afterwards. "What these guys have been through the last 24 hours has been incredible. It's been bonding. It's been emotional for many of them. It's made them so resilient. They played connected today like they were connected yesterday when we got a hundred-some people off an airplane, it seemed like, in two minutes."

Michigan's reward was a date with the #1 seed in the conference, Purdue, in another 24 hours. The Wolverines came out that next day and shot the ball well again. DJ Wilson gave Michigan 18 first half points and a one-point lead at the break by attacking Purdue's traditional big man tandem of Caleb Swanigan and Isaac Haas. "We talked about it a lot coming into the game, how they play two bigs," Wilson said later. "We're mobile. We're agile. Taking them off the dribble is a real good option for us."[7]

The team lost their touch in the second half, shooting one for 11 from deep, but held on just enough to have a chance to tie it late. A Zak Irvin layup with four seconds remaining gave them the opportunity to play overtime. Irvin scored Michigan's next two baskets as well, to put them up three in overtime. Walton and Duncan Robinson knocked down free throws to seal the crucial upset. Irvin's renaissance as a late-game shot-maker felt particularly redemptive after a rocky junior year shooting the ball. Beilein had heard the calls to take the ball out of Irvin's hands, but he stuck by him. "I said I'm not turning to anybody else. We've got a team. Zak Irvin is in there and will take shots because he makes shots. We have a lot of confidence in him. I wouldn't do that if he hadn't shown extreme selfless leadership during the entire four years here."[8]

With the win over Purdue, Michigan had now assuredly punched their ticket to the Dance. But they had their eyes set on a conference championship first. Twenty-four hours later, another game, this time against Minnesota. Derrick Walton was dominant against the Gophers. Twenty-nine points, nine assists, five rebounds, and only a single turnover. He scored 14 of Michigan's final 20 points as they won 84–77. He was beginning to look like the type of guard that could carry a team in March.

Wisconsin, the #2 seed, was waiting for the Wolverines in the Big Ten Championship. It was Michigan's fourth game in four days, immediately following the traumatic plane crash. Given the emotional roll they were on, many had a sense of destiny about the team finishing the job. Both teams shot the ball well in the first half, with Walton and Wisconsin's Bronson Koenig exchanging seven three-pointers between them. The Wolverines led by one at the break, and Billy Donlon stepped in with his defensive adjustments. After shooting 5–7 in the first half, including 3–3 from long distance, Michigan's defense didn't allow Bronson Koenig to make a single field goal in the second half. Additionally, Donlon switched DJ Wilson onto Ethan Happ, which slowed down their star big man significantly. The Badgers didn't score a point until five minutes into the second half and didn't make a field goal until more than eight minutes had gone by. By that point, given the level that Michigan's defense was playing at, the game was essentially over. Wisconsin shot 27 percent from the field in the second half, and the 71–56 final represented their second lowest scoring output of the season. The team was elated afterwards and celebrated on the court with family and friends. It was the program's first Big Ten Tournament championship since 1998. Derrick Walton had scored 22 with 7 assists and 6 rebounds. He described their mentality coming out of the break as a difference maker. "Before the half even started, we talked about how important the first two possessions of the half is, the first four minutes of the half," Walton said. "We came out firing. We made some consecutive stops. We hit tough shots."[9]

The theme of the week had been clear once Michigan arrived in Washington. After surviving the crash, why not just go and win the whole thing? "Once we landed in D.C., we agreed that why can't this be the greatest story ever told," Zak Irvin said at the champions' press conference. "Everybody had that mentality: Why not us? When we were tired and fatigued, whatever it might be, that was the extra push we needed to win this championship."

Strength and conditioning coach Jon Sanderson believed Beilein's leadership was a key ingredient. "This is my eighth season with Coach Beilein, and his teams grow through adversity," he said. "We get better with adversity. His positive outlook whenever we lose a game, the way he turns it into a positive by pointing to what we need to get better at. And so this team takes adversity and responds with a positive outcome."[10] After disappointing finishes the previous two seasons, Michigan had returned to the Beilein status quo of demonstrating significant development over the course of the season. Following the lead of their always grounded head coach, the Wolverines were able to withstand as much adversity as just about any college team would face. By winning four games in four days following the plane crash, the Wolverines had put the college basketball world on notice that they would be an uncomfortable draw in the NCAA Tournament.

After the Wisconsin triumph, Michigan found out they would head to Indianapolis as the #7 seed to face #10 seed Oklahoma State the following Friday. The Cowboys presented a stylistic adjustment from what Michigan had been playing against in the Big Ten. They ran with a high tempo, up and down the floor, and never met a shot they didn't like. Crashing the offensive glass and an aggressive risk-taking defense rounded out the team's profile. Oklahoma State was led by lightning-fast point guard Jawun Evans, who could take the ball the length of the court as quickly as any player in the country. Following the opening tip, Evans got off to a rushed start and turned the ball over twice and missed a layup. After a short breather on the bench to allow him to slow down, he settled into the flow of the game. Both teams held true to some of their primary tendencies. Oklahoma State outrebounded Michigan 22–12 in the first half but also turned the ball over eight times compared to Michigan's two turnovers. Derrick Walton didn't find his shot in the first half, but he managed the game well, dishing out six assists and protecting the basketball. Michigan led 41–40 as both teams adjourned to their locker rooms. Walton and Evans traded baskets to start the second half, foreshadowing how the rest of the contest would unfold. Offense was the name of the game from that moment on, with both teams shooting over 60 percent from the field in the second half, as well as over 60 percent from three-point land.

Walton drained a three-pointer with 9:10 on the clock to give Michigan a six-point lead—its largest up to that point. Evans immediately answered with a layup. A few minutes later, Walton hit another three to give Michigan an eight-point lead. Oklahoma State kept hanging around though, eager to put the ball up on the rim quickly and hit the offensive boards. When Walton knocked down a jumper with under a minute left to give Michigan a seven-point edge, it seemed like it might finally be over. A quick 7–2 run kept the Cowboys in it and made it a two-point game with 10 seconds remaining. Michigan would need to make its free throws to close the game out, and they were able to get the ball in the hands of their senior point guard to do just that. Derrick Walton had arguably been the most reliable free-throw "finisher" in recent Michigan history. Few players had consistently knocked down as many to put a game on ice. True to form, Walton made them both.

The Cowboys' furious tempo continued unabated, allowing them to score five points in the last 10 seconds. However, three of them came on an inconsequential three-pointer after DJ Wilson had added two free throws of his own to finish off the win. The 92–91 win had displayed an extreme contrast in styles and had proven a core tenet of John Beilein's offensive philosophy: three is worth more than two. Walton had knocked down six three-pointers to Evans' single make, and the entire Wolverine squad had made 16 to Oklahoma State's seven. Despite being out-rebounded 40–21, that difference in shooting from distance allowed Michigan to advance. Walton had continued his incredible surge, finishing with 26 points and 11 assists, while DJ Wilson chipped in 19 points and four blocks. Walton's teammates were asked in the postgame press conference what it was like to watch his second-half emergence. "It's a lot of fun, first and foremost, to know you've got that rock that you can always count on. He's been so good, and we go as he goes. So hopefully, he's got more left in the tank," Duncan Robinson shared.

"He's a heck of a point guard. He makes things easier for all of us because he attracts so much attention to himself, which frees up everyone else. He's been on a tear, and I know he's going to continue to do it," said the co-captain Irvin.

Two days later, Michigan would have the chance to avenge their 2013 national championship loss, as they took on the #2 seed Louisville Cardinals and their scandal-plagued head coach Rick Pitino. Louisville was led by future NBA star Donovan Mitchell and featured a variety of shot-blocking big men. The Cardinals jumped out to an early 15–8 lead and held on to it for much of the first half. Walton struggled, shooting 1–8, and Louisville held a 36–28 lead at the half. The one area Michigan did have some success was with their offensively skilled big men attacking Louisville's shot-blockers. Wilson and Wagner shot 7–12 and kept their team above water. The two continued that trend, opening the second half with Michigan's first ten points. Louisville held serve though, and still led by nine. Soon the rest of Wagner and Wilson's teammates picked things up, and Michigan began to close the gap. Irvin and Abdur-Rahkman scored 12 sandwiched around a Wilson three-pointer as the Wolverines went on a 15-4 run to take the lead with 8:54 remaining. For much of the rest of the game, Michigan rode Wagner's best performance to date in his career at Michigan. He used a wide variety of post moves to keep Louisville's aggressive defenders off-balance. Rather than settling from long-distance, Wagner repeatedly took the ball to the hoop and finished with layups or got to the line. His last hoop gave the Wolverines a six-point edge with 1:18 remaining.

Derrick Walton didn't play his best game, but, with 29 seconds remaining, he answered Donovan Mitchell's layup with one of his own, putting the Wolverines up four. Despite Walton's poor shooting night, he still found ways to help his team and finished with seven rebounds, six assists, and—most importantly—no turnovers. Mitchell kept coming at Michigan, adding two more quick layups, but each was answered by a pair of DJ Wilson free throws that let the Wolverines hang on for a 73–69 win. Wilson finished with 17 points, but his partner down low had stolen the show. Wagner shot 11–14, good for 26 points, and made quite the impression on his opponents. "He was a nightmare matchup for us,"[11] said Louisville forward Deng Adel.

"He's going to have a great career,"[12] agreed Jaylen Johnson.

It was a different type of win for Michigan, which didn't go unnoticed by the players. "We only shot six threes today and we won. So it's awesome. We played gritty basketball, and I think we can be proud of that,"[13] Wagner pointed out.

Derrick Walton agreed. "That's been our identity in the last month and a half, finding different ways to win. Whether it's the three-ball or not, it's finding multiple different ways to win and taking what the game gives us."[14]

There also was a sense of karmic justice served in knocking off Louisville. It would wind up being the last game Pitino ever coached at the school, as he became ensnared in the FBI investigation into "pay-to-play" arrangements in college basketball. It was certainly not Pitino's first brush with impropriety. The NCAA eventually forced Louisville to vacate their 2013 title as penalty for its involvement in the scheme. But when the vacating of the title was later announced, the always classy John Beilein wasn't interested in trying to claim it for his own. "No, we didn't win that one," Beilein said. "It was fair and square. They didn't have six guys on the court…. We had our chance, and we couldn't quite get it done."[15]

Vanquishing Louisville put Michigan back in the Sweet 16 for the third time in five years. Their next stop was in Kansas City to face the #3 seed Oregon Ducks. Dana Altman's team had only lost five games all season and featured a three-guard lineup with some general similarities to Michigan. Both teams wound up shortening their rotation for the game, each playing just six

The always emotive Moe Wagner shares his mood after Michigan upset Louisville to go to the Sweet 16 in the 2017 NCAA Tournament. D.J. Wilson (#5) and Zak Irvin celebrate in the background (photograph by Marc-Gregor Campredon).

players for more than 10 minutes. Oregon opened up with a 5–0 lead that was immediately answered by consecutive DJ Wilson three-pointers. The two teams traded baskets with Michigan led by Walton's 11 first-half points and seven assists. The Ducks answered with Tyler Dorsey's 12 points. Oregon maintained their small halftime lead deep into the second half. They had identified Duncan Robinson as a defensive liability and were able to consistently isolate against him and attack successfully. Michigan's senior cocaptains led the charge down the stretch, as a Walton three-pointer gave his team the lead with 4:24 left in the game. Irvin followed with his own three, and then each added a two-point bucket to put Michigan up 68–65. Oregon power forward Jordan Bell's strength and athleticism were a factor throughout the game as he dominated Michigan's leaner interior players. The next possession exemplified his contribution as he raced down low to retrieve Dylan Ennis' missed free throw and quickly put it in to pull Oregon within one.

After a Derrick Walton miss, Tyler Dorsey scored to give Oregon the lead with one minute remaining. After both teams traded misses, Michigan inbounded the ball with nine seconds left and a chance to win. There was little question who would be taking the shot. Derrick Walton dribbled the ball over half court, went with a quick cross-over to create some space, and ducked forward before stepping back into his shot. His feet looked to be on the three-point line, and it was an off-the-dribble jumper that he had been consistently knocking down the second half of the year. Only this time he didn't. The ball bounced off the front iron as time expired and Oregon escaped with a 69–68 win. Zak Irvin was just as surprised as those of us watching. "It looked good from my angle," he said after the game. "No one else on this team that we wanted taking that shot. He's been on a run and he's such a great player. I'm proud of him."[16]

Despite the disappointing finish, it had been a tremendous run over the second half of the season. Their star player had a chance to win it—just like any Michigan fan could have hoped. But sometimes the shot doesn't go in. Like all of John Beilein's great Michigan teams, they had gotten better throughout the season. They overcame the unique adversity of surviving a plane crash together, played as a unit, and gave the university a team they could be proud of. Derrick Walton sounded every bit the senior captain he was in expressing his appreciation afterwards: "It's the tightest bunch I've been around in all my years of playing basketball. Just a very selfless group. I had the joy of being a part of it and being one of the leaders."[17]

His partner Zak Irvin stepped up with 19 points and 8 rebounds in the game, including 14 points scored in the second half. He addressed his teammates in the locker room following the game: "It's been a hell of a ride. I appreciate each and every one of you. There were a lot of memories made. I wish you all nothing but the best in the future. I love you."[18]

As usual, John Beilein was ready to provide perspective to his players at the end of an emotional season. "You've been through a lot, and you are better men for it," he said. "I've never been prouder of a group of young men. This is a real team! Value every minute in life going forward."[19]

Chapter 10

Off-Season Adjustments

With the culmination of another season came the annual news of departures and arrivals throughout the program. It was Moe Wagner and DJ Wilson's turn to make a decision about the NBA. Both had received significant interest after their impressive development during their sophomore seasons. DJ Wilson decided to leave and became the 17th pick in the 2017 draft. The Milwaukee Bucks had made a habit of drafting long and athletic prospects, and the bouncy Wilson with his 7'3" wingspan fit the bill perfectly. Charles Matthews, the transfer that would figure prominently in Michigan's future, pointed out that John Beilein had done it again. "Nobody in America thought DJ was going to be a [first-round pick]," Matthews told *The Athletic*. "Now look at him."[1]

Indeed, development was a primary factor in Wilson's decision to originally attend Michigan. "I was in awe of their player development and how well Michigan developed both their guards and their bigs, getting them ready for the next level,"[2] Wilson said.

Strength coach Jon Sanderson played an essential role in allowing Wilson to get the most out of his athleticism. Much of Wilson's first few years at Michigan were spent re-working his movement patterns to allow his body to function properly. "DJ, as long and lanky as he was, in our initial evaluations we saw some valgus tendencies. The knees collapsed inward and were knock-kneed," Sanderson shared. "It was exercise, drills and a whole protocol that we put together for DJ. His vertical jump has improved by eight inches."[3]

Wilson was realistic about the challenges ahead but felt that he had been well prepared by his time in Ann Arbor. "It's never going to be easy. But if I have learned anything at Michigan, perseverance pays off. It has truly been a blessing to have had the opportunity to attend Michigan, and I will forever be grateful to Coach Beilein and his staff for taking the chance on me," he shared in a press release announcing his departure.

His roommate and close friend Moe Wagner considered his options and came to a different decision. In many ways his deep set of offensive skills combined with his length made him an ideal fit in the modern NBA. But his erratic defense and marginal rebounding ability still left something to be desired. Wagner put his name in for the NBA draft but did not sign with an agent, leaving him the option to opt out. He attended the NBA combine but shot 1–8 from behind the three-point line, and ultimately listened to the feedback he received from the process. The NBA advisory committee told him that "I wasn't in the top 20 for sure. So, it was very, very risky. The second round doesn't guarantee you anything," he said. "I'd rather play another two years here at the University of Michigan, take another step toward my bachelor degree and have a good time here. I would've hated myself if I'd found myself in the D (NBA Development) League next year. I would rather play in college." For Michigan fans who had felt frustrated by other players leaving in the past under similar circumstances, this logic was music to their ears. Wagner also revealed some of the pressure he had felt after his standout performance against Louisville, "After the Louisville game, it became an international story. It was different for me because I'm from Germany and people there go crazy about this kind of stuff. I'm not saying that's why I played terribly in the Oregon game, but there definitely was a lot more pressure on my shoulders in the Oregon game. Now, I had a whole different level of interest coming to me and coming at me that I had to learn to deal with, and it wasn't easy."[4]

So his development path would continue under the careful tutelage of John Beilein and the Michigan staff. And the goals seemed pretty clear. He needed to improve as a rebounder after averaging just 4.2 boards a game. His defense had to take a step forward and he had to limit his exposure to foul trouble. "Coach Beilein and I always had these conversations: be a big that can shoot and not just a shooter that is big. There's a significant difference there,"[5] Wagner said. Using his natural energy as a positive and not becoming "emotionally drunk" as he put it, was also a priority. Finally, improving his leadership meant a lot to Moe and the staff. "I had been a leader under the radar but wasn't held accountable for the mistakes. I was very ambitious to take on that challenge and be consistent. I hadn't proven that yet."[6]

John Beilein was thrilled to have Wagner back for another year and felt that he was going about it the right way. "All I know is, going into it, he has the right attitude,"[7] the coach said before the season.

Having lost their senior point guard Derrick Walton, Michigan wasn't exactly sure who would be taking over that spot. While Zavier Simpson played in every game his freshman year, his minutes were restricted and his limitations seemed clear. Despite winning Mr. Basketball in Ohio his senior year of high school, Ohio State had chosen not to recruit him. With his shorter stature and a bit of a knuckleball for a jump-shot, some fans wondered what John Beilein had seen to prioritize Simpson ahead of Michigan State's Cassius Winston. Flashes of his defensive ability were evident, but few expected him to become a core component in his sophomore season.

Incoming freshman Eli Brooks would also be an option at point guard, but Beilein didn't want to bank on a true freshman succeeding in his first college action. That situation led him to take his first and only graduate transfer at Michigan. On paper, Jaaron Simmons seemed like a perfect fit. Simmons had started off his college career at the University of Houston. He had a promising freshman year including a matchup where his team prevailed versus Shabazz Napier and the soon-to-be national champion Connecticut Huskies. After a coaching change at Houston, he transferred to Ohio University where he became their lead guard and scored over 1000 points. He averaged 15.9 points and 6.5 assists on a 20-win Ohio team in 2016-17. Beilein described his excitement in the press release that announced Simmons' arrival, "His playmaking and vision on the floor are outstanding and he can really score the ball, too. Best of all, Jaaron is a terrific young man and teammate who we are excited about coaching next year."

Charles Matthews had completed his mandated redshirt year following his transfer and was ready to contribute to the 2017-18 Michigan team. While he had played in every game his freshman season at Kentucky, his production was limited to less than two points per game. He came to Michigan in search of the development that so many other players had enjoyed under Beilein. "Coach Beilein and the program has become well-known for developing guards," Matthews said at the time of his transfer. "Having this next year to develop not only my game but my overall strength is something I want to take full advantage of. I want to learn the offense and should be a seasoned vet so when it is my time to step on the floor, I will be ready."[8] Rumblings about the athleticism he flashed in practice during his redshirt year had begun to trickle out. John Beilein, rare to overhype, invoked the names of Tim Hardaway, Jr., and Glenn Robinson III when describing Matthews' ability. The former highly sought-after recruit seemed an excellent match for the Michigan program and expectations were high going into the season. Among the other new players who would share the floor with Matthews were incoming freshmen Jordan Poole and Isaiah Livers.

For the second consecutive season, there would be some new coaches on the bench next to John Beilein. After the progress Michigan's defense showed down the stretch in 2016-17, things looked promising under Billy Donlon's direction. But a unique set of circumstances led to Donlon moving on to serve as Chris Collins' assistant at Northwestern. The deep history Donlon shared with Collins—the two were high school teammates—along with the chance for Donlon to live with his father in Chicago made the opportunity about more than just basketball. It was no surprise that Beilein was fully on board with Donlon doing what was best for him and his family. Additionally, former Michigan assistant Lavall Jordan had called and asked Jeff Meyer to come join him at Butler. That left Beilein with two important openings to fill. The events of the last few months changed his mentality in the hiring process. "I wanted coaches who are great with today's generation of kids and have great relationships with players, who gravitate to them," said Beilein. "They don't care how much you know until they know how much you care about them. That team played so well in February and March, but particularly in March because there was such a great bond with them and the coaches."[9]

Surprisingly he ended up finding both his replacements at the same school. Luke Yaklich and DeAndre Haynes were both highly recommended by Illinois State head coach Dan Muller. In his search for a new defensive coordinator, Yaklich was not a name that was originally on Beilein's radar. The Illinois State assistant was only a few years removed from coaching high school basketball, and he and Beilein had never crossed paths. They seemed like a good match given that their backgrounds and styles were incredibly similar, except for one thing: Yaklich has made his career with as relentless an appreciation for the defensive side of the ball as John Beilein had for the offensive side. When Yaklich was a high school player at Lasalle-Peru Township High School in Illinois, his first practice with coach Gary Sonnenberg involved no basketballs. Strictly defensive work, man to man principles. He grew to love it. He became a successful high school coach and teacher, just as Beilein had many years ago. He found success following those principles he learned from Sonnenberg who he credits as "the assistant coach who instilled defense in my mind as a player."[10] Yaklich paid it forward, instilling defense in his players' minds.

One of those former players from Joliet Township High School, Jaquan McGee, told *The Athletic* about Yaklich's impact. "Once we noticed that people were scared to play us because of our defense, we took teams out of their rhythm," McGee said. "It really threw them off. And once we noticed that, man, we took off."[11]

Yaklich got his first opportunity to work at the college level as an assistant at Illinois State. There he put together solid defenses culminating with Kenpom's 19th best Adjusted Defensive Efficiency ranking in the country in the 2016-17 season. From there his head coach Dan Muller took the unusual step of reaching out to John Beilein to recommend both Yaklich and DeAndre Haynes. Muller believed in his friend Yaklich's ability so much that he was willing to lose him because he knew how successful he could be competing at a higher level. Beilein said Muller told him, "These guys deserve this opportunity. They want to play in the Big Ten. Do not let me get in the way of that."[12]

Beilein's interview process with Yaklich was an exhausting drawn-out affair. It was multiple meetings and multiple phone calls. It took time and work for Beilein to get comfortable with the idea of hiring someone he didn't know. Yaklich even had video put together of his coaching style from Illinois State practices to help Beilein gain comfort. At the end of the process, Yaklich checked all the boxes. "It took me a long time," Beilein says. "But I wanted a teacher, right? I wanted a guy that thought defense and knew defense, a relationship-builder. He was a high school teacher and a brilliant one. I want to be known as a teacher and mentor, not *the coach*, the guy that taught. This guy, that's what he does."[13] Early returns suggest a match-made in heaven; two former high school teachers that love the game and are full of integrity and work ethic.

Brian Cook of Mgoblog summed the whole situation up perfectly: "That is incredible on many levels. Beilein listened to a cold call about a couple of guys he didn't know, did the requisite research to bridge that gap, and hired both of the Illinois State guys on offer. And the guy who'd hired them in the first place and saw them build a team that absolutely should have gotten an at-large NCAA bid in the MVC was selfless enough to kick that process off."[14] A hearty thank you to Coach Dan Muller at Illinois State, indeed.

Beilein shared that appreciation towards Muller. "Dan is a champion. Dan is a first-class guy. I have an utmost respect for him and how he handled this."[15] Muller was just getting to know DeAndre Haynes when he left to join Yaklich and Beilein. Haynes was a Detroit native who was thrilled to have the opportunity to return home. He graduated from Southwestern High and went on to star at Kent State as a four-year starter and was named MAC player of the year in his senior season. After playing in Europe, he returned to Kent State and began his coaching career as an assistant for the Golden Flashes. He had only just been hired by Illinois State, yet to coach in-season there, when the chance to move to Ann Arbor presented itself.

"Coaching basketball at the University of Michigan has always been a dream of mine," Haynes said in the press release announcing his hire. The timing of the transition couldn't have been better, as Haynes' mother was experiencing health problems, and he would now be able to move with his wife and children close to his parents. Haynes' primary responsibility would be working closely with Michigan's guards, a task that had particular importance given the need to replace Derrick Walton at the point guard position.

The addition of the two young assistants completed Michigan's personnel changes over the offseason. This was the group that would seek to build on the success of the 2016-17 team. A number of important contributors had moved on and it would be up to others to replace their production and leadership. Challenges would inevitably arise. But in the early days of the 2017-18 team's practices, it became clear that the program's leader had adjusted his mindset to better handle those challenges. The plane crash just months ago had forced John Beilein to reevaluate things. He realized that more than ever, he needed to embrace the moment. Moe Wagner felt the entire team had adopted that message. "Enjoy every day because it could be your last," he said. "You have the job of being in the gym, and it's a beautiful job to have. It's a blessing. That's how we approach it, and that's how he approaches it."[16]

Beilein confirmed the slightly altered approach while also acknowledging this year's group had a lot of work to do. "Yes, I am [having more fun]. I do understand, however, that this is going to be a year where I better try and have fun because we're really in a rebuild in some areas of the program."[17]

Michigan made one final addition to their family just before the season got underway. On November 6, 2017, in a special ceremony and press conference attended by the entire team, Jude Stamper signed a National Letter of Intent to join the Michigan men's basketball program. Jude was born with a rare condition called Arthrogryposis Multi-Congenital disorder, which severely limits his ability to bend his joints. He had already had to endure ten surgeries at Mott Children's Hospital and made frequent use of a wheelchair. Jude's serendipitous path to wind up a member of the Wolverines seems almost too good to be true. His mom happened to catch the local news the day the Michigan football team introduced Larry Prout, Jr., a young man that has endured spina bifida, as an honorary member through a program called Team IMPACT. That led her to look into the program and submit an application on Jude's behalf. Team IMPACT's mission is to "connect children facing serious and chronic illnesses with college athletic teams, forming life-long bonds and life-changing outcomes." John Beilein happened to attend a Michigan men's soccer game and met Aiden Hansen and his family. Aiden was linked up with the soccer program through Team IMPACT, and Beilein was immediately intrigued by the idea of adding a new member to his program. Soon after a connection was made between Jude and Michigan basketball—"That's how it went down," Jude's mother Courtney said. "I call it divine intervention."[18]

"We are so very pleased to welcome Jude to the Michigan basketball family," Beilein said as he introduced Stamper. "Jude brings great passion and enthusiasm to this program and we are honored to have him on our team. We will continue to work hard toward another championship and know that Jude's presence will be an important part of our journey."

Duncan Robinson was similarly enthusiastic about Jude's addition. "It is great for him, but I am just so excited to have him around us and the perspective that he brings on a day-to-day basis. I think this is going to be an incredible opportunity for both of us."[19]

The Stampers weren't sure what would come after the press conference. They thought that receiving some tickets might be the extent of their interaction with the team. Instead Jude and his family were welcomed with open arms beyond their wildest dreams. Jude's mom explained, "When Jude was first drafted, we didn't quite know what to expect. We didn't know how much Jude was going to be involved in the program. I think Coach Beilein and this team have taken it to the next level for us. They include him at practice, they interact with him at practice. Coach Beilein comes up to him right away."[20]

Jude ate pre-game meals with the team, visited the locker room before and after games, and would later lead the team in "The Victors" after a win over Rutgers. The players exchanged texts with him, played video games together, and asked him for words of encouragement. Beilein explained the players' relationship with Jude. "It's not like, 'hey there's this kid with some challenges that we're helping out as a charity.' No, he's their friend right now, they respect him."[21]

The Stamper family is very clear about how tremendous an experience this has been for Jude. "It feels great. I've loved Michigan my entire life, so it feels really great. It's just an honor to be able to be on a team, even though I'm not able to play on one for basketball or sports. It's really cool," Jude said. His mom was even more emphatic. "What greater way can you feel loved and included and part of a team? Those are the things that Coach Beilein and this team, they'll never understand what they're doing for my son."[22]

The Wolverines also benefited from their relationship with Jude. "This young man brings energy to us every day, and he's really been an inspiration to our team,"[23] Beilein said. Duncan Robinson agreed. "Whether it's a tough loss, or a tough practice, or you're just having a bad day, and you look over and you see him [with] everything he's been through at such a young age and he's still smiling ear to ear, it's pretty hard to get down on yourself.... He's a special kid and he's meant a lot to us."[24] That extra dose of perspective was needed as the beginning of the 2017-18 season saw its share of bumps in the road.

Chapter 11

Remodeling

At the start of the 2017-18 season, Beilein did not sense a Final Four team. "Back in the preseason, if you would've said this team would win 30, I'd have told you to come watch us practice. I really felt that this was a re-modeling type of year,"[1] he said later.

Michigan won the first three games of the year but trailed in the second half of each against inferior opponents in North Florida, Central Michigan, and Southern Mississippi. They went on to lose in Maui to a mediocre LSU team that exposed chinks at the point guard position. For the first time in eight years, Michigan couldn't rely on Darius Morris, Trey Burke, or Derrick Walton to run the show. Zavier Simpson had started the game but played an empty 10 minutes, picking up four fouls without scoring a point. His hesitancy on offense often left the Wolverines playing four against five on that end of the court. Jaaron Simmons played a similarly empty 15 minutes. Eli Brooks had a few brief flashes but was outplayed down the stretch. The three combined to shoot 1–5 with four turnovers to match their four assists in 42 minutes. That would clearly not be a winning formula from one of the most important positions on the floor. The coaching staff met early the next morning and discussed how to address the poor production. Brendan Quinn of *The Athletic* did a great job detailing the decision-making process: "Assistant coach DeAndre Haynes spoke up, saying that when he played at Kent State, an underclassman took his starting job for a game and it 'got my attention.' Haynes said he was in favor of sitting Simpson and starting Brooks."[2]

Beilein listened to Haynes' instincts and made the change, inserting Eli Brooks into the starting lineup for that day's game. Due to the loss the day before, Michigan found itself in the loser's bracket playing an overmatched Chaminade team. They beat the Division 2 team handily 102–64. Charles Matthews had his second straight terrific performance, never missing a shot from the field. Duncan Robinson found his stroke against the lesser opponent, knocking down four buckets from long distance. Freshman Jordan Poole played his first extended minutes, and demonstrated his potential for instant offense, scoring ten points in nine minutes. Despite the lineup change at point guard, the struggles continued at the position. Simpson bounced back to play a bit better, dishing out four assists and recording two steals without turning the ball over. Brooks shot 1–5 from the field, while Simmons played 11 minutes with only a turnover and a foul to show for it.

That win lined Michigan up against a mediocre VCU team. The team needed a win to salvage what had been a disappointing trip so far. Michigan struggled in their half-court sets but was able to use VCU's aggressiveness to their advantage, getting out effectively in the fast break to take a six-point lead into halftime. That lead disintegrated in the middle of the second half as Michigan's still suspect defense allowed VCU to go on an 11–0 run entirely on free throws and points in the paint. The Wolverines matched VCU's 11–0 run with one of their own but timed it better—finishing the game with their flourish for a final of 68–60. It hadn't been particularly pretty, but the developing group had shown some grit in pulling out an important win. The point guard battle continued to be an open question. Though Brooks started again, Simpson played the final six minutes. Simmons looked like the odd man out, seeing just two minutes of action. The defensive effort had been solid, though the execution was lacking at times. But Yaklich was excited to receive a text from Wagner during the trip, saying, "I can't have that many defensive plays where I say woulda, coulda, shoulda. I need to be a better leader."[3] Wagner understood this team would be measured by the growth they showed over the course of the season. "I think we're a very young team, and that shouldn't be an excuse," he said. "But I think we have a long way to go in terms of how to play to win and in a mature way."[4] He had shown improvement in his rebounding and his leadership early in the season, having addressed some of the weaknesses NBA scouts had pointed out to him. His desire to be accountable to his coaches and teammates was an important step toward building the defense Yaklich planned for.

The team returned home for a non-competitive blowout win over UC-Riverside. Three days later, they traveled to Chapel Hill, North Carolina, for a much-hyped matchup against the defending champion North Carolina Tar Heels. It became apparent that Michigan was not yet up to the challenge. Leaning heavily on Wagner and Matthews once again, the game was close for much of the first half. The two combined for 21 of Michigan's first 29 and it was a tie game with eight minutes left before the break. From there, the Tar Heels took over. They began knocking down shots and running up and down the court on the fast break. The Dean Dome became very loud, very quickly. After a 16–3 run, a shell-shocked Michigan team was on the ropes. That burst continued after halftime as Michigan put up limited defensive resistance. UNC distanced themselves by as many as 29 before some garbage-time baskets made the 86–71 final score closer than the game had been played. All the themes of the early season were evident: lackluster point guard play, poor team defense that allowed 51 points in the first half, and another strong performance from Moe Wagner. If Michigan was going to reach their goals in 2017-18, it was clear there would need to be marked improvement across the roster. "I don't think we were ready for the quickness, the speed, and the precision that they run with. And we weren't locked in defensively. I can't tell you why, but we need to shore it up," Beilein vented in his post-game comments.

The Wolverines didn't have much time to make corrections. The Big Ten Conference Tournament was starting a week earlier because conference commissioner Jim Delaney and the Big Ten wanted New York City to host, and the standard conference tournament weekend was already booked by the Big East. This dictated that conference play would also begin early. Michigan opened its conference slate at home against Indiana on December 2. The Maize and Blue faithful were finally treated to the first glimpses of the team's potential against a decent opponent. A foul by Charles Matthews 14 seconds into the game led to Beilein's standard quick hook, and Jordan Poole checked in for the first extended minutes of his career. The offense didn't miss a beat. Poole quickly knocked down a three-pointer, and two minutes later he did it again. They were sandwiched around threes from Robinson and Abdur-Rahkman and the Wolverines had a 16–2 lead. Michigan maintained a comfortable lead the rest of the way for a 69–55 victory in their Big Ten opener. Beilein gave credit to his staff afterwards: "DeAndre Haynes did a great job with the scouting report and our kids lived that scouting report. They did a great job." The defense had played one of their best games, limiting Indiana to seven three-point attempts and just 40 percent shooting overall.

Poole's play had been a revelation, as the freshman drained five three-pointers and totaled 19 points. His bench celebrations with Isaiah Livers, and the young teammates' self-assigned nickname of "The Drip Boys" (along with Ibi Watson), had made him an early fan favorite. His care-free approach to the game combined with his obvious talent perpetuated that excitement. "[The coaches] constantly stress 'shoot the open shots,' and not hesitate. You don't need to tell me twice,"[5] the young guard explained afterwards.

Poole had grown up in Milwaukee and his unique personality was evident at an early age. "We always encouraged individuality," his mom Monet Poole said. "He didn't want to go to parochial high school because he was so fun and so different. The parochial school kind of wants you to walk a fine line. It would've smothered him."[6] Former assistant Bacari Alexander first identified Poole as a Michigan target. It didn't take long for Beilein to agree—besides Poole's obvious talent, he also offered a projectable frame and wouldn't be turning 18 until after he had graduated high school. Once a formal scholarship offer was made, Beilein's track record as a developer and an offensive genius then paid dividends. Poole's high school coach, Jim Gosz, knew all about the Michigan's proficiency in those areas and encouraged Jordan and his parents to jump on the opportunity.

After he committed, Beilein went to see him in a game and Poole didn't make a single basket. Fortunately, Michigan's head coach trusted his original evaluation. "It was a not a great performance, but I knew what I saw earlier and I knew his capabilities."[7] Without that conviction, Michigan's 2017-18 season may have played out much differently.

As positively as things were trending for Poole, Jaaron Simmons' season was moving in the opposite direction. He received no playing time for the first time all season in the Indiana game, and he was clearly on the outside looking in on a point guard job that he had expected to be his. Beilein's system can be challenging to pick up, and no one player controls the ball the way Simmons had become accustomed to at Ohio. The adjustment was not as smooth as Simmons or the coaching staff had hoped. "I've never seen stuff like this ever in my life, the things we do," he admitted. "We got a lot of plays, we got a lot of different terms. I've never heard of none of this stuff."[8]

It had quickly become apparent that Simmons was not going to simply be a plug and play replacement for Walton. John Beilein spoke openly and honestly to Simmons about the adjustments he would need to make and used data from early-season practices to back up his points. "I wanted to show that he has to be a better player if he wants to get on that court and that his defense has to really be better as well. Jaaron can be a really good player, but if he's not going to guard people, and if he's not going to take care of the ball and make good decisions, then repetition [in practice] doesn't mean anything. He gets that, and he's worked really hard, but he's had some tough practices. He's better than that. And we know it. That was the message."[9]

After playing double-digit minutes the first five games of the season, his playing time was drying up. It was a situation that had the potential to cause a problem in the locker room, but Simmons would have none of it. "I'm not used to sitting on the bench," he said. "But at the same time I'm going to be there to support my teammates whether I'm out there playing or sitting on the bench cheering."[10]

Two days after beating Indiana, the Wolverines traveled down to Columbus, Ohio, to face their rivals. Ohio State had a new head coach in Chris Holtmann and appeared to be in rebuilding mode. Despite having the talented Keita Bates-Diop on the roster, Holtmann had offered former Wolverine walk-on Andrew Dakich a scholarship and was playing him extended minutes. Michigan came out rolling as the expectations about both teams appeared to be playing to script. Behind seven first-half three-pointers, Michigan led by 20 with 1:30 left before the break. Ohio State closed with a 7–0 run but the Wolverines appeared to be comfortably in control. That end of half momentum seemed to spark the Buckeyes though, and they opened the second on a 9–0 tear, cutting Michigan's 20-point lead down to four. Suddenly the Maize and Blue had no answers. They shot 5–29 in that half. Their three upperclassmen leaders Wagner, Abdur-Rahkman, and Robinson combined to go 0–15. There wasn't much positive to take away from the collapse. Just as the team had seemed to figure things out against Indiana, they gave up a 20-point lead to their rivals to lose by nine. John Beilein was measured in his post-game comments as usual but identified the need for his team to grow. "We did a lot again what we did in the North Carolina game and the LSU game—when things got a little tough, we really had trouble stepping up. That's a big area we have to work at. Somehow we have to get them to understand the importance of [embracing] that part of the game and [getting] it done."

With five days off prior to matchups with UCLA and Texas, it was a fair bet that practices would feature a heightened intensity from both staff and players. While the Bruins had lost draft picks Lonzo Ball and TJ Leaf from the previous season, they were 7–1 and ranked #23 in the country. Michigan's NCAA Tournament resume was looking a little light without a signature non-conference win, so the game took on greater importance than most December outings. Charles Matthews would be playing that day with a heavy heart; his grandmother, Mary Thomas, had passed away two days earlier. While she had been in hospice care the last few weeks, Matthews had struggled in games against Indiana and Ohio State. Now he would have to move forward knowing his grandmother was gone.

In a nationally televised game on CBS that was marketed as Star Wars Day at the Crisler Center, the afternoon appropriately took on twists and turns deserving of Hollywood. The Wolverines jumped out to a 5–2 lead after a dunk by Matthews and an Abdur-Rahkman three-pointer. Abdur-Rahkman would not score again in the half despite seven more attempts. A few minutes later, Matthews knocked down a jumper before foul trouble relegated him to the bench for the majority of the first half. Moe Wagner kept Michigan in the game while the rest of the team struggled to make a shot. Their 33 percent shooting percentage in the first half said it all. The 30–27 halftime deficit would have been worse if not for UCLA's sloppiness with the ball, resulting in 12 turnovers. Their big man, Thomas Welsh, scored 13 points and grabbed 8 boards to pace the Bruins. Welsh then hit a three to start the second half and UCLA took off. By the time Aaron Holiday knocked down his own three-pointer out of the first media timeout, the Bruins had blitzed Michigan into a 15-point differential. The Wolverine faithful were left grumbling about the similar Ohio State run to start the second half five days earlier. The next 20 minutes would be one of the first clear indicators of the 2017-18 team's ability to overcome adversity. At the previous timeout Coach Beilein had implored Matthews to give him more. In his press conference later, he shared his message in the huddle: "You've been the MVP for UCLA so far. We want you to be the MVP for us." And just when things could have gone off the rails, Charles Matthews took over. He scored the next eight points of the game to quickly trim the lead back to a more manageable seven-point difference. The two teams then played roughly to a stalemate over the next seven minutes. With 5:27 left, Aaron Holiday scored two of his game-high 27 to put UCLA up six points. The much-maligned point guard position for Michigan then showed a spark of potential. Eli Brooks set up Wagner for a three-pointer and followed with a layup of his own the next possession. Simpson soon relieved him and hit a contorted running hook shot in the lane to narrow the lead to two. Then after another Matthews missed free throw (he was 2–10 for the game), Simpson picked up his teammate by exploding into the passing lane to steal a pass from Holiday, and quickly laying it up at the other end.

UCLA still led 64–63 with 18 seconds left. The Bruins knocked down a single free throw at the other end, giving the Wolverines one final shot. Brooks re-entered the game for Simpson, and aggressively took a handoff from Abdur-Rahkman and drove to the hoop. He was fouled hard and rewarded with two free throws that could tie the game. Brooks was 3–6 from the line on the year and was yet to make two in a row in his brief college career. He stepped to the line and coolly made them both. The offense-defense substitution pattern continued as Simpson checked back in for UCLA's final possession in regulation. The emerging defensive stopper knocked the ball away from Holiday, which disrupted their offensive flow and resulted in an errant final shot attempt. After trailing by 15 in the second half, Michigan had forced overtime. When the extra period started, it seemed as though the Bruins had already conceded defeat. Back to back threes from Simpson and Matthews pushed Michigan out front. During a late game timeout, Beilein later revealed that he had encouraged Matthews, telling him that his grandmother was looking over the team. Simpson finished with six points in overtime in the best performance of his young career, as Michigan won 78–69. The team was ecstatic afterwards. Beilein asked Brooks and Simpson to lead the team in singing "The Victors" to celebrate the developing tandem's successful performance. The head coach hoped this game could be a steppingstone. "When we really needed to suck it up and get some work done at the end, we got it done. I'm hoping it's a huge benchmark for our team as we go forward,"[11] Beilein said.

Simpson, in particular, had a standout performance. He scored 15 points on a very efficient 6-9 shooting. His four steals were the only thing that slowed down Aaron Holiday all game. Despite losing his starting job in Hawaii, he had persevered and maintained a winning attitude for the team. Matthews was proud of his teammate, saying he "never pouted" and "was never a cancer in the locker room."[12]

Simpson followed his father Quincey's great advice. "I told him to keep his head up, keep working. I told him to be a good teammate and challenge and compete daily in practice. It's adversity."[13] Though Brooks was still the starter, Simpson was often on the court at the end of the game. He had played more minutes than his counterpart the last two games. If he could continue to overcome his hesitancy on offense like he had against the Bruins, his defensive tenacity offered the potential to really impact Michigan's ceiling in the 2017-18 season.

A trip to Austin, Texas, followed just three days later. The Wolverines had a chance to demonstrate that the UCLA comeback was more indicative of the team's future than their Ohio State collapse. The Longhorns were led by former VCU coach Shaka Smart and featured a highly acclaimed seven-foot shot blocking center named Mo Bamba, who had strongly considered attending Michigan before settling on Texas. In a low-scoring game, Muhammad-Ali Abdur-Rahkman led the way with 17 points and 10 rebounds. At one point, Abdur-Rahkman spun through the lane only to encounter the lengthy Bamba in his path. He lofted the rock skyward over Bamba's outstretched hand, off the glass and in. That evening was one of the first glimpses of his consistent scoring ability that the Wolverines would come to depend on later in the season. The defensive effort limited Texas to 37 percent shooting and provided a hint that Michigan was slowly growing into a team that could win a game at either end of the court. The only negative in the 59–52 victory was a rolled ankle that would keep Moe Wagner out the next two contests.

The first of those games was against Detroit Mercy as part of a college basketball triple-header played at Little Caesar's Arena in downtown Detroit. The day before, Matthews and DeAndre Haynes had flown back to Chicago to be at the services for his recently deceased grandmother. After a morning scramble to get back in time for the game, the two arrived at the arena just before game-time. Detroit was led by former members of the Michigan family: head coach Bacari Alexander and forward Kameron Chatman. The Wolverines showed no interest in taking it easy on their overmatched opponent and torched them wire-to-wire. In Moe Wagner's absence, Jon Teske showed what he was capable of with 15 points and 10 rebounds. "He's gotten incrementally better with his athleticism and his understanding of the game," Beilein said. "But what I really like is that he never stuck his nose in, and he's really sticking his nose in now. That's been a big difference. He's getting what I call traffic rebounds, and he's never got those."[14] Zavier Simpson continued his surge and stuffed the stat sheet with 12 points, seven assists, five rebounds, and two steals without a single turnover. "I think that by trying to do less, he's doing more,"[15] his head coach said.

After an understandably slow first half, Matthews scored 17 in the second half. He expressed his appreciation for the support he had received from his coaches and teammates. "When you see people caring about you outside of basketball—that makes you run through brick walls for them,"[16] he said.

As the calendar turned into 2018, optimism around the program began to grow. Michigan's trajectory seemed positive, and it's always smart to bet on a John Beilein team over the second half of a season. One could even imagine a deep tournament run after watching the second half against UCLA, or the first half in Columbus, Ohio. But it was those other halves that gave pause. And the entire games against LSU and North Carolina. The team's consistency was definitely lacking, and many players needed to establish more defined roles. The future began to come into focus as the team resumed the conference portion of the schedule. They got off on the right foot in Iowa the day after New Year's Day. After a slow six minutes found Michigan trailing by two, Beilein inserted Zavier Simpson and freshman Isaiah Livers into the game. Livers immediately had two assists with a dunk sandwiched in between. Then Simpson had an assist and an old-fashioned three-point play, followed soon by back-to-back three-pointers. By the time Livers checked out, Michigan had gone on a 21–4 run and would remain comfortably in control the rest of the evening. Simpson never left the floor the rest of the half, and the two stayed on the court for most of the second half as well. The two young players had shown steady improvement throughout the year and now were blossoming at the perfect time. Jon Teske also contributed 24 solid minutes as Wagner's minutes were limited so he could fully heal from his ankle injury. The success of Beilein's teams over the back half of the schedule was typically predicated on emerging players stepping forward, and the youth on Michigan's roster appeared to be ready to do so.

Given how well the team played with Livers and Simpson on the court, it naturally raised questions about whether those players should move into the starting lineup. Simpson already had been trending in that direction for a few games. His 15 point, seven assist, zero turnover performance in Iowa City clinched the adjustment. Livers offered a stark contrast at the four-position to Duncan Robinson, the current starter. His advantage in physicality and athleticism made him a more natural fit, and better suited to matchup defensively with opposing fours. "Isaiah should be playing more in the future. He's been working on that jump shot, his numbers are good in practices [but] he hasn't done it in games. Maybe this is a breakthrough," Beilein said afterwards.

Both players would figure more prominently going forward, but it was Simpson who had earned back his starting job four days later against Illinois. Not only did he start, but he rarely left the court. As Simpson's minutes picked up, his voice as one of the team's primary leaders grew as well. "He's a tough dude, and you want him on your side," Beilein said. "He just has a really good attitude toward life and is just growing and getting better. He's also a little bit of spiritual leader for us."[17]

Simpson pointed to the work he did with DeAndre Haynes as essential to his recent improvement. "Coach DeAndre has a lot of good drills that are confidence builders. When you're working out with him, you pick up a lot of little things that help your game. He's working with me a lot on my finishers and my floaters."[18]

It all traced back to that benching in Hawaii. "The biggest thing for [Simpson] was that when he was on the bench he took the time to see the game from there. Then, he could come in and play a little better,"[19] said Haynes.

Simpson saw a familiar face in the opposing coach's seat when he returned as a starter. Brad Underwood, former Oklahoma State coach, had taken over Illinois' program. The previous year, his Cowboys had almost upset Michigan by playing at a frenetic pace. Illinois had learned to play at that same pace and, early in the game, took an eight-point lead over the Maize and Blue. At that point, Livers checked in and quickly made his impact felt again. He knocked down a three-pointer and then had three dunks to give Michigan a two-point lead. The final of those three dunks was a highlight alley-oop thrown by Jordan Poole from behind the three-point line. "I got the pass and kind of peeked at him at half-court," Poole said. "We made eye contact, and I'm looking like, 'I'm just going to throw it to the rim, big boy. You've got to go get it.' When he got it, it had me super excited, and it brought a lot of energy to the crowd."[20] Poole also had a strong performance, scoring 11 points, and inserting his trademark energy into the proceedings. Michigan shot 64 percent in the second half and pulled away for the 79–69 win. Much of the roster contributed, including Wagner who looked completely healthy, scoring 14 points to go along with seven boards.

After two solid efforts to start 2018, the degree of difficulty was about to rise. Michigan was scheduled to face #5 Purdue and #4 Michigan State the following week. These two games would provide a telling gauge for whether the team's steady improvement over the past few weeks was enough to hang with the conference's heavyweights. The Purdue game was a thrilling battle right down to the wire. Both teams played high level basketball throughout the contest. The favored Boilermakers led by seven at the half on the strength of that many three-pointers. They quickly upped it to 13 after the break, but the Wolverines responded with three straight three-pointers—one by Matthews, and two by Livers. Michigan kept hanging around and finally tied it on a Charles Matthews three-pointer from the corner, off a beautiful feed from Simpson with just under eight minutes remaining. Purdue's cold-blooded lead guard Carsen Edwards answered right back with a three of his own. Then Simpson took his turn from distance, knocking down long balls on the next two possessions. After a Vince Edwards three-pointer tied it up at 69 with 2:28 remaining, both teams went cold. Matthews rebounded a Purdue miss with 28 seconds left and had a chance to break the tie in Michigan's favor. After milking some clock, Matthews penetrated to the hoop and had the ball knocked innocently away with six seconds left. The referee at the scene properly awarded the offensive team the ball, as referees have done on similar plays since James Naismith first invented the game.

Then they decided to stop the game to look at the replay. After more than a five-minute delay that killed the wonderful pace of an exciting basketball game, they found super slow-motion footage that suggested a Matthews' fingertip had actually grazed the ball last. Purdue was awarded the ball, and they proceeded to throw it down low to their mammoth center Isaac Haas. He was fouled by Wagner, made one of two, and Purdue survived a late Matthews' Hail Mary that rolled around the rim, to win 70–69. Beilein was frustrated, but professional as always, in his comments afterwards. "I thought he was going to lay that ball in with five seconds left—he had leverage, he had everything. I don't know where the ball got slapped down. He said it did not go off of him, but apparently it must have." Despite the tough finish, Michigan left the game knowing that they could hang with anyone. They carried that attitude with them into the Breslin Center four days later.

Chapter 12

Broken Ankles

The opening tip against Michigan State featured an adjustment in the starting lineup. Livers had played well once again against Purdue and would start instead of Duncan Robinson going forward. That couldn't have been an easy decision. Robinson had been named a captain of the team and was in his senior season. But for whatever reason, his usual success from the three-point line wasn't there. He shot well against Michigan's clearly inferior opponents, but over the season's first 18 games he was 10 of 48 (20.8 percent) when Michigan faced a legitimate foe. Beilein shot him straight. "Look at your stats. In big-time games you're shooting 25 percent. We showed him the stats of all the opponents, he was the worst three-point shooter on our team. I said, 'I owe it to the rest of the guys on the team, let's bring you off the bench and just come in there with some swag ready to knock down shots.'"[1] It was obviously a bitter pill to swallow, and it left Duncan somewhat reeling. This year was supposed to be the culmination of all his hard work, and now he had lost his job to a freshman. "It was one of the few times that I have not been 100 percent on board with his attitude," Beilein told *The Athletic*. "He sulked for a couple days, I thought."[2]

Robinson didn't disagree: "I thought I maybe let it get to me for a sec, but I had to heighten my sense of urgency and understand that this is it. This is my senior season, and I wasn't going to go out like that."[3] The game against Michigan State presented an ideal opportunity to make the adjustment because Livers could provide better defensive support against the Spartans' NBA prospects Miles Bridges and Jaren Jackson. Beilein could then choose Robinson's matchups more carefully off the bench.

In the Michigan locker room before the game, Beilein pointed to the close loss to Purdue as motivation. "You can't cheat this game. All those things that we regret, that I regret, that you regret from the Purdue loss … not today. Let's go!" Once the two rivals took the court, Bridges and Jackson got off to a good start with a couple early dunks, but then it was Moe Wagner that made his presence known. On the road in front of a hostile crowd, he came out and scored 11 of the Wolverines' first 18 points. Both teams competed back and forth. Michigan State had some emphatic finishes at the rim that whipped their crowd up and made for a very loud building. But every time, Michigan seemed to come back with a bucket at their own end. The way Michigan matched Michigan State's physicality and aggressiveness was a welcome sign. Despite shooting a dismal 36 percent in the first half, the Wolverines were only down by three thanks to a 17–4 advantage in points off turnovers. At halftime, Beilein brought the positivity and emphasized staying consistent. "Here's the story—they're going to win the highlight tape and we're going to win the game!"[4]

In a game plagued by foul calls, the referees struggled to identify the proper balance of when exactly to blow their whistles. The first eight points of the second half came at the free throw line. Just after the first media timeout of the second half, Duncan Robinson found himself defending Jaren Jackson in the post—a matchup that is heavily tilted in Michigan State's favor. This case was no exception, as Jackson worked his way around him for an easy layup. Wagner came over late to help out and picked up a foul, his third. Jackson completed the three-point play and Michigan's best player headed to the bench. Down two on the road and without Wagner, Michigan would need Jon Teske to step up with some solid minutes. He immediately pulled down an offensive rebound and made two free throws after getting fouled to tie the game. A few minutes later, he grabbed another offensive board and put it back in. By the time Wagner checked back in for Teske five minutes later, Michigan had weathered the storm and led by one. On his first offensive possession back, Wagner put Nick Ward through the wringer with a spinning drive punctuated by a head fake and a layup. Ward was whistled for the foul and Wagner completed the three-point play.

Abdur-Rahkman followed with his own three-point play in Michigan's next possession to push the lead to five. A brief six-point burst by the Spartans culminated with Jaren Jackson free throws that gave the home team a one-point lead with 8:24 on the clock. It would be the last time Michigan State was ahead that afternoon. On the next possession, Wagner popped out to the three-point line as Simpson drove and was rewarded by his teammate with an open look that he calmly drained. Those two repeatedly stepped up down the stretch to control the game. Matthews rejected Bridges' dunk attempt as the Wolverines flexed their newfound defensive intensity. Simpson found his way to the basket, late in the shot clock, for a layup at the other end. A similar sequence soon followed as Wagner made two free throws, Michigan's defensive energy forced a turnover, and Simpson hit a runner in the lane to stretch the lead to eight. As Simpson's offensive confidence had grown during the season, so too did the bag of tricks that he showed off. Various floaters, runners, and different angled layups were all deployed to defuse shot blockers' attempts to return to sender.

With under four minutes, Wagner posted up Nick Ward. He spun away and bounced off the opposite leg into his best Dirk Nowitzki fade-away. Nothing but net. At the other end of the court, Ward tried to return the favor. Wagner stayed square and vertical, absorbed the contact, and got a piece of Ward's shot. His abuse of Ward culminated on the offensive end with one of the signature plays of the season. Wagner received the ball at the top of the key, took one dribble to his right, before reversing course with a behind-the-back dribble to his left. As Ward tried to regain his balance and stay in front, he simply wasn't athletic enough to do so, and collapsed in a heap in the middle of the lane. It was the same play that had inspired Beilein to offer Wagner his scholarship three years earlier. Wagner continued his path unabated to the hoop and finished the easy layup. Ward rose from the floor, rightly embarrassed, as announcer Gus Johnson exclaimed as only he can, "Ankle-breaker ... whoa!"

That final indignation seemed to zap whatever spirit the crowd and the team could muster to defend their home court. Although a free throw shooting marathon ensued before the clock struck zero, the outcome was never again in doubt. Wagner had posted an all-time performance in a matchup with plenty of history behind it. Despite fighting through foul trouble that limited him to 27 minutes, he had scored a career-high 27 points. A never-ending sequence of spin moves and head fakes kept Michigan State's assorted big men struggling to keep up. He offset those drives and posts on the interior by sinking three of four from distance. He fouled out with 18 seconds left and walked up and down the bench high fiving his teammates while smiling from ear to ear. He had taken the liberty all game to display his emotions, and even Tom Izzo couldn't take exception. "He earned it. He's Scott Skiles—he talked it, he walked it," Izzo admitted in his press conference.

Simpson, meanwhile, had temporarily put to rest any question about whether he or his long-time nemesis Cassius Winston was the correct target for Michigan. Simpson posted his own career-high with 16 points. He also set up his teammates with five assists and zero turnovers. His emerging elite defense had stifled Winston, who turned the ball over four times amid a quiet 3–7 shooting performance. Beilein was ecstatic as he entered the locker room and players doused him with the ritual big-win water shower. "How about those Wolverines baby!" he shouted. "Quote me what I said at halftime. They're going to win the highlight tape," he continued. "And we're going to win the game!" his players answered. Beilein smiled and said, "They had some great dunks. But it's two damn points. That's it. You have to have that mindset."[5]

The 2017-18 Michigan Wolverines had their signature victory, but more importantly they now carried the confidence that if they kept improving, they could beat any team in the country. Assistant coach Saddi Washington was starting to sense something special. He told Beilein afterwards, "This team may be different. This team has some of that grit you may need to win games like that."[6]

Beilein saw it too, as he shared with the assembled media: "I think that was evident today a couple times to us. In timeouts and things like that, whenever they'd make a little run or it was going the other way, somebody would come up with a big hoop or a big stop."

Michigan's next challenge was its cramped schedule. The Michigan State game was the first of four games scheduled over eight days. The Wolverines hosted Maryland just two days after the emotional win. With all the factors lining up to create a classic "trap-game" scenario, Michigan played their part in the first half and found themselves down 10 at halftime to a lesser opponent. Poole and Wagner each hit three three-pointers in the second stanza to resuscitate the Wolverines. As Maryland coach Mark Turgeon would emphasize after the game, "They're impossible to guard. Let me say that again: They're *impossible* to guard with Wagner." The game seemed to be in hand when Simpson tallied a layup for a five-point lead with 26 seconds left. But Maryland's Anthony Cowan quickly answered with a three-pointer and Simpson drew a foul on the ensuing inbounds. Simpson's free throw shooting was the one piece of his game that hadn't improved much over the course of the season. It presented a serious end-of-game concern for Beilein and staff. That concern was manifested when Simpson missed both. A Kevin Huerter three-pointer for Maryland gave them a sudden one-point lead and only 3.2 seconds showed on the clock. Isaiah Livers took the ball out under the basket with the length of the court in front of him. Livers had a high school pitching background at Derek Jeter's alma mater Kalamazoo Central, and was known for his ability to deliver a fastball. And as we would see again later in the season, he threw a strike to Abdur-Rahkman streaking up the court. This time Abdur-Rahkman would keep the ball, drive to the hoop, and get knocked down—earning two shots from the free throw stripe.

The young man from Allentown was known for his stoic demeanor. It was never better exemplified than on these game-deciding free throws. Registering zero emotion on his face, Abdur-Rahkman calmly knocked down both shots for the win. To top it off, those points gave the senior 1000 in his career. The lack of expression in such a tense moment so perfectly personified Abdur-Rahkman that a picture of him preparing to shoot the free throws became an internet meme among Michigan fans. Only occasionally was he the star of a game, but he was always a dependable contributor that could be counted on in the clutch. Moments like these were all thanks to Dave Rooney's recommendation years ago. Back home in Pennsylvania, Rooney, the basketball aficionado, and Abdur-Rahkman's father, Dawud, had begun meeting for coffee once a month. "We have a lot in common. Matter of fact—a lot more in common than I'd ever think,"[7] Rooney said. Four years earlier, when Beilein had told Abdur-Rahkman and his father about Rooney's recommendation, they had no idea who Beilein was talking about. But having received limited attention from other schools, they were thrilled to have the opportunity to play at Michigan.

"It's just a crazy story, man ... how this all happened,"[8] Dawud said. It sure is. The impression a young John Beilein made in 1978 on a fellow coach in upstate New York led to a recruiting tip in 2014, which led to Michigan finding their senior captain and the school's all-time leader in games played. It also led to an unusual friendship and deep level of appreciation between Rooney and the Abdur-Rahkman family—and had just allowed Michigan to avoid a frustrating home loss.

Following the suspenseful Maryland victory, the team soon traveled to Lincoln, Nebraska. Whether you blame it on the longer distance trip or the condensed schedule, the team played its worst basketball of the season and lost 72–52. A home game against conference doormat Rutgers provided a chance for the Wolverines to regroup. Duncan Robinson made four three-pointers and the defense held Rutgers to a 33 percent shooting percentage and just 47 points, while registering 62 of their own. That Saturday afternoon also featured a special connection to the team's close friend Jude Stamper. Beilein and staff, along with the BTN broadcast crew and many Maize Rage members, wore Stamper's signature bowties to promote awareness of his medical condition. After the game, Stamper led the team in singing "The Victors."

It was also a day that served to connect the emerging team with many of Michigan's greats from the past. John Beilein invited 100 former players to partake in the festivities. Rudy Tomjanovich took a liking to Moe Wagner and the two celebrated the win together afterwards. Wagner explained, "I know a little bit about the way Rudy played, and he was a tough player. It was a pleasure to meet him."[9] Tomjanovich scored 29 points and grabbed an astounding 30 rebounds in a game against Loyola of Chicago in 1969. Wagner would do his best to match that performance against the Ramblers later in the season.

Jalen Rose also spoke to the team and expressed what he had seen from them so far. "They're all hungry," Rose said. "The thing I appreciate about this team is that they continue to get better. Look no further than how they played against Michigan State. It showed that this team has a lot of promise."[10]

It was an exchange that impacted the current team. "It meant a lot," said Duncan Robinson. "You don't realize how many people are rooting for you and care about you. To have them come back and say these things to our faces after the game was really cool."[11] Knowing that the whole Michigan family had their back, the current Wolverine squad headed to Purdue to try and avenge their earlier loss against the Boilermakers. Both teams played like the elite offenses they had the potential to be. Both shot over 60 percent and you couldn't really blame either defense. The ball was moving quickly and players were knocking down shots. Vince Edwards, who John Beilein had aggressively recruited years before, scored a career-high 30 points for Purdue. Abdur-Rahkman answered with his own career-high 26 points.

There were 24 lead changes throughout, though Purdue maintained at least a four-point lead over the final eight minutes. It was the rare loss that was tough to be too upset about. The Wolverines played great and Purdue played even better. They looked like two of the better teams in the country. Beilein discussed the game plan in his press conference afterwards, which had yielded success for Michigan against dominant post players. "We were trying to play one-on-one in the post, and if Haas scored 40 points and he had 20 [two-point baskets] it was ok with us. But we weren't going to give them the three, we couldn't do that. They were just too good."

Michigan left West Lafayette hoping for one more chance later in the year to finally slay the giant. Before that could happen, Michigan had to focus on the final eight games on the conference schedule. A strong finish would position them well in both the Big Ten Tournament and the NCAA Tournament, while also providing valuable momentum for a growing team. "We have a long way to go in this season with eight games left," Beilein said. "We're going to have to win a lot more games and get better. And the only way we can do that is if we continue to practice and continue to self-correct some of the habits that we have. And the coaches have to continue to look at the game and try to grow as well. And of course that's me included."[12]

Chapter 13

Defensive Growth

Their defense proved up to the task in their next win, a 58–47 final at home against Northwestern. The Wildcats didn't score a single point in the final seven minutes of the first half, and it was the second time in three games that Michigan held an opponent under 50 points. The Wolverines had shot poorly but were still able to win, a welcome change from seasons past. "This whole press conference should be about our defense. It was exceptional," Beilein said afterwards. "I told our guys it's as good as we've played right now and it had to be."

Luke Yaklich's teachings seemed to be taking hold. There had been glimpses throughout the year of an impressive defensive capability. The team's effectiveness seemed to be steadily improving at the right time. Yaklich's plan combined an analytic approach with old-fashioned defensive principles and a healthy dose of increased demands. "We try to get to 70% contest rate for our defense, and then we want to rebound at 75% or better," Yaklich said. "I feel like we're going to be in the top 25% of the country if we can get to that level."[1] Those goals provided the analytical expectations for the group, but Yaklich's genius laid in teaching his players how to reach them. "You are your habits. From a defensive standpoint, the hardest thing to do is guard the ball and close out—those two things we practice religiously every day," Yaklich said. "You keep building those habits each and every day to create a team that slowly and continually builds momentum on the defensive end and confidence in one another."[2]

The early part of the season, however, did not portend the success they would eventually experience. Nine of their ten worst defensive efforts of the season (as measured by Adjusted Defensive Efficiency), were in the rear-view mirror at this point. This was a slow build, as players gradually came to better understand their roles and the level of energy that great defense requires. "At least in my time here, I feel we've always been criticized for not getting after it at that end," Duncan Robinson said. "But this team has just completely transformed that mentality."[3]

The key to the whole operation was Zavier Simpson's resurgence as the starting point guard. Simpson served as the tip of the spear by matching up with, and usually shutting down, the opposition's lead guard. His play inspired others and let them slot into roles that they were more comfortable in. His return as the team's primary point guard after some early season struggles tracks very closely with Michigan's ascent to an elite defensive team. "I think Zavier laid the foundation for our defense," Yaklich said. "From there, other guys began adding two or three bricks at a time. Then when it helps you win a couple games, that's how you build a whole wall."[4]

His teammates agreed. "I think it starts with Zavier. He brings it every single game and every single day in practice and raises everybody's level,"[5] Duncan Robinson said. The opposition recognized it too. "Simpson 100 percent prides himself on his defense,"[6] Michigan State's Miles Bridges said.

Because of the standard that he set, Simpson was able to demand more of his teammates. "My energy is contagious. I'm getting on people about mistakes. I tell them before the play that we're gonna get a stop,"[7] he said. There would still be some poor defensive outings in the next few games, but the idea of Michigan somehow having developed a shutdown defense in the middle of the season was now a thing. So was the goal of becoming a player-led team.

Prior to the Minnesota game, Beilein emphasized the principles that would be necessary for this team to continue progressing. "Here's my job as a leader right now. My job is to become a servant very soon. All the coaches are leading you, so we can serve you once you all are leading yourselves," Beilein said. "We need more leaders, so we can step back and tell you what to do next, and you go lead the team."[8]

Yaklich defined what he saw as a player-led culture. "When they hold each other accountable to what they know the coaches are teaching them, because it's going to help them get to the point where they want to go," he said, "that's it."[9]

The Wolverines did need players to step up and lead, but first they just needed someone to step up and hit a free throw against Minnesota. Michigan's standard man-to-man defense regressed for much of the game, which left them in a 10-point hole. With 12 minutes left, they resorted to a rarely used zone look that sparked a 23–8 run and put them up five with 28 seconds left. Minnesota knocked down two jumpers sandwiched around a Robinson turnover to tie it in the final seconds. Overtime wouldn't have been necessary had the Wolverines not posted a 12–28 free throw shooting line. Thanks to Derrick Walton and Zak Irvin, the prior season's team shot the ninth best free throw percentage in the country. This year's group was one of the poorest

Division 1 free throw shooting teams in the nation. Matthews and Simpson were the two biggest culprits, but just about everyone suffered at some point. Three of those free throw misses came in overtime, which allowed the Gophers to tie it up with 11 seconds remaining. But Abdur-Rahkman, the player John Beilein called "as cool as the other side of the pillow,"[10] took the inbounds pass and carefully ambled up court. Then he perfectly timed his drive and netted a spinning layup plus one at the line to provide the final winning margin. "It was a great move and that's what we expect and need from our leader, and I'm very happy with the way he responded today and stepped up,"[11] Wagner said afterwards about his teammate.

At their next outing in Evanston, Illinois, it appeared that momentum had propelled the Wolverines through their first half. The team jumped out to a 13–3 start over Northwestern and held on to carry a three-point lead into halftime. But then their offense stayed in the locker room after the break. Just three players made a field goal in the second half, and only Wagner made more than one. Meanwhile Northwestern's Bryant McIntosh and Scottie Lindsey combined to shoot 7–9 from beyond the three-point line on their way to 42 points in the game. Michigan's offensive struggles left them unable to match that duo's performance and Northwestern prevailed 61–52. It would be their last loss for quite some time.

Zavier Simpson had missed all four of his three-point attempts and was mired in a 1–14 slump. His percentage of late was beginning to resemble the aesthetics of his jumper. But of greater concern was Charles Matthews' struggles in his hometown of Chicago. Going back to the first Purdue contest, Matthews was shooting just below 40 percent and had topped out at 15 points just one time. His five-point, three turnover, four foul effort against Northwestern was his second single-digit scoring performance over the nine-game stretch. His early season success suggested a potential breakout as Michigan's leading man. But some of his old habits caught up to him. In the past, his troubles protecting the basketball had led to the nickname "Turnover Matthews," along with a lot of time spent running the Crisler Center stairs as punishment. Once again, he was playing tentatively and letting the game speed up on him. "I think it's more mental than anything," Matthews said. "I'm overthinking out there. I can't play basketball when I'm worrying about what's a good shot and what's a bad shot. I have to stop playing like that— stop playing not to make mistakes, and start being aggressive."[12] Through the close of the regular season, Matthews would continue to search for the right balance. If Michigan was going to make a post-season run, they would need Matthews at his best.

Fortunately the team was able to quickly flush the Northwestern game with a statement performance at Wisconsin—a venue that had historically been a tough place for the Wolverines to win. Jumping out to a 15–2 lead loosened up any nerves and served as a reminder of how tough this team could be when their shots were falling. Those shots continued to fall as Michigan put together one of its best offensive performances of the season. Robinson knocked down four three-pointers and Wagner also added three in a 20-point, nine-rebound performance against Ethan Happ. Happ scored 29, but 18 came in the second half when Michigan controlled the game and was content to let him work hard in the post for two. Beilein's preferred strategy against Purdue was realized effectively against Wisconsin. Three is worth more than two, after all. The 83–72 win left the #20 ranked Wolverines at 20–7, as they entered the final stretch of the regular season.

Though it went unnoticed by many, Jaaron Simmons played 10 minutes in the win against Wisconsin—the most he had seen in a game since December. He had quietly reclaimed the backup point guard spot from Eli Brooks, and though his minutes were limited, he had carved out a role. "We put him on the scout team and he did some really good things," Beilein said. "He's handled it like a champion. I told his parents they should be so proud of how he's handled it."[13]

While he battled his struggles adjusting to a new system, Simmons still sought to help those around him. He became an important sounding board for Charles Matthews, who was now facing his own struggles. "We had a lot of late-night talks, late-night drives, we talked to each other all the time," Simmons said. "I just wanted to keep his spirits up."[14] Those late-night drives were a theme for Simmons, who made it a point to bring a few of his younger teammates along for them, "There have been some long conversations—some real conversations. I like talking to them. I've told guys where I've been and what I've been through. I tell them how they can get through it. You know, some guys need to hear that things are never as bad as they seem."[15]

The ability to stay positive and persevere resonated with his younger teammates. Isaiah Livers said, "When I get down, I always think about how Jaaron's handling his situation. This is his last year, and he's not doing—in his mind—what he thought he'd be doing right now. But it's incredible. I really hope to have a mature mind such as his."[16]

"Not a lot of guys can go through what he's been through, being the top player in the MAC and having such success here and not having the time he would like," said Abdur-Rahkman. "You don't see it on his face or his attitude or anything, how he treats anybody on the team. He's buying in completely."[17] Now Simmons' leadership and focus on incremental improvement had earned him a spot in the rotation. The coaches seemed to see it coming because of the positive mindset Simmons carried himself with.

"The guy has been tremendous," assistant coach Saddi Washington said. "Obviously, he wants to play more and contribute more, but his attitude throughout this season and throughout this process has been like no other."[18]

"His attitude has never wavered. What that kid gave up to come and play for us—it hasn't worked out the way either of us dreamed but at the same time he's in there every day working his tail off,"[19] Beilein said. Simmons followed up his Wisconsin effort with 12 steady minutes against Iowa, scoring five points and dishing out four assists. He hit a three-pointer and set up three more to aid Michigan's 12–2 advantage from deep. Beilein continued to emphasize that winning the three-point battle is part of their game plan, and that meant taking them away from the opposition defensively as well. "Don't let them hit threes. It's been a secret to Wisconsin's [success] for years," he said. "Just watching over time, between what Billy Donlon and I talked about last year, and with Luke [Yaklich], it just became part of our defense now. If they're going to score twos, they're going to be tough ones—but they're not getting open threes."[20]

Six of Michigan's three-pointers came off the fingertips of Duncan Robinson. Having made 10 of his last 15, he seemed to be returning to his level offensively. While that was somewhat to be expected, his emergence defensively came as a complete shock. "The job that Duncan is doing right now on strong four-men is really something," Beilein said in his post-game comments following the 74–59 win. "It reminds me of Zak Irvin when we gave him a mismatch by weight, and he would just outwork the other guy. For him to be matched up on [Tyler] Cook and hold him to 10 points and score 18 himself—that's a pretty good night."

Michigan's defensive development was due to contributions up and down the roster. Zavier Simpson led the charge. Matthews played very strong defense at the wing position, and Abdur-Rahkman provided his typical steady contributions on both sides of the ball. Wagner listened to the NBA's critiques of his game, got stronger and walled up better on the interior. He also learned to avoid some of the ticky-tack fouls that plagued his ability to get into the flow of the game. Jon Teske turned into one of John Beilein's best rim protectors in his time at Michigan. But no player symbolized Michigan's defensive renaissance as much as Duncan Robinson. "We used to mess with him," Abdur-Rahkman said. "We used to call him Uncan. Because there was no 'D' in D-uncan."[21] And it was true. Michigan's season ended in the 2017 Sweet 16 with a one-possession loss in which Oregon ruthlessly targeted Robinson inside and out. He's never been known for his strength or his athleticism, and it would have been understandable for Michigan to simply accept his deficiencies and hide him on the defensive end.

But in one of the most impressive examples of Yaklich's coaching acumen, he helped turn Robinson into a solid post defender at the college level. Yaklich recognized Robinson lacked the foot speed to defend quicker players on the wing. He compensated by adjusting the defense to allow Duncan to stay underneath even as offenses tried to draw him out. Down low he was able to use his length and improved technique and earn the "D" back in his name. Yaklich, unsurprisingly, gives the credit to Robinson: "You have to start with a want-to. Early on when we started, Duncan knew he had deficiencies. He knew he had to improve, off the ball and guarding the first two or three dribbles. To his credit, he had moments this year, when he didn't play well defensively. He would come back and watch film and he'd come back to me with ideas. In daily drills, he was really cognizant of all the finer points that have allowed him to become a better rebounder, or have allowed him to become a better post defender or on the ball defender."[22]

Robinson's emergence as a defender that could hold his own was yet another small piece of development that gave the team an opportunity to grow into something great. Beilein couldn't help but marvel at his improvement. "What we've found is this skinny little kid that came from a Division 3 school has been really good at playing physical defense in the post."[23]

Chapter 14

Finishing Strong

On Sunday afternoon, February 18, Michigan welcomed Ohio State into Crisler Center for Senior Day. The Buckeyes had been unranked when the teams had played earlier in the year and had used the comeback victory over Michigan as a stepping-stone that now brought them into Ann Arbor as the #8 team in the country. The Wolverines slotted in at #22 at this point. Prior to the game Michigan honored its outgoing seniors. Abdur-Rahkman, Robinson, and Simmons all received the ovations one would expect. But there was one other outgoing senior to recognize, and he received the biggest applause of all. As Austin Hatch walked out on the court with his grandparents and his fiancée Abby, it was yet one more milestone on his incredible journey. Even if he didn't make his impact on the court, he left everybody associated with the program better off for having been around him. "People keep thanking us, or showing great appreciation for honoring this scholarship and doing all these things," Coach Beilein said. "I say, 'Wait a minute, we're getting the blessing here. We're around a young man that is just incredible to be around.'"[1]

Hatch had spent his time as an undergraduate assistant seeking to make an impact on the program in any way he could. "My goal is to be the best—I don't know if you want to call me a practice player or a role player—because I guess I have a role," Austin said. "I want to be the best person who's ever filled the role that I'm filling as an encourager, a motivator, an inspirer. I want to be the best person to ever fill that role in the history of college basketball."[2]

Hatch provided his teammates with a level of perspective that will guide them for the rest of their lives. According to Abdur-Rahkman, "How positive he is is just truly inspiring. That's all you could really ask for."[3] Zavier Simpson put it simply: "You can't be around him and not have a good day."[4]

The relationship forged between Hatch and Beilein clearly goes beyond that of the standard player-coach dynamic. "I could go all day about how in awe I am of Coach Beilein for the way he's treated me," Austin said. "I don't think that it's an accident that I committed to play at Michigan nine days before [the first plane crash in 2011]. What if I had taken two weeks later to commit? I was on my death bed. There's not a better place I could be given the circumstances. And even if nothing had happened, there's not a better place I could be, not a better man I could play for. Coach Beilein talks about what I've given to him and the impact I've had on the team, but that's nothing compared to the way he's impacted me."[5]

Hatch will move forward in life with the lessons he learned in Ann Arbor, seeking to motivate others. "I have to use the gifts I've been given to give back to other people,"[6] he says. He planned to make public speaking part of his way of giving. Sharing his lessons of pushing forward through adversity with grit and a growth mindset is an important part of his message. "To be able to spread perspective and encouragement [is great]," Hatch says. "I don't go into a speech saying I hope every person in here leaves thinking different about things. If one person out of that audience leaves thinking a little bit different, then I've done my job."[7] Most importantly, he's focused on the legacy left behind by those he's lost: "I'm sure they'd be proud of me just being here. But I think they would probably be more proud of my outlook on life. They're still with me every day, still having a profound impact on the man I am and hope to become."[8]

His time in Ann Arbor would leave an indelible mark. Coach Beilein put it best: "It's one of the greatest stories I think that I've ever been associated with and am pleased to be a part of."[9] Once the game tipped off, it appeared the formal honoring of Hatch and the lingering frustration from Michigan's earlier collapse in Columbus gave the Wolverines an edge from the very start. While the offense took some time to get going, the defensive tenacity was present from the very first possession and resulted in a steal by Zavier Simpson. The team would record steals on four of Ohio State's first five possessions.

To trigger the offense, Michigan went to their microwave. When Jordan Poole first checked in, Ohio State led by three. He knocked down a three-pointer on their next possession, then followed it up with a transition layup. A few minutes later he completed a four-point play. He had one more three-pointer in him before halftime. His offensive pyrotechnics jumpstarted Michigan to a five-point halftime lead. Poole's final three-pointer came with 6:25 left in the game and pushed Michigan's lead to eight. Keita Bates-Diop made a free throw on the next possession, but Ohio State could not trim the lead any closer after that. Following Poole's crucial 15 points off the bench in the win, Ohio State coach Chris Holtmann acknowledged him afterwards: "He's a really talented freshman. As a matter of fact, we said in the scouting report that he could be an X-factor for them. He's really gifted."

Poole had battled through erratic playing time for much of the season, toggling between offensive outbursts and defensive breakdowns. Teammates compared his instant offense to other notable bench scorers like former Detroit Piston Vinnie "The Microwave" Johnson and NBA player J.R. Smith. They also scratched their heads at some of his eccentricities. "We had no idea what to make of him,"[10] Brent Hibbitts said. Some of Poole's defensive breakdowns appeared against Ohio State too, but John Beilein had developed him about as much as he could in the short-term. Michigan had officially reached the part of the season in which they needed to sink or swim with the talented freshman.

Duncan Robinson had once again competed really well against a more physical and athletic player in Keita Bates-Diop. The Big Ten Player of the Year got his 17 points but had to shoot 5-17 to get there. "[Duncan] should be known for the job he did on Diop," Beilein told the media after the game. "He was absolutely terrific, he and Isaiah Livers. Did they shut him down? No, but they changed the momentum of the game when they took the top scorer in the league and marginalized him a little bit." Michigan's development was beginning to get noticed by outsiders as well. During the CBS halftime show, commentator Seth Davis presciently announced he liked the Maize and Blue as a potential Final Four team.

Two games remained on the regular season schedule, both winnable but both on the road. Michigan was now 5-1 in its last six games and with two more wins had the chance to play themselves into a strong NCAA Tournament seed. Robinson and Poole continued their marksmanship at Penn State three days later. Michigan's two best shooters combined for 32 points off the bench. Wagner chipped in four three-pointers of his own to create a large enough cushion for victory to withstand the Nittany Lions' late run and prevail 72-63. Among Robinson's 19 points was the dagger three-pointer that stretched the lead to nine with a minute and a half left. Robinson's defensive game also continued its ascent as he accumulated three blocks—easily a career high for the lanky shooter. Speaking afterwards about Poole's strong performance, which included some tremendous post-dunk mean-mugging for the camera, Beilein described his approach with the talented freshman. "He's got so much confidence, we can teach the other stuff. We can't teach his DNA right now," he said. And Beilein shouldered some of the blame when asked why Poole was just breaking out now. "The coach is playing him more. He's showed us that defensively and offensively, he's about making the next right play more than he was earlier in the year. Now we'll play through a mistake, because we know that they are not as common as they were."

The one negative to Michigan's victory was that Charles Matthews continued his slump, missing all five shot attempts and being held scoreless for the first time all season. His movements at the offensive end of the court were clouded in hesitancy, seeming to suffer a split-second gap between mind and body. Finding the version of Matthews that Michigan had seen early in the season would be an important element for any post-season success. A first half blowout at Maryland soon afforded Beilein some opportunities to help Matthews search for himself. The very first possession of the game ended with the dreaded words "Turnover Matthews." He was held scoreless in the first half as seemingly every other teammate made it rain. But with a 30-point spread at the break, Beilein utilized the second half to call some plays designed for the man all too frequently referred to as "The Kentucky Transfer." The results were encouraging as he scored 11 points on 4–5 shooting and added four rebounds. Perhaps more importantly, he only had a single turnover. "That was big. He's worked on it, he's been working after practice, he's been working on his own, been working with the coaching staff. It's just big to have him [knock down some shots]," Beilein told the press corps.

The first half blowout that preceded Matthews' strong play was as positive a finish to the regular season as Michigan could have hoped for. The Wolverines scored 54 points in just 33 possessions. Abdur-Rahkman seemed to cement his status as a focal point of the offense, scoring a career-high 28 points on the game and getting within range of a triple-double with eight rebounds and seven assists. "As the year went on, we began to realize as a staff that he can do so much more than we were probably allowing him to do," Beilein said. "He's basically right now become a guy we play through, like we would a Tim Hardaway, a Trey Burke, or Nik Stauskas."[11] Poole missed his first three-pointer upon entering the game, but as usual he was unfazed. He went on to convert three from distance and was fouled in the act of shooting on another. Simpson had a solid effort running the show, while his backup Simmons posted his season-high with seven points. Robinson and Teske made important defensive contributions. Michigan had officially found another gear. They'd won seven of their final eight regular season games and would be heading into post-season play with the wind at their backs. The coaching staff had carefully cultivated and developed the players into roles that best suited their skill sets and readiness. Luke Yaklich had built Michigan's best defense in years and it seemed to be improving by the game. They allowed the fewest points per game in the conference and were ranked eighth nationally in that category. According to Kenpom, their Adjusted Defensive Efficiency was the 11th best in the country at the time; the program's previous high under Beilein was 37th. The potential for a magical run was certainly in place.

Chapter 15

Taking Over the Big Apple

This year, there were no issues getting the team to New York City for the Big Ten Tournament. They arrived without incident on Wednesday night prior to their first-round game against Iowa. Their dismal loss at Nebraska in January proved to be the tie breaker that the 13–5 Cornhuskers needed to receive a first-round bye instead of the 13–5 Wolverines. In the opening round matchup against Iowa, Michigan almost got sent home immediately. The afternoon started out positively enough when Wagner and Abdur-Rahkman scored 13 of the team's first 22 points to give Michigan a five-point lead. But soon thereafter, Abdur-Rahkman was called for his second foul and headed to the bench. A few minutes later, Wagner was whistled for his second foul and joined Abdur-Rahkman. Both would remain seated for the rest of the half, and their absence allowed Iowa to turn the game around and enjoy their own five-point lead when the teams returned to their locker rooms.

Allowing Iowa 40 first-half points was not something in Coach Yaklich's defensive plans, so inevitably adjustments ensued. With Wagner and Abdur-Rahkman back on the court to start the second half, Michigan went on an immediate 11–0 run, all on baskets at the hoop. But before either team scored another point, and just three minutes into the half, each picked up their third foul and returned to the bench. This time their teammates weathered the storm better. Jon Teske disrupted shots and created an obstacle for the Hawkeyes at the basket, while Poole had a few strong drives to the hoop. When Beilein deigned the timing appropriate for his two stars to return, Michigan led by seven. But in a game plagued by frequent whistles, it only took a few minutes for Wagner and Abdur-Rahkman to get sidelined again with their fourth fouls.

To make matters worse, Michigan shot horribly from long range all game, finishing 3–19 with all three coming from Robinson. Fortunately, all three makes came at opportune times, including the first two coming just after his teammates received their fourth whistle. His big shots put Michigan up eight. Wagner would return, only to foul out with 4:37 remaining in regulation. It was unfortunate timing to have his foul-prone ways from earlier in his career resurface. Thankfully, Teske had been prepared for this and stepped in with important defense and rebounding. Michigan led by six when Wagner left, and with two minutes left, Matthews drained a shot with his foot on the three-point line to push it back to six. Teske then blocked a shot at the other end.

After a stagnant offensive possession, Iowa came down and hit a much-needed three-pointer with one minute left to make it 67–64. Michigan immediately gave the ball back to them, getting whistled for a five-second violation on the inbounds pass. Two missed three-point attempts later, Abdur-Rahkman was driving the other way to the hoop and fouled just before laying the ball off the glass and in. The basket that could have sealed the win was waved off, and instead Abdur-Rahkman went to the line for a one-and-one opportunity. He missed the first free throw and Iowa had one last chance. Zavier Simpson had lived in Iowa point guard Jordan Bohannon's shirt for much of the game, limiting him to a 2–10 shooting performance so far. Coming the day after Bohannon had scored 25, it was a defensive effort that Michigan needed. But in his last possession in regulation, Bohannon instead chose the path of least resistance and launched the ball from one of the few places Simpson didn't guard him—about 30 feet away from the hoop. He drained it. Game tied 67–67. A final Abdur-Rahkman layup attempt harmlessly bounced away, and Michigan was forced to play another period in a game they had numerous chances to end.

In overtime though, their newly reliable defense was up to the task. After scoring a basket on the first possession, Iowa didn't score another field goal the rest of the game. Abdur-Rahkman fouled out in overtime but Matthews assured him they would prevail. "Hold your head high and we're going to make sure we come out of this with a win,"[1] he told him. Robinson's textbook timing for Michigan's lonely three-pointers continued, as he nailed his final one the next time down the court. As usual, the foul shooting down the stretch wasn't pretty, but it was enough and Michigan pulled it out 77–71.

Wagner had been limited to 16 minutes, and Abdur-Rahkman to 22. Matthews' confidence seemed to return to its early season levels as he carried Michigan often in their absence. His 16 points and eight rebounds were much needed, but his zero turnovers in 41 minutes was arguably most telling of all. "It was a huge game for Charles," Beilein said afterwards. "Knowing he had [so many players] in foul trouble, just to step forward and do what he can. Unbelievable." The one positive result of the foul trouble was that Wagner and Abdur-Rahkman would be well rested for the quick turnaround against Nebraska 24 hours later. Beilein also emphasized: "We have got to be better than this tomorrow to have a chance."

15. Taking Over the Big Apple

Fortunately, they were. Whether they were playing loose after a close call or they got all their long-distance misses out of the way, Michigan looked like a completely different team against Nebraska. After jumping out to a 9–5 lead, the Cornhuskers shot just one for their next 20 as the Wolverine defense tightened the screws. Meanwhile the three-ball fell with impressive regularity. Looking refreshed, Abdur-Rahkman was 5–5 from long range and Wagner posted 20 points and 13 rebounds. Simpson was an effective floor general at both ends of the court, and Robinson added four three-pointers of his own. A theme was beginning to emerge around the program. When just about anyone on the team answered a question, they spoke about being "connected." The defensive intensity led by the team's resident "pitbull" Simpson had become contagious, and the whole group had found joy in working together as a unit. "When you have veteran guards like Muhammad and Charles, and Moe's improved so much as well defensively, I think when we come together and stay connected on defense, it makes all the difference," Robinson said after the game.

Beyond the defensive resurgence, the team was made up of quality kids that enjoyed being around each other. "We hang out outside of basketball. We're not just a basketball team," said Abdur-Rahkman. "We hang out and we're more like brothers. We always look out for each other, and that builds chemistry."[2]

The importance of staying connected and fostering those relationships was something that Beilein had come to strongly value: "There were some times [earlier in my career] when I probably didn't have the relationship with a player that I would like to have had. I've learned a lot about that and still work at it. Everybody is the same way, no matter where you work, you have to prioritize relationships with whoever you're working with or for, because that's how it all gets done. And I think our best teams had great relationships with the coaches, and had great relationships with each other."[3] In many ways the 2017-18 team was living proof of that lesson and the ability to stay connected would be a critical point of emphasis as the team moved deeper into the post-season.

The progression forward would start with the heavyweight rematch that the Michigan State Spartans had openly hoped for. "I definitely won't be disappointed to get another opportunity to go out there [against Michigan]," Cassius Winston said. "I think I dropped the ball the last game."[4] The setting couldn't have been better for the two long-term bitter rivals. Madison Square Garden on a Saturday afternoon, broadcast on CBS; the winner would go to the Big Ten Championship the following day.

Zavier Simpson heard Winston's pre-game chatter loud and clear and gave him an immediate reminder of what he was capable of. Simpson canned a three-pointer on the opening possession and glared at the Michigan State

Zavier Simpson (left) and Isaiah Livers (right) move in to separate a frustrated Nick Ward (44) from Charles Matthews at the Big Ten Tournament. Michigan went on to defeat Michigan State 75–64 in the semi-final matchup (photograph by Marc-Gregor Campredon).

bench. Then he took Winston to the rack twice for layups to score 7 of Michigan's first 10 points. Charles Matthews sunk two three-pointers of his own, as the two combined to put the Maize and Blue up 13–4. Matthews also took the liberty to attempt to get in the heads of a few Spartans and was successful with one at the very least. The next time down the court, Nick Ward put his shoulder down to bully Jon Teske to the hoop. Matthews came from the weak side to help and he and Teske inadvertently knocked Ward to the ground. As the foul was called, Matthews stood tall over a fallen Ward who scrambled to his feet to return the favor. Matthews grinning from ear to ear at a flustered and angry Ward became an iconic image that symbolized Michigan's weekend.

To the Spartans' credit, they battled back from that nine-point deficit, and the lead was traded back and forth in a low-scoring first half. What the half lacked in aesthetics, it made up for in heated competition. The two teams combined to shoot a dismal 33 percent and Michigan State led 29–26 as they retreated to their locker rooms. Wagner had missed all seven shot attempts and was a little too quick to settle from long distance, where five of his misses came from. His coach needed him to get going and told him so at halftime.

"Hey, Moe, are you going to make a shot? Because right now you're stinking the place up. Just make one shot,"[5] Beilein said.

Upon emerging from the locker room, Wagner quickly heeded his coach's advice. He started off by splitting a pair of free throws. A Miles Bridges dunk gave Michigan State its biggest lead at four, but that was quickly answered by an Abdur-Rahkman three-pointer. On the next possession, Simpson delivered a textbook wraparound pass to set Wagner up for an easy layup after slipping a screen. Wagner went at the hoop and banked it in the next time down, and then finished the sequence with a beautiful open-court euro-step to give Michigan a 9–0 run and a five-point lead. Although there were almost 16 minutes left, it was a lead that they never relinquished. Five different Wolverines scored in double figures. Simpson finished with 15 points and seven rebounds, while also hounding Winston into a 3–10 shooting performance. Most importantly, he was 6–8 from the line late in the game, as Michigan State attempted to exploit his kryptonite. "It was a sweet sight to see Zavier's [foul] shots just go right through the middle," Beilein admitted in his press conference. Abdur-Rahkman scored 15 and stepped up any time Michigan needed a bucket or a stop. Matthews added 12 points and six rebounds to his Spartan-antagonizing performance.

Robinson showed off just how much he had transformed as a player late in the game. With one minute left, Michigan was moving the ball around to try to avoid a foul. Robinson received a pass and drove towards the hoop. He was shoved hard but maintained his balance and finished the layup and drew the foul. That's not a play that he could have finished earlier in his career, but thanks to the tutelage of Jon Sanderson he now had the strength to do so. Although shots at the rim would never be his forte, Robinson had managed to raise his percentage of shots there in each season of his Michigan career per hoop-math.com. At the other end of the floor, he showed off his new defensive chops, stealing the ball to ice the triumph.

Wagner finished with 15 points and 8 boards while Nick Ward, Michigan State's big man who seemed to intentionally trip Wagner the previous year, scored just six points in only 10 minutes played. The "rivalry" between those two served as catnip to Michigan fans and in many ways symbolized the recent differences between the programs. Ward came in as the highly ranked recruit, Wagner as the unknown. Ward was the burly bruiser whose style fits better in the 1980s whereas Wagner was the more skilled player with a soft touch that could find a home in any modern offense. Wagner was developed into a post-season hero and future first-round pick, while Ward was limited to 18.9 minutes per game that season due to his lack of conditioning, his propensity for drawing technical fouls, and Tom Izzo's inconsistent substitution patterns (best demonstrated a few weeks later when Michigan State's season ended in a loss to Syracuse with the largely anonymous Ben Carter receiving more playing time than 4th overall draft pick Jaren Jackson). In their four head-to-head matchups, Wagner averaged 17.8 points and 6.5 rebounds to Ward's nine points and four rebounds. Most importantly, Michigan won three of the four with an average margin of victory of more than 16 points.

Now Wagner was on to more important things—like dealing with Purdue's Isaac Haas in the Big Ten Championship. Just 24 hours later, the two teams matched up for the third time on the season. Michigan had gone 10-1 since their last meeting and was riding an eight-game winning streak with confidence at a season high. The game started with Haas posting Wagner and collecting a layup on the first possession of the game. Wagner answered with a three. The battle was on. At Purdue's end, Haas collected an offensive rebound and Wagner drew a whistle for a foul on the put-back. On a John Beilein team, a foul this early typically led to a seat on the bench—and this time was no exception, as Jon Teske replaced Wagner. The young man they used to call "Big Sleep" for his low-energy persona looked transformed. On his first possession Teske darted around the court, and actively set screens for a variety of ball-handlers. Simpson eventually found him underneath, and while he didn't convert his first opportunity, he pounced on the offensive rebound and finished the job. Teske employed the same formula the next time down. After screening and re-screening for ball-handlers five different times, Abdur-Rahkman found him slipping to the hoop for a dunk. A pick and roll with Simpson on the following possession led to two Teske free throws. A Michigan big man was having an impact on the game early—it just wasn't the player anybody expected. The Wolverines had trailed by two when Teske entered; by the time he took a seat they led Purdue by seven. Teske would add six more in the half, including a very pure stroke from the top of the key that he hadn't shown much of before.

Beilein and Purdue's coach Matt Painter were known for their cat-and-mouse strategy games when facing each other. This time, Painter had his defenders show temporary help on screens and slow the ball-handler with a "hard hedge" rather than simply switch everything as they had done earlier in the season. Michigan looked prepared for this adjustment. Throughout the first half, the Wolverines seemed to understand what Purdue was doing and how they wanted to attack it. The ball was consistently moving, and they were getting the open looks they wanted, as exhibited by their ten assists without a single turnover. If not for a 3-11 performance from the three-point line, the Wolverines might have blown the game open already. Even so, Michigan led 38-33 at halftime. If they started making their threes, then they would be Big Ten Champions.

After trading a couple of two-point baskets to start the second half, that's exactly what happened. A Wagner steal led to a transition opportunity where

15. Taking Over the Big Apple

DeAndre Haynes (left) and Moe Wagner walk beside John Beilein through the streets of New York on their way to Madison Square Garden for the Big Ten Tournament Final against Purdue in 2018 (photograph by Marc-Gregor Campredon).

he found Abdur-Rahkman open from the wing. His father Dawud was in attendance and raised a celebratory fist as the shot found the bottom of the net. One minute later, another Wolverine steal led to Abdur-Rahkman in transition and he found Simpson open on the opposite wing to put Michigan up 11. A few minutes later it was Wagner's turn. He started by attacking a closeout, showcasing a quick first step for an easy layup. Next up was a simple pick and pop three-pointer that he drained. Finally, the coup de grace. Michigan had the ball out-of-bounds under their own hoop with just three seconds on the shot clock. As Duncan Robinson struggled to find an open target, Wagner rushed from the block to the corner, calling for the ball. Robinson obliged and Wagner received the ball with his back to the hoop and his energy moving away from it. Without ever stopping, he spun and threw up a fadeaway from behind the arc that was pure the moment it left his hand. Michigan was up 14 and the party was on. Purdue's head coach thought Wagner was the difference-maker on Michigan's team. "Those guards are good but not everybody has a guy like Wagner that can stick threes, drive the ball, and play with passion," Painter told the media in the aftermath.

There was one more sequence with six minutes left that served as the final exclamation point. Robinson blocked a shot on the defensive end, and

John Beilein cuts down the net following Michigan's second straight Big Ten Tournament title in 2018 (photograph by Marc-Gregor Campredon).

then Simpson drove hard to the hole at the other end. He had the presence of mind to find a trailing Teske behind him. The emerging sophomore charged to the hoop and dunked right on Isaac Haas. It would have been pretty much impossible to imagine any of those three contributing those particular plays just months earlier. Teske headed back to the huddle, red-faced and hollering, full of emotion that no one had ever seen before. Simpson strutted, straight-faced and confident. "I was so happy when he popped off after that dunk. I got so excited," Wagner said afterwards about his teammate Teske. "I know how good he is. I play against him every day. That was long overdue."

Some shaky free throw shooting down the stretch made the final 75–66, and before long the confetti was falling. Wagner was named the tournament's Most Outstanding Player, and his mother Beate might as well have been named most outstanding fan. The CBS cameras frequently found her celebrating as Moe knocked down big shots. It was readily apparent where Moe had gotten his emotional expressiveness from. It was the second trip she had made from Germany to see her son play in person for Michigan—the first having been the prior season's Big Ten tournament. She had now watched both teams win four games in four days to win in consecutive years.

Abdur-Rahkman made the All-Tournament team and probably had just as strong a case for Most Outstanding Player as Wagner. For a player that often got overlooked, Beilein made clear just how important he is. "He has just answered the bell on so many big shots. So many big stops," Beilein said. "He is everything we could ask for. I told him sincerely, 'Muhammad, you are playing as good as any guard has played here. Just keep doing what you're doing.'"[6] His decision making played a critical role in the team's offensive success throughout the season; per Kenpom he would finish the season with the eighth lowest turnover rate in the country among players that had logged at least 40 percent of their team's minutes.

Michigan now had a victory over every other team in the Big Ten. According to the advanced metrics at barttorvik.com, Michigan was the best team in the country since February 7. It was becoming clear to all that there was something pretty special going on here. Broadcaster Terry Mills noticed it. He was asked if this team was similar to his 1989 national championship team. "Players are holding each other accountable and playing with defined roles," he said. "Those are the biggest things."[7]

All the Michigan fans that had flooded Madison Square Garden over the weekend stuck around to celebrate the victory. They were treated to John Beilein speaking as Jordan Poole flamboyantly blew confetti off the back of Jim Nantz' head. "The Big Ten is an incredibly competitive league, and we got better and better as the year went along. These kids are so dedicated, and sacrifice a lot, just for the team." Invoking Bo Schembechler, Beilein added, "The team, the team, the team."

As the broadcast closed, the team of Nantz, Grant Hill, and Bill Raftery discussed Michigan's potential in March. "You saw great chemistry from that Michigan team last year, but this team—something special, they defend," Hill said. "They're going to be a tough out for an opponent."

"We might be seeing them at the end of March and beginning of April," Raftery concurred. Those three would become quite familiar with Michigan before the season was done.

Chapter 16

Late Nights in Wichita

After playing their best basketball of the season in the Big Ten Tournament, Michigan had a full 10 days off before facing their next opponent. It was a challenge to keep the team on track, but one that suited Beilein well. He had dealt with a similar situation at some of his earlier coaching stops and took advantage of the time to focus on a couple of his core tenets—development and fundamentals. He considered giving them a few days off but instead leaned on his staff. "I was advised to not take two days off by our performance team because it would throw off their bodies so much,"[1] Beilein said. The team held an open scrimmage to simulate a game setting. Despite his quiet weekend in New York, Jordan Poole was still firing away every time he was open. He hit a buzzer beater at the end of the first half, then sunk a game-winning deep three-pointer as the clock expired. In case there was any question, the young man was not afraid of taking a big shot, something that would serve Michigan well in the tournament. On Selection Sunday, they learned they would be heading to Wichita as the #3 seed in the West bracket. Their first-round opponent would be the University of Montana.

With a very late start on Thursday night, in an arena that felt lethargic compared to the prior weekend in New York City, the Wolverines showed the rust that was to be expected. Before they could even score a point, Michigan racked up three turnovers, three fouls, and missed four shots. Two of those fouls belonged to Zavier Simpson, which forced him to the bench. When Jaaron Simmons checked in for Simpson with Montana leading 10–0, the situation seemed dire at the first media timeout. After the game, John Beilein talked about that moment: "It didn't look good for Michigan at that time. I told them all we need is one basket here, and then let's win the next four minutes. And we did that." Matthews finally broke the seal, and Poole followed by hitting a three-pointer. A Teske free throw completed a 6–0 run that quelled any panic amid the fan-base.

Simmons took advantage of his opportunity with three layups at the hoop, the last of which narrowed the lead to three. His shift, which registered a plus eight, had steadied the team. Later Saddi Washington would say, "We had a veteran guy who could step [up] in the moment and right the ship for us. To have that is priceless, especially at this time of year."[2] There was still plenty of work left to be done of course. Abdur-Rahkman hit a three-pointer to give Michigan its first lead just a few minutes later. He and Matthews combined for the Wolverines' last 12 points of the half to give Michigan the 31–28 advantage. During that stretch, Michigan seemed to figure out Montana's trap-heavy defense and Matthews benefited by getting open underneath for some easy finishes.

Just after both teams returned to the court, there was a power outage at the scorer's table that caused an extended delay. Eventually, Michigan set to work widening their lead by holding Montana scoreless for ten minutes. The lead got pushed into double digits, and Michigan held on from there. They limited the Grizzlies to a total of 19 points in the second half and just 32 percent shooting on the game. It certainly wasn't their prettiest outing of the season, but they did what a #3 seed is supposed to do to a #14 seed. Matthews posted numbers with 20 points and 11 rebounds, continuing his positive trend. They were necessary in a game where none of his other teammates' performances really stood out.

Michigan had held serve and would need to do so again in two days. The second-round test would pit them against a hot Houston team led by the talented Rob Gray, who had just dropped 29 points on San Diego State in their first game. The Wolverine coaching staff got to work slicing up Houston's video with the quick turnaround. They realized what a handful Gray was going to be for Michigan's defense. "He just can get his own shot. He sees the floor well," Beilein said. "A lot of guys can shoot their jump shot, but when they get in among the big fellows, can they still get their hands to the rim? He does that. So just a really clever player."[3] Fortunately Michigan had a pretty solid defender at Gray's position that relished the opportunity to guard him. Late at night on St. Patrick's Day, 2018, Zavier Simpson would get his chance.

For the second straight game, Michigan quickly fell behind after the opening tip, with Houston taking a 6–1 lead. Duncan Robinson then knocked down consecutive baskets from NBA range to give the Wolverines their first lead. After a strong take to the basket by Matthews, and Simpson's lightning quick hands creating a transition bucket for Abdur-Rahkman, Gray got himself on the board with his own NBA distance three-pointer. Robinson answered with yet another, shooting in easy rhythm off a pass from Moe Wagner. A minute later, Jordan Poole got in on the action, seeing the ball go through the net for the first of three times on the evening. Gray answered that one as well, off the bounce and with his back foot on the enlarged center court logo.

The two teams continued to punch back and forth throughout the first half and entered halftime tied at 28. Gray's two three-pointers had been important, but Simpson had hounded him into nine other misses in the half. Both teams shot poorly overall.

Houston's two leading scorers, Gray and Indiana transfer Devin Davis, got the Cougars started in the second frame with baskets in the paint. Wagner, who had been plagued by foul trouble in the first half, hit a three-pointer off a feed from Simpson. The battle continued with neither team holding a lead bigger than three until Gray scored five quick ones on his own to put Houston up six. Wagner answered immediately with a pick and pop three from Abdur-Rahkman and was fouled in the process but missed his free throw that would have completed a rare four-point play. Only two points were scored over the next five minutes, as the game turned into a defensive slog.

Two physical teams with some eager whistle-blowers led to a lot of free throws down the stretch. Teske made four key ones, and Robinson and Abdur-Rahkman knocked down their own on a night when Michigan couldn't afford any free throw mishaps. Rob Gray made a number of tough shots and proved to be a serious challenge even for Simpson. But Simpson was able to take the ball away when Gray tried to split a screen and immediately hit a streaking Wagner in transition for the 59–57 Michigan lead. With two minutes left, Devin Davis converted an important three-point play, and fouled out Duncan Robinson in the process. Robinson had done yeoman's work defending more physical players but burned all his fouls in the process. Houston now led 60–59.

Davis then blocked a Wagner attempt at the other end, but Michigan was able to corral two offensive rebounds on the possession as Wagner ultimately tipped it in to grab the lead back. Davis continued his aggressive work on the glass, getting fouled rebounding a missed Matthews three-pointer with 44 seconds remaining. He sank both free throws to make him a perfect 6–6 from the line and to give the Cougars a one-point edge. Michigan put the ball in Abdur-Rahkman's hands late in the game, as they had so many times earlier in the year. He drove to the basket, spun around, but couldn't quite shake the defender. He still went up with the shot and banked it off the glass, only to see it rattle out. Matthews soared up right underneath the hoop and cleanly tipped it right back onto the iron—only to also have it roll out. Davis pulled down yet another strong rebound and was fouled once again. With 24 seconds left, he would have two shots at the line. He finally missed a free throw, before connecting on the second to make it 63–61 Houston.

Abdur-Rahkman got one more opportunity, this time with 10 seconds left as he drove by Gray to the left and found an opening at the hoop. He seemed to switch the ball to his right hand at the last second, and that was just enough to throw off the timing of the layup and cause the ball to bounce out. It appeared that this just wasn't going to be Michigan's night. Yet again, Davis pulled down the rebound for Houston and was fouled. With two made free throws the game would be over. Once he missed the first, Michigan immediately felt new life. Then incredibly, after playing great all night and shooting 9–10 from the line, Davis missed the second as well. Wagner grabbed the rebound and Michigan immediately called timeout.

The Wolverines took the ball out with 3.6 seconds left, underneath their own hoop and down two points. Beilein used the timeout to dial up the play (called "Indiana") that they'd been practicing since the season started, in preparation for a moment just like this. As the two teams broke their huddles, Gray told Jordan Poole he was about to be going home. Just as he had done against Maryland earlier in the season, Isaiah Livers and his high school pitching background made the strong throw to a streaking Muhammad-Ali Abdur-Rahkman in the backcourt. Two dribbles up-court and an expected double-team closed on him. The threat of a slip to the hoop by Ibi Watson drew Poole's defender off the three-point line. Abdur-Rahkman recognized the opening and delivered a perfect strike on Poole's hands. All that was left was draining a 30-footer with the season on the line. Legs splayed out at the top of his jump, the shot was true from the moment it left his hands. And then he celebrated as only Jordan Poole could, running laps around the court and dodging his teammates seeking embraces until they finally chased him down on the other side. The next day, video surfaced of him making pretty much the exact same buzzer beater in high school, just like he had in Michigan's open scrimmage the week before. John Beilein was right—you can't teach this kid's DNA.

The intersection of Beilein's preparation and development was, once again, a success. In this case, it saved Michigan's season. Moe Wagner later revealed in an article in *The Players' Tribune* just how well prepared they had been. "There's four seconds left and Houston's at the line, up two. Not great. And at first, to be honest, I'm thinking, *Oh no, this might be over.* But then all of a sudden, it's like—it hits me. I realize, *Wait ... I've been here before. I've already done this play, this EXACT SAME play, countless times.* Every single one of us had. We'd all practiced it so much that it felt like habit. And when I say 'this play,' I'm not even just talking about the final inbounds sequence where Jordan hit the buzzer beater. I'm also talking about everything before that—everything else that Coach Beilein had prepared us for. Coach B would have us practice our body language. He'd have us practice walking into and out of the huddle. He'd even have managers practice acting like fans who would be heckling us—to test our focus during timeouts. It's wild, right? The highest-stakes moment of any of our lives ... and the truth is, I think we mostly all just felt super calm and prepared. Jordan will be the hero forever for that shot against Houston, and he deserves it. But I'm telling you: Without the little things that Coach B had prepared us for all year, the season is over. That play never happens."4

Survive and advance. That's exactly what Michigan had done. They shot 36 percent for the game; prior Michigan teams didn't have a chance when they shot that percentage. But this group had dug in defensively and executed under the most challenging of circumstances. They had rightly earned their way to the Sweet 16. After the game, the players displayed incredible relief just to be able to continue playing with each other. "That was the only thing on my mind, get another game or two or three or four for our seniors," Wagner said.

Robinson felt helpless on the bench after fouling out. "You see your career flashing before your eyes, and I didn't want to go out that way," he said. "I'm thankful that I'm still writing this legacy that we've got going."5 There was still one more highlight left in the evening. When questioned about Poole in his postgame interview, we got to hear John Beilein explain on national TV that the precocious freshman had "an overdose of swag." Truer words have never been spoken.

Chapter 17

Party in Los Angeles

After putting on a show in the biggest city in America a few weeks earlier, the Michigan Wolverines now hoped to stage a rerun in the second biggest city. With the largest alumni base in the world, and arguably the proudest, Michigan can always count on vocal support in different parts of the country. Los Angeles would be no exception. Consider Moe Wagner impressed. "Everywhere we go we have a huge fan base, and it feels like a home game. New York, Wichita, and now Los Angeles. It's a pretty special thing that I wasn't aware of,"[1] Wagner said. The day after Jordan Poole hit his game winner, #7 seed Texas A&M knocked off #2 seed North Carolina, creating a potentially easier path for Michigan to the next round. The Aggies featured some talented big men and often played zone defense. Beilein drew the natural parallel between Texas A&M and Syracuse's style and personnel. It was a system he was familiar with, and one that he had beaten in the postseason before.

Michigan's first weekend in the tournament featured two poor offensive performances—they hoped to turn that around in Los Angeles. Wagner's early foul trouble in recent games had limited his minutes, as well as the team's offensive upside. To combat this, Michigan devised a creative technique to keep him in the lineup. "Some of our defensive drills today he's going to hold tennis balls in his hands so that he's not putting his hands on people,"[2] Beilein said during their week of practice. This strategy paid dividends. During the Texas A&M game, Wagner was on the court for a full 30 minutes and proved to be a handful for the Aggies' bulkier big men.

Texas A&M guard TJ Starks came into the game with nowhere near the resume of the more talented guards Zavier Simpson had shut down. Yet, he still made the mistake of providing Simpson with bulletin board material. "I think I'm unguardable, unstoppable,"[3] Starks said prior to the game. No doubt Simpson heard him. Michigan's first basket of the game came when he recorded his first steal and worked it ahead for Wagner to eventually finish a transition basket. Simpson would go on to tally a remarkable six steals in the game. On their next possession, Jordan Poole received a pass from Simpson a few feet behind the three-point line. He sized up his man, jab-stepped at him, then rose up and drained it—swag personified.

It took about five more minutes for the Wolverines to get into full onslaught mode, but once they did, it was a deluge. When the rarely used Ibi Watson sank a corner three to go up 19–6, that was a pretty good sign this might be Michigan's night. On the next possession, Duncan Robinson removed any doubt when his three-pointer bounced high in the air off the back iron and dropped straight back down and through. Wagner hit a three to put Michigan up 18, and he let everyone know the Maize and Blue mood as he raced back on defense with his tongue wagging. Everybody got in on the action. Michigan played as efficient an offensive half of basketball as they had all year, exemplified perfectly by their 14 assists to just one turnover. The ball whipped around their end of the court. At times they passed up high percentage two-point looks only to keep rotating it around the perimeter to drain yet another three-pointer. Seven different players made one and they shot 10–16 from distance in the half. It was beautiful basketball. Even TBS announcer Reggie Miller, one of the greatest three-point shooters of all time, couldn't get enough of it. He was just about openly laughing on air at their sheer proficiency displayed in the 52–28 first half thumping.

The second half was simply a perfunctory affair at that point. Michigan scored eight in the first minute and a half (including two more three-pointers) to break whatever spirit Texas A&M had left. The evening brought to mind the 2012-13 team's tournament game against Florida. There were plenty of two-point buckets to go around as well. Charles Matthews had seven of them in an 18-point performance. The game seemed to be slowing down for him. He had a number of jump-stops on two feet where he stayed patient and balanced before converting. Abdur-Rahkman, true to form, quietly led all scorers with an efficient 24 point, seven assist, five rebound outing. Michigan emptied the bench at the end of game for a few more highlights. Big man Austin Davis had only scored 17 points all season, but he came lumbering down the floor and was on the receiving end of a powerful alley-oop that may have registered as seismic activity. Walk-on C.J. Baird, who had started the season as a team manager, got his opportunity as well. With 31 seconds left, he pulled up off the dribble from about 25 feet away and buried it. The bench reaction looked as if they had just won the whole tournament. It was one of those great sports moments where everyone watching could relate to the every-man getting his chance to make an impact. It also revealed just how much the team valued the players at the back end of the roster and the contributions they made. Baird's job on the scout team that week was, somewhat comically, to emulate the explosive and powerful future first-round pick Robert Williams.

It's a responsibility that Baird took seriously. "That's one of the best things Coach Beilein has taught us, how important the scout team is to every game."[4]

Charles Matthews served on the scout team the year before and agreed about its importance. "Those guys have a tough job. They have to learn the other team's offense and got to be ready to execute against us every day. They come prepared to practice every single day."[5]

And getting to see Baird knock down the shot also revealed something essential to this team's success in the way they celebrated. "It was a great moment for everyone. I just looked at our bench and they were going crazy. That's the sign of a great team," Coach Beilein said afterwards as he answered media questions. "Those are great moments. Those are the ones I may remember more than others."

Meanwhile Texas A&M coach Billy Kennedy succinctly summed up his feelings in the opening statement of his post-game press conference. "It felt like we ran into a buzz saw." That evening in Los Angeles evolved into a celebration for the team, all the fans in attendance, and all those watching all over the world. But by the next morning, Beilein and staff had moved on and were focused on their Elite Eight opponent, Florida State.

The Seminoles presented some similarities to the Texas A&M squad Michigan had just beaten, but where the Aggies had strength and size, Florida State possessed an almost absurd level of length for a college basketball team. They featured two seven footers in Ike Obiagu and Christ Koumadje—the second of whom stood 7'4". All told, 12 players on their roster were listed at 6'6" or taller. Florida State liked to block shots and get out and run. That came through in Michigan's scouting report. "Their defense is terrific," Beilein said beforehand. "They prioritize it, and they have great length to do it."[6]

In the game's opening moments, Matthews quickly made his impact felt. He got himself in great defensive position and stayed vertical on Terrance Mann, who nevertheless made a tough basket over him. On the offensive end, he took a dribble handoff from Wagner and charged at the hoop with bad intentions. He elevated off two feet and finished with two hands and hit an accompanying free throw. A minute later on the defensive end, he provided weak-side help and swatted Braian Angola's shot away. Abdur-Rahkman made Michigan's first three-pointer of the game to take a 10–4 lead, three minutes into it. It was almost another three minutes before they scored again, but when they did, it was again Matthews who initiated the action. He deflected a Florida State pass away and immediately broke out, receiving a pass from Abdur-Rahkman and finishing with another dunk. Matthews then added another old-fashioned three-point play to put Michigan up 15–10, only to be answered by a 7–0 Seminole run. The first half continued as a nip and tuck affair with a plethora of turnovers and a lot of missed three-pointers on Michigan's part. Once again, the Wolverines' defense was up to the task. They forced an incredible

(Left to right) C.J. Baird, Austin Davis, Eli Brooks, Isaiah Livers, Ibi Watson, Jordan Poole (sitting), Jaaron Simmons, and Jon Teske celebrate during their Elite Eight contest against Florida State in 2018 (photograph by Patrick Barron).

14 turnovers in the first half alone and didn't allow their opponent a single fast break point. The offense, on the other hand, was lacking. Wagner did not score a first-half field goal, and Abdur-Rahkman was the only player to hit a first-half three-pointer. Matthews had done work to keep them afloat on that end of the court, to go along with his stellar defense, and that was enough for a 27–26 lead at the break.

The team defense continued to lead the way in the second half. After Florida State scored on their first possession, they were stopped the next seven times down the court. That allowed Michigan to go on an 11–0 run over the next five minutes. The first basket in that run came on an Abdur-Rahkman drive that drew two defenders, opening up space for an easy layup for Wagner—his first field goal of the game. The next was a Matthews' pump fake into a step-back three-pointer where he calmly reset his feet and delivered. Defensive tenacity combined with effective shooting from inside the arc kept Michigan in front the rest of the way. With 4:15 left, Phil Cofer made two free throws to close the gap to three. The Wolverines then scored on their next three possessions to seemingly ice the game. First, Matthews scored on a mid-range pull-up. Then Simpson eschewed a Teske screen and blew by his defender for a layup on his own. The next time down, Simpson's actions

Charles Matthews cuts down the net in Los Angeles after scoring 17 points and collecting eight rebounds against Florida State (photograph by Patrick Barron).

mirrored the play before only to finish this time with a dish to a wide-open Robinson in the corner for three. A 10-point lead with 2:25 is typically secure if a team can make their free throws, but that was clearly not Michigan's specialty. Simpson missed the front end of a one-and-one and split another pair. Abdur-Rahkman did the same. All the while Florida State chipped away, and after a scramble possession of missed three-pointers, a Cofer tip narrowed the lead to two with 24 seconds remaining. Michigan was finally able to get the ball into the hands of their best free throw shooter, and Robinson converted both of his to provide the final score of 58–54.

The Wolverines had won their 13th straight game to go to the Final Four, despite their offense posting its lowest points per possession of the season. The defensive performance was truly elite, and the numbers were jarring. Florida State had 15 turnovers and just 16 baskets on the game. They didn't score a single fast break point. Michigan did not allow a field goal from the ten-minute mark until almost two minutes remaining. While many might call it an "ugly" win, Yaklich had a different take. "We've had some grinder games this year and people call them ugly and I call them beautiful."[7]

Jon Sanderson put it succinctly: "This is the best defensive team we've ever had, and it's not even close."[8] Duncan Robinson agreed. "Since I've been in a Michigan jersey, we've never been able to play defense at this level."[9] That

(Left to right) DeAndre Haynes, John Beilein, Ibi Watson, Zavier Simpson, Muhammad-Ali Abdur-Rahkman, Charles Matthews, and Luke Yaklich are visible in the foreground as the entire team gathers amidst falling Maize and Blue confetti after earning a trip to the 2018 Final Four (photograph by Patrick Barron).

defense allowed them to overcome a 4–22 shooting performance from long range, including 0–7 from Wagner.

Matthews was deservedly named the West Region's Most Outstanding Player, completing an incredible in-season evolution. His journey was a classic example that the development process never stops under John Beilein. All throughout his mid-season struggles, he bought in to continually striving to improve. He spent time after practice diligently working on simple fundamentals. DeAndre Haynes told the media, "You see him driving, landing on two [feet], the pivots he did to get guys up in the air ... all that you guys see is things that he's been working on in practice, and he's finally doing it in games and it's working for him."[10]

His coaches and teammates couldn't be happier for him and his development. "He struggled at the end of the season. He just went back to work—no attitude," Wagner detailed. "Coach Beilein took his time, they went back to work together and now he's putting numbers up."[11]

Beilein pointed to his humility in his post-game comments. "For him to come in and just buy in, I'm talking 1,000 percent, to culture, to individual workouts, scouting reports, to all the things that sometimes guys who are recruited so highly have a hard time buying into. So many times they've been told they're the greatest, and now you say, 'No, these are weaknesses we're going to work on,' there are blind spots. There has been none of that. He is just trying to get better."

The celebration was on. Beilein insisted on a picture with his staff and their families out on the court. "That's pretty cool. Not a lot of head coaches would do that or think about the families and kids,"[12] Jon Sanderson said. Nets were cut, and the team showered Beilein with a cooler of water when he entered the locker room. A dance party ensued on the bus ride back to the hotel with the unlikely duo of Beilein and Poole at the center of it. The Wolverines now truly were "Champions of the West" and were on their way to the Final Four.

Chapter 18

Sending Cinderella Home

The Michigan men's basketball team had made it to San Antonio, a scenario that seemed highly unlikely for large stretches of the season. Unity, passion, appreciation, integrity, diligence, and accountability had led to an incredible finish. The newfound dedication and focus on defense had added a completely new attitude to the program. All of that would hopefully be enough to overcome this tournament's Cinderella team, the Loyola Ramblers. The small Jesuit school in Chicago had a 98-year-old team chaplain named Sister Jean that had become the most famous member of their traveling party. She offered a great story that the media had seized on to, but her name didn't find its way into the scouting report. Luke Yaklich had coached against Loyola in the Missouri Valley Conference the previous season. He gave Beilein a quick synopsis after the win against Florida State. Beilein said of the report, "They're a lot like us. They have a bunch of good kids. They play together, they play defense. They have a bunch of guys that can shoot."[1]

Once Beilein had a chance to look at the film, he was in agreement. "[Their offense] is a thing of beauty. This is not Princeton in any way, but they cut on and off—they cut without the ball. They dribble with the ball. They post. I think having the great, not good, but great passing center has really had a great impact on them. And they've got shooters everywhere."[2] Michigan had the edge in talent, but they would have to go prove it on the court. Their defense had gotten them this far, while the offense had really only stepped up once in the tournament. Another rough day shooting the ball might be one too many. By the time Saturday finally rolled around, both teams were eager to get on the Alamodome floor.

Michigan's coaches primed their team in the locker room beforehand with some inspirational speeches. Saddi Washington emphasized the team's core values. "Unity. Passion. Appreciation. Integrity. Diligence. Accountability. That's why we're here. If you want to know a man and who he is, look at his foundation. If you want to know a man and who he is and what his story is, look at his foundation. We come to work and we do our job every day. We ain't flashy, we just believe in this team. We believe in Michigan!"[3]

He handed off to Yaklich, who spoke in his gruffest tone. "You dominate the simple! Those are the things that are going to win this game, and are going to help us lock them up. You've done it all before. You guard those guys tonight the same way you guarded every single team—with a chip on your shoulder. You are going through every single screen! It's on tonight fellas because we are going to stay true to who we are, stay in character, stay connected, and be the hardest playing bunch of pit bulls that have ever stepped on a Final Four floor!"[4]

Beilein kept it simple, invoking Rudyard Kipling's "Law of the Jungle," to remind his charges to play for each other. "The strength of the pack is the wolf, and the strength of the wolf is the pack."[5]

Judging by the opening tip, Moe Wagner took all their words to heart. Cameron Krutwig appeared to win the tap against Isaiah Livers, pulling it back towards his teammates. Instead, Wagner stepped in and ripped the ball away to claim possession for Michigan. It was the first of many times he would aggressively attack the undersized Ramblers. Loyola quickly revealed they would be switching all screens defensively. That strategy left Matthews in the corner with a significant athletic advantage against Krutwig. He jab-stepped once. Then again. And once more. Confident Krutwig couldn't contest, Matthews rose and fired for the game's first three points. But the points wouldn't come as easily as the game progressed. About 12 minutes in, the Wolverines' offense officially stagnated. Michigan struggled to adjust to Loyola defenders switching every screen, and their scoring devolved into little more than Wagner's put-backs over smaller defenders that had switched on to him. Wagner's effort and aggressiveness kept them in it when they needed it most, but it would not be enough to give them the lead. Loyola's buzzer-beating put-back just before halftime pushed them up 29–22 and added a little more hop to Cinderella's step.

The Ramblers hadn't made a single three-pointer in the half yet had the lead, thanks to Michigan's brutal 9–31 shooting performance. Abdur-Rahkman led the way having missed all seven of his attempts. Zavier Simpson looked more like the player he'd been earlier in the year, scoreless and with three turnovers to his name. The whole team combined for eight turnovers and only a single assist. Wagner, Matthews, Teske, and Poole were the only players to log a point, and Teske and Poole had just two and one respectively. While it was a brutal half offensively, the team had seen enough challenges this year to know this was adversity they could handle. "The captains came into the room," Isaiah Livers stated, "and they said, 'This isn't over. We've got 20 minutes left to play, and we know what we can do. Let's go get to it.'"[6] Jordan Poole followed up as the hype man and reminded each player individually what they were capable of.

All that good mojo was put to the test as the half opened with Krutwig completing a three-point play and extending the lead to double digits. But Wagner immediately answered with a dribble drive into an authoritative slam off two feet. Robinson soon added a three-pointer, whittling Loyola's lead down to five. For a while, Michigan could get no closer. Although their offensive efficiency had much improved and their defensive effort had been amplified, Loyola kept making tough contested shots. It seemed like the Wolverines would eventually break through, but the longer the game went on, you couldn't be so sure.

Down 45–37 with 11:25 left and needing a spark (or perhaps some swag), Beilein called Poole's number. Nine seconds later, Poole showed off his quick first step and body control to sneak in a layup. At the other end, Poole pulled down the defensive rebound and eventually Robinson knocked down a three to pull within that many. Krutwig scored to momentarily staunch the Ramblers' bleeding, but Poole then used a Wagner screen and raced by the sluggish Krutwig to score another layup. The Wolverines returned to their end of the court after forcing a turnover, and Simpson fed Wagner down in the post. As Loyola trapped him, he patiently dribbled out to the corner, turned and hit a fade-away three-pointer to tie the game. It was eerily similar to one he had hit a few weeks ago to put the Big Ten Championship on ice. "That's like the same shot Moe hit in the Big Ten Tournament when time was winding down and he drove to the corner and shot some crazy shot that went in,"[7] Livers said later.

Michigan then forced Krutwig into his second straight turnover. Poole followed with two free throws. Loyola turned the ball over again. Wagner continued his tour de force with a left-handed bounce pass to a back-cutting Matthews, who gathered and stepped around a defender for the reverse layup. The Alamodome was as loud as it had been all evening. Matthews took the ball away from Clayton Custer at the other end. After a Michigan turnover, the Wolverines forced Loyola to do the same. Five straight possessions for the Ramblers had resulted in five straight turnovers. Poole couldn't quite put down a three-pointer to add the exclamation point, so Wagner cleaned it up the old-fashioned way by tipping it in and drawing the foul. Michigan had gone on a 17–2 run over almost seven minutes and held Loyola scoreless for the last four minutes and 36 seconds. The expected run had finally arrived and it completely flipped the game on its axis.

When Wagner drained a three-pointer from the top of the key at the three-minute mark, it pushed the lead to eight. Ninety seconds later, Loyola rushed to trap and allowed Matthews to leak out all alone. Abdur-Rahkman lofted it ahead and Matthews tied the ceremonial bow on the victory by slam-

The CBS broadcast team of (left to right) Bill Raftery, Jim Nantz, and Grant Hill accept Moe Wagner's apology after the Michigan big man leapt onto their table while pursuing a loose ball out of bounds in the 2018 Final Four against Loyola (photograph by Bryan Fuller).

ming it home. Even C.J. Baird got in on the action once again, recording a block in the closing seconds. Michigan was going back to the national championship game, with Wagner largely to thank. All of his improvement over the past year had culminated in a pinnacle performance on one of the biggest stages in sports. His 24 points and 15 boards had carried Michigan in a game they trailed by as many as 10 in the second half. He joined elite company in Larry Bird and Hakeem Olajuwon as the only players to score 20 and rebound 15 in a national semi-final game. "He was just physically dominating, which is something we haven't seen from him at all times," observed Robinson. "He usually does it with his skill. So, to dominate in a different way was pretty special. He was great for us."[8]

Also crucial was that Wagner racked up only a single foul on the evening, with three steals to his credit while contributing to Krutwig's six turnovers. "I tried to do my job, tried not to foul and stay solid, build walls and grab rebounds. And it worked out,"[9] Wagner said. His energy also led to a humorous moment when he chased down a loose ball over the announcer's table and almost ran over Grant Hill, Bill Raftery, and Jim Nantz. Hill's priceless reaction as the 240-pound German barreled towards him quickly became immortalized as an internet meme. Raftery's glasses were broken in the process and the crew had some good laughs on the air. Wagner apologized to Raftery in his on-court interview, saying, "I'm sorry, Coach. I hope that's the only thing that broke."

Yaklich's defensive plan had once again been executed. Loyola only attempted 10 three-pointers all game compared to 28 by Michigan. Stifling three-pointers had been a focus all year, and this game was no exception. "We made a concerted effort to take away the three," Beilein said in his press conference. "And a little bit like an Isaac Haas type of idea—where that kid's going to get two on Moe, but we're not going to give these great three-point shooters [opportunities]. They make seven a game, we limited them to one."

The celebration moved to the locker room. It was slightly more subdued, because their gaze quickly shifted to the ultimate challenge that was just two days away. "That was about all of our core values right there," Beilein said in a post-game speech. "We had unity, right? Our diligence and persistence was incredible. Nothing was going well. So, I have a great appreciation for where we were. We held each other accountable, right? And we played with passion, baby. We played with *passion*. So, I just loved the way you won it—not just that you won it, but the way you won it."[10]

Chapter 19

One Final Game

Bracket busters along the way had created an easier path, relatively speaking, for Michigan to reach the national championship. That would not be the case in the last game of the season. The Wolverines were playing the best team in the country in Villanova. The Wildcats, in a tournament rarity, were yet to even play a close game on their path to the finals. Villanova's head coach Jay Wright and John Beilein knew each other very well. Their mutual respect dated back to their days in upstate New York at Rochester and Le Moyne. They shared similar approaches and philosophies to program building and playing style. Wright's program was uniquely positioned at the sweet spot of talent and experience, led by the Wooden Award winner, Jalen Brunson. Beilein had recruited Brunson and knew him well. At one point, Michigan looked like a potential favorite to land him. "I voted him as well as the player of the year," Beilein told the media in his availability the day before the game. He added, "He plays like a guy that's played forever and just outsmarts everybody."

Villanova had also patiently developed Mikal Bridges from a role player into a lottery pick over three years. Talented youngsters in Omari Spellman and Donte DiVincenzo had taken redshirt years that had allowed them to grow into their current roles. Upperclassmen Phil Booth and Eric Paschall had also redshirted earlier in their careers and now provided leadership and reliability. Beilein had taken notice of those additional years of development Villanova enjoyed. "I can't believe how many guys have redshirted for a bunch of reasons, I'm sure. That makes them a much older team and that's really an advantage today in college basketball,"[1] he said. Both programs prided themselves on recruiting high-character kids that understood team basketball and offered potential to develop. Both passed the ball freely and had big men that could shoot from outside. And now that Michigan's defense had taken its leap, both programs relied on defenses that knew how to get a stop. And on Monday, April 2, only one of them would be crowned national champions.

Each team's star appropriately made his impact felt immediately. Brunson, who despite playing point guard also doubled as one of the best post players in the country, backed down Simpson for the first bucket of the game. Wagner matched him with an up and under move for his own two. Brunson came back with a turn-around jumper from in close, and Wagner hit two free throws. Abdur-Rahkman poked a ball away and took it himself to give Michigan its first lead and one they would maintain for the next 12 minutes of action. On Brunson's next shot attempt, Matthews jetted from the other side of the court to pin it against the backboard in an impressive feat of athleticism. Wagner soon hit a long-distance three-pointer and then a spinning, driving layup that started beyond the three-point line. He had scored nine of Michigan's first 11 and looked primed to repeat his virtuoso performance from two nights prior. Abdur-Rahkman matched Wagner's deep three to make the score 14–8.

It seems unbelievable in hindsight, but Donte DiVincenzo had been in the game at that point for close to five minutes without hearing his name called once. Unfortunately for Michigan, it soon became a name that they will never forget. He answered Abdur-Rahkman's shot with the first of many three-pointers from NBA range. The two then traded driving layups with DiVincenzo adding a free throw to his to tighten the score to 16–14. Jordan Poole then checked in, and as he was wont to do, immediately scored with an athletic take to the hoop for a three-point play. Poole then found Wagner on a nicely run pick and roll, and the Wolverines held their largest lead of the evening at 21–14.

Villanova quickly answered with a 9–0 run bookended by DiVincenzo jump shots. The second of those came off the bounce from a deeper spot than any shot all night. At that point it became abundantly clear he was going to be a serious problem for Michigan. A few minutes later, DiVincenzo added another three and a drive to the hoop. Michigan kept coming though. Wagner had a beautiful feed to a cutting Matthews for a dunk to make it 30–28. Up to that point, the game resembled Michigan's last finals appearance against Louisville. Both teams were firing on all cylinders and the night seemed destined to be a well-played shootout, complete with a bench player knocking down multiple first half three-pointers. But the sheer range that Villanova shot from created problems that even Michigan's now elite defense struggled to solve. Once they were forced to extend farther out to take away three-pointers, everything underneath then opened up. Villanova took advantage.

Brunson dribbled down into the post while Matthews aggressively pursued DiVincenzo around the perimeter in an effort to take away any airspace for the hot shooter. All it took was a simple back screen to spring him free. Brunson made the easy pass to a cutting DiVincenzo for the dunk. Their next hoop came when Spellman started to screen for DiVincenzo up top but then dove down to the hoop. Both Wagner and Matthews closed out on the potential three-pointer leaving Spellman wide open to receive the dish and slam it home. DiVincenzo seemed to be everywhere. At the defensive end, he sprinted from well behind the play to block a Simpson layup so hard it was wedged in between the rim and the backboard. He jumped so high that he still had time to use his opposite hand to try and pull it down, to no avail. Still, the jump ball arrow favored Villanova. It was inbounded to Brunson, who let it roll up the court untouched to conserve some time. He scooped it up at midcourt, took a few dribbles, and launched yet another long three-pointer. That one was a dagger that completed a 7-0 run, good for a 37-28 lead heading into halftime and completed a significant momentum shift in Villanova's favor.

Beilein and staff had their work cut out for them in trying to make half-time adjustments to stop the best offense in the country. There were no easy answers. Wagner began the second half with a wraparound layup to give Michigan a momentary boost. But over the next 90 seconds, Villanova quickly responded with a 7-0 run and pushed the lead out to 14. The Wildcats had matched their burst right before the half with another one just after it and were now completely in control. Eric Paschall and Mikal Bridges began getting in on the action as well, both from behind the three-point line and on layups in the paint.

Michigan had one more push left, and it started with an Abdur-Rahkman three-pointer and a Matthews' dunk. Matthews had an opportunity for another dunk soon after, but he was met at the apex of his vertical for a two-hand block by none other than Donte DiVincenzo. It was a stunning display of athleticism to perfectly time the leap of the highest jumper on the Wolverine squad. Simpson collected the block and was fouled, hitting both free throws. A Wagner dunk, and a Matthews' steal and layup completed an 11-5 burst that closed the lead to 12. One more stop and a score and Michigan could pull within single digits. Eighteen seconds later, DiVincenzo dribbled forward and rose up from very deep once again for three more. Fifty-two seconds later, using a Spellman screen, he did it again. Just like that, the lead was back to 18. Michigan competed hard the rest of the way, but Villanova simply wasn't going to be beaten. Not with that many weapons on the court, and not with DiVincenzo showing the ability to score at will at all three levels.

Michigan would have needed one of their better shooting performances to hang around, but instead were 3-23 from beyond the arc, including one for their last 19. Luke Yaklich's defense had finally been cracked for the first time in over two months. Even with Zavier Simpson holding the National Player of the Year Brunson to his lowest scoring output of the season, DiVincenzo's performance was simply too much to overcome. "Even if we had played our best, it would have been very difficult to win that game with what

DiVincenzo did, it was an incredible performance," Beilein said in his media availability afterwards.

The redshirt sophomore's 31 points were the most in a title game since 1989, when Seton Hall's John Morton and Michigan's Glen Rice scored 35 and 31, respectively. It was also the most points ever scored by a player off the bench in a Final Four game. DiVincenzo used that dominant performance as a springboard to the first round of the NBA draft a few months later. There was no shame in losing to the unequivocal best team in the country. Villanova would go on to have four of their players selected in the first 33 picks of the NBA draft. Along with their natural talent, those four were also among the most polished players to be selected. "That team right there, could win a lot of Final Fours, not just the 2018 one,"[2] Beilein said.

The locker room was understandably somber and emotional afterwards. But there was also a sense of pride and accomplishment beneath the sadness. This team had been unranked at the beginning of January and hadn't even received any votes. They rattled off 14 straight wins with a suffocating defense, sound team principles, and the formation of a deep bond that would last the rest of their lives. "It's more than basketball. It's a brotherhood," said Abdur-Rahkman. "We're a family. And tonight was rough, but we'll always remember this run, this team. We're 33–8 and nobody expected us to be here. And we're just always going to remember each other and being part of this team."[3]

Their other senior captain, Duncan Robinson, echoed his counterpart's sentiments. "We gave everything we had every day. We were all in. As a leader of this team, that's all I can ask for. For me to have been a part of it, I'm just incredibly grateful and thankful."[4]

Beilein deeply appreciated the mindset that Robinson had brought to the team, and the legacy he would leave. "He is so into Michigan winning. That's all he cares about. Here's a kid that—you know, a lot of kids can't even get to an NCAA Tournament. This kid went to the championship game at Williams, and now he's been to the Sweet 16 and [a national championship game]. In his four years, he's had a pretty good four years of college basketball."[5]

Though Wagner was a junior, it seemed likely he would be heading to the NBA next year. For now, he was only thinking about his teammates. "I'm proud of this team, the way we fought, the way we competed," he said. "The way we've grown over the year is just something that you don't see that often."[6]

Beilein often spoke of the special relationship he had with Wagner. He searched for the right words to express how much he valued the talented junior's contributions. "Moe, as a captain, you were absolutely tremendous," said Beilein. "So much energy you gave us. It's incredible."[7]

The coaches did their best to console the group, and to convey how meaningful the entire experience had been. "You guys had an unbelievable season … you won't know the impact right now. But 10, 15, 20 years down the line, people are going to talk about this team. So, be proud of that,"[8] insisted Saddi Washington.

"I'm as proud of this team as any team I've coached in all these years," said Beilein. "I appreciate how you bought into what we're doing. We weren't perfect, but we were pretty close to perfect. I thank all of you for being great representatives of the greatest university in the world."[9] With that, the 2017-18 team gathered for one last singing of "The Victors."

Beilein faced the media afterwards and, as always, displayed a level of perspective all too uncommon in major college sports. "This is why I coach: To be in that locker room right now with these kids and to have this opportunity to tell them 'This is life.' This is a great part of life. You have these highlights, and then all of a sudden, in the blink of an eye, your season is over and there's sadness. But in the long run, there's a lot of joy in what we just went through." Despite the disappointment, Beilein focused what made this Michigan team so special. "They just had such substance," he said. "That was just incredible growth because they were connected. And that's what I'll remember about this team. That is a very sad locker room right now, not because we lost the game, but because they know something special just ended."[10]

Chapter 20

Thank You, Michigan

Although Michigan's season ended in a loss, it was an undeniable success. Despite low expectations from outsiders, they wound up finishing as one of the last two teams standing. They did it through hard work, a relentless commitment to improvement, and a complete transformation on the defensive side of the ball. While the team returned from San Antonio to Ann Arbor together, a number of players were ready to move on. Moe Wagner had capitalized on his decision to return to Michigan for his junior year by improving the weaknesses in his game and leading his team on an incredible journey. He finished the season ranked 46th in the country in defensive rebounding percentage—an impressive 64 percent improvement from the previous season. His defense, while not elite, had strengthened substantially under the tutelage of Luke Yaklich. Though foul trouble had still occasionally pushed Wagner to the bench, he was able to stay on the court for more minutes than the year before. He also increased his assist rate and lowered his turnover rate to complete his impressive development under John Beilein. Having addressed the flaws that NBA teams had pointed out to him during the previous year's draft process while simultaneously taking Michigan to the national championship game, it was now time for Wagner to level up. He announced his decision to enter the NBA draft in a detailed letter to coaches, teammates, and fans in *The Players' Tribune* entitled "Thank You, Michigan." He summed up his gratitude for his university nicely: "Michigan will always be this place where, if you work hard enough, and you work together enough—you can become your best self."[1]

After showing up on campus as an unheralded recruit, Wagner completed his story at Michigan like many before him—he became a first-round pick in the NBA draft. Former Michigan basketball player Rob Pelinka, who was now the Los Angeles Lakers GM, selected him 25th overall. Pelinka later revealed that former Spartan great and NBA Hall of Famer Magic Johnson led the charge, saying, "Selecting Moe Wagner was a big target for Magic." He went on to tell the assembled Laker media something that Michigan fans already knew very well: "You guys are going to love Moe Wagner because he literally lights up a room when he walks into it."[2]

Beilein was in the green room at the draft with Wagner and his family to lend his support. He was perhaps most noticeable for the way he quickly dodged out of view of the cameras once he realized Moe and his family were getting their moment on television. Wagner believes his time in Ann Arbor was the ideal development setting for an NBA career. "I've talked to my friends that are in the NBA now," he said. "And they say 'you're going to be surprised how prepared you already are just with what you've experienced the last three years.' So I feel very good and obviously Coach Beilein is a huge part of that."[3]

The senior leaders on the team also followed Wagner into professional basketball. With all that Duncan Robinson had accomplished after being discounted at every stop along the way, nothing he achieves should come as a surprise anymore. Despite going undrafted, he latched on with the Miami Heat to play for them in the NBA Summer League. After shooting 20–34 from deep in his first six games, he essentially forced the Heat's hand. They signed him to the same two-way contract that they had signed Derrick Walton to the previous year. "Obviously, shooting is at a premium in the NBA, so that's what attracts you at first, but he's very competitive on the defensive end, he's really smart, he knows angles and knows how to put himself in the right position," Heat summer league head coach Eric Glass said. "And he really has a good feel for the game: he knows when to make an extra pass, he knows when to put the ball on the floor, [and] he knows when to help on defense."[4]

A thrilled Beilein tweeted how Duncan made it happen: "We are all so proud of [Duncan Robinson]. His climb to the NBA from Division 3 was simple but not easy. He made it simple by just working hard each day to do his best. Very dedicated to his work habits and teammates. He thanked the coaching staff daily too. A Leader and the best!"

Muhammad-Ali Abdur-Rahkman suffered unfortunate timing and required surgery to repair a stress fracture in his ankle just before the NBA draft. Once healthy, he signed a contract with the Canton Charge, the Cleveland Cavaliers' affiliate in the G-League. It would surprise no one in the Michigan basketball family if he eventually found his way onto an NBA roster. Jaaron Simmons signed with the Swiss professional team Union Neuchâtel. In the end, his individual performance wasn't what he had envisioned when he came to Michigan. However, his personal growth and his demonstrated ability to overcome adversity will always be remembered. He got to help cut down some nets as part of the greatest team he ever played on, and in the process served as a great teammate and leader. "I came here to learn, I came here to grow," he said. "Obviously I came here to play and it hasn't been *exactly* what I wanted in that regard. But at the same time when you're winning it trumps everything."[5]

Austin Hatch married his college sweetheart and former Michigan volleyball star Abby Cole shortly after graduation. He then began a position working in franchise development for Domino's. He also continued his public speaking career, sharing the incredible story that has impacted so many inside and outside of the Michigan family. Charles Matthews initially declared for the draft but did not hire an agent. After going through the NBA's workout and combine process, he ultimately decided to continue his tutelage under John Beilein for another year. Assistant coach DeAndre Haynes expressed his excitement about watching him continue to grow: "The sky is the limit. He just has to keep working. He is so athletic. He can shoot the ball. We are going to keep working on his craft, but he's going to be a star."[6]

While Matthews worked his way through his decision-making process, Beilein was simultaneously wrestling with his own life decision. The Detroit Pistons had invited him to interview for their vacant head coaching position. The lifetime head coach who had led teams at every other level was intrigued by the idea of ascending that final step and coaching in the NBA. The league had evolved to feature the ball movement and spacing that Beilein had prioritized for years; its current style suited his offense perfectly. Getting the chance to coach the most talented players on the planet without relocating was an opportunity that he had to at least consider.

For the Pistons, it made perfect sense to be calling Beilein. As a franchise that lacked a defined culture and struggled with player development, Beilein's strengths met their needs perfectly. In terms of achieving NCAA Tournament success while developing players at the same time, Michigan's head coach had few peers. Since 2013, no program had won more tournament games than Michigan and only two had produced more first-round picks. And those schools had done it by signing McDonald's All-Americans by the boatload, while Beilein had never dipped his toe in that water. But after engaging in extensive conversations with the Pistons and gathering more information, Beilein ultimately decided to pull his name out of consideration. He soon thereafter signed a rolling five-year extension that athletic director Warde Manuel hoped would keep him in the head coach's chair at Michigan until he retired. "This is the time that I've stayed longer in one place and I really have grown," he said. "I've fallen in love with Ann Arbor, the Michigan people, the thousands and thousands of our alums that follow men's basketball, and I've realized this is a heck of a job I have."[7]

While Matthews and Beilein had struggled with crucial decisions, the drumbeat of development continued on for the rest of the team. Zavier Simpson returned home to Ohio and spent the summer working with his father on improving his shooting percentage. "We just want to go back to ground zero to work on his mechanics," his dad Quincey said. "Get his release point higher—getting that left hand off the ball so much and having that window available for him—and then try to perfect the mid-range game."[8] Simpson also found a new friend that summer. He had taken such a liking to his identity on the team that he actually adopted a pitbull in the off-season. Apparently, his apartment complex manager was not a basketball fan though, and Simpson eventually had to leave Sosa with his aunt in Ohio.

Jordan Poole, Isaiah Livers, Jon Teske, and Austin Davis attended Camp Sanderson to drive essential strength and athleticism gains. Livers felt the summer spent in Ann Arbor would pay dividends, "We stayed in the spring and summer, got better, got bigger, and learned a lot more."[9]

Teske took it one step further, working under Sanderson's tutelage for a full 16 weeks over the summer. With Wagner moving on, Teske's development loomed as an important storyline to the 2018-19 season.

Coming off the theatrics of his buzzer-beater in Wichita and the attendant celebrity that followed, Jordan Poole entered an important summer. While he had shown flashes of his considerable upside during a freshman season played entirely as an 18-year-old, Michigan needed Poole to become more consistent to help the team reach its potential. While he had the tools to become an elite shooting guard on the offensive end, the rising sophomore needed to eliminate his defensive miscues and become a more consistent player. Beilein was excited to watch the rising sophomore's growth. "Jordan Poole has a very high ceiling and he's learning every single day. I can't wait to continue to coach him, get him to understand what winning basketball looks like, what Muhammad and Duncan and Moe have really appreciated."[10]

A slight adjustment to NCAA rules also gave the coaching staff some valuable additional practice time with those players that stuck around in the summer. Saddi Washington pointed out that change was particularly valuable for Michigan. "The additional two hours of skill development that we were able to have with our players this year was huge for a program like ours that really values the player development piece."[11]

Michigan's incoming freshmen also arrived on campus for an introduction to Sanderson's program. Beilein and staff had assembled what looked to be one of the more complete recruiting classes during his tenure. "They're all going to be good," Beilein said, "but are they going to be the Trey Burke good where their freshman year they're getting 15 a game, or are they going to be the Moe Wagner good or D.J. Wilson where they average two [points] their freshman year and they average 15 their junior year and they're still NBA players."[12]

Ignas Brazdeikis was the highest rated of the bunch and entered with expectations to contribute right away. The Lithuanian-born Canadian developed a friendship with Nik Stauskas and received a detailed scouting report on the program from the former NBA first-round pick. "We actually live only 15 minutes apart from each other back home so we just started to work out together and built a connection from there," Brazdeikis shared at the team's media day. "He gave me a lot of insight on what it's like to be here, so he kind of pushed me to show me the good things at Michigan and it really did help."[13] The powerful wing actually had an offer from Michigan to attend the previous season but instead chose to do an extra year of prep school to ensure his readiness. Upon his arrival, Brazdeikis (known as Iggy) demonstrated his motivation by telling Luke Yaklich, "I want to be an elite two-way player, Coach. You can hold me accountable to that."[14] That confidence and desire combined with his college ready skill-set and strength would allow Brazdeikis every opportunity to make an immediate impact.

David DeJulius offered the look of a future floor general. His body type and game offered some similarities to Derrick Walton. The four-star recruit out of Detroit dominated Michigan State recruit Foster Loyer in a high school matchup. DeJulius admitted that their matchup meant a little something extra to him, "I'd be lying if I said I didn't [take it personal]. It was, for sure. It's a Michigan-Michigan State thing, and I felt like it was time to give Michigan fans something to talk about."[15] When Loyer went on to receive the state of Michigan's Mr. Basketball award, it undoubtedly stoked DeJulius' competitive fire even more.

Brandon Johns was an athletic big man from East Lansing that turned down Tom Izzo and Michigan State to instead be a Wolverine. He made himself an early fan favorite when he described Izzo's reaction to his decision. "Yeah, he went on a whole rant," Johns said. "That was not what I expected. It wasn't easy."[16] Colin Castleton was a skilled big man from Florida lacking in physicality. An apprenticeship under the joint leadership of Jon Teske and Jon Sanderson beckoned, with potential for playing time if everything went well. Finally, Adrien Nunez was a late developing shooting guard out of New York City. Standing 6'5" with a quick release and a smooth three-point shot, Nunez looked like a good fit for Beilein's offense.

Those newcomers were indoctrinated over the summer into the program's culture and values. Isaiah Livers looked back on that process from before his freshman season as an essential component to his development. "Coach B took all us young guys through a process in the summer leading up to fall. Just every day he was talking about the growth mindset. Every day he was just trying to [get us to] learn something new and trying to perfect it and put it into your craft."[17]

Unfortunately, Beilein did not have the chance to be as involved in the transition process with this group of recruits. His yearly physical revealed a heart problem that required immediate treatment. "I do a routine stress test every year, and I actually missed it the first time because I had to go recruiting. That's sort of the way I live my life. I had the first part of my physical, and they said it was time for the stress test. I said I only have 30 minutes, I have to catch a flight, so they said let's do it later. And I actually wasn't going to do it," Beilein explained in his first press conference upon his return. Fortunately, his doctor insisted, and the stress test discovered an issue with his heart that required double bypass surgery. Beilein was in good hands with a world-class medical facility on campus and the surgery and his recovery were a complete success. Reflecting later in that same press conference, Beilein recognized what a tumultuous time he had just gone through: "This has been as unique a nine months as anybody could have in their life between a great run to the national title game and winning the Big Ten Tournament, having an opportunity to at least discuss being the Detroit Pistons' coach, and then being shocked by the need for a double bypass."

The timing of the surgery meant that Beilein would have to skip the 2018-19 team's trip to Spain in August. Although there was a brief discussion of cancelling the trip, Beilein insisted they go on without him. "There was probably a five-minute span where we all discussed should we do the trip or not once we found out. And I was 100% on board, let's do the trip, this is what we all need. With these five freshmen, you can't pass on this opportunity. And I'm so glad we stayed united in that."[18]

Saddi Washington took the helm as head coach as the next edition of Michigan basketball crossed the pond to begin the new season's journey with three exhibition games against European professional teams. With stops in both Madrid and Barcelona the trip revolved around basketball, but also involved sightseeing and an ideal opportunity to bond as a group and lay the groundwork for a successful season. In between games, the Maize and Blue-clad athletes drew stares from perplexed Spaniards as they wandered Las Ramblas and toured the Palau Nacional and La Sagrada Familia. With limited practice time, the rust was apparent as the team won just one of their three contests. The biggest development from a basketball perspective was the immediate emergence of Brazdeikis, who led the team in scoring on the trip. The freshman's on-court success caught everyone's eye but so did his focused demeanor off of it. He quickly earned the respect of the team's leaders, as Zavier Simpson later detailed: "During film sessions when Coach Beilein or any other assistants are talking to him he's just engaged, and as a freshman that shows a lot of maturity."[19]

The team returned stateside understanding the work they had to do. Saddi Washington summarized the benefits at the team's media day: "It was big-time. From the perspective of being able to have those ten extra days of practice was invaluable. To be able to go over and play against actually professional guys was an eye-opening experience. When you come off the season that we came off of—I think we're a pretty grounded team—but to see another level of play and to see how far we have to go, it motivates our guys going into the season."

As important as their on-court experience had been, the trip also offered a chance to indoctrinate the five freshmen into the team dynamic. "It was good outside of basketball. We got a chance to connect as a team, get to know each other better and develop that relationship, so we're able to hold each other accountable for on the court actions,"[20] Zavier Simpson said.

The assistant coaches' ability to step up when Beilein was unable to make the trip to Spain owed itself to the preparation their head coach provided. "Coach had started delegating more even prior to that," Saddi Washington said. "The last couple of years I think he has had confidence in the staff to do our jobs and do it at a high level. That's the expectation. When we had to adjust to the sudden change this summer, I think everybody just embraced their roles and tried to make it an environment where Coach could be proud of the staff that he has put together."[21] It was a trend that first began with entrusting the team's defensive strategy to Billy Donlon and gradually developed into encouraging the players to hold each other accountable and grow into a player-led unit. The stability of the program in his brief absence spoke to the culture that Beilein had created, going all the way back to its humble beginnings in that Belgian conference room eight years earlier.

"Everyone knows what to expect," sophomore guard Jordan Poole said. "It's more of a culture that [Beilein] has built, more than it's just him. When he's not here, it's the same thing and the same energy."[22] Back in Ann Arbor, those clearly defined expectations encouraged the players to take on a greater leadership role when fall practice began. Zavier Simpson and Charles Matthews quickly established themselves as team leaders and made it clear that the toughness and defensive focus that allowed the team to reach the national championship would be a priority moving forward.

Beilein was delighted by the assertiveness of his captains, saying, "I can't get a word in sometimes because I want to tell Iggy what to do and Charles is telling him 'this is what coach wants.' What he used to think was corny a little while ago, now he's preaching it to the other guys. It's great. To watch him and Zavier coach—they might as well be on my staff now."[23]

Chapter 21

Underrated Once Again

Those early signs of accountability throughout the program portended a good future for Michigan's 2018-19 season. However, with a surface-level glance the national media highlighted the departures of Wagner, Abdur-Rahkman, and Robinson and voted Michigan #19 in their pre-season poll. Despite Beilein's track record of development and success along with the return of a number of core contributors, Michigan again would have to prove their doubters wrong on the court. They got to work doing just that on November 6, 2018, against Norfolk State in the opening game of their season. Michigan dominated their outmatched opponent defensively and did enough offensively to win comfortably 63–44. The night was most memorable for the raising of their two banners from the previous season; one for the Big Ten Tournament title and the other for reaching the Final Four. The meaning of those team accomplishments resonated deeply for Beilein. "Those banners aren't going away," he said afterwards. "They're going to be up there forever. We'll all be dead and gone and they're still going to be up there. That's what special for these kids to walk in here 30 years from now and look at those banners and know they were a big part of it. Hopefully we'll have a lot more up there by that time, but that's something that is never going to go away and that's huge."

The win that night was also the 800th of his storied career. True to form, he was less interested in discussing his individual milestone. "It's 800 wins, it'll go with those other basketballs that are back there," Beilein told the media after the game. "It was nice to have a poster and so many people congratulate you. I do appreciate all the people that have been a part of this." The following game against Holy Cross played out similarly with a suffocating defense leading the way to a 56–37 victory. The Wolverines' offensive performance was raising some questions as the team had shot a dreadful nine for 45 from three-point land in their first two contests. Improved shooting would be needed in the next game; their first real test, a national championship rematch against NCAA Tournament winner Villanova.

Despite losing four stars from the previous season's team, Villanova had received the benefit of the doubt and was ranked 8th in the pre-season AP poll—a stark contrast to Michigan's placement. The matchup was a headliner of the Gavitt Tipoff Games—a series that paired up teams from the Big Ten and the Big East. The game would also serve as the grand opening of the refurbished William B. Finneran Pavilion, the cozy on-campus facility where Villanova played many of their games. Although he hadn't been part of the Michigan program the prior April, Iggy Brazdeikis relished the opportunity to play the Wildcats in such a marquee setting. "As soon as I saw we were playing them, I circled that game on my schedule. I'm just super excited to play that game, and show that we could actually beat them and that we're better than them," Brazdeikis had said on media day. "That game is going to mean a lot more to me, and I feel like the rest of the team as well." It would soon become clear that the entire team had this game circled as soon as the schedule came out. During warmups, Villanova made the poor decision to attempt some intimidation of a fired-up Michigan team. Villanova guard Phil Booth crossed onto Michigan's side and bumped into Jordan Poole. Poole's Wolverine teammates rushed to his defense, and both teams eventually needed to be separated. The boisterous Brazdeikis later explained, "They tried to clown us in the beginning when they just stood in front of us and we were like, 'What? Who do you guys think you are?' We're not going to back down from anybody."[1]

Once the game tipped off, announcer Gus Johnson set the stage for the closely watched rematch: "Great chess match between two of the best coaches in America: Jay Wright and Professor John Beilein." Michigan's offense immediately looked revived from their lackluster early-season outings. On the first possession of the game, Jordan Poole used a screen by Jon Teske to work backdoor. Zavier Simpson hit him with the pass for an easy layup. The next time down Teske found a cutting Charles Matthews for a dunk. After two Villanova free throws, a missed Matthews' three was slammed home by the precocious freshman Brazdeikis. Seventeen seconds later Simpson handled a rebound and launched it up-court to a streaking Matthews for a transition layup. Matthews followed that up with a turnaround jumper against an overmatched Collin Gillespie to quickly make it 10–2.

The two teams traded a few baskets before Eli Brooks, back in his home state, knocked down a three-pointer. Isaiah Livers got in on the action with a transition three from the wing. Poole was fouled underneath while the shot was in the air, so Michigan also received the ball out of bounds. Another simple fade-away by Matthews completed a five-point possession and pushed the lead out to 22–8. A few minutes later Livers missed a layup, but Matthews was there to finish with an emphatic two-hand slam that he punctuated with a primal scream heard throughout the Pavilion. The onslaught continued with another Livers three. Then Jordan Poole jab-stepped twice before launching and connecting on his own from NBA distance. After another Villanova turnover, Brazdeikis spun by Gillespie on the baseline and Jermaine Samuels flopped feebly as the ambidextrous freshman finished the "and-one" with his right-hand while falling to the ground. Livers and Simpson rushed over to help him up after Simpson had taken a moment to crouch over him demanding that he keep his foot on the gas. Another Matthews' basket completed the 10–0 run and put Michigan authoritatively in front 39–13.

At halftime, the Pavilion's namesake, Bill Finneran, addressed the disgruntled crowd telling them "this is the worst game you're going to see here." If the Wildcats hadn't given up, it seemed their fans had. Michigan came out in the second half and quickly established they wouldn't be letting up despite the comfortable lead courtesy of the 44–17 first-half blitzing. They scored the first five points of the second half, giving them what would be the largest lead of the evening. A few minutes later Jordan Poole knocked away a pass at midcourt. After briefly possessing it, he feared he couldn't touch it again without a traveling violation being called. So instead he set about boxing out two Villanova players until Simpson arrived, picked it up and hit a running Livers for a layup. It was the type of determined effort play rarely seen by a team up 27 points. A few minutes later, Villanova's frustration bubbled to the surface. After a patented rip steal by Simpson, Dhamir Cosby-Roundtree grabbed him and added an extra shove as they were separated. Matthews and Brazdeikis rushed in immediately to protect their leader, as the toughness and closeness of the group was readily apparent. "Right or wrong, we've got to stick up for each other, we're gonna ride or die for each other," Matthews said. "You watch the clip, all five of us came in that huddle. That's just how we're raised."[2]

Despite almost 13 minutes remaining on the clock, the game was over. Villanova would never get closer than 25 as Michigan completed an authoritative early season beat-down. The Wolverines put the college basketball world on notice that the previous season was not a fluke—they had returned again as championship contenders. John Beilein was of course eager to temper any such talk, insisting afterwards "this is a November win—that's all it is. Just like a November loss—that's all it is. And you try and grow both ways." But the sheer level of dominance was undeniable. While Michigan had shot only a meager 5–17 from three-point range, their defense had imposed its will on Villanova and offensively they had gotten whatever they wanted at the hoop. They outscored Villanova 26–2 in points off turnovers, scored 44 points in the paint, and held the Wildcats to 31.8 percent shooting overall. The 0.72

points per possession Michigan held Villanova to would be, far and away, the Wildcats' worst performance all season.

Matthews led the way with 19, but it was Brazdeikis' 18 points and seven rebounds that really drew notice. Coming into the game, his matchup against burly redshirt senior Eric Paschall looked to be an exploitable one for Villanova. Brazdeikis was known for his offensive game, but his defense had been somewhat of a question mark. In his first true test, despite giving up more than two years in age and 40 pounds in weight, he repeatedly moved his feet and walled up as Paschall tried to bully him. Villanova's co-captain ultimately struggled his way to a 3–14 shooting night. It was a performance John Beilein greatly valued, saying afterwards "his endurance and his toughness today were outstanding."

Michigan's captains were similarly pleased with the freshman's outing, but made it clear they would not be letting him rest on his laurels. "We're going to stay on him. We don't let Iggy take any plays off," Matthews said while seated next to Beilein afterwards at the dais. "He's an extremely talented player and we don't want him to slack on any parts of his game. One thing about Iggy is that he has pride and I think that's half the battle with defense right there." The team's intensity in shutting down the defending champions' offense suggested a defensive ceiling even higher than the previous season. The points per possession allowed in each of the first three games would rank among Michigan's best performances from the season before.

Jay Wright certainly didn't disagree. "Their defense was very physical, very aggressive, and really locked in to their scouting report," he said in his post-game press conference. "I just really like their team. Great togetherness, great execution." The Wolverines returned to Ann Arbor feeling good about themselves, but also fully aware that it was just a single game and they had plenty of work to do. A few days later, they were off to the Mohegan Sun resort in Uncasville, Connecticut, for the Naismith Memorial Basketball Hall of Fame Tip-off Tournament. Playing in a sterile neutral environment against a weak George Washington squad was exactly the type of game that could trip up a team coming off a headline victory. Instead, Matthews scored 25 points, Jordan Poole canned five three-pointers, and Zavier Simpson added four of his own and the Wolverines cruised to an 84–61 victory.

The following day the Wolverines locked in defensively against Providence, holding the Friars to a dismal 28 percent shooting rate. Brazdeikis scored 20, while Teske added 17 and knocked down his first career three-pointer. The big man's smooth stroke hinted at potential upside to Michigan's offense; one didn't need a very deep memory to recall how Moe Wagner's pick-and-pop three-pointers unleashed the previous season's offense. John Beilein pushed Teske in practice and in games to take that shot. "What I hope is that is his first three of many," Beilein said afterwards. The variety of options at the offensive end were illuminated over the back-to-back days and, for Beilein, it called to mind some of the great teams he had coached in the past. "I think what's most impressive is we had Jordan Poole and Charles Matthews had great nights last night as far as scoring. They had great nights tonight, but it wasn't in scoring—it was in other areas. And now Jon [Teske] and Iggy [Brazdeikis]—Jon and Iggy didn't score last night. That's the way our best teams have been built. Trey Burke has it one night, Tim Hardaway has it the next night, Glenn Robinson has it the next night. And that's the way we have to continue to do this."

Chapter 22

A Contrast in Tempos

Coming off the dominant week, Michigan jumped ten spots to #8 in the AP poll. They enjoyed five days off before welcoming Chattanooga to town for a perfunctory 83–55 blowout. They rose one more spot in the rankings before the next important test of the season. One year after the North Carolina Tar Heels handled Michigan easily in their own building, it was time for the ACC–Big Ten Challenge rematch at the Crisler Center. It was the first time the two storied programs had ever played each other in Ann Arbor. Roy Williams' team featured a balance of talented freshmen and experienced winners. Luke Maye and Kenny Williams had won a national championship in their time at Chapel Hill. Coby White and Nassir Little had played in the McDonald's All-American Game just eight months prior. White had immediately made a name for himself in college basketball, coming off a 33-point performance in a loss to Texas. The 6'5" point guard was the all-time leading scorer in North Carolina high school basketball history; he presented exactly the type of challenge that Zavier Simpson relished. The contrast in tempo between the two programs was expected to be a key to the game. As the Wolverines had seen firsthand the year before, North Carolina was capable of scoring points in a hurry. They were quickly reminded of this when White hit Garrison Brooks running in transition for a layup on North Carolina's first possession. "It is tough to control the pace of this team. They're going to force their pace and we're going to have to adapt at times,"[1] Beilein had said beforehand. That fast tempo continued as both teams responded to the energy of a sold-out crowd. White kept pushing the pace, finding Brooks again as well as hitting his own tough shot. Luke Maye knocked down a couple of jumpers and grabbed a few rebounds. Brazdeikis finished at the hoop and was fouled, and took the opportunity to flex for the crowd. Charles Matthews was good for two more of his midrange turnarounds. Just after the first media timeout, Isaiah Livers hit a three to pull Michigan within two at 13–11.

Carolina answered with an 8-0 run and the script began to resemble the previous year's contest. But a steal and layup by Zavier Simpson changed the momentum in Michigan's favor. On their next possession, Brazdeikis slalomed his way to the hoop and finished with his right hand while drawing a foul. He followed it up with a three from the wing the next time down. Ten seconds later, after UNC rushed upcourt, Jon Teske blocked a shot and Michigan raced the other way. A Poole pump-fake led to an open three from Eli Brooks to complete an 11-0 run and gave Michigan its first lead at 22-21. The rambunctious crowd at the Crisler Center was rocking. After a Nassir Little jumper, Brooks and Brazdeikis each had a nifty off-hand finish at the rim. Then Matthews jumped a passing lane and finished with a breakaway dunk to ignite the crowd again and put the Wolverines up by five. But the Tar Heels kept hanging around and, with a series of tough shots that put the visitors up 33-31, Coby White demonstrated why he was so highly regarded. However, a strong finish to the first half left the Michigan faithful feeling good at the break. A Matthews three with 42 seconds left was followed by a steal at the other end that featured the seven-footer Teske diving on the ground for a loose ball and pushing it ahead to his point guard who found Jordan Poole in the corner. He hit nothing but net to send the Wolverines to the locker room leading 39-35. John Beilein later pointed to that as an important moment in the game: "We needed something going into halftime just to get us going."

An energized Michigan team emerged from the break with a varied offensive attack. Teske hit Brazdeikis for a layup and then blocked another shot at the other end. Michigan came down and got a third chance to score after two offensive rebounds. Poole pump-faked Garrison Brooks onto his heels, re-set his feet, and then knocked down a three with his efficient quick release. On their next possession, Poole drove and hit Iggy for a three. With the outside shooting well established, Simpson and Teske set to work on attacking the interior. On two consecutive trips, a rolling Teske scored out of the ball-screen off pretty feeds from his point guard. After that sequence, both teams went to the huddle for the first media timeout with Michigan up 51-39.

Freshman Leaky Black came out and hit a three for Carolina, and then made the inexplicable decision to talk some trash to Matthews and Simpson. Matthews attacked him the next play and was fouled, making both free throws. Black then turned it over on UNC's turn down the court. Simpson took the ball straight to the hoop but missed his layup. Fortunately, Matthews was waiting for it on the other side and slammed it home with two hands and drew a foul, as the crowd once again exploded in celebration. It was so loud that no one on the court actually heard the referee's whistle. "When Charles had the dunk off the rebound and the guy clearly blew his whistle in front of me and put his hands up, and I couldn't hear him—then I said, 'wow it is really loud in here,'" Beilein marveled afterwards.

Leaky Black's torment continued at the other end. The crowd resumed its deafening roar as Teske volleyball spiked Black's shot attempt into the Carolina bench. The UNC freshman still hadn't learned his lesson though—he then tried to take Matthews to the hoop, only to have the high-flier reject him once more. On the television broadcast, ESPN's Dan Shulman exclaimed "It's turned into a block party here in Ann Arbor!" The rout was on—the lead was soon stretched to 22 after Black was unceremoniously removed from the game and sentenced to watch the last 11 minutes from the bench. His chirping had only served to motivate Matthews, who seemed to relish when an opponent tried to talk trash. "I think a little chatter and confrontation is good for the game," Matthews said. "I have fun with it."[2] The packed house at Crisler also had fun with it, reveling until the very end. The final reverberation came as Poole hit a step-back from 25 feet in the last minute of the game and Dick Vitale exclaimed on the broadcast, "Are you serious?! It's been a Maize and Blue night!"

Brazdeikis had continued his dazzling introduction to college basketball, posting numbers against another premier opponent. He finished the night with 24 points on 9-13 shooting. He and the crowd fed off each other symbiotically. "I loved it. I expected a big crowd but when everyone started yelling and screaming, my emotions were so high. There's not a better feeling in the world."[3] After numerous years of an occasionally tepid home-court advantage, Michigan fans now packed Crisler both early and late. Coby White knew he was in enemy territory, saying "this is by far the toughest environment I've ever played in. It was loud, they had the crowd behind them."[4]

The exuberant fans witnessed Jordan Poole tie his career-high by draining five triples and Jon Teske tie his career-high with five blocks. Matthews had scored 21 and added seven rebounds, but he wasn't riding high afterwards. The team's leader instead pointed out the room for improvement. "It was 20 points above our average [in points allowed]," he said. "This wasn't a championship for us. Happy to win, happy it's over with. On to the next one."[5] High expectations had clearly become a hallmark of his and Zavier Simpson's watch. North Carolina would go on to earn a #1 seed in the NCAA Tournament and Michigan's 1.21 points per possession would stand as the best offensive performance the Tar Heels allowed all regular season.

Three days later another ranked opponent came to town for the first conference game of the season: the Purdue Boilermakers. Although Purdue had lost four starters from a team that had defeated Michigan twice the previous year, lead guard Carsen Edwards was back and talented enough to win games on his own. Another energetic crowd greeted the Wolverines' opponent and Michigan's shooters quickly fed off that atmosphere. Jordan

22. A Contrast in Tempos

Ignas Brazdeikis displayed an unusual level of confidence from the moment he arrived in Ann Arbor. The precocious freshman led all scorers with 24 points in Michigan's 84–67 win over North Carolina on November 28, 2018 (photograph by Marc-Gregor Campredon).

Poole's hot hand remained from the North Carolina game. He showcased his full offensive arsenal, starting with a three-pointer off crisp ball movement just two minutes into the game. Matthews followed his lead the next time down, sinking his own three from the top of the key. With the threat from distance established, Poole then back-cut on a defender that was over-pursuing him for an easy layup. One minute later, Poole drew the 7'3" Matt Haarns on a mismatch and rose up off the dribble over his extended hand and connected. A three from Brazdeikis on the wing soon extended the early lead to 10.

Simpson made the talented Edwards work for his but couldn't prevent a couple of tough driving layups that got Purdue back into it temporarily. As soon as Edwards went cold, Purdue had a tough time hanging around. A turnover and a couple missed jumpers by the Boilermakers' star guard allowed Michigan to separate themselves. Poole showed out from long-range once again—this time off a baseline out-of-bounds set and an authoritative screen from Jon Teske. Brazdeikis immediately followed with a steal and dunk as the crowd thundered its approval. Michigan had made six of their first seven threes after Matthews hit his next one. Once Matthews tossed up an alley-oop to Teske the next time down, Matt Painter was forced to call an immediate timeout. The 10–0 run took just 1:36 off the clock and put Michigan up comfortably 31–16. They would go on to stretch it as high as 20 and never closer than 12 the rest of the way before ultimately winning 76–57. It was their eighth straight win with a double-digit advantage.

Poole shot a perfect five of five from outside the three-point line but also added a number of alluring drives to the hoop and a nice feed to Simpson on the baseline for an assist. However, it was another facet of his game that excited John Beilein. "His numbers defensively right now are really good, as we chart contested shots and missed assignments. So now, his relationship with me is I'm giving him a little bit more leash because I realize he's bought in on those other things," the head coach said after the game. "Defense was not a priority and now it's becoming a priority for him."

Teske knocked down both of his threes as part of a 17-point, eight-rebound performance that left Matt Painter impressed. "Jon Teske has come a long ways. He has bypassed a lot of people, in my opinion, that he competes against," Painter said in his post-game presser. "He's got a bright future. He's really, really helped them not just defensively, but also offensively because he can knock down that 17-footer, and he can play at the rim." Beilein's player development had struck again with a big assist from Saddi Washington.

The assistant coach in charge of the big men had rebranded Teske as "Big Nasty" in an effort to inspire more rough and tumble play from the gentle giant. That effort was beginning to be rewarded. His performance in the previous season's Big Ten Tournament against Purdue had hinted at a breakout but now Michigan was seeing his potential become fully realized. Knocking down multiple threes in the game was the result of a diligent plan to extend his range. "He's got a very clean stroke and he's worked a tremendous amount in the spring and summer," Washington said. "That has empowered him to take those shots, and I think as he sees the ball go in more, he'll have even more confidence to take those shots."[6] His ability to shoot offered a potential game-changer for Michigan's offense if he could find consistency. But it was his defense that had ratcheted up the Wolverines' already stout unit.

Teske's 85 inches of height magnified by his long arms allowed him to alter numerous shots around the rim. But what really set him apart from most big men was his ability to move his feet. Much of Luke Yaklich's ball-screen defense was built around Jon Teske's ability to hedge out against the ball screen and buy the on-ball defender precious time to work their way around the screen and back onto their man. Teske was then agile enough to recover back onto his matchup who had typically rolled to the hoop. That approach required all five players to do their job and offer help, but without a mobile

Matt Haarms stands in the background as Jon Teske demonstrated to Eric Hunter, Jr., his transition from gentle giant to dominant center in Michigan's 76–57 win over the Boilermakers on December 1, 2018 (photograph by Marc-Gregor Campredon).

big man up top it simply doesn't work. Beilein pointed out the importance of that attribute, saying, "We like his feet. He's very unique for a 7'1" guy to have a size 13 shoe. So he really can move his feet. We're not hesitant about switching a ball-screen late."[7]

Perhaps most importantly, Washington's rebranding campaign had seemed to impact Teske's intensity. The first glimpse of that development was seen last year against Purdue at Madison Square Garden as he hollered to the heavens following a slam dunk over Isaac Hass. That emotive intensity was now emerging on a regular basis, much to his teammates' delight. "I'm so proud of him," Isaiah Livers said. "He wasn't doing that, he wasn't looking to score. He was looking to pass up wide open shots and wide open dunks, and now he's looking to dunk on people's heads. That's what he's been doing all off-season and I'm very proud of him."[8]

Team leader Zavier Simpson played an important role in Teske's comfort level. Their on-court chemistry was clear, but Simpson also took particular pride in getting teammates to come out of their shell. The big man's evolution was clear as day to the team captain. "Jon was a guy, who as soon as he said one word, would turn red," Simpson stated. "Now he's going around the locker room making jokes and stuff, knocking down three-pointers on the court and talking a little trash."⁹ Michigan's success with player development came in many forms. While Teske had clearly improved from the traditional strength and skills perspective, his teammates and coaches had also helped him grow more comfortable in his own skin. That growth would continue to pay dividends for Teske and his teammates throughout the rest of the season.

Chapter 23

A Freshman in Name Only

Although Ignas Brazdeikis had been a high schooler the previous April, he mirrored the toughness and resilience of his teammates who had competed for a national championship. With standout performances against Villanova and North Carolina, Brazdeikis' transition to the college game had been shockingly seamless. He appeared to be the rare freshman whose mental game wasn't compromised by the sudden media attention and accolades. Brazdeikis believes that a unique childhood spent in three different countries under the careful watch of a driven father had created the necessary conditions for his particular persona. "Moving around a lot gave me toughness and confidence that I could overcome any obstacle that comes my way,"[1] he said.

Brazdeikis was born in Kaunas, Lithuania and lived in his family's homeland for the first three years of his life. In search of better opportunities, his parents moved their family to Chicago briefly before heading north of the border to Canada. A few stops later, they settled for good in Oakville—a Toronto suburb with a Lithuanian diaspora. All along the way, Brazdeikis took cues from his father. Upon first glance, it's clear the chiseled Sigitas Brazdeikis provided the genetic impetus for his son's impressive physicality. He spent his recreation time in the mixed martial arts ring and brought his young son along with him to train. It was there that the younger Brazdeikis first learned many of the traits quickly recognizable on the basketball court: confidence, strength, and resiliency. Sigitas also taught his son the meditation and visualization techniques that Iggy continues to employ to this day.

When the younger Brazdeikis transitioned from martial arts to the hardwood at an early age, his talent eventually propelled him all the way to Orangeville Prep. The top Canadian high school basketball program boasts NBA alumni Jamal Murray and Thon Maker. With Orangeville, Brazdeikis traveled throughout the United States, taking on many of the best teams that the Lower 48 had to offer. In 2017, he scored 31 points as his team took down #1 ranked

Oak Hill at the Jordan Brand Invitational. He scored 50 points two different times playing in the 2017 Cali vs. Canada Showdown. He also traveled internationally a number of times to play for Team Canada in various FIBA events. Though he had the option to enroll in college for the 2017-18 season, Iggy instead chose to prepare himself fully for Day 1 of college basketball by spending an extra year at Orangeville. When he entered college as a 19-year-old freshman aided by a lifetime of training with his father, Brazdeikis had as much brute strength as Jon Sanderson had ever seen in a new arrival. All that muscle, however, left Brazdeikis with some tightness that could be a hindrance on the basketball court. "This was a huge weak link for Iggy,"[2] Sanderson explained. The freshman was disappointed by a prescription that took him out of his beloved weight room but shifted his focus towards an aggressive routine of yoga and flexibility that would prepare him to move laterally on the court and do his part contributing to Michigan's defensive prowess. His ability to move his feet and stay in front of Eric Paschall in the signature win at Villanova was a direct result of that summer diligence.

While he was hard at work prioritizing looseness and flexibility, he was also demonstrating his ability on the court to his new teammates in their summer workouts and then on the trip to Spain. They quickly realized he would be an important contributor in the team's effort to return to the national championship. It was also eminently clear that he carried himself a bit different than most freshmen. "He's aggressive—an aggressive freshman. Confident—a lot of confidence. He's got swag too—not as much as me, but he definitely has a lot of swag,"[3] said Jordan Poole. If Brazdeikis fell short of having the same overdose of swag that his teammate possessed, it wasn't by much.

Isaiah Livers took notice as well. "You don't hear of a lot of freshmen coming in and talking like (MMA fighter) Conor McGregor. His philosophy is based on Conor McGregor, and I think that's where all of his confidence comes from."[4] A childhood spent training to step in the ring had led Brazdeikis to a very different role model than most of his competitors had on the basketball court.

When it was time to pick a uniform number for the season, he knew exactly which one he wanted after having stayed with Moe Wagner the previous year on his official visit to Michigan. "I watched Moe last year and I loved the passion he had on the court. He would stick his tongue out during games and stuff so it was just amazing to watch. I was like, 'Man I could really do that too.' That's the kind of player I am. [An] emotional, confident, passionate player like Moe. He wore number 13 so I thought I might take his jersey and continue that legacy."[5] Indeed, his emotive mannerisms on the court and willingness to play the villain in hostile environments were reminiscent of Wagner.

Iggy brought all of these distinctive elements with him to the newly refurbished Welsh-Ryan Arena to take on Northwestern in Michigan's first Big Ten road test. It was a venue that had caused problems for Michigan in the past, including their last defeat outside of the national championship game, roughly ten months prior. If the fans in the building hadn't heard of Brazdeikis yet, by the end of the night they would certainly know his name. A quick 7–0 start by Michigan suggested a potential blowout, but a banked in three-pointer by Dererk Pardon reminded everyone of the bad fortune the Wolverines seemed to suffer in Evanston. The senior had only made a single three-pointer in his career prior to the ugly bank shot. Brazdeikis' first points didn't come until eight minutes had elapsed in the first half. Off a Zavier Simpson feed, he knocked down an open three from the left wing. He left his left arm extended and then backpedaled down the court while slicking his hair back. A moment later he sat down for a breather and wound up watching the Wildcats go on a 7–0 run to pull within three points. Twenty-five seconds after checking back in, he hit a baseline runner. On the next possession, he charged downhill from the top of the key, only to hit a baseline fade-away. John Beilein had said, "My hope is that as he grows, he could be like a Manu Ginobli type of player,"[6] and on those possessions it was easy to see the comparison.

Three minutes later, he drained another three-pointer from the wing off a cross-court pass from Jon Teske. Again, he left his arm extended and then clenched his fists as he retreated on defense. That shot put Michigan up 10, a lead they would stretch to 12 on a Charles Matthews slam with 1:56 left before the break. Northwestern responded with a 7–1 run to close the half, capped by an improbable 25-foot step-back from Vic Law. A series of old-school post maneuvers by Pardon had kept the Wildcats hanging around, but it was the flurry of highly contested jumpers that pulled Northwestern within range at 36–30. They were exactly the types of shots Luke Yaklich hoped to force yet they had somehow found the bottom of the net.

Early in the second half, Brazdeikis went hard to the hoop for a layup and a foul and immediately flexed his biceps to the disapproving crowd. That taunt was definitely Zavier Simpson approved: "I want him flexing on dudes every chance he gets."[7] After a Simpson steal, Michigan drove back down and Brazdeikis rebounded a Teske miss and put it back in. Back on the defensive end, he immediately stole the ball from Ryan Greer, and quickly outlet passed up ahead to Jordan Poole for a dunk. The 9–0 run fueled by the freshman to start the half gave Michigan its biggest lead of the game at 45–30.

The feisty Wildcats kept battling back though, this time with a 7–0 run of their own. Every time Michigan needed a big hoop to stop a run, Brazdeikis was happy to oblige. He charged downhill from the left wing so fast that he found himself behind the backboard, but was able to stretch his right hand back out to flip it in. Brazdeikis' ability to use both hands was a trait that Beilein had identified early on. "He can throw a baseball with both hands," the head coach said. "It's very advantageous for him when he goes to the basket and he can go with either hand."[8]

But that hoop only slowed the Wildcats momentarily, as they immediately responded with an 8–0 run to pull within two points. As the Welsh-Ryan denizens celebrated, Beilein called timeout to settle down his team. Iggy charged out of the timeout looking to answer but missed two consecutive layups on the same possession. Simpson reclaimed some momentum with one of his elusive drives to the hoop for a layup. Next time down he threw an alley-oop to Brazdeikis but the timing wasn't quite right; instead the freshman landed with the pass and fought his way to a basket. Unable to get over the hump with traditional tactics, Northwestern's head coach Chris Collins and his defensive assistant Billy Donlon resorted to a calculated gamble and challenged Simpson to beat them from the three-point line. They pulled a defender off Simpson and instead played five against four on everyone else, daring Simpson to shoot. Encouraged by Beilein, Simpson obliged. Over the next three and a half minutes, he missed four three-pointers and Michigan's ball movement fell stagnant—clogged up by the additional defender Northwestern gained by sagging off the Wolverine point guard. After Vic Law hit back-to-back long threes to finally give Northwestern a 52–51 lead, Beilein had no choice but to remove Simpson for the final six minutes.

After Northwestern added another basket and Michigan had been held scoreless for over six minutes, the game seemed to be slipping away. Brazdeikis stepped up once again, connecting on an open three to tie the game up. Eli Brooks then hit his own crucial three and Brazdeikis split a pair of free throws to answer a pair of Wildcat baskets and tie the game at 58. A few minutes later, Poole rejected a Teske ball-screen and blew by his man, finishing with a dunk that provided the winning margin of 62–60 as Northwestern's heavily contested heaves finally started bouncing out. Michigan had avoided getting tripped up again in Chicago and remained perfect on the season. Beilein effusively praised his mature freshman to the media after the game: "That's why he came to Michigan. He watched Nik Stauskas make a lot of those big shots, and he wanted to be in this element and play in front of that crowd today. That's who he is and that's why we love him."

Chris Collins, who had embarrassingly gotten down on all fours at midcourt during the game to plead with his team, couldn't help but agree. "I just love his spirit," he said in his press conference. "He's a warrior, he's tough, he makes shots, he gets to the basket, and he competes. He's a really fun guy to watch play." The strategic gamble taken by Collins and former Michigan assistant Billy Donlon had given their team a window to steal the game, but Michigan and Brazdeikis had done just enough to close it out.

Brazdeikis stayed on the attack afterwards, saying "I love environments like this. It was really hostile out there. The crowd was really into it. They punched us in the face in the second half. We got knocked down, but I feel like this game brought us more together. I feel like we grew a lot and it shows how tough we are." He spared no candor when asked how good his team was, answering, "We can go all the way. We can win the whole damn thing. No doubt."[9] So far his play was backing up his strong words and brash persona. He ranked in the top ten in Kenpom's Player of the Year standings—a metric "designed to identify the most valuable player in the game, free of reputation and future potential." His strong start had mirrored his team's success. With their early conference wins and the bulk of their non-conference challenges behind them, an undefeated Michigan seemed well-poised in December to pursue their championship goals.

Chapter 24

The Calendar Turns

A soft end to the non-conference schedule gave the Wolverines four more notches in the win column to close out one of the most memorable calendar years in Michigan basketball history. The program had gone 34–5 in 2018, including a remarkable 27–1 over their last 28 games. They had ended the 2017-18 season as the second-best team in the country, and now ended 2018 as the #2 ranked team in the country. After a 68–55 home win over Penn State to kick off 2019, Michigan took on their fourth ranked opponent of the season in #21 Indiana. The pre-game hype centered on the matchup between Charles Matthews and talented freshman Romeo Langford. The young guard from New Albany, Indiana, was already being hyped as a potential lottery pick, which explained the numerous NBA scouts in attendance. Matthews immediately demonstrated that he planned to show the 19-year-old a thing or two. On Indiana's first possession, he trailed the freshman through a ball-screen and poked the ball away for his first steal. A frustrated Langford held Matthews to prevent an easy fast break and was called for his first foul just 33 seconds into the game. After Michigan took the ball out, Jordan Poole opened up his bag of tricks, pulling up from the elbow for a one-legged fadeaway. Poole then rebounded Indiana's next miss and Matthews split two defenders in the frontcourt, but was knocked down by Indiana's other star, Juwan Morgan. A few trips later down court, Matthews got on the board with a corner three. Then in a span of 12 seconds the game changed drastically. Juwan Morgan found himself guarding Jordan Poole 25 feet from the basket on a switch and couldn't help himself from reaching in. Morgan took a seat on the bench with his second foul as the Wolverines had the ball side-out. After the inbound, Michigan strategically worked the ball around to Matthews on the wing. He identified a flat-footed Langford in front of him and immediately blew by him to the hoop for a two-handed slam. The young freshman compounded his error with a half-hearted late contest that drew his second foul. Beilein later revealed Michigan's intent in his post-game comments: "That was a designed play to see if we could get that second foul," Beilein said. "And Charles has a tendency for taking the ball strong then right at the end—not be as strong with it. That was a strong baseline drive, and that's who he can be. If there's a block [or] charge at the end, so be it. But when you get to the rim, you're one of the elite athletes—maybe the quickest athlete on that court out there today—you've got to do that."

Indiana's two best players were now seated on the bench. Indiana reserve Al Durham hit a three that would comprise all of their scoring for the next four minutes. It was quickly answered by an NBA-range three by Poole, with an assist to Matthews. The motivated captain then extended his pressure on his new defensive mark Zack McRoberts and forced him into a travel. Poole followed with another three, on a step-back from the wing. On Indiana's next possession, Matthews demonstrated his mastery as both an individual and help defender on one of the best defensive teams in the country. He chased McRoberts around a base-line screen, but identified a cutting Devonte Green as having a step on Zavier Simpson. When Green received the back-door pass he found an elevating Matthews prepared to harm any shot attempt. He thought better off it and dished out to McRoberts who quickly rotated the ball to Justin Smith on the wing. Michigan's elite wing defender then scrambled to close out on Smith, who moved the ball along to Durham. A quick first step got Durham by Brazdeikis, but Matthews was there with the help and knocked the ball away. He recovered it and proceeded to go one on three in transition and finished with the layup. In the span of five seconds, Matthews had defended four different Indiana players and ended up with a steal.

The Poole and Matthews show continued unabated as the former hit a rolling Austin Davis for an easy bucket. After that basket, Archie Miller was left with no choice but to re-insert Langford and Morgan with 13 minutes remaining in the first half. Matthews greeted their return by immediately jumping a passing lane and finishing with an easy two-handed slam. That completed a 12–0 Michigan run in just over two minutes of play that essentially decided the game. The lead would eventually get pushed as high as 19 as Michigan dominated the first half in front of their home crowd and led 44–29 at the break. A couple momentary pushes in the second half brought Indiana within single digits but Michigan always had an answer. When it reached seven, Zavier Simpson brought out the running hook shot—his third of the game. A series of Jordan Poole twos showcased his range of offensive weapons and provided a welcome departure from his occasional reliance on the three-ball. The final insult was a devastating crossover that embarrassingly sent McRoberts to the ground in a heap. Poole calmly knocked down the jumper as his fallen foe stumbled to his feet. He would finish with an efficient

18 points and, after a slow start to the season, seemed to be finding himself. Poole had made 53 percent of his threes over the last 12 games while shooting a high volume (36 of 68) and had augmented his long-range success by both getting to the hoop and setting his teammates up. Michigan went on to close it out 74–63, and they did so without a second half three-pointer. Their 1.26 points per possession would stand as the team's highest total all season. Langford wound up scoring 17, though most his buckets came in the second half when the game was already out of reach. Matthews scored 18, grabbed six rebounds, had four steals, added two assists, and did not turn the ball over once. Knowing that the eyes of next-level talent evaluators were watching, the cagey veteran had eagerly embraced the matchup. With Isaiah Livers missing the game due to back spasms, Brandon Johns gave the team his best minutes of the season. The freshman had looked unsure in all of his earlier appearances and had managed just one field goal all year. Although the tentativeness was still present at times, he finished at the hoop when opportunities presented themselves and scored eight points and added eight rebounds. He was rewarded by leading "The Victors" in the locker room after.

In light of Simpson's multiple hook shots throughout the afternoon, much of the post-game questioning centered on the evolution of that technique. Turns out he had just started experimenting a few years ago in open gym, motivated to find a way to get the ball up on the rim past his shot-blocking teammate D.J. Wilson. "The hook was kind of an accident on a fast break where I kind of threw it high," Simpson said. "Then I started practicing it for finishing layups in situations like that—with a defender that's bigger than me who has a high chance of blocking it. It kind of felt natural and then I started just trying to perfect my craft." He spent many an hour the previous summer honing the challenging shot with his father, Quincey. Now the results were having an impact on Michigan's season. As Simpson put it, "I'm just proud that it's part of my bag."[1]

His coach couldn't help but smile when asked about it. "He works on it—we do it every day," Beilein told the media afterwards. "The only way the smaller guards can score right now in front of a jump wall is the old-fashioned hook. So we work on it and you'll probably see a lot of it in the future. It's soft and nice, Kareem would be proud." He went on to point out the shot's efficiency: "If he keeps shooting and getting a point per possession on that one, we'll take that all the time."

The Wolverines won their next contest at Illinois 79–69, thanks to strong efforts by Zavier Simpson and Jon Teske. Simpson filled out the box score with 16 points, eight assists, five rebounds, and two steals. Teske posted a double-double with 13 points, 11 rebounds, along with four blocks.

Michigan was coming to expect, in every game, strong performances at both ends of the court from their starting point guard and center. A round-table debate soon ensued among the contributors at Mgoblog.com about who Michigan's most important player was. A reasonably strong case was made for every core contributor, but in the end the general agreement was that Teske and Simpson stood above the rest. Much of that was due to their importance in the ball-screen game at both the offensive and defensive end. The game had evolved to the point where often the very first question when putting together a defensive game-plan was deciding how to handle the opposition's ball-screen game. Teske gave Luke Yaklich options because of how well he moved his feet for such a big man. He was able to hedge out onto the opposition's point guard and take away the vision needed to deliver a pass. That bought time for the relentless Simpson to recover back onto his man and control the point of attack. Offensively, the two offered unique challenges for a defense to guard as Beilein explained. "In the trend of college basketball today, a lot of times it comes down to a two-man game and everybody else is on the periphery," he said. "When you get those two guys in the right space, they're really a very productive duo. I think that between the pick and pop and the pick and roll, they feel each other. One guy can get wherever he wants with the ball and the other guy is a huge target to throw to."[2] Most of Michigan's possessions were now flowing off the two of them, which created openings for others to thrive. A chemistry had clearly formed between them, with an unspoken understanding of how to work off each other.

At first glance, the two Ohio juniors seemed like an unlikely pair. Teske was naturally quiet and unassuming despite his immense stature, and Simpson was compact and incredibly intense. But every point guard needs a big man and vice versa. "I think we first met and had some interaction at the Ohio vs. Kentucky [high school] all-star game, and right then and there I felt like we clicked," Simpson said. Both had seen limited action their freshmen seasons before becoming important components in Michigan's deep tournament run their sophomore years. And now both had continued developing into arguably the team's most important players. Simpson, as captain and floor general, encouraged Teske to just play his game and let him take care of the rest. "I tell him all the time, 'Don't worry about playing off me, let me play off you.' So if you pop or roll, you just do it and I'll find a way to make it work."[3]

Teske's offensive game had flourished as a result of following his teammate's instructions. He had learned firsthand that Simpson knew how to deliver the ball just the way his coach wanted it: on time and on target. "He has great court vision so he always knows where I am. I kind of have a feel for where he's gonna go. If he's going to drive to the lane, I'll pop out,"[4] Teske said.

While the improvement the tandem had shown over the course of their careers had become the norm at Michigan, it certainly wasn't standard practice elsewhere as opposing coaches often pointed out. "I don't think Coach

[Beilein] gets the credit that he deserves for the way his players develop," South Carolina coach Frank Martin said after the teams met in December. "The growth of his players—I grabbed [Zavier] Simpson yesterday when we got here for our practice [and] he was shooting around and I said, 'I was watching our film from two years ago. You and Teske were like two little kids. I was watching the film and now I'm watching you guys play and it's unbelievable how much better you guys are and how different you look.' John does an unbelievable job making his players better during their career. I think you see that with the guys who have come through here and have gone on and played in the NBA, how they continue to grow once they get there."[5]

After the Illinois game, the Illini head coach Brad Underwood was in agreement. "Zavier Simpson, in my opinion, is the MVP of the league to this point," he said. "You take him away from that team and they're not No. 2 in the country." He recalled Simpson's play against his previous team, Oklahoma State, in Simpson's freshman year. "He couldn't play in the NCAA Tournament game. We picked him at half court. He couldn't play." That was a very different player from the one who he had just faced. "I think it's a testament to John's program. Look at Simpson and his growth. Look at Teske and his development. It's a tribute to their assistant coaches, their staff, in what they do. We're striving for that every single day with our guys."[6]

The primary flaw remaining in the pair's play was inconsistent shooting from deep, where the two had combined to shoot 27 percent up to that point. Northwestern had almost exploited that weakness in their first meeting and given the lack of other strategies for the out-gunned Wildcats to pull off an upset, they tried it again in Ann Arbor in Michigan's next contest. Simpson missed his first two three-pointers of the game, making him 0–7 against Northwestern on the season, and likely had many a grumbling fan itching for him to stop shooting. But with the encouragement of his coach and teammates, he kept letting it fly and knocked down his next one. Then he hit another. Teske joined in on the fun, making three of his own before halftime. The Wolverines went into the break with a comfortable 50–28 lead thanks to a 34–14 run started by the first Simpson three-pointer. It was more of the same in the second half, with Simpson knocking down three more three-pointers, with his first step-back three included among them. To the delight of his teammates and the crowd, Simpson even felt compelled to shoot a heat-check three. That one fell short but soon enough the final horn sounded as the Wolverines had won 80–60.

Beilein felt that the rout was due in part to Simpson's incredible resilience. Michigan's point guard didn't like being exposed in the first meeting and Beilein believed that Simpson had carried that grudge into the game. "This young man is really special as far as the type of grit and determination he has," he told the media. "You put a challenge in front of Zavier Simpson

Minnesota's Jordan Murphy tries in vain to block Charles Matthews' game winner as time expired on January 22, 2019 (photograph by Marc-Gregor Campredon).

and he's going to eventually win." He certainly had responded, finishing with 24 points, five rebounds, four assists, and three steals. His partner-in-crime Teske finished with 17 points, 11 rebounds, three steals, and two blocks. The pair had combined with their teammates to lead Michigan to its best start in program history, with a 17–0 record. Ranked #2 in the country, the team had six days off before traveling to Wisconsin on Saturday, January 19. During that time, #1 Duke had fallen to Syracuse, meaning that the top-ranked spot in the country was up for grabs. The excitement about Michigan's potential to grab the top spot for the first time since 2013 merged with debate about whether Virginia—the nation's only other unbeaten—could leapfrog them with a win over Duke Saturday night. All of that discussion was immaterial unless the Wolverines could get a win in what had historically been a very challenging venue in the Kohl Center.

Beilein's teams at Michigan had gone 2–8 in Wisconsin's home gym, none of the disheartening losses more memorable than when Ben Brust's last-second prayer from half-court in 2013 sent a game to overtime that Wisconsin would eventually win. Misfortune seemed to follow Michigan in the Badger State, and it seemed apropos that their incredible winning streak came to an end against Greg Gard's plodding unit that seemed to bring out the worst in Beilein's teams. The Badgers thrived by pulling their opponent into a drawn-out half-court affair, and Michigan walked right into their trap, with the Wolverine offense bogging down to a miserable 0.82 points per possession in the 64–54 loss. That figure represented the team's worst offensive day since the day before Thanksgiving in 2016 at South Carolina. Wisconsin's star Ethan Happ racked up 26 points, 10 rebounds, and seven assists as Michigan waited until too late in the game to attempt to exploit his weakness at the free throw line. Ignas Brazdeikis was held scoreless in his quietest performance of the season. Beilein described the post-game locker room vibe in his press conference afterwards. "We always sing the fight song after every win. It's the first time these guys had never sang the fight song [this season]," he said. "It was sort of really quiet in our locker room. I think it's been 49 weeks since we lost a game that wasn't called the national championship game. That's pretty good. It was February 6th.... And now it's January 19th. That's a hell of a run and now it doesn't mean anything. Now we've got to go back and we've got to find a way to beat Minnesota on Tuesday."

Beating Minnesota proved to be more challenging than expected as the hangover extended late into the second half of that game when Michigan's offense again hit a wall. After taking a 57–47 lead with 4:51 remaining, the Wolverines seemingly forgot how to score. All five starters missed at least one shot as Minnesota chipped away at their lead. With 31 seconds left, Gabe Kalscheur nailed his third three of the evening to tie it up. As the stunned Crisler Center crowd looked on, Michigan called timeout and drew up a play for their fearless freshman Brazdeikis. With seven seconds left, he drove hard to the hoop right into a pile of Gophers. As he was swarmed, Eric Curry got a piece of his shot and knocked it away—right into the waiting hands of Charles Matthews. The team captain, with the game on the line, stared at the exact shot he had struggled with since Big Ten play had started. As noted on Umhoops.com, he had missed his last 24 mid-range looks in conference play. With the clock ticking down, Matthews didn't hesitate—he elevated and knocked down the game-winner. Although the finish was thrilling, a 59–57 win at home against a mediocre Minnesota team did not meet the team's heightened internal expectations and the post-game locker room mood was subdued. "I'm happy but I don't feel like we played that well today,"[7] a somber Matthews said. A trip to Bloomington beckoned and offered an opportunity to get back on track playing the type of basketball they knew they were capable of.

Chapter 25

Culture Is the Only Way

Michigan's return engagement at Indiana came at a tenuous time for their hosts' once-proud program. The Hoosiers had not won since Michigan had handled them easily in Ann Arbor and were dealing with a rash of injuries. Although their head coach Archie Miller was only in his second season after achieving mid-major success at Dayton, the fanbase was beginning to grumble about the lack of progress. His brother Sean was embroiled in scandal at the University of Arizona, where the program was under formal NCAA inquiry following the FBI's investigation into college basketball corruption. While there was no evidence that linked Indiana's program, it was the kind of connection that didn't help matters as Indiana devolved on the court. With a packed house at Assembly Hall, a takedown of the 5th ranked team in the country would be the perfect way for the Hoosiers to change the narrative. That possibility had the Friday night crowd of 17,222 energized and hopeful early on. Beilein admitted after the game that the environment had made an impression on him: "That place was charged up like I remember it was in '13 when we came here as the number one team in the country. And you couldn't hear yourself think."

The night got off to an inauspicious start due to a shot clock that malfunctioned just after the opening tip. When the game resumed after a long delay, it appeared that someone had forgotten to let the Hoosiers know. Even with the frenzied crowd behind them, the team played flat and appeared disinterested defensively. Zavier Simpson knew exactly how to take advantage of the situation. He patiently probed the defense and either scored or assisted on 12 of Michigan's first 17 points as they throttled Indiana to a 17–0 start. The Hoosiers did not score a single point until Al Durham made a pair of free throws seven minutes into the game. They didn't score their first field goal until Durham converted almost three minutes later. The crowd grew audibly frustrated—not just by the score but by the program's seeming inability to return to previous heights. It was an emotion that Michigan fans could recall from the days prior to Beilein's arrival. Although Archie Miller's team showed a few mild signs of life as the game chugged along, the opening spurt had essentially decided their fate. Romeo Langford must have been pleased to be done with Charles Matthews for the season. His opposite number limited him to nine points on 3-12 shooting. Ignas Brazdeikis had gotten back on track with a 20-point outing while Jordan Poole had continued his sudden cold streak by reverting to long jumpers and step-back threes. The win went down as Michigan's largest ever at Assembly Hall. It was the fewest points Indiana had scored in a game since 2010—and their 0.7 points per possession would finish as the third lowest by any team in a Big Ten game all season. Archie Miller didn't mince words in his post-game press conference. "[Michigan] came in here and did what they want, when they wanted, how they wanted, and it's really disappointing," he said. "Our team in general right now is soft and for whatever reason we're also scared."

The juxtaposition between the two programs was quite clear. John Beilein had solved the problem that Miller now faced: how do you return a former great back to the upper echelon of college basketball? When asked this question after the game, Beilein revealed, "It is really hard to maintain this and the only way you can do it is culture." While he usually received attention for his flexible and creative offensive sets or his ability to discover underrated talent (and rightly so), Beilein understood that the environment was an essential difference maker. The selfless play and commitment to improvement that Zack Novak, Stu Douglass, and Jordan Morgan embraced had become gospel for Michigan. Moe Wagner, Duncan Robinson, Muhammad-Ali Abdur-Rahkman had perpetuated their example in 2017-18, and now Zavier Simpson and Charles Matthews adopted the missionary zeal. The core values those players exemplified were evident at the William Davidson Player Development Center where the entire program pursued the simple goal of trying to get better every day.

For some on the outside, culture can be a nebulous concept that is often used as a post-hoc explanation for winning. But those inside the program swore by it and had numerous examples to prove it. Beilein and staff carefully instilled culture from the moment freshmen arrived on campus. Their core values were plastered throughout the team's facilities and frequently discussed. As Michigan celebrated their Final Four win over Loyola the previous year, Beilein carefully emphasized how each core value had impacted the team's success. After Michigan's loss to Villanova two nights later, it would have been natural to mourn the missed opportunity to claim glory; instead, the players focused on the end of their journey together and how much they appreciated one another.

In many ways the program had changed. Michigan had transitioned from a finesse three-point shooting team into a defensive-oriented squad built on toughness. It had gone from a program limited to recruiting a certain caliber of player to one that was developing a much broader appeal. Beilein had evolved from a dominant presence reticent to cede control to a coach who started delegating to the rest of his staff. Throughout every change, the culture that was first designed in a Belgian conference room had remained a constant thread throughout the program. The complete adoption of those values had enabled Beilein to rely on his players to teach each other. "That's how you build a program—the [teams] are player-led because of the leadership at the top—but they didn't come in as leaders, they learned from the other upperclassmen,"[1] Beilein had said a few weeks earlier. That dynamic—combined with the coach's talents as a developer—allowed new players to step forward each season into bigger roles.

Zavier Simpson had struggled to find his footing his freshman season. Accustomed to substantial playing time, his transition to Michigan was a bit of a rude awakening. But in Derrick Walton, Simpson found a leader who lived all of the program's values. With the benefit of hindsight, Simpson understood his importance. "I give a special shout out to Derrick for the player I am today," he said. "I did not just listen to him, I learned from him. He was my mentor."[2] After serving his apprenticeship and earning the lead guard spot, Simpson now essentially served as the team's lifeblood. He paid forward those lessons that he learned from Walton by inspiring David DeJulius and the other freshmen. He taught them to simply focus on what they could control and to adhere to Beilein's principle of achieving incremental improvement. "Keep learning every day—that's what it's about right now. Our minds are nowhere else but just every single day keep learning,"[3] Simpson said in the lead-up to the season.

Isaiah Livers had contributed his freshman season by carefully watching how his upperclassmen teammates went about their work. He had realized that he was just a small part of something much greater than himself. When Livers spoke, he did so with the awareness of someone much older than a college sophomore. "Last year I learned that it's not all about you. Your decisions affect the team. Anything you do outside the court can affect the team. On the court, your attitude can affect the team," he said. He too had embraced the idea of paying it forward by helping his new teammates achieve that same type of growth. "I'm just passing on the torch of leadership from Duncan. He taught me everything the right way, and how to be a leader. So I try to help out Brandon, Iggy, Dave, Colin, Jaron—anybody new to the team, I try to help them out the best I can."[4]

There were endless examples throughout the years of older players taking younger ones under their wings, or just simply setting an example for how things should be done. The beauty of that approach was that it had a multiplying factor; Beilein correctly believed that a positive culture breeds itself. As such, he targeted players that could propel others forward. "It's a purposeful way we recruit," he said. "To get a kid who's going to embrace this thing—that it's all about the team. It's not something that we have to preach. Do we have to teach it? Yeah but we don't have to preach it. Because it's natural. They come from great moms and dads, great families."[5] Learning the attention to detail that was expected in all their actions, becoming a supportive teammate, and understanding proper work habits on and off the court were just a few of the ways that the entire program educated its newest members. "Inch by inch you get 1% better every day and who knows what can happen,"[6] was just one of many basic instructions Beilein gave his players. Delivered humbly and lived authentically by the program's ultimate leader, Beilein's mantras allowed his players to improve and slowly learn to be accountable for themselves and to one another.

Chapter 26

The Pride of Lima, Ohio

No one had anticipated the Ohio State game more than Zavier Simpson. The point guard, who had been named the 2016 Ohio Mr. Basketball winner, resented that the university had declined to offer him a scholarship. The Michigan family shared his contempt and braved the glacial conditions outdoors to bear witness to the solitary matchup of the season between the two ancient rivals. With a 9 p.m. Tuesday night start and a wind-chill of -17 degrees, the university allowed students into the arena early so they did not have to suffer in the dangerous weather. In the locker room beforehand, Beilein emphasized to his charges that this would be the only time the two teams played. "We have one time to play these guys this year, on our court, right now!" he said. "That's why we're going to win, because we have no other freaking option. Just go win. We win because we're fighters and we believe in defense. We're going to be relentless tonight. You win when you play with the people in the room. Not for yourself, not even for Michigan, you play for the freaking guys in this room!"[1]

Early on in the game, an announcement was made that, due to the weather, classes were cancelled for the next two days. This only contributed to the crowd's liveliness and a house party feel spread throughout the stands. Less than welcoming chants were extended to the Buckeyes all evening. After the game, Beilein would marvel at the atmosphere: "It's just amazing to get that kind of energy in the building when it's below-zero [outside]," he said at his press conference. "A 9 p.m. game on a Tuesday night—to have that kind of energy in the building. I'm sure it had something to do with the opponent, at the same time I think it has a lot to do with what these kids have accomplished this year." Despite that energy, the Buckeyes hit five of their first seven shots to claim a 12–6 advantage. Second-year head coach Chris Holtmann had built a fringe NCAA Tournament team around burly-bodied 6'9" 270-pound Kaleb Wesson. For all of Wesson's strengths as a space-eating

Ignas Brazdeikis looks on, next to Ohio State's Keyshawn Woods (32) as Zavier Simpson drives past Kaleb Wesson on an unforgettable night for the Wolverines' floor general. Simpson posted a triple-double and added a memorable block when he caught Wesson from behind (photograph by Marc-Gregor Campredon).

post player, he could be exposed by his limited mobility and penchant for fouling. He started strong in Ann Arbor though, scoring seven of the team's first 12 and adding two rebounds, two blocks, and an assist in getting his team off to the early lead. Michigan struggled initially against Ohio State's zone defense look but soon pulled even and the two teams traded leads for much of the first half. With just over two minutes remaining before the intermission, Simpson executed one of his trademark slow-to-fast sneaky drives to the hoop for his second basket of the night and a one-point Michigan lead. At the other end he corralled an air-balled three-pointer from Kaleb Wesson's older brother, Andre. Simpson pushed it up-court and found Brazdeikis on the wing for a transition three. After sinking the shot, Iggy turned to the boisterous denizens of Crisler and rubbed his fingers together—gesturing the international money signal in celebration. Simpson then hit a streaking Charles Matthews for a transition layup, which completed a game changing 7–0 run to end the half and gave Michigan a 32–26 lead.

After the break, Simpson and crew slowly lengthened that lead. Once he found Jordan Poole for a catch-and-shoot NBA three with 12:36 remaining, Michigan had finally pushed the lead to double-digits at 44–33. A few possessions later, Simpson skied to grab an errant Buckeye shot only to get knocked over by Kaleb Wesson at the apex of his leap. The two had history going back to a state championship battle in high school that was won by the Wesson brothers. Simpson would soon exact his revenge. After contesting a missed Brazdeikis three a few minutes later, Wesson leaked out behind Michigan in transition. He received the outlet pass at the free throw line, took a cursory look at the much smaller Simpson trailing him, deemed him a non-threat and went up for the dunk. That turned out to be a foolish miscalculation by Wesson. The smallest player on the court stuck with the biggest man, put out his left hand, and blocked Wesson's dunk attempt from behind. After the game, Beilein offered an interesting comparison, "It reminded me of the block in the national championship game but let's not talk about it," referring to Trey Burke's rejection six years before. This time the referees got it right and let them play on.

Simpson soon got Wesson on a switch at the offensive end. Once again, the Ohio State big man deemed him a non-threat and receded back into the paint. Simpson responded defiantly by draining a three to extend the lead to 12. At that point, Simpson had officially taken up residence in his opponent's head. Once Ohio State had the ball, Wesson leaned into a pick in an attempt to knock Simpson over. When that was ignored, he hit Jon Teske needlessly on the rebound and was whistled for his third foul. Simpson took the break in the action to let the referee know he didn't appreciate the screen and Wesson started barking back at him. Poole and Teske interceded on Simpson's behalf. Technical fouls were issued to both parties, along with Jon Teske. The initial personal foul along with the technical gave Kaleb Wesson four on the day; Chris Holtmann sat him on the bench and left him there for the rest of the evening. Michigan scored the next four to take an 18-point lead and ostensibly finish off their rival. All that was left was a late pursuit for the record books.

A running straight-away hook off the glass gave Simpson 11 points, 11 assists, and 9 rebounds. At the ensuing timeout, two assistant coaches alerted him that he needed one more rebound to finish with a triple-double. The jubilant crowd was also aware and when a Jaedon LeDee runner bounced into a pack of Michigan players, Isaiah Livers pulled back to let Simpson gain possession, and the 12,707 in the building erupted. "I could hear the fans. I was like, 'OK, let me back off.' Honestly, if I had went for it he would have took my arm off anyway,"[2] Livers said.

It was just the sixth triple-double in program history. That he had accomplished it without a single turnover made it even more impressive. The 49 points allowed was the fewest by Michigan to an Ohio State team since a January 29, 1949, game at Yost Field House, exactly 70 years prior. Holtmann could do little in his post-game press conference but tip his cap to the diminutive floor general that had just dominated the court. "He's a tremendous, tremendous player," he said. "He really is. He deserves a lot of credit for how he impacts winning."

Ann Arbor had yet to thaw out from the deep freeze when the team headed to Iowa a few days later to face their next conference opponent. Early foul trouble for Jon Teske earned him a seat on the bench and he was limited to a single minute of first half action. Without Teske's presence in the middle, Iowa was able to outrebound Michigan in the first half 26-12 and their two big men Luka Garza and Ryan Kriener shot 6-8 for 15 points. Meanwhile, the four players that took a turn at center in his absence for the Maize and Blue combined to score zero points, gathered zero rebounds, and accrued five personal fouls. A frustrated Beilein admitted afterwards, "We can't find a backup five." That first half dug them a hole from which they couldn't recover, as they fell to the Hawkeyes 74-59. If there had been any doubt remaining about Jon Teske's importance to this Michigan team, the Iowa game rendered the verdict final.

An easy win at Rutgers followed, with the Wolverines prevailing 77-65. On his 66th birthday, Beilein passed Johnny Orr for the most conference wins in school history. As usual, he took it in stride and deflected any praise. "If I'm compared to Johnny Orr at any time, that's a heck of a compliment," Beilein said afterwards. "I think if he were still alive he would say, 'I've had really good assistant coaches and I've had really good players.' And I'm going to say the exact same thing. At an incredible university." Following the win, the team's sights quickly moved on to their upcoming game against Wisconsin. The players talked openly about how the mental image of Wisconsin's fans storming the court had stuck with them. Their opportunity for revenge came four days later.

Chapter 27

Constant Adaptation

In advance of the rematch, Beilein took the time to point out the similarities between the two teams' approaches, which often made Wisconsin such a challenging opponent for his team. "Look at their stats and our stats overall and we're doing the same thing. They might foul a little bit more than us, but we don't go to the foul line a lot. Everything's almost virtually the same," the head coach said. "It's called winning basketball. You don't turn it over, you make your foul shots, you don't foul people, [and] you don't give up threes. It's winning basketball. How they see it and how we see it."[1]

On the defensive side of the ball in particular, Luke Yaklich had adopted one of Wisconsin's traditional tenets—taking away three-point opportunities and forcing tough twos. One only had to dig into the data to know it was a sound strategy. Beilein explained, "As analytics have gone through this, everybody has picked up on what Bo Ryan was doing for a very long time. I wasn't coaching like that when I first got here. I probably wasn't running a lot of ball screens at that time either. Coaches evolve."[2] Not many coaches had evolved to quite the degree that Beilein had. Earlier in the season, he had bemoaned the varying defenses his team faced due to more detailed advanced scouting reports. With his tongue planted firmly in cheek, he quipped: "Damn computers have screwed everything up."[3] While he liked to play the role of the grumpy old man yelling at you to get off his lawn, the truth was John Beilein had come to adopt every advantage modern technology could offer. During practices and games, his players wore special monitors on their back made by a company called Catapult that provided detailed measurements on their movements and exertion levels. He leaned on a team of performance experts, often consulting with them in the middle of practice, to determine the proper balance between practice and rest and recovery. As a result, he was able to rely heavily on his core rotation without a fall-off late in games or over the course of the season. At the team's practice facility, he had special technology installed to measure the arc on his player's shots and provide real-time feedback to allow them to make adjustments to achieve an ideal level and ultimately improve their shooting. Every drill and scrimmage at practice was filmed and meticulously charted by student-managers to track progress and provide real data to show his players their areas for improvement.

He made constant reference to the detailed video and statistical information he garnered from Synergy Sports and the way it informed the staff's decision-making. Though he hadn't necessarily been an early adopter of in-depth analytics, he was always looking for an advantage. After all, this was a coach that had been using video to help coach his high school junior varsity team more than 40 years earlier. "One of my first jobs was a social studies teacher, and there was not a position for me unless they created these other opportunities, so they made me the first audio-visual director," Beilein said. "So I started filming my JV team and it seemed like exponentially they were getting better. Ever since then, I have been an incredible film watcher, as far as getting 20 clips to show to the team from practice so that they can see their progress."[4]

While coaching Team USA in the summer of 2013 at the World University Games in Russia, Beilein had impressed his peers with his talent as a film session maestro. Beilein would use his own computer and cut his own clips there, much like he often does with his Michigan program. "You get 12 guys together in Russia and they're looking at film sessions and they're wondering, 'What the heck are we doing here?'" said Davidson head coach Bob McKillop, who was also serving as a Team USA coach. "And John is doing a magnificent job of getting their attention and streamlining the way he cut the film so that it becomes attention-grabbing to the guys that were watching it."[5]

That constant progression was visible in pre-season practices as Beilein worked to address the free throw shooting woes that had plagued the 2017-18 team. Prior to that season, Beilein had never had a team at Michigan shoot below 70 percent from the line, and his previous four squads had all finished among the top 41 teams in the country. The 2017-18 team shot 66 percent—poor enough for 326th in the nation. By all accounts they had worked on it tirelessly, but the results simply hadn't come. To ensure that the 2018-19 team wouldn't suffer the same fate, he resorted to more creative and unconventional techniques. As DeAndre Haynes shared at the team's media day before the start of the season, Beilein had brought in a professional to assist the team with meditation and visualization. "We've been doing a lot of meditation. Coach B brought a guy in the other day and we were all in the media room and he actually put a lot of people to sleep—he just showed us how to relax," Haynes said. "He's going to be working with the team and working with some of the guys on their free throws and I think it's working." It seems unlikely that too many other 66-year-old coaches were having their teams learn to meditate and visualize, but the unique approach brought results. Though some players were admittedly slow to warm to the idea, most eventually bought in—especially as the results started showing up. Despite having lost some of their better free throw shooters like Duncan Robinson and Muhammad-Ali Abdur-Rahkman, the 2018-19 team finished just above 70 percent for the season and moved up to 192nd in the country. While that was still Beilein's second-worst free throw shooting team at Michigan, it was enough improvement to transform the watching experience from abject fear into mild unease when a game wound up being decided at the line.

While opponents were able to exploit Zavier Simpson during his sophomore season with late-game fouls, he had improved his percentage at the line from 52 percent to 67 percent. This advancement continued throughout the year, with his free throw percentage climbing to 75 percent in conference play. As the player Michigan wanted in control in a close game, his development at the line was essential. "I like positive visualization," Simpson admitted. "I just try to keep my mind positive. I don't like to think about negative things."[6] Beilein frequently complimented his point guard on the work he was doing behind the scenes. Charles Matthews took an important step forward from 55 percent to 65 percent, and Jordan Poole and Isaiah Livers also saw small improvements as their volume taken also increased. Wins over Western Michigan, Illinois, and Rutgers, had all involved Michigan taking care of business at the free throw line late to maintain control.

Wisconsin-Michigan battles typically involved few free throws as the programs were two of the most foul-averse teams in the country. But the slight edge would go to Michigan in the rematch as they made seven of their nine while the Badgers missed their only two attempts, and that subtle difference wound up very close to the final margin. The script was pretty much the same as it had been in the first meeting, which John Beilein encapsulated in his post-game comments. "It's really just exactly what happened in Madison," he said. "The score there was 27-25 at the half, this time it was 27 all. Got to be six minutes or so in the game and they got away from us. Six minutes to go in this game, four minutes, and we got away from them." Charles Matthews' mid-range game accounted for many of his 16 second-half points and led the way to the 61–52 Michigan victory.

Jon Teske matched up with Ethan Happ and came out on top. His 17 points and 12 rebounds only told part of the story, as Michigan outscored the Badgers by 17 while Teske was on the court. Though he had a center that had demonstrated he was capable of handling Wisconsin's All-Big Ten performer, Beilein wanted nothing to do with Happ anymore. "Ethan Happ said to me after the game 'I hope to see you again this season.' No, Ethan, I don't want to see you again the rest of my life,"[7] he joked.

After the emotional win over Wisconsin that had a dose of well-earned revenge to it, Michigan traveled to Happy Valley, Pennsylvania, to play an 8:30 p.m. weeknight game in front of a sparse crowd. What seemed like an opportunity for a letdown going in quickly proved to be the case once the game started. Beilein had implored his team beforehand that this would not be a cakewalk. "They're really playing well," he said. "Their record just doesn't show it. We're gonna have our hands full."[8] Penn State did play well, though the referees' wonky whistles didn't help matters. Only three first-half fouls were called on a Penn State team that carried a fairly high foul rate on the season, and John Beilein finally reached his tipping point on the last play of the half. Jamari Wheeler decked Zavier Simpson with a moving screen and Beilein was apoplectic in a way rarely seen. He was abruptly ejected from the game, earning his first dismissal in 40 years—dating all the way back to his time at Erie (New York) Community College. Without their head coach and trailing 40–27 at the break, Michigan fought back but didn't quite have enough. Penn State eventually closed it out by a score of 75–69.

Charles Matthews had scored a very efficient 24 points to go along with 6 rebounds but took no solace in his individual performance. He fumed to the media afterwards, ticking off the team's issues. "There was no sense of urgency, lack of focus, lack of effort," he said. "Time is running short," Matthews went on. "There ain't no more, 'We'll fix it later.' Time is now."[9] It was implicitly understood that this would be the redshirt junior's last year in the program, and he was desperate to go out on top. With the team mired in a 5–3 rut after the 17–0 start, his frustration was clear. While his offensive game could be inconsistent, Matthews' intensity and effort could never be questioned, nor could his dedication to the team.

With Maryland and Minnesota next on the schedule, Michigan faced consecutive teams that employed two-post offenses. Beilein's teams had thrived employing just a single conventional big man, and most of modern basketball had followed suit. But Mark Turgeon and Richard Pitino's teams were two of the remaining clubs still utilizing a traditional power forward. Michigan's victories over both squads relied on their staff effectively teaching the players a recent point of emphasis in the NCAA rulebook: the principle of verticality. It was the latest addition to what was now fully established as one of the best defenses in all the land. Remnants of this development were evident back in the early-season win over Purdue. Beilein took particular zeal that night in his post-game press conference in praising Jordan Poole for his "jump wall." He went on to explain the principle of verticality: as long as a defender stays vertical—that is, balanced straight up and down with arms extended to the sky—defenders could jump to contest an oncoming offensive player without fear of a foul. Poole relayed that Yaklich had also exuberantly celebrated him for the play. All that praise for one small moment in a game that Poole had scored 21 points and went 5–5 from three. Looking back it

Jon Teske got the best of All-American Ethan Happ in Michigan's 61–52 home victory over Wisconsin on February 9, 2019. The Badgers' Kobe King looks on (photograph by Marc-Gregor Campredon).

makes sense—a player that had been scattered at best on defense as a freshman successfully executed a tough play that they had worked on extensively in practice, much to his coaches' delight.

Teske was the poster boy for staying vertical and providing 85 plus inches of length to shoot or pass around. His ability to anchor Michigan's elite defense while avoiding fouls was especially crucial given the limited depth backing him up. At the end of the season there were only two players in the country that sported a fouls committed per 40 minutes lower than Teske with a block rate as high as his. And Brandon Clarke of Gonzaga and Jalyn Hinton of Jacksonville were respectively five and eight inches shorter than Teske. Beilein explained the process of coaching Teske into a verticality master. "It's gone from no knowledge of it as a freshman because I don't even think it's a high school rule, to trying it but not being able to do it as a sophomore, and now he's becoming an expert at it and it's really helped us because it keeps us out of foul trouble."[10]

Against both Maryland and Minnesota, the referees properly officiated verticality to the Wolverines' advantage. One can easily imagine Beilein, after carefully studying the technical details of the rule, conferring with the referees to clarify the letter of the law. All that preparation allowed his interior players to slow Maryland's star center Bruno Fernando and his fellow 6'10" teammate, freshman Jalen Smith. The Terrapins rolled into Ann Arbor just a game behind the Wolverines in the conference standings and ranked 24th in the nation. Teske proved quite the rude host, holding Fernando scoreless in the first half. Isaiah Livers and Iggy Brazdeikis walled up against their taller opponents and would occasionally add a false step or two to disrupt the twin towers' rhythm. That defense was essential in getting out to a double-digit lead, at which point they essentially strangled the game to death, winning 65–52. The win gave Michigan its 22nd straight home victory, tied for the second longest streak in program history. They had once again held an opponent to their worst offensive performance of the season to date. Maryland's 52 points were the fewest it had scored in a game since joining the Big Ten.

The Minnesota game played out similarly. Jordan Murphy struggled with his bully-ball style to finish against length in the first half. Minnesota's other big man, Daniel Oturu, added many of his points when Teske was in foul avoidance mode. After his foul trouble in the Iowa game, Teske had honed his skill for modulating his aggressiveness according to the game situation. Often an opposing big man might have some early success in the post as Teske played possum and hoarded his fouls. But as the game developed and Teske's risk of foul trouble decreased, he played with an easier aggression. The big man detailed that approach, saying, "The first couple minutes, you can't be too aggressive. At the same time, you're just not gonna give them a layup. So you just gotta wall up." He went on, "As the game goes on, you can be a little bit more aggressive depending how many fouls you have."[11]

Utilizing that technique allowed Teske to rack up five blocks against the Gophers while only accruing two fouls. Beilein raved about that combination in his press conference after the 69–60 win over Minnesota. "It's not only the five blocks but the ones he affected," he said. "It's just huge what he's doing at the rim for us and not fouling at the same time." The Michigan center also contributed three second-half three-pointers that provided the final margin of victory. Charles Matthews provided his standard shut-down defense on the wing. Matthews didn't have single point scored on him in the Maryland contest, and then hounded Minnesota's leading scorer, Amir Coffey, into a 2–15 shooting performance. Their defensive prowess had led them to victory all season. But in many ways, that season was just beginning. In a strange scheduling quirk, Michigan and Michigan State would play twice over the last four games of the season. With those two late season contests immediately followed by the post-season, the determining stretch of Michigan's season was set to begin.

Chapter 28

Spartan Battles

Following the departure of NBA lottery picks Jaren Jackson and Miles Bridges, this latest edition of Spartans' alchemy had actually improved thanks to the players developing a better understanding of roles and embracing a shared purpose. Though Nick Ward and Josh Langford were both injured and unavailable, Cassius Winston and his Spartan brethren were still ranked in the top ten nationally. Frustratingly it seemed like the injuries, at least in Ward's case, actually improved the team overall. Most importantly, the two bitter rivals were tied at the top of the conference and this game would have championship implications.

Despite the history of success at both schools, February 24, 2019, was just the third time they had met with each team ranked in the top 10. Beilein and Izzo had clearly established both programs among the nation's best, with both a ceiling and a consistency rarely achieved. Since Stu Douglass had knocked down his fateful three at the Breslin Center in 2011, the programs had traded winning streaks back and forth with Beilein claiming the slight edge, having won nine of the 16 games since. In winning the previous three games, Beilein's modern approach utilizing a mobile big man like Moe Wagner had triumphed over Izzo's more traditional post players. But in light of Nick Ward's injury, this year's group of Spartans was better suited to handle Michigan's ball screens with the more agile Xavier Tillman taking Ward's minutes.

The initial moments of the game revealed that Izzo also made a strategic alteration taking advantage of this adjustment in personnel. Michigan State's defense switched on every Wolverine screen. That tweak caught Beilein and Michigan by surprise and proved to be an important element in the game. "Tom has never done a lot of switching of ball screens or even lifting ball screens like they did," Michigan's head coach acknowledged after the game. "They're daring some of our guys to shoot." By switching defenders, Michigan

State created some mismatch opportunities for Michigan to exploit and in the early going they did just that. Teske was able to corral a few offensive rebounds over smaller players either for a put-back or to get to the free throw line. The Spartans also sagged under screens frequently and allowed jump-shots. Early on, when Kenny Goins and Tillman both stayed back on a Teske screen, Ignas Brazdeikis recognized it and eagerly took the open look from the top of the key to give Michigan a 10–6 lead. Zavier Simpson received the same treatment and hit his first three with 11:22 left in the first half to narrow a Michigan State lead to 22–20. That Spartan lead had come in large part thanks to Cassius Winston. The junior point guard was a different player from the one Simpson had harassed into losing efforts the year before. He controlled the ball much of the game, similar to Simpson for Michigan, but with the added threat of the three-pointer and the ability to get his floater off in the lane. With Winston at the helm, Tom Izzo's offense looked more similar to John Beilein's than ever before. Winston ran ball-screen after ball-screen and anytime Michigan made a mistake, he was ready to capitalize. "I think that they have changed their offense dramatically," Beilein observed. "They used to throw the ball in the post, throw the ball in the post and play a lot out of that, and I think that's probably a lot of ways people have prepared for, and now it's probably 100 different ball screens by the same guy."[1] The success Luke Yaklich's defense had enjoyed all year by having Teske hedge out hard on a screen and then retreat to cover his man wasn't quite the same with Winston in charge. He was able to put defenders into conflict, forced to choose between helping on the rolling Tillman and staying with their own man at the three-point line. Winston's ability to quickly read the help defender's intentions and deliver passes around Teske's length changed the equation. Goins and Tillman were the primary beneficiaries in the first half, scoring a combined 21 points, including 3–4 from beyond the three-point line by Goins. His emergence as a shooter was yet another example of Izzo adjusting his team's approach to more closely resemble Beilein's—by developing and encouraging his big man to shoot from distance, their offense had better spacing and options. In his first three seasons, Goins had only attempted a total of 15 threes, but he would go on to finish his senior season 56–159 (35 percent) from beyond the arc. The back-and-forth between two similarly talented teams continued throughout the half, ending with the Spartans leading 39–37.

The second half opened with Brazdeikis charging into the lane as he often did, this time drawing two free throws in the process to tie the game at 39. A pretty Winston runner courtesy of a Matt McQuaid dish put MSU back on top. Poole answered with a backdoor cut for a layup thanks to a Charles Matthews assist. It was one of the few bright spots for Matthews in the game; after suffering an ankle sprain in the first half, he stayed on the court to log 28 minutes but was clearly not at full strength. Brazdeikis was fouled shooting a three by McQuaid on Michigan's next possession and hit all three free throws to put the home team up 44–41. After Simpson and Winston exchanged free throws, the Michigan State point guard tossed up another challenging runner that found the bottom of the net. Beilein described Winston's ability to find daylight in his press conference afterwards, saying, "He gets into nooks and crannies. His mid-range game is one of the tops in the country." Jordan Poole had the response from Michigan, using his change of direction to fly by McQuaid for an and-one layup. A Brazdeikis baseline drive and slam past Goins followed, and the crowd roared to life as Michigan found itself in control 51–45.

But from that point on, the offense suddenly dried up. Over the next ten minutes, the Wolverines managed just a single field goal. Their defense held off the Spartans for the first few minutes, but soon enough McQuaid had pump-faked Poole off his feet and leaned into a three-point attempt to draw three shots at the line. He sunk all three and Michigan State had regained the lead 52–51. It was one of a number of defensive mistakes Poole made in a matchup against a less talented player. McQuaid had experience in his favor and used it to his advantage. Earlier in the game, an eager Poole had flown by a similar pump fake and McQuaid simply reset his feet and hit a three. Later in the first half, Poole had flopped to the floor on a McQuaid drive, leaving him wide open for a step-back three. And now McQuaid had once again used Poole's over-aggressiveness against him. Up until that point, the game had been remarkably even. The two teams had been tied for a total of almost six minutes, Michigan held the lead for 11:22, and Michigan State ahead for 10:49. Simpson and Winston continued to go at each other, with Simpson driving for a half-hook and Winston answering with another runner. That put the Spartans up 54–53 with 10:12 remaining, and they didn't relinquish the lead the rest of the way. After successfully attacking the mismatches Michigan State's defensive strategy presented earlier, the Wolverines reverted to settling for deep jumpers rather than driving the lane or feeding Teske against smaller defenders. Michigan State shot 0–8 from three-point land in the second half, but it didn't matter because Winston had been so effective carving up their defense inside the arc. "Our ball-screen defense has been terrific all year [until now]. Cassius Winston was terrific. He destroyed our ball-screen defense," Beilein lamented afterwards. Winston completed the effort by making nine of ten free throws over the last 2:03 to close out the Spartan victory.

Michigan's offense had gone stagnant at the worst possible time. In the hunt for a culprit, much of the fanbase focused its displeasure on Jordan Poole. The young sophomore had seemingly spent the year oscillating from a remorseless gunner to a hesitant and passive floor spacer struggling to find the right mix. His penchant for gambling defensively often left him out of place and forced his teammates to scramble to cover for him. Perhaps because of his significant natural talent, his inability to stay consistent and make the simple play frustrated close observers as much as any player in recent Michigan history. On top of that, his three-point shooting had cratered after a dominant streak earlier in the season. Ever since the calendar had turned to 2019, Poole had shot 29 percent from three-point land. Many of those came from a few feet behind the line—a fact Beilein would often point out in an effort to improve his guard's shot selection. Following the season, Poole's father Anthony revealed to journalist Brendan Quinn that his son had essentially decided he would be moving on to professional basketball at the halfway point of the season—right when his shooting percentage tanked. When Beilein spoke of welcoming early entry candidates to Ann Arbor as long as they were willing to "unpack their bags," this was the exact situation he was trying to avoid. As impressive as Winston had played, the contrast between the simple plays made by McQuaid and the mistakes made by Poole were a primary factor in the loss.

The sophomore shooting guard continued his fluctuating pattern of performance in an easy 82–53 win over Nebraska. Poole, who never met a shot he didn't like, didn't attempt a single first-half field goal. Early in the second half, he was knocked to the floor after finishing an explosive fast break dunk for his first basket of the game. As he was getting up he showed two fingers and mouthed, "That's two," to the ESPN cameras, possibly a message to the constant critics regarding his shot selection and tendency to settle from distance. Freshman Colin Castleton flourished in his nine minutes, collecting 11 points with a steady diet of under-control head fakes and up-and-under moves. The long lean center kept the ball high around the rim and finished. Once Nebraska doubled down, he recognized it and passed out. He was showing early signs of being another Camp Sanderson success story. His teammates were believers. "You guys are gonna see a lot more of 'Swaggy C,' as we call him," Isaiah Livers said. "That's the future. I'm trying to tell you guys, he's next."[2]

Charles Matthews was honored that night for Senior Day. Matthews had one remaining year of eligibility, but he was on track to graduate in the spring. After his flirtation with the NBA draft the prior season, all parties involved understood his desire to move on to the next stage of his career. Unfortunately, his ankle injury against Michigan State had been more serious than initially thought and he was unable to take the court one last time at Crisler. It was the first break in the team's good fortune in health; they were the last remaining team in the country to have started the same five players all year.

Matthews had proven to be a perfect fit for the Michigan program in his two seasons. Having lost three crucial players in Derrick Walton, Zak Irvin, and DJ Wilson the year he became eligible, Matthews picked up the slack and helped Michigan achieve an impressive 58-12 record to that point. Along the way he had clearly become a Beilein favorite for his hard work and humility. "He's one of the best kids I've ever coached," Beilein said after the game. "He just does the next right things. His mom and dad are so solid in who they are and how they've raised those three boys." He was accompanied by those parents, Charles and Nichole, onto to the court and was given a framed version of his #1 jersey as the fans and his teammates and coaches sounded their appreciation. The wide margin of victory provided an enjoyable close to a very successful 17-1 season at Crisler.

Next up was a return engagement with the Maryland team they had just beaten two weeks before. The Terrapins played under the tutelage of their head coach Mark Turgeon. The former backup point guard at Kansas led a talented but very young team, checking in on Kenpom as the 5th least experienced team in the country. He had enjoyed success on the recruiting trail over the years at Maryland, including his 7th ranked freshman class, but had yet to break through onto the national scene in March. With just one trip to the Sweet 16 in his eight years in College Park, the fanbase was beginning to pine for their storied past under Lefty Driesell and Gary Williams.

With Charles Matthews still resting his injured ankle, it was a game the short-handed Wolverines had to win to keep their Big Ten championship hopes alive. Although Matthews didn't take the floor, he quickly identified Maryland's defensive approach. "He was the first one—within ten seconds he said 'they're cross-matching the four and the three [positions].' I didn't even notice that yet and he was already on it," Beilein said afterwards in praise of his astute captain. Michigan's counter was to dial up their star freshman against Maryland's smaller defender, Darryl Morsell. Brazdeikis, who had enjoyed hostile road atmospheres all year, played with the rugged aggression that helped define his game. He consistently took the ball right at Morsell and used his strength and balance to finish with a basket or draw the foul. Before the game was over, he drew nine Maryland fouls without committing a single one himself. Frustrated by the freshman's confidence and effectiveness, the Xfinity Center's crowd chanted, "You are ugly!" early in the game while Brazdeikis was at the free throw line. The public address announcer relayed Mark Turgeon's request to stop the chant, perhaps for its utter lack of creativity more than anything else. Brazdeikis, meanwhile, was unmoved and continued to flex and flash his money signal to his haters on the way to a 21-point, seven-rebound performance.

The defense and Zavier Simpson kept Michigan in front 28-24 after a low-scoring first half in which they shot just 1-11 from beyond the arc. Simpson controlled the ball as usual, scoring or assisting on nine out of ten Michigan first-half field goals. Among those baskets were a number of effective pick and roll dishes to his favorite target, Jon Teske. Simpson also added a few of his patented hooks over the outstretched hand of Bruno Fernando. The Maryland center racked up a number of emphatic volleyball spike blocks on the day but was helpless in the face of Michigan's barely six-foot point guard's sky hook. Simpson closed the first half with a full-court dash through the teeth of the defense for an up and under layup as the buzzer sounded.

Two quick Simpson fouls, which were out of character for the point guard, began the second half and landed him a seat on the bench just a minute and a half after the break. By the time he checked back in with 11:01 remaining, the Terrapins had outscored Michigan 18–11 and now led 43–41 with a rejuvenated crowd behind them. Simpson soon added another hook, and Maryland did not score a single field goal in his first eight minutes back on the court. The plus 14-point differential he registered in such a crucial road game once again demonstrated his immense importance on both ends of the court. With five minutes remaining and the ball in Simpson's hands, the offense returned to its bread and butter as Teske set a screen for his point guard at the top of the key. Having been burnt one too many times by Teske rolling to the hoop, both Aaron Wiggins and Fernando sagged down to defend the big man. That left Brazdeikis, the Terrapin fans' chosen villain, open as he rotated from the corner to the wing. After receiving the Simpson dish, he drained the three in front of a closing Wiggins. The Lithuanian-Canadian blew kisses to the crowd in homage to his predecessor from the same community. "I've seen [Nik Stauskas] do that against Michigan State, so I was like 'These guys are on me. I might just blow them a little kiss too,'"[3] Brazdeikis said later.

On their next possession, with the shot clock winding down, Simpson hit one last hook to put his team up 53–45. "I mean, the kid makes four sky-hooks. Are you kidding me?" Mark Turgeon would marvel afterwards in his press conference. Maryland knocked down some late threes to keep the game superficially close, but the Wolverines remained in control with the assistance of their newfound reliable free throw shooting. Their last four points came at the line as part of a 13–15 performance from the stripe. Brazdeikis hit the last two and then ripped the ball away from Anthony Cowan to provide a fitting closure to the hard-fought 69–62 win. With 12 points, 10 assists and just one missed shot, Simpson had played another outstanding game. His four hooks were particularly impactful in light of the final seven-point margin. Beilein was again thrilled with his point guard's performance and signed off on the latest nickname he had heard: "Captain Hook was unbelievable today," he said in his post-game press conference. "That one can stick. He's the captain and he's got a hook." It was the Terrapins' first Big Ten loss at home and the Wolverines had kept alive their hopes for a conference championship.

With six days off before the final test of the season in East Lansing, the Maize and Blue had plenty of time to try and correct their mistakes from the previous meeting. Both teams enjoyed a pleasant surprise during the week when Minnesota upset league leader Purdue, ensuring the Michigan–Michigan State winner at least a share of the conference throne. The Wolverines' earlier struggles to feed Jon Teske down low when guarded by a smaller defender was a hot topic. The solution was so obvious that Beilein was happy to answer it irreverently. "We're not going to throw it to him. We want to shoot step-back threes the whole time. No throwing it in to the 7'1" guy on the 6'0" guy. Absolutely not. Step-back three—that's our plan," he said with a smile in his press conference at the beginning of the week.

The ESPN broadcast started with a split-screen of the just completed North Carolina win over Duke, displaying both of what John Beilein had taken to calling the two preeminent rivalries in college basketball. Charles Matthews was still not on the floor, but his fellow wings, Brazdeikis and Poole stepped up early in his absence to get Michigan out in front. A fast break dunk and an early three from both were sandwiched around a Simpson hook to give Michigan its first 12 points and a six-point lead. Brazdeikis kept coming, once again thriving in an angry road environment. He attacked an overmatched Thomas Kithier on a switch for a layup and then hit a pull-up transition three from a few feet behind the arc on the left wing. This gave the Wolverines a 17–7 advantage and also quieted the Breslin Center crowd. Foul trouble for both teams sent key personnel to the bench. Brazdeikis and Isaiah Livers both sat the last 10 minutes of the half after earning their second fouls. Despite having to dig deep into their bench, Michigan maintained control. When Cassius Winston drew his second foul and headed to the bench with 7:34 remaining and Michigan ahead 29–21, the road team seemed poised to stretch the lead.

Winston's importance to his team was hard to overstate and his replacement Foster Loyer was a massive downgrade. But in what was to become a recurring theme of the contest, a questionable call immediately benefited the Spartans on their first possession without Winston. While trying to escape Zavier Simpson's pressure defense, Loyer fell down untouched—clearly traveling in the process—and was somehow granted two free throws for his clumsiness. Loyer struggled to stay in front of Simpson on defense, giving up two layups leading to Michigan's biggest lead of the game at 35–23 with 3:12 left in the half. But over those last three minutes, the Spartans closed the half with a disheartening 6–0 run. Before the game, Beilein would have welcomed the idea of a 35–29 halftime lead but failing to extend their lead in Winston's extended absence felt like a huge missed opportunity.

With both teams back at full strength after the break, Michigan held serve for the first eight minutes pushing the score to 50–45. Brazdeikis had returned from his foul-induced exile and scored seven of their first 13 in the half. But in a frustratingly similar pattern to the first meeting, the offense then fell stagnant. Xavier Tillman once again stoned their ball-screen game by switching and staying in front of Simpson, and the Wolverines' went without a field goal for more than seven minutes. Over that time, Winston hit his stride and began scoring and distributing much like he had in the first matchup. By the time Jordan Poole finally broke the drought with a three with five minutes left, Michigan was down ten and would never draw closer. Once again, missed opportunities were abundant in a game that Michigan had previously controlled. The Wolverines had missed too many layups, while Michigan State had converted theirs. Michigan had again struggled to find Jon Teske on mismatches down low. The home cooking served up by referees Keith Kimble, Lamont Simpson, and Terry Oglesby that resulted in a 30–7 free throw discrepancy didn't help matters, but there was plenty of blame to go around for the disappointing 75–63 loss. Izzo correctly pointed to his team's ability to survive the end of the first half as a key component of the victory. "I think what won the game for us was only being down six at halftime," he said afterwards. "Because that thing could've been 16." Winston had led the way with 23 points while Kenny Goins tracked down 16 rebounds and hit three important threes along the way.

Michigan's disappointment afterwards was obvious. Michigan State and Purdue were the Big Ten regular season champions, but Beilein, as always, took the longer view and emphasized that his team still had opportunities ahead of them. "We'll take the lessons we learn from this game, apply it to the Big Ten tournament, see if we can win that again," he told the media afterwards. "If we can't, apply it to the NCAA tournament and just keep getting better." Michigan headed to the post-season 26–5 with a 15–5 conference record; a level of success that anyone would have welcomed coming into the year.

Chapter 29

The Green River

After emerging victorious in Washington, D.C., and New York City in the previous two Big Ten Tournaments, Michigan hoped to add Chicago to its list of vanquished cities and become the first team ever to win three times in a row. Unlike the past tournaments, they would only need to win three games to do so, having earned a double-bye as the #3 seed. Iowa comfortably defeated Illinois on Thursday, so the #6 seed Hawkeyes were Michigan's opponent for a late Friday night start. The formula for Michigan to exact revenge was simple—avoid the issues that had plagued them back in Iowa City. That meant staying out of foul trouble, limiting the opponent from three-point range, and hitting the open shots that Iowa's 111th ranked defense allowed. Michigan thrived on all three fronts, though Iowa managed to hang around for the first ten minutes. From that point on though, the lead was steadily stretched by crisp ball movement and good shooting. A 13-4 run to close the half—fueled by threes from Matthews, Livers, and Simpson—sent Michigan to the locker room confidently with a 40-27 lead. The Wolverine big men had not accrued a single foul and Iowa had not made a three-pointer, while Michigan shot a healthy 7-16 from three. Iowa was fortunate just to be that close, though that luck wouldn't last. Jordan Poole converted one of his trademark four-point plays early in the half, and once Brazdeikis and Eli Brooks followed with their own threes, the rout was on. Zavier Simpson completely bottled up Jordan Bohannon, holding him without a point and registering yet another double-double with 10 points and 11 assists. The ball whipped around the way John Beilein preached, evidenced by the 24 assists on 28 made baskets. Brazdeikis finished the game as Michigan's top scorer with 15, and he also led the way in exuberant celebrations. Charles Matthews looked understandably rusty in his return, shooting just 1-9 from the field. However, the rest of his teammates picked up the slack shooting over 50 percent. As soon as it ended, Beilein and staff were already focused on the next game, which was coming fast. "Quickest turnaround I've probably ever had as a coach to be sitting here right now at 11:00 [at night] with a 2:30 game [tomorrow], but we'll do our best," he pointed out at his press conference.

That turnaround was made more manageable by the fact that Minnesota had upset Purdue yet again. Playing a #7 seed that they had recently beaten comfortably on the road was certainly preferable to taking on the #2 seed Boilermakers. The scouting report on Minnesota hadn't changed since the last time Michigan played them; the Gophers simply didn't match up well given their poor perimeter shooting and Michigan's ability to slow down their post players without help. Beilein sported a 9-1 career record against Minnesota's coach Richard Pitino, and this game would be the Gophers third in three days. All signs pointed to a Michigan win and that is exactly what happened as the game played out similarly to the contest the night before. Jordan Poole came out of the gates playing well, first finding Brazdeikis for a pick and pop three to open the scoring. Michigan's next three baskets all came courtesy of Poole using his deft footwork to dance through the defense for three consecutive layups, each more aesthetically pleasing than the last. The last ten minutes of the half featured a dominant 25-6 run by the Wolverines with balanced scoring at all three levels predicated on ball movement and their typically tenacious defense at the other end. After Simpson finished a full-court push through traffic for the final points of the half as the horn sounded, Michigan left the floor with their chests out and their confidence at an all-time high. This was a team that could make serious noise in the NCAA Tournament if they were able to maintain this level of play.

The second half was more of the same. Isaiah Livers was the star in the box score with 21 points in just 22 minutes off the bench, shooting 8-10, including four three-pointers. Beilein saw Livers' increased minutes as the silver lining in Charles Matthews' injury. "All of a sudden Isaiah had to be out there for 35 minutes, and it gave him confidence coming off the bench now to do what he does. He's taking the ball to the basket a little bit more," Beilein said post-game. "What we like about Isaiah, he can play either position and give people rest. But it's been—his defense continues to get better. He's become a very, very good defender, and he's just a young, young sophomore." Though he was easy to overlook at times, Livers had played an essential role all season serving as the Swiss Army knife for the team. His ability to sub in at the three, four, or five positions was what allowed Beilein to keep such a short bench and stick with his core six players for the majority of the minutes. Always with a smile on his face, Livers clearly enjoyed the game and his teammates. He spoke often in his coach's vernacular about having a growth mindset and the importance of the team's culture. He had clearly bought in and as a result had steadily improved in his time in Ann Arbor. As the team's best three-point shooter (he would finish the year at 43 percent) and a good athlete,

29. The Green River

Iowa's Luka Garza is unable to affect Zavier Simpson's patented hook shot at the 2019 Big Ten Tournament (photograph by Marc-Gregor Campredon).

he seemed poised for a breakout junior season. But first, there were more urgent matters to take care of. With the Wolverines' dominant 76–49 victory, they pressed on to the finals the next day. And to nobody's surprise, Michigan State stood in their way.

Outside the United Center, the Chicago River was ominously dyed Spartan green for St. Patrick's Day—exactly one year after Jordan Poole had made his miracle three against Houston to keep Michigan alive. All eyes were focused on the last conference championship game in the country, which featured two heavyweights going down to the wire. Brazdeikis continued his fearless play under the bright lights and opened the game with a three. Cassius Winston and Xavier Tillman returned to their ball-screen game and Teske and Simpson were forced to switch responsibilities. The Spartans quickly gave a tutorial on the lesson Michigan had been struggling with—how to attack the smaller defender down low. Tillman sealed off Simpson, and Winston delivered a perfectly placed pass for an easy layup. Their next time down, Matt McQuaid continued to be a thorn in the Wolverines' side and hit his first of too many threes on the day. Brazdeikis continued his aggressive play and drew an all-important foul on Tillman. The mobile big man took a seat on the bench and was replaced by Nick Ward, who had just returned to action after missing the last month. Michigan immediately took advantage of Ward's

Isaiah Livers drives by Jordan Murphy as part of his season-high 21-point performance in Michigan's 2019 Big Ten Tournament win over Minnesota (photograph by Marc-Gregor Campredon).

defensive deficiencies as Brazdeikis sized him up for a three that Ward couldn't close out on. The freshman scored his team's first nine points of the game. The Spartans survived Tillman's first stint on the pine without incident, climbing ahead 17–11 just after he checked back in. But a minute later, the sophomore from Grand Rapids was whistled for his second foul and spent the final nine minutes of the first half spectating. In Tillman's extended absence, Michigan State looked more like the team Beilein's offense had broken down consistently the season before. With the slower Ward and Thomas Kithier left to fill his shoes, gaps in the Spartan defense opened up and the Maize and Blue rattled off a 10–0 run. But McQuaid kept his team close, hitting two more threes for their only points the rest of the half. The 20–6 run heading into halftime put Michigan up 31–23. They had held off Cassius Winston thus far, limiting him to three points and four assists—but there were 20 minutes of basketball yet to be played.

McQuaid found himself yet another three to open the half, and Zavier Simpson lined up his hook shot at the other end. Tillman reminded everyone he was back in the game by anticipating it and blocking it out of bounds. It was the first time all year anyone had blocked what had seemed unblockable—this guy really did have Michigan's number. But the Maize and Blue retained possession and, after inbounding the ball, Jordan Poole came around a Teske screen and rose up off balance for a pull-up three. Brazdeikis soon followed with his own and then added two free throws. The 8–0 spurt made the score 39–26, giving Michigan, once again, an illusory comfortable second-half lead against Michigan State. The Spartans began their climb back slowly, chipping away with McQuaid leading the way offensively and Tillman tightening the screws on Michigan's ball-screen offense. And just as they had done two times before, ten minutes later the game was tied on a herky-jerk Winston layup off the glass as he fell to the ground. This time though, Michigan didn't back down. Simpson gave Winston a taste of his own medicine with a tough body-control layup and Michigan was back up 57–52 with three minutes remaining. But at the other end, with a devastating sense of déjà vu, Matt McQuaid once again got Jordan Poole up in the air and drew a three-shot foul—making all three. Isaiah Livers responded with a crucial three to retake the five-point lead. It briefly seemed like a crisis averted until McQuaid nailed another bomb—his seventh of the game. The shooting guard had begun his senior season having made a total of 14 career starts and had averaged six points per game the season before. Now he had scored 27 points on Michigan in the Big Ten Championship. The Wolverines were unable to answer, and Tillman and Winston followed with their own baskets. One last opportunity remained with nine seconds left as Zavier Simpson inbounded to Jordan Poole hoping he could re-enact his theatrics from 365 days before. Michigan State had a foul to give and Poole anticipated Winston committing it. As Winston moved in, Poole put up a shot and clearly drew contact in the act of shooting. What should have been three free throws and a chance for the 83 percent shooter to tie it was instead a harmless air-ball as the referees egregiously swallowed their whistles.

Michigan's locker room was once again understandably devastated; three times they had held second-half leads only to fall each time. Although this had been their best effort of the three, once again Winston, Tillman, and McQuaid had pulled it off. "They are just a bad matchup for us," Beilein acknowledged to the media afterwards. If imitation truly is the sincerest form of flattery, then Beilein could take minor solace in Michigan State achieving this success only after adopting many of Michigan's tenets. Employing a mobile big man and working the offense primarily out of the ball-screen were keys to Michigan's success in the matchup the year before; now Izzo had utilized those techniques to his advantage.

Chapter 30

A Trip to Des Moines

The frustration and disappointment evident in the Wolverine locker room would remain despite the good news that the loss had not affected their seeding in the NCAA Tournament. The brackets were revealed immediately after the Big Ten Championship was played, and it appeared the selection committee had simply penciled both finalists in as #2 seeds. Michigan State's prize for winning was placement in the same region as Duke and their wunderkind freshman Zion Williamson. The quick turnaround led to a strange dynamic that the Michigan coaching staff had to address: despite earning a coveted seed in the NCAA Tournament, the players were consumed by their third failure against the Spartans. "There's some disappointment there, dealing with the loss in that environment and that type of game," said assistant coach Luke Yaklich. "We had to remind them, 'We're a two seed. It didn't work out on Sunday the way we wanted it to, but there's a lot of teams that would love to be in our position. And you have an opportunity to go out there and win a tournament game.'"[1]

After the incredible start to the season and a back-loaded schedule featuring three contests with Michigan State over 22 days, Michigan's 6–4 late-season record had led to the popular narrative that the team had simply peaked too soon. But in reality, advanced metrics painted quite a different picture. Bart Torvik's analytics found Michigan to be the best team in the country since February 13, a similar story to the season before. Over the month of March until this point, the Wolverines ranked in the top ten nationally for both offensive and defensive efficiency. Charles Matthews noticed, saying, "That's something that we've shown on multiple occasions. So now we've just got to do it six times. Literally. Let's just do it six times. We've done it more than six times all season long, and I feel like the whole country knows how scary we can be clicking on all cylinders."[2]

Michigan's first opportunity to prove how well they were playing came

30. A Trip to Des Moines

Montana's Michael Oguine and Kendal Manuel defend the talented but streaky Jordan Poole during Michigan's 74–55 win in the first round of the 2019 NCAA Tournament (photograph by Patrick Barron).

in Des Moines, Iowa, on Thursday, March 21. Coincidentally, they were joined by the Spartans in Iowa despite being placed in different regions of the bracket. A repeat engagement with the Montana Grizzlies beckoned—Michigan's first-round opponent from the year before. Montana returned many of the same players that had taken an early 10–0 lead in their first meeting, though they would be without their leading scorer and rebounder Jamar Akoh who had missed the previous 12 games with a knee injury. The Grizzlies had managed to reel off a 10–2 record in that time with a small lineup featuring no player taller than 6'7". That lack of size would be put to the test against Michigan and Jon Teske. Due to that height deficiency, Montana essentially ceded the jump ball to start the game.

It quickly became clear that it would once again be Michigan's defense that would be the star of the evening. The team's intensity and effort at that end of the floor was evident on every possession. They held Montana to one for their first nine field goal attempts, and the overmatched Grizzlies didn't score their tenth point until just 6:09 remained in the first half. Charles Matthews converted his first five attempts, looking like his old self for the first time since his ankle injury, while leading the Wolverines to a 34–21 halftime lead.

The Grizzlies started the scoring out of the locker room with a three-pointer by Sayeed Pridgett, and he then followed it up with a whirling dervish of a drive around Teske to close within eight. But before anyone could get the slightest bit nervous, Michigan reasserted itself with three-pointers by Poole and Matthews, as well as a baseline jumper by the reinvigorated Matthews and a beautiful hook alley-oop from Simpson to Teske for a 10–0 run. It would never get closer than 14 and the Wolverines pushed the lead as high as 27.

One lighthearted moment occurred later in the half as Brazdeikis completed one of his powerful drives through traffic and stood over a defeated Timmy Falls while flexing and yelling, "And one!" though no foul was called. At the other end, Ahmaad Rorie quickly blew by Brazdeikis for his own layup. As Iggy retreated up-court by the Montana bench, their entire team stood and flexed back at him to achieve some minor solace after his brash antics had tormented them all night long.

After the under four-minute media timeout, Beilein essentially declared the game over by inserting his backups. A minute and a half later, Montana coach Travis DeCuire agreed, and began to empty his own bench. Soon enough the win was official, 74–55 Michigan. It hadn't been a perfect outing, but Michigan's defense had been sharp, limiting their opponent to just 0.81 points per possession. That figure would have been even lower if not for a number of garbage time baskets by the Grizzlies. With a few less turnovers and slightly better fortune from long distance, Michigan may have had an offensive outing to match. As it was, they shot 59 percent on two-point field goals on the strength of numerous dunks and layups. Matthews led the way with 22 points and 10 rebounds, playing with the aggression and confidence seen in the previous post-season run. Simpson added 10 assists and did not have a second-half turnover after an unusual four in the first half. Those 10 assists allowed him to pass Michigan's last elite point guard, Trey Burke, in the school's all-time record book. Charles Matthews was excited to find out afterwards about another milestone for his fellow captain, telling the assembled media, "We just found out that he set the school record—the first guard to have eight 10-assist games in a season."[3]

DeCuire, Montana's coach, paid his respects to one of the greats in his post-game comments saying, "It's a game of adjustments. I think Beilein is probably one of the best in the country at making adjustments." With the win, Michigan had assured themselves of going the entire season without ever suffering consecutive losses. Their resilience had been a defining trait all season and would help them prepare for the short turnaround before a Round of 32 matchup against Florida.

The Gators were led by head coach Mike White, who was in his third season at the helm. Florida strangely seemed to be a yearly Michigan opponent in either football or basketball, easily their most common out-of-conference Power Five foe in recent memory. Although the matchup had long been dominated by Michigan, the Wolverine faithful were still smarting from one of Florida's only victories—a disappointing Peach Bowl blowout just months before. Like Michigan, this Gators' group was also a defense-oriented squad and ranked 14th in the country in defensive efficiency. They achieved that rank by adjusting seamlessly between a 1-2-2 zone press, a 1-3-1 zone in the half-court, and traditional man-to-man. That ability to morph mid-play concerned Beilein. "That is the challenge," he said. "Sometimes they change defenses in the middle of a [possession]. They throw the ball in and they are in zone and they may change it in the middle of it. You have to play with heads up." Their press, in particular, seemed like it could present a challenge for Michigan. Penn State had slowed the Wolverines' ability to initiate their offense with a similar look in their upset win back in mid–February. One of Mike White's assistant coaches, Darris Nichols, had played under Beilein at West Virginia. Beilein said he was "as close to him as I am any of my former players."[4] The Gators' other assistant coach, Jordan Mincy, had been DeAndre Haynes' teammate at Kent State and the two remained close. With the familiarity among the coaching staffs and similarities in their profiles as defensive-minded squads, Florida offered some difficulties beyond a standard #10 seed.

Like they had done two days prior, Michigan opened the scoring on Saturday evening. Ignas Brazdeikis drove hard from the wing for a two-handed slam complete with his typical demonstrative celebration. Jalen Hudson responded with a three for Florida. After a patented Simpson to Teske pick and roll dunk, Keyontae Johnson hit another three. That was an ominous sign for a Michigan team that seemed likely to win unless the underdog found good fortune from beyond the arc. Simpson and Teske got back to work for another dunk. At the first media timeout the Wolverines led 8–6, and John Beilein had to be happy with their offense to that point. They were moving the ball and taking what the defense gave them without forcing the issue. He must have been even happier after their first possession out of the timeout when the ball rotated crisply to an open Jordan Poole, who drained the three and drew a foul, going on to complete the four-point play. The talented scoring guard found himself in rhythm to hit his next shot, capping off an 11–0 Michigan run and giving the #2 seed a 15–6 lead.

After their own point guard to center pick and roll dunk by Kevarrius Hayes, Florida began employing their multiple defensive looks by shifting to a 1-3-1 zone. Poole, likely restarting the shot selection debate in living rooms across Michigan, immediately took a heat-check three from about four feet beyond the line. Florida tracked down the rebound and their talented freshman, Noah Locke, knocked down his own three-pointer. On their next opportunity down the floor, Jalen Hudson lucked out and banked in a three from straightaway with Poole closely contesting. Simpson lessened the resulting frustration by hitting his own fairly unlikely three-pointer. Eli Brooks then auditioned for the role of the "outlier" John Beilein had been asking for with a confident drive to the hoop resulting in a layup. Another Locke three tightened the game to 20–17. Beilein had recruited the sharp-shooting freshman before he chose Florida, and it looked like yet another spot-on evaluation as the guard eagerly stepped up in his first NCAA Tournament. A few moments later he made a turnaround jumper to pull Florida even at 21. A layup by Kevarrius Hayes put them up two and completed a 17–6 run for the Gators. Simpson and Matthews responded, ripping off a combined 6–0 spurt. The underdogs came down and made their sixth three of the evening, this time from Andrew Nembhard. Yet another talented freshman Gator, Nembhard was an Ontario native that had been playing with Ignas Brazdeikis since fifth grade. Now the two Canadians, who had started every single game for their teams, were matched up in an NCAA Tournament game.

Isaiah Livers soon made his first shot of the night—a three from the right corner, courtesy of a Simpson drive and dish. That basket sent the Wolverines to the locker room ahead 32–28. Michigan had largely outplayed the Gators in the first half but had been unable to pull away. They had gotten good looks, but only hit 4–13 from three-point land. On the other hand, Florida had shot 50 percent from long range despite ranking 225th in the nation in that category. The Wolverines hadn't allowed an opponent to make 10 three-pointers in a game all year, but Florida had already hit six. With a little regression to the mean, Michigan seemed poised to pull away in the second half. Charles Matthews, though, wasn't leaving anything to chance. His teammates gave him credit for an inspiring halftime speech that spurred them forward. "He just told us that it's all about winning and that's what we need to do right now and nothing else matters except winning,"[5] Brazdeikis shared.

The anticipated regression started immediately. Beilein dialed up a pick and pop on the first play of the second half in an effort to get Brazdeikis involved. Following his dunk to score the first points of the game, the freshman had missed his next five shots. After catching this feed from Simpson, he let it fly. The ball landed gently on the front rim and bounced back up in the air before eventually finding its way through to start the second half with a fortunate roll. It was the first sign of an evening-out of the three-point luck between the teams. Their next time down, Poole recognized a mismatch as guard KeVaughn Allen attempted to defend Teske. Poole made the entry pass that had proved so difficult in the Michigan State losses and Teske finished. The Wolverines' defense followed that up by forcing a Florida five-second violation on a baseline out-of-bounds play. With momentum at their back, Michigan headed to their end of the floor for another impressive possession. After the ball whipped around, Jordan Poole passed up a shot and instead sliced hard to the hoop and wound up getting three the old-fashioned way. After another Florida turnover, swaggy Poole returned with a step-back three completing a 14-0 Michigan run that put his team up 43-28.

Just as it appeared the Wolverines were ready to pull away, the Gators answered with their own 9-0 streak. Poole halted the run by once again drawing a foul while shooting a three. The game soon settled into the defensive slog that many had predicted; Michigan's defense consistently forced Florida into late shot-clock looks but, offensively, they were having trouble executing. Eli Brooks checked into the game and a minute later, he cut into the lane with confidence and put in a runner. At the other end, he charged in among the trees to rip away a defensive rebound and pushed the ball in transition, drawing a foul. When he returned to the bench, the Michigan faithful showed their appreciation.

With under nine minutes left, KeVaughn Allen finally got in on the action. Florida's leading scorer had been completely negated by Charles Matthews' elite defense. His shot narrowed the lead to 48-41 but Florida would get no closer. A few minutes later, Simpson thread the needle to a streaking Livers in transition who took off from the middle of the free throw lane and went right through Nembhard for a violent two-hand slam. The finish made its way onto SportsCenter's Top Ten Plays that evening and served as a capstone for the festivities. Livers had a few similar opportunities earlier in the year where he cocked back with one hand and lost control. In that instant, he was reminded of his wise coach's words. "Coach B said, 'Go up there and finish with two, and I guarantee you that it's going to go in,'" he said. "I went up, and I don't know how I thought about it in that moment, but I went up with two and just put the ball in the basket."[6] Development never stops; what appeared to be pure instinct was actually learned behavior.

As the buzzer sounded and "The Victors" played following the 64-49 victory, announcer Kevin Harlan stated, "Things are looking good for Michigan. They are heading to the Sweet 16 for the third straight year." Indeed, it was the Wolverines' fifth Sweet 16 appearance in seven years—an unprecedented level of success that no one could have imagined when Beilein first arrived in Ann Arbor.

After the hot-shooting first half, the Gators had indeed faded to a 3-14 second half from long distance. That regression fittingly left them within a percentage point of their season-average three-point percentage. Jalen Hudson had led them in scoring with a measly 11 points. Their total of 49 represented Florida's lowest scoring output of the season. Simpson had fallen a single point, rebound, and assist short of an NCAA Tournament triple-double and never once left the court. Jordan Poole had a resurgent 19 points on 4-9 shooting from three. For a player that had borne the brunt of the criticism for Michigan's losses to Michigan State, it was an important step back into good

Charles Matthews (1) closes in on Florida's Kevarrius Hayes as Zavier Simpson (3) rips the ball out of his hands. The Wolverines' defense led the team all season and held the Gators to just 49 points, their lowest output of the season (photograph by Patrick Barron).

graces. All that was left was the celebration Charles Matthews had asked his teammates to imagine at halftime. Jon Sanderson served as Beilein's fullback upon entry to the locker room and greeted a waiting Colin Castleton with a cup of water to the face. Castleton returned the favor to a trailing Beilein as everyone in the program joined in and left yet another locker room drenched with their revelry. "A shower like this makes all the sweat you put in with the guys supremely worth it,"[7] Luke Yaklich said afterwards.

The impressive defensive effort had made Florida into believers. "I can see why they're number one in college basketball for defense," Jalen Hudson said. "They were super solid. Everything we tried to run or the mistakes they made, they had to cover them so fast. And they had the seven-footer and even when you did get in the paint it was tough and he was blocking them."[8] Although the details varied from game to game, Michigan had been winning this way all year long. With a few exceptions, they hadn't spent their season running teams out of the gym with blowout victories. Their opponents generally hung within striking distance, but as the Wolverine defense constricted and the lead hit double digits it rarely returned. During the broadcast, CBS documented that Michigan had spent the second most time in the country ahead by 10. Fifteen other schools had larger average margins of victory, whereas Michigan just steadily forced its opponent to tap out.

Their two team captains had driven the team all year, and the first week of the NCAA Tournament was no exception. "[Simpson and Matthews] were just champions this week," Beilein said. "Believe me, we were all salty after our loss last Sunday in the championship game and that's a quick turnaround. Everybody was upset. That could've tore us apart. But it actually brought us together. That's great leadership."[9]

Seeing Zavier Simpson up close allowed Mike White to see what all the fuss was about. "It's hard to appreciate how good Zavier Simpson is on film," the Florida coach told the media after the game. "Incredibly impressed with his toughness, accountability, leadership, the way he barks at his teammates, the way they respond to him. The guy just doesn't make any mistakes. He is out there plugging away, playing the game, offensively and defensively—really, really good." The Michigan point guard really was a marvel to watch. He was one of the more impactful players in the country, but he did it in a most unconventional way. Offensively, he controlled every possession despite not being a classic scorer. While no such statistic is kept, he seemed like a good bet to lead the nation in the ratio of time with the ball in his hands divided by points per game. Once Michigan gained possession, he raced ahead at full speed before typically coming to a hard stop at the three-point line. That ability to shift gears, both physically and mentally, allowed him to probe the defense for weaknesses and blind spots. He was built strong and low to the ground and used those attributes to pivot and step through to make brilliant yet challenging passes into tight windows in the faces of double teams. The addition of his highly successful hook shot along with other creative finishes in his bag of tricks forced defenses to respect him enough as a scorer to open up the rest of Michigan's offense.

His teammates loved every minute of it. "His vision is ridiculous," Brazdeikis said. "It seems like he has eyes in the back of his head. I love playing with him."[10] After a sophomore season that displayed his free throw shooting as an exploitable weakness, his hard work and willingness to adopt new techniques transformed him into a player everyone wanted taking late game free throws. With 6:34 remaining against Florida and a seven-point lead, Simpson was fouled and went to the line for a one-and-one. In a situation that would have had Michigan fans reaching for the antacids a year before, Simpson calmly swished both ends, and Florida only scored four more points the rest of the way.

Defensively, Simpson challenged his teammates to match his desire every single day in practice. His technique was impeccable. Again, where some would see his small stature as a negative, he utilized it as a strength. His low center of gravity allowed him to get in front—and stay in front—of any matchup. He anticipated oncoming screens and leveraged his way around them whenever possible. As good as he was with his feet, he may have been even better with his hands. He seemingly showed his hands up high to the referees at all times, except for those moments when he suddenly ripped the ball away from a confused opponent. His incredible hand strength was never more on display than earlier in the season at Minnesota. Following one rebound by Daniel Oturu, Simpson snuck in and pounded the ball out so hard that the 6'11" 250-pounder had to be removed from the game with an arm injury.

If that wasn't enough, in between timeouts, Simpson could often be seen coaching up the referees on what he planned next. That they listened and engaged willingly only spoke to his tremendous basketball acumen along with an advanced level of emotional intelligence. Regardless of the statistical distribution at the end of a given game, he was Michigan's focal point at all times. As DeAndre Haynes put it, "When you've got a point guard like that, the sky's the limit."[11]

Chapter 31

Going Back to Cali

Much like the year before, it was on to California for the regional final, a fact not lost on Jordan Poole. "I'm just trying to get to some nice weather," Poole said. "It's been snow out there in Michigan. I'm not with it. Even Coach B said, 'Let's try to find a way to get to California.'"[1] And just like the year before, they were joined by Gonzaga and Florida State and their opponent was a team from Texas—this time, the Texas Tech Red Raiders. Their head coach, Chris Beard, had served as an assistant at the university under Bob Knight and considered that period his formative experience as a coach. From there he had lived the life of a basketball vagabond, coaching in a low-budget semi-pro league for a season before jumping to McMurry University, and then to Angelo State, Arkansas Little-Rock, and finally settling in Lubbock, Texas.

There he had built a roster in his image with a group of well-traveled and often underappreciated players who fit into Beard's aggressive defensive system. Two of his starters, Matt Mooney and Tariq Owens, were graduate transfers at their third college. Mooney, the point guard, had accepted the only scholarship offer he got out of high school and went to Air Force. He soon moved on from there to South Dakota and became a coveted graduate transfer option for many programs across the country after the 2017-18 season. Among those was a certain program in Ann Arbor. "I think I'm going to give Michigan a serious look,"[2] Mooney said at the time. Owens, a bouncy beanpole of a center, had started at Tennessee, before transferring to St. John's, and ultimately completing his journey with Beard. Shooting guard Davide Moretti had taken the path perhaps never traveled, growing up in Bologna, Italy and moving to Lubbock, Texas, for his college years. And Beard's best player was sophomore Jarrett Culver, a local kid who had been severely underrated in the recruiting process. After registering as the 312th ranked player in his class, Culver was being projected by many as a lottery pick after the season. Beard had gotten the underappreciated group to band together and buy in to his "no middle" defensive scheme, which naturally prioritized keeping the ball out of the middle of the floor. On-ball defenders funneled the ball to the wings and baselines, where help was waiting. From there, they were able to use their length and aggressiveness to force turnovers, registering among the best in the country in that category. It was a very different defensive scheme than what Michigan ran, but the results were similar: the two programs had traded the top spot in defensive efficiency at various points throughout the season.

With the pairing of two elite defensive teams, most were expecting a hard-fought, low-scoring game that would appear ugly to the casual fan. For much of the first half, it wasn't just them that found it ugly. The late-night start was repeatedly pushed back as earlier games ran late and the Honda Center dealt with a power outage. Once the game began, CBS struggled to connect their audio feed, so viewers were subjected to the in-studio team awkwardly narrating the action from thousands of miles away. There weren't many baskets for them to speak about, and by the time the audio feed from the arena was restored at the first media timeout, Michigan had already turned the ball over three times—but did have four of the measly six points scored. They added their fourth turnover on their next possession as Brazdeikis threw it into traffic to a rolling Teske. Ironically the talented freshman had rarely passed all season, and it was the type of dish that would have been wide open against less active opponents. Michigan's defense locked up Texas Tech at the other end, forcing a Culver air-ball and a 24-second shot clock violation. Jon Teske got to work on the offensive glass, gathering two boards on the same possession and each time dishing out to a wide-open shooter—but neither Eli Brooks nor Brazdeikis could cash in. Teske was undeterred and sprinted back on defense to provide help to Brooks and block Deshawn Corprew's attempt. One more sprint to the other end immediately ensued, and Teske was fouled as Simpson threw an alley-oop up to him. The big man was visibly and understandably winded after this tremendous display of effort, and Beilein subbed in Colin Castleton to give him a quick breather. By the time the second media timeout rolled around, only six more points had been scored and the game was tied. Officially a slog, it continued unabated as both teams combined to go five for their first 29 and 0–8 from three. Michigan had six turnovers against just three field goals. For once, a Jordan Poole step-back three didn't seem like such a bad option, but that didn't go in either. Moretti soon hit the game's first three-pointer, putting Texas Tech up 13–8. Given the style of play, what would ordinarily seem to be an easily overcome deficit loomed much larger.

Unlike Michigan's defensive principle of limiting opponents' three-point attempts, Texas Tech's aggressive pursuit of turnovers with help defense meant shooters were often open when offenses rotated the basketball. As a result, they finished the year 241st in the country at limiting three-point attempts. Once those threes went up though, their opponents connected at the 12th worst rate nationally. Although there is limited analytic evidence that defenses can significantly affect three-point shooting percentage, Texas Tech had ridden that trait to their defensive success. Against Michigan, that same trend frustratingly continued. The Wolverines certainly weren't the greatest three-point shooting team, but their core players were more than capable of knocking down open looks. Most of their nine first-half attempts were good looks at the rim, but they couldn't get a single one to fall through. A few of them looked halfway down before popping back out. When Matt Mooney hit an absurd fade-away three off the backboard from the corner as the shot clock expired to go up 18–12, it was clear that good fortune from distance was firmly on the Red Raiders' side. A late four-point run with baskets by Moretti and Culver ended the half, and Michigan's struggling offense stared uncomfortably at the 24–16 scoreboard. Their 16 points were the lowest first-half output in NCAA Tournament history.

The second half got off to an inauspicious start as Teske missed two free throws after getting hacked by Norense Odiase, and Matt Mooney hit a pull-up in the lane. It felt like if Michigan could get just one three to go through, the offense could play more freely. But instead Charles Matthews air-balled an attempt, and Moretti came down and sunk his own to go ahead 29–16. Brazdeikis had gotten stuck in rotation and froze up trying to decide whether to stay with a 30 percent three-point shooter in Culver or close out on the 46 percent shooter Moretti—he made the wrong decision. A sky-high alley-oop from Moretti to the high-flying Owens followed, and the Italian guard soon hit another three. The game was over shockingly early. "What really hurt us was the first four minutes [of the second half]," Beilein explained in his press conference. "We had two turnovers and two missed foul shots and they answered every time with a couple of threes and another basket. And all of the sudden an 8-point lead was a 16-point lead in seconds. We're a defensive team. We're not a great offensive team and coming back from that was going to be really hard." Even after Texas Tech had pulled away, the three-point shot still wouldn't fall for Michigan. Just like he had done the year before in a Sweet 16 game in California against a school from Texas, walk-on C.J. Baird hit a three in his one minute of play. The year before, that had been one of 14 threes that he and seven other teammates combined to make. In this one it was the only three Michigan made all night on 19 attempts.

While the 63–44 margin was a surprise, Michigan ultimately falling in the tournament due to a struggling offense was an understandable outcome. All year, teams that had been able to effectively switch screens on defense had stifled the Wolverines into isolation situations. It was the same formula

Michigan State had used. "We're not a great isolation team," Beilein said. "We're not a team that can score one-on-one. We need ball screens. We need things. And that's what they made us do all day is isolate us."[3] The lack of a reliable go-to scorer that could put the team on his back caught up to them. Early on in the season, Michigan's variety of leading scorers in any given game was espoused as a strength—but in reality it was ultimately a fatal flaw. And while some three-point luck was to blame, the game simply wasn't close enough to point to that. Against the best defenses they faced, the offense had bogged down. Their toughness, resilience, and unity could never be questioned, but ultimately this iteration of the Wolverines didn't have the offensive playmakers needed to win it all. That John Beilein managed to put together the 24th most efficient offense in the country with this group was a testament to his coaching and his players' ability to play as a team.

The disappointment ran deep, but a surprising sense of perspective provided a more reasonable view. "There's going to be a team that wins the NCAA Tournament," Jordan Poole said, "and everyone else is going to be in tears. So, right now, it's hard, it's tough. But in a couple days we'll look back at a team that had a 17–0 start, a Michigan record. Who does that? We had back-to-back 30-win seasons. That's amazing."[4] And he was right. The ability to feel such immense disappointment after a 30-win Sweet 16 season was the ultimate proof of just how far John Beilein's program had come. Their seven losses were the fewest in a season since the Fab Five era, and their 89 wins over three seasons was the most in any three-year period in school history. Texas Tech proved to be a great team, defeating Gonzaga and Michigan State and taking Virginia to overtime in the national championship game. The Red Raiders' final Adjusted Defensive Efficiency was the best ever recorded by Kenpom, dating back to 2002. It was the third straight year the team that ended Michigan's season went to the Final Four. John Beilein's crew finished the year as the 6th best team in the country according to Kenpom and the 4th best team according to Bart Torvik.

It was also a group of young men that the university and its fans could be proud of. Graduating senior Charles Matthews had left his legacy on the program as a player, but also as a person. "Charles has been a model of leadership and a model of who you want to be in society,"[5] C.J. Baird said about his veteran teammate. Unanimously respected throughout the program, he had rebounded from a challenging situation his freshman year at Kentucky and developed his game under Beilein's careful tutelage. Now having won 63 games in two seasons and soon to earn his degree, he was off to pursue his professional basketball dreams. In a statement released by the program, Matthews conveyed his gratitude: "I cannot express what Coach Beilein, the coaching staff, my teammates and everyone involved in the program means to me. I am here and in this position because of all of you. Thank you Michigan basketball!" In a devastating turn of events, Matthews tore his ACL while working out for the Boston Celtics and wound up going undrafted as a result. The injury occurred just as Matthews was drawing praise in NBA circles for his elite defense throughout the pre-draft process, and hopefully after a full recovery he will receive an NBA opportunity.

His fellow captain Zavier Simpson had matched Matthews' leadership with a more vocal style that commanded the respect of those around him. His dominant presence established expectations for everyone in the program. Rare to crack a smile, Michigan basketball may not have ever had a player so obsessed with winning. At the end of the season banquet, he was rightly awarded as the team's Most Valuable Player. And with his leadership and unique all-around game returning for his senior season, Simpson looks poised to become the program's all-time winningest player.

Simpson's pick and roll partner and fellow Ohioan, Jon Teske, will also return for the 2019-20 season. The two will likely run hundreds more ball-screens together. Although Teske entered college as a gentle giant, with his teammates and coaches' encouragement he transformed into a shot-blocking rim-runner that mimed bow-and-arrows after made three-pointers. Off the court he maintained his humble Midwestern nature, and deep down he was still the Big Sleep. When describing how he had utilized Michigan's team meditation sessions, he simply explained, "I love naps, so I kinda just take a nap."[6] With continued development, the potential for an All-Big Ten season loomed in his future.

The team's precocious freshman Ignas Brazdeikis had arrived in Ann Arbor on a mission and had delivered on all fronts. As the Big Ten Freshman of the Year, the team's leading scorer, and a player that never shied away from pressure situations, his season was everything John Beilein could have hoped for. As the coach explained, it was his work away from the limelight that really stood out. "He is an easy guy to coach. It's 'Yes, Coach' all the time. And he tries to make changes to try to get better. I love his growth. He actually came in this year as not a kid who you'd think was a shooter, and he wasn't. He was a driver. Now he's got a great mixture to both, rebounding, and the next step is to get him to be continuous on the floor."[7] That next step will take place away from Ann Arbor. Brazdeikis decided to move on to the NBA, becoming John Beilein's first ever one-and-done player, and was selected 47th overall by the New York Knicks. Never one to shy away from the spotlight, Brazdeikis should be right at home in Madison Square Garden.

Jordan Poole made a similar decision shortly after Michigan's season ended. As arguably the most naturally talented player on the roster, the 19-year-old certainly offers the potential that NBA teams covet. Perhaps it was that potential combined with his often-iffy shot selection that caused Poole to draw the ire of frustrated Michigan fans when things didn't go well.

As a result, his legacy at Michigan feels a bit incomplete. But like Matthews, Poole also won 63 games in his only two seasons—nobody had ever won more over a two-year stretch in program history. He also gave the program one of its most memorable moments with his buzzer-beating three against Houston in 2018. The Golden State Warriors recognized Poole's upside, and selected him 28th overall—making him the eighth first-round pick to play under John Beilein at Michigan. For a young shooting guard that likes to launch from distance, Poole couldn't have found himself a better organizational fit.

His close friend Isaiah Livers would be sticking around and was assured of moving back into the starting lineup. Livers had steadily grown over the course of his two seasons and seemed poised to take a leap into a breakout junior campaign. After his runaway train dunk on Florida, NBA draft analyst Sam Vecenie tweeted, "God I'm going to have to pay attention to Isaiah Livers as a real NBA prospect next year, aren't I?" Indeed, that seems quite likely. Most importantly, with Livers, Simpson, and Teske leading the way, Michigan basketball's leadership and culture is in good hands moving forward.

Chapter 32

The End of the Beilein Era

For the second straight year, a national accolade was bestowed upon Beilein at the conclusion of the season. At the Final Four, he was aptly honored with the John Wooden "Keys to Life" Award, which was "presented annually to a member of the college or professional basketball community who lives out qualities exemplified by Coach Wooden; outstanding character, integrity, and leadership on the court, in the work place, in the home, and in the community." Fittingly, Austin Hatch presented him with the award. On hand to pay their respects were not just his current staff, but also numerous former assistant coaches who were still grateful for the time spent learning underneath their mentor.

John Beilein and staff had built something truly special at Michigan by bringing in the right people and teaching them the right lessons about basketball and about life. Saddi Washington explained the secret. "The culture keeps repeating," he said. "Seniors graduate, coaches take other jobs, players go pro.... But the culture never graduates."[1] For all his acumen as an evaluator, a developer, and a brilliant offensive mind, John Beilein's real genius lay in his ability to get individuals to place their team ahead of themselves and to simply focus on doing the next right thing.

Saddi Washington was not the only one to notice Beilein's skill as a culture builder. In May, the Cleveland Cavaliers made the shocking announcement that they had hired John Beilein as their new head coach. In a press release, Cavaliers GM Koby Altman stated: "John is one of the most accomplished and innovative basketball minds and leaders in the entire game. He has a unique ability to create an outstanding culture that will promote the development of young players and provide a solid structure to the entire program; not to mention the fact that John Beilein wins everywhere he goes." Cleveland, a young team in the midst of a rebuild, prioritized development in their hunt for a new head coach, as well as the ability to be a "culture-driver."

Beilein is clearly established among the best coaches in the world in those categories. His close relationship to Cleveland Assistant GM Mike Gansey—a former player at West Virginia and close family friend who he considered to be like a son—provided added comfort for both sides in the new alliance.

Many had assumed that after withdrawing his name from consideration for the Pistons job the year before, Beilein would finish out his career in Ann Arbor. At 66 years old—with a long history of success behind him and what essentially amounted to a lucrative lifetime contract at Michigan—why would he ever leave? But that assumption ignored the evidence of what drove Beilein his entire career. He has always been a builder—a coach intrigued by the challenges presented by new opportunities. "When people said—why are you going to Canisius? Why are you going to Richmond? Why are you going to West Virginia? Those are all like train wrecks," Beilein had explained the summer before. "And I said, that's why I'm going. Tell me I can't do something and I'm about to do it."[2] The situation in Ann Arbor appeared dire when Beilein first arrived, but he saw a chance to craft something great—after 12 seasons, he unequivocally had. Now he sees something similar in Cleveland.

As a master in player development, his skillset historically seemed better suited to the college game. But as the NBA shifted to become a younger and younger league, executives had begun to embrace the need for development at the professional level. With the most talented players exiting the college game at their earliest opportunity, the NBA was a chance for Beilein to develop players over a longer duration than the year or two that was becoming all too common at the college level. He pointed out that dilemma at the end of season banquet before leaving Michigan: "It's a sad state of things when you say, oh, I hope he's not too good as a freshman."[3]

At his introductory press conference in Cleveland, he expressed excitement that his time spent on growing his players' games was no longer limited by NCAA restrictions. "I'm so excited about the possibility of working with them in the off-season without limitations," he said. "I'm not limited by hours." All the extra components of being a college coach—monitoring grades, managing a roster, and adhering to the peculiar NCAA rulebook—took away from what he loved best. "That's what makes me tick—being on that floor with those guys, being in a film session with them, and watching them grow as players," he shared.

The latest developments in college basketball couldn't be ignored in his decision either. The FBI's recent investigation into the sport revealed rampant cheating across the college basketball landscape. Wiretap recordings caught both Sean Miller at Arizona and Will Wade at LSU involved in providing financial payments to players. Each coach received a mild reprimand before being reinstated and resuming their signing of top-ranked recruits. Although the push to tweak the amateur model and provide financial compensation to players is rightfully gaining steam, Beilein has always adhered to the rules as they are written. His high ethical standards left him at a distinct disadvantage; with coaches paying no price for brazenly breaking the rules, his frustration with the system could only have grown. In an effort to empower the players in lieu of financial compensation, the NCAA is now allowing them to have formal relationships with agents and has eased the process of transferring between schools. Those developments are certainly positives for the players but have made roster management a painful year-round exercise. The classy Beilein is hesitant to delve into these issues, but his comments suggest it was at least a consideration. "I believe college basketball is going through a transition right now and needs to really evaluate itself and what's best for the sport," he told the Cleveland media when questioned about it.

Beilein's success in Cleveland will be largely dependent on the type of roster the front office can provide him with. Young players he will inherit such as 19-year-old Darius Garland, 20-year-old Collin Sexton, 22-year-old Ante Zizic, 24-year-old Cedi Osman, and 26-year-old Larry Nance, Jr., offer varying levels of promise, but much more talent will be needed to eventually turn things around. Undoubtedly, Beilein will help everyone in a Cleveland Cavaliers uniform grow into a better player. It's what he has done his whole career, and it's why many of his coaching peers were thrilled for him. "I have quite a few contacts in the NBA, head coaches that I know fairly well, and they all reached out and said you're going to love it," Beilein said. "Brad Stevens said the NBA just got better today. It's just really complimentary things."[4]

While the NBA may have improved, college basketball lost one of its best. The Michigan community felt a sense of sadness over his departure, encapsulated well by Jordan Morgan: "Michigan didn't just lose a basketball coach. It lost a role model, a key figure, somebody that really epitomized what Michigan is about. He was more than a basketball coach and that's why I think everybody is so disappointed not in him but in losing him. That will be hard to replace."[5]

Stepping into his void is former Michigan star Juwan Howard. After leaving Ann Arbor following his junior year, Howard was the 5th pick in the NBA draft. He spent his rookie season completing correspondence courses to earn his degree. At the end of his 19-year career, he won two NBA championships with the Miami Heat and immediately transitioned into an assistant coach with the organization. After six seasons in that role, he garnered plaudits throughout the industry for his work developing young Heat players and earned multiple interviews for NBA head coaching vacancies. Once the opening at Michigan presented itself, he was an obvious candidate. While Howard and Beilein come from vastly different backgrounds, both are universally respected and have a passion for development. Hopefully Howard can build on his predecessor's success while uniting the program's past and present.

Once the shock of Beilein's departure subsided, nobody could rightfully begrudge his decision. He had wholeheartedly committed to Michigan for 12 seasons and, as he had done at every single coaching stop in his career, enjoyed unprecedented success. Two national championship games, two Big Ten regular season titles, two Big Ten Tournament championships, eight NBA first-round picks, and 829 wins, all achieved in a manner that embodied the University's motto—"The Leaders and the Best."

His time in Ann Arbor was a perfect match between coach and university. He fit in just as easily with his fellow teachers as he did with his fellow coaches, and his adherence to the rule book and constantly doing the next right thing endeared him to an incredibly proud alumni base and student body. His constant desire to grow and evolve, along with the perspective gained from some challenging life events make him an inspiration for others. He will continue to mentor and teach young men to become better basketball players, better teammates, and better people—it just won't be at the University of Michigan.

Given Beilein's obsession with incremental improvement and his desire to see the very best in his players, it is only natural that he applies the same standard to his own life. As he climbed from high school through every rung of college basketball and transformed passed over recruits into first-round draft picks, Beilein showed an inability to remain in stasis. It's been an amazing journey that started from humble beginnings, and while the stage has continually gotten bigger, the humility has always remained. The safe bet is that he will continue to slowly but surely outperform expectations in the next stage of his career. It's a guarantee that he will continue to do the next right thing, and that he will teach his players to as well. For that reason, even after moving on, the larger Michigan family will always be proud to call John Beilein their coach.

Chapter Notes

Preface

1. Mitch Albom, "Why'd John Beilein leave Michigan? There's a simple reason," *Detroit Free Press*, May 14, 2019, https://www.freep.com/story/sports/columnists/mitch-albom/2019/05/14/john-beilein-cleveland-cavaliers-michigan-basketball-mitch-albom/1189468001//.

Chapter 1

1. Moe Wagner, "Still Alive," *The Players' Tribune*, March 23, 2017, https://www.theplayerstribune.com/en-us/articles/moritz-wagner-michigan-basketball-airplane.
2. "Men of March: John Beilein," *CBS Sports Network*, aired January 10, 2018.
3. Moe Wagner, "Still Alive," *The Players' Tribune*, March 23, 2017, https://www.theplayerstribune.com/en-us/articles/moritz-wagner-michigan-basketball-airplane.
4. "Men of March: John Beilein," *CBS Sports Network*, aired January 10, 2018.
5. Brendan Quinn, "This is John Beilein," MLive.com, November 12, 2014, https://www.mlive.com/john-beilein/.
6. Dan Wetzel, "Michigan's John Beilein a descendant of soldiers that inspired 'Saving Private Ryan,'" *Yahoo! Sports*, April 2, 2013, https://sports.yahoo.com/news/ncaab—michigan-s-john-beilein-a-descendant-of-soldiers-that-inspired—saving-private-ryan—205604686.html.
7. "NCAA Men's Final Four," ASAP Sports Transcripts, April 7, 2013, http://www.asapsports.com/show_interview.php?id=88266.
8. Brendan Quinn, "This is John Beilein," MLive.com, November 12, 2014, https://www.mlive.com/john-beilein/.
9. Steve Kornacki, "So Far, So Fast: How Beilein Took U-M from Obscurity to Title Game in Three Months," Mgoblue.com, April 1, 2018, https://mgoblue.com/news/2018/4/1/mens-basketball-so-far-so-fast-how-beilein-took-u-m-from-obscurity-to-title-game-in-three-months.aspx?path=mbball.
10. "NCAA Men's 2nd and 3rd Rounds: Auburn Hills," ASAP Sports Transcripts, March 22, 2013, http://www.asapsports.com/show_interview.php?id=87780.
11. Tim Keown, "Director's Cut," *ESPN*, March 5, 2013, http://www.espn.com/mens-college-basketball/story/_/id/9014486/michigan-wolverines-head-coach-john-beilein-never-too-prepared-espn-magazine.
12. "NCAA Men's Final Four," ASAP Sports Transcripts, March 29, 2018, http://www.asapsports.com/show_interview.php?id=138938.
13. "NCAA Men's Final Four," ASAP Sports Transcripts, April 1, 2013, http://www.asapsports.com/show_interview.php?id=88137.

14. "NCAA Men's Final Four," ASAP Sports Transcripts, April 7, 2013, http://www.asapsports.com/show_interview.php?id=88266.
   15. Associated Press, "Beilein gets $1.3M per season from Michigan," *ESPN*, April 6, 2007, http://www.espn.com/mens-college-basketball/news/story?id=2825254.
   16. John Niyo, "Beilein, Michigan take high road to Final Four," *The Detroit News*, March 25, 2018, https://www.detroitnews.com/story/sports/columnists/john-niyo/2018/03/25/niyo-beilein-um-take-high-road-final-four/33271509/.
   17. Adrian Wojnarowski, "David Griffin," *The Woj Pod*, April 4, 2018, https://art19.com/shows/thewojpod/episodes/e4455054-9488-41ca-9a8e-fd209139cbba.
   18. "NCAA Men's Regional Semi-Finals and Finals: Los Angeles," ASAP Sports Transcripts, March 23, 2018, http://www.asapsports.com/show_interview.php?id=138752.
   19. "NCAA Men's 2nd and 3rd Rounds: Auburn Hills," ASAP Sports Transcripts, March 22, 2013, http://www.asapsports.com/show_interview.php?id=87780.
   20. "NCAA Men's Regional Semi-Finals and Finals: Los Angeles," ASAP Sports Transcripts, March 22, 2018, http://www.asapsports.com/show_interview.php?id=138721.
   21. "Michigan head coach John Beilein addresses the media (6/26)," YouTube Video, 30:57, posted by "Isaiah Hole," June 26, 2018, https://www.youtube.com/watch?v=kmaTaq_8R0E.
   22. "NCAA Men's 1st and 2nd Rounds: Wichita," ASAP Sports Transcripts, March 16, 2018, http://www.asapsports.com/show_interview.php?id=138367.
   23. Shawn Windsor, "U-M's Beilein a teacher looking to learn new ideas," *Detroit Free Press*, October 3, 2015, https://www.freep.com/story/sports/college/university-michigan/wolverines/2015/10/03/michigan-wolverines-john-beilein-teacher/73270532/.
   24. Associated Press, "Michigan's John Beilein: Still coaching thanks to ability to adapt," March 12, 2018, *ESPN*, http://www.espn.com/mens-college-basketball/story/_/id/22738209/john-beilein-michigan-wolverines-cites-ability-adapt-key-longevity.
   25. "NCAA Men's Regional Semi-Finals and Finals: Los Angeles," ASAP Sports Transcripts, March 24, 2018, http://www.asapsports.com/show_interview.php?id=138853.
   26. "Men of March: John Beilein," *CBS Sports Network*, aired January 10, 2018.
   27. Adrian Wojnarowski, "David Griffin," *The Woj Pod*, April 4, 2018, https://art19.com/shows/thewojpod/episodes/e4455054-9488-41ca-9a8e-fd209139cbba.
   28. Brendan Quinn, "Does John Beilein make sense for the Pistons? Do the Pistons make sense for John Beilein?" *The Athletic*, June 1, 2018, https://theathletic.com/377257/2018/06/01/does-john-beilein-make-sense-for-the-pistons-do-the-pistons-make-sense-for-john-beilein/.
   29. Rod Beard, "Celtics' Brad Stevens lauds UM's John Beilein as 'one of the best,'" *The Detroit News*, June 5, 2018, https://www.detroitnews.com/story/sports/college/university-michigan/2018/06/05/boston-celtics-brad-stevens-john-beilein-one-best/674522002/.
   30. Nick Baumgardner, "The John Beilein Episode," *The Michigan Rant*, June 4, 2018, https://player.fm/series/the-michigan-rant/the-michigan-rant-the-john-beilein-episode.
   31. Brendan Quinn, "Michigan AD Warde Manuel says he never gave any thought to John Beilein's job security," MLive.com, March 18, 2017, https://www.mlive.com/wolverines/index.ssf/2017/03/michigan_ad_warde_manuel_says.html.

Chapter 2

   1. "Big Ten Elite: 1989 Michigan Basketball," *Big Ten Network*, 45:01, aired January 14, 2014, https://www.btn2go.com/video/big-ten-elite-1989-michigan-basketball.

Chapter 3

   1. Nick Baumgardner, "Underdogs forever: Zack Novak, Stu Douglass at core of Michigan basketball resurgence," *The Ann Arbor News*, February 23, 2012, http://www.annarbor.com/sports/um-basketball/underdogs-forever-zack-novak-stu-douglass-at-core-of-michigan-basketball-resurgence/.

Notes—Chapter 4

2. Michael Rothstein, "Novak, Douglass Lead Revival," *ESPN*, February 24, 2012, www.espn.com/colleges/michigan/basketball/story/_/id/7609316/zack-novak-stu-douglass-foundation-michigan-wolverines-revival.
3. Josh Bartelstein, "We On: An Inside Look at Michigan's Final Four Run" (Blog Into Book, 2015), Foreword by Zack Novak, https://www.amazon.com/We-Inside-Michigan-Basketballs-Final-ebook/dp/B00EZCLA76.
4. Max Marcovitch, "For Beilein, All That's Left Is a Title," *The Michigan Daily*, April 15, 2018, www.michigandaily.com/section/basketball/john-beilein-michigan-coach-legacy-culture.
5. B.R.J O'Donnell, "Coaching Players for Life," *The Atlantic*, August 21, 2017, www.theatlantic.com/business/archive/2017/08/beilein-mentoring/536994/.
6. Josh Bartelstein, "We On: An Inside Look at Michigan's Final Four Run" (Blog Into Book, 2015), Inside This Book, https://www.amazon.com/We-Inside-Michigan-Basketballs-Final-ebook/dp/B00EZCLA76.
7. B.R.J O'Donnell, "Coaching Players for Life," *The Atlantic*, August 21, 2017, www.theatlantic.com/business/archive/2017/08/beilein-mentoring/536994/.
8. Diamond Leung, "John Beilein Explains Michigan's Five Core Values, Forming UPAID Acronym," MLive.com, August 17, 2013, www.mlive.com/wolverines/index.ssf/2013/08/john_beilein_explains_michigan.html.
9. Brian Cook, "The Aneurysm of Leadership," *Mgoblog*, January 28, 2011, www.mgoblog.com/content/aneurysm-leadership.
10. Nick Baumgardner, "A Program Turning Point? Zack Novak Reflects on His Signature Moment in East Lansing," *The Ann Arbor News*, February 4, 2012, www.annarbor.com/sports/um-basketball/a-program-turning-point-zack-novak-remembers-his-signature-moment-in-east-lansing/.
11. "Big Ten Elite: 2013 Michigan Basketball," *Big Ten Network*, 50:11, aired January 2015, www.btn2go.com/video/big-ten-elite-2013-michigan-basketball.
12. Ibid.
13. "NCAA Men's Final Four," ASAP Sports Transcripts, April 7, 2013, http://www.asapsports.com/show_interview.php?id=88266.
14. Michael Rothstein, "Novak, Douglass Lead Revival," *ESPN*, February 24, 2012, www.espn.com/colleges/michigan/basketball/story/_/id/7609316/zack-novak-stu-douglass-foundation-michigan-wolverines-revival.
15. Ibid.
16. Jim Carty, "The Un-Fab Two—A Tale of Two Hoosiers," *Ann Arbor Observer*, January 2012, annarborobserver.com/articles/the_un-fab_two.html#.W7eveWhKjid.

Chapter 4

1. "NCAA Men's Regional Semi-Finals and Finals: Indianapolis," ASAP Sports Transcripts, March 27, 2014, http://www.asapsports.com/show_interview.php?id=97626.
2. Amy Whitesall, "Inside Athletics: On the Recruiting Trail," *Michigan Alumnus*, 2013, alumnus.alumni.umich.edu/inside-athletics-on-the-recruiting-trail/.
3. Max Marcovitch, "For Beilein, All That's Left Is a Title," *The Michigan Daily*, April 15, 2018, www.michigandaily.com/section/basketball/john-beilein-michigan-coach-legacy-culture.
4. "NCAA Men's Final Four," ASAP Sports Transcripts, April 1, 2018, http://www.asapsports.com/show_interview.php?id=139019.
5. "NCAA Men's Final Four," ASAP Sports Transcripts, April 7, 2013, http://www.asapsports.com/show_interview.php?id=88266.
6. "NCAA Men's Final Four," ASAP Sports Transcripts, March 30, 2018, http://www.asapsports.com/show_interview.php?id=138971.
7. "NCAA Men's Regional Semi-Finals and Finals: Indianapolis," ASAP Sports Transcripts, March 29, 2014, http://www.asapsports.com/show_interview.php?id=97718.

8. Gary Parrish, "Is John Beilein the Best at Turning Lowly Recruits into Lottery Picks?" CBSSports.com, April 6, 2017, www.cbssports.com/college-basketball/news/is-john-beilein-the-best-at-turning-lowly-recruits-into-lottery-picks/.
9. Sam Webb, "Former Michigan Assistant has Seen Major Changes in Beilein," 247sports.com, March 30, 2018, https://247sports.com/college/michigan/Article/John-Mahoney-assisted-John-Beilein-during-his-first-three-years-at-Michigan-and-has-noticed-his-former-boss-adapting-with-the-times-116856224/.
10. "Big Ten Elite: 2013 Michigan Basketball," *Big Ten Network*, 50:11, aired January 2015, www.btn2go.com/video/big-ten-elite-2013-michigan-basketball.
11. Gary Parrish, "Is John Beilein the Best at Turning Lowly Recruits into Lottery Picks?" CBSSports.com, April 6, 2017, www.cbssports.com/college-basketball/news/is-john-beilein-the-best-at-turning-lowly-recruits-into-lottery-picks/.
12. "NCAA Men's Regional Semi-Finals and Finals: Indianapolis," ASAP Sports Transcripts, March 29, 2014, http://www.asapsports.com/show_interview.php?id=97718.
13. "Big Ten Elite: 2013 Michigan Basketball," *Big Ten Network*, 50:11, aired January 2015, www.btn2go.com/video/big-ten-elite-2013-michigan-basketball.

Chapter 5

1. "MAN 5010 B 2.8 Every Role Matters in Teams," Vimeo Video, 2:04, posted by "Massey Services," May 16, 2018, vimeo.com/270187962.
2. "NCAA Men's 2nd and 3rd Rounds: Auburn Hills," ASAP Sports Transcripts, March 23, 2013, http://www.asapsports.com/show_interview.php?id=87871.
3. Nick Baumgardner, "Michigan's John Beilein Celebrates Program Benchmark with Family in 'Knock down, Drag out Party'," MLive.com, March 27, 2013, www.mlive.com/wolverines/index.ssf/2013/03/michigans_john_beilein_celebra.html.
4. "NCAA Men's Regional Semi-Finals and Finals: Arlington," ASAP Sports Transcripts, March, 29, 2013, http://www.asapsports.com/show_interview.php?id=88074.
5. *Ibid.*
6. "NCAA Men's Final Four," ASAP Sports Transcripts, April 4, 2013, http://www.asapsports.com/show_interview.php?id=88182.
7. "NCAA Men's 1st and 2nd Rounds: Wichita," ASAP Sports Transcripts, March 15, 2018, http://www.asapsports.com/show_interview.php?id=138317.
8. Nick Baumgardner, "Michigan's Jordan Morgan Has His Redemption Moment—Twice—in Final Four Win over Syracuse," MLive.com, April 8, 2013, www.mlive.com/wolverines/index.ssf/2013/04/michigans_jordan_morgan_has_hi.html.
9. "Big Ten Elite: 2013 Michigan Basketball," *Big Ten Network*, 50:11, aired January 2015, www.btn2go.com/video/big-ten-elite-2013-michigan-basketball.
10. "NCAA Men's Final Four," ASAP Sports Transcripts, April 8, 2013, http://www.asapsports.com/show_interview.php?id=88297.
11. "Big Ten Elite: 2013 Michigan Basketball," *Big Ten Network*, 50:11, aired January 2015, www.btn2go.com/video/big-ten-elite-2013-michigan-basketball.
12. Nicole Auerbach, "After Loss, Michigan Appreciates Past, Relishes Future," *USA Today*, April 9, 2013, www.usatoday.com/story/sports/ncaab/2013/04/09/championship-michigan-behind-the-scenes/2066245/.
13. "NCAA Men's Final Four," ASAP Sports Transcripts, April 8, 2013, http://www.asapsports.com/show_interview.php?id=88297.
14. "Big Ten Elite: 2013 Michigan Basketball," *Big Ten Network*, 50:11, aired January 2015, www.btn2go.com/video/big-ten-elite-2013-michigan-basketball.

Chapter 6

1. Adrian Wojnarowski, "David Griffin," *The Woj Pod*, April 4, 2018, https://art19.com/shows/thewojpod/episodes/e4455054-9488-41ca-9a8e-fd209139cbba.

2. Sam Webb, "Michigan B1G's Top Performing Bball Program; Recruits Noticing?" *247sports*, May 25, 2018, 247sports.com/college/michigan/Article/Over-the-last-six-seasons-no-program-in-the-Big-Ten-can-match-Michigans-on-court-and-draft-success-118513723/.

3. Brendan Quinn, "Old Faces, New Places: This Is Charles Matthews' Moment, Again," *The Athletic*, November 3, 2017, theathletic.com/143050/2017/11/03/old-faces-new-places-this-is-charles-matthews-moment-again/.

4. "MAN 5010 D 4.13 Instilling a Learning Mindset," Vimeo Video, 1:23, posted by "Massey Services," July 29, 2018, vimeo.com/270200339.

5. "Coach John Beilein—It's Worth It (Narrow Way Café & Shop)," YouTube Video, 20:00, posted by "David Merritt," January 21, 2019, https://www.youtube.com/watch?v=pHuFqNil9Z0&t=2s.

6. Nick Baumgardner, "Michigan's Jaaron Simmons, Charles Matthews Learned System Together," *Detroit Free Press*, March 17, 2018, www.freep.com/story/sports/college/university-michigan/wolverines/2018/03/17/michigan-basketball-ncaa-tournament-charles-matthews-jaaron-simmons/433901002/.

7. "Coach John Beilein—It's Worth It (Narrow Way Café & Shop)," YouTube Video, 20:00, posted by "David Merritt," January 21, 2019, https://www.youtube.com/watch?v=pHuFqNil9Z0&t=2s.

8. Rod Beard, "Michigan's Beilein Still Coaching up His Players," *The Detroit News*, February 10, 2015, www.detroitnews.com/story/sports/college/university-michigan/2015/02/09/michigans-beilein-still-coaching-players/23148519/.

9. Gary Parrish, "Is John Beilein the Best at Turning Lowly Recruits into Lottery Picks?" CBSSports.com, April 6, 2017, www.cbssports.com/college-basketball/news/is-john-beilein-the-best-at-turning-lowly-recruits-into-lottery-picks/.

10. Everett Cook, "The Architect: How University of Michigan's Jon Sanderson Builds Better Basketball Players," *STACK*, March 13, 2014, www.stack.com/a/jon-sanderson.

11. Mark Snyder, "Michigan's Jon Sanderson, John Beilein Development Boosts NBA Interest," *Detroit Free Press*, March 21, 2017, www.freep.com/story/sports/college/university-michigan/wolverines/2017/03/21/michigan-wolverines-basketball-jon-sanderson-john-beilein-nba-draft/99426592/.

12. Ibid.

13. Rod Beard, "Michigan's Beilein Still Coaching up His Players," *The Detroit News*, February 10, 2015, www.detroitnews.com/story/sports/college/university-michigan/2015/02/09/michigans-beilein-still-coaching-players/23148519/.

14. Jeremy Fallis, "Mental Health Wellness Plays a Role in Beilein's Championship Success," *Athletes Connected*, March 7, 2018, athletesconnected.umich.edu/mental-health-wellness-plays-a-role-in-beileins-championship-success/.

15. Tim Keown, "Director's Cut," *ESPN*, March 5, 2013, http://www.espn.com/mens-college-basketball/story/_/id/9014486/michigan-wolverines-head-coach-john-beilein-never-too-prepared-espn-magazine.

16. John Niyo, "Beilein, Michigan take high road to Final Four," *The Detroit News*, March 25, 2018, https://www.detroitnews.com/story/sports/columnists/john-niyo/2018/03/25/niyo-beilein-um-take-high-road-final-four/33271509/.

17. Nick Baumgardner, "Michigan's NBA Prospects Seeking Advice from Draft Board, John Beilein Being 'Proactive' with Process," MLive.com, April 11, 2013, www.mlive.com/wolverines/index.ssf/2013/04/michigan_nba_prospects_seeking.html.

18. B.R.J O'Donnell, "Coaching Players for Life," *The Atlantic*, August 21, 2017, www.theatlantic.com/business/archive/2017/08/beilein-mentoring/536694/.

19. Nick Baumgardner, "John Beilein's Two First Round Picks a Major Recruiting Chip, Big Moment for Michigan Basketball," MLive.com, June 28, 2013, https://www.mlive.com/wolverines/index.ssf/2013/06/column_john_beileins_two_first.html.

20. "McGary, Robinson to Continue Collegiate Careers at Michigan," Mgoblue.com, April 18, 2013, https://mgoblue.com/news/2013/4/18/McGary_Robinson_to_Continue_Collegiate_Careers_at_Michigan.aspx?path=mbball.

21. "NCAA Men's Final Four," ASAP Sports Transcripts, April 2, 2018, http://www.asapsports.com/show_interview.php?id=139039.

Chapter 7

1. David Fox, "Michigan's Nik Stauskas, Texas' Isaiah Taylor earn weekly honors," *Athlon Sports*, January 27, 2014, https://athlonsports.com/college-basketball/michigans-nik-stauskas-texas-isaiah-taylor-earn-weekly-honors.
2. Ace Anbender, "The All-Beilein Teams: Giants," *Mgoblog*, June 10, 2017, www.mgoblog.com/content/all-beilein-teams-giants.
3. "NCAA Men's 2nd and 3rd Rounds: Milwaukee," ASAP Sports Transcripts, March 22, 2014, http://www.asapsports.com/show_interview.php?id=97458.

Chapter 8

1. Jeremy Allen, "Read President Obama's full speech from his University of Michigan visit," MLive.com, April 2, 2014, https://www.mlive.com/news/ann-arbor/2014/04/read_president_obamas_full_spe.html.
2. Daniel Feldman, "John Beilein's Refusal to Leave," *The Michigan Daily*, June 27, 2014, www.michigandaily.com/sports/daniel-feldman-john-beileins-refusal-leave.
3. Brendan Quinn, "The Peculiar Story of Michigan Recruit Muhammad-Ali Abdur-Rahkman, Dave Rooney and the Phone Call That Changed Everything," MLive.com, May 10, 2015, www.mlive.com/wolverines/index.ssf/2014/04/the_peculiar_story_of_muhammad.html.
4. "NCAA Men's Final Four," ASAP Sports Transcripts, April 1, 2018, http://www.asapsports.com/show_interview.php?id=139019.
5. Steve Kornacki, "How Muhammad-Ali Abdur-Rahkman Got His Name and Got His Game," Mgoblue.com, March 16, 2018, mgoblue.com/news/2018/3/16/mens-basketball-kornacki-how-muhammad-ali-abdur-rahkman-got-his-name-and-got-his-game.aspx?path=mbball.
6. Ibid.
7. Tim Layden, "The Transfer Story of Michigan's Duncan Robinson Is Not Your Average One," SI.com, March 29, 2018, www.si.com/college-basketball/2018/03/29/michigan-duncan-robinson-roots-williams-college-final-four.
8. Ibid.
9. "NCAA Men's Final Four," ASAP Sports Transcripts, March 30, 2018, http://www.asapsports.com/show_interview.php?id=138971.
10. Tim Layden, "The Transfer Story of Michigan's Duncan Robinson Is Not Your Average One," SI.com, March 29, 2018, www.si.com/college-basketball/2018/03/29/michigan-duncan-robinson-roots-williams-college-final-four.
11. Brendan Quinn, "What Slump? Duncan Robinson and the Psychology of Makes vs. Misses," *The Athletic*, January 9, 2018, theathletic.com/207087/2018/01/09/what-slump-duncan-robinson-and-the-psychology-of-makes-vs-misses/.
12. Ibid.
13. James Hawkins, "Austin Hatch receives touching 'Senior Day' send-off," *The Detroit News*, February 18, 2018, https://www.detroitnews.com/story/sports/college/university-michigan/wolverines/2018/02/18/austin-hatch-receives-touching-senior-day-send/110587918/.
14. Steve Kornacki, "Austin Hatch: A Storybook Ending Achieved After Unimaginable Tragedy," Mgoblue.com, February 27, 2018, mgoblue.com/news/2018/2/27/mens-basketball-austin-hatch-a-storybook-ending-achieved-after-unimaginable-tragedy.aspx.
15. Dana O'Neil, "Austin Hatch Is an Uncommon Man," ESPN.com, February 9, 2015, www.espn.com/mens-college-basketball/story/_/id/12299896/michigan-wolverines-basketball-player-austin-hatch-survived-two-plane-crashes.

16. Steve Kornacki, "Austin Hatch: A Storybook Ending Achieved After Unimaginable Tragedy," Mgoblue.com, February 27, 2018, mgoblue.com/news/2018/2/27/mens-basketball-austin-hatch-a-storybook-ending-achieved-after-unimaginable-tragedy.aspx.

17. Ibid.

18. "Miraculous: The Austin Hatch Story—ESPN," YouTube Video, 16:06, posted by "Dan Arruda," September 7, 2016, www.youtube.com/watch?v=AmKUpj97ZB8.

19. Kyle Rowland, "Story of Michigan's Austin Hatch Remains an All-Time Account of Perseverance," *The Toledo Blade*, March 21, 2018, www.toledoblade.com/College/2018/03/21/Austin-Hatch-story-remains-an-all-time-account-of-perseverance.html.

20. Dana O'Neil, "Austin Hatch Is an Uncommon Man," ESPN.com, February 9, 2015, www.espn.com/mens-college-basketball/story/_/id/12299896/michigan-wolverines-basketball-player-austin-hatch-survived-two-plane-crashes.

21. "Miraculous: The Austin Hatch Story—ESPN," YouTube Video, 16:06, posted by "Dan Arruda," September 7, 2016, www.youtube.com/watch?v=AmKUpj97ZB8.

22. Steve Kornacki, "Austin Hatch: A Storybook Ending Achieved After Unimaginable Tragedy," Mgoblue.com, February 27, 2018, mgoblue.com/news/2018/2/27/mens-basketball-austin-hatch-a-storybook-ending-achieved-after-unimaginable-tragedy.aspx.

23. Ibid.

24. Tim Hackett, "Embraced by a Home Away from Home, Moritz Wagner Is Finally Ready for a New Challenge," SI.com, June 12, 2018, www.si.com/nba/2018/06/12/moritz-wagner-michigan-nba-draft-john-beilein-dirk-nowitzki.

25. Brendan Quinn, "How John Beilein Snuck off to Germany to Meet Moritz Wagner and 'Look Him in the Eye,'" MLive.com, June 14, 2015, www.mlive.com/wolverines/index.ssf/2015/06/moritz_wagner_john_beilein.html.

26. Brendan Quinn, "When Moe Wagner Met Michigan: How Chance, a Film Clip and an Email Changed Everything," MLive.com, March 16, 2017, www.mlive.com/wolverines/index.ssf/2017/03/when_moe_wagner_met_michigan_t.html.

27. Joel Anderson, "Moe Wagner's Michigan Career Really Is a Dream Come True," ESPN.com, April 1, 2018, www.espn.com/mens-college-basketball/story/_/id/22922995/ncaa-tournament-final-four-moe-wagner-michigan-wolverines-career-really-dream-come-true.

28. "NCAA Men's Regional Semi-Finals and Finals: Los Angeles," ASAP Sports Transcripts, March 23, 2018, http://www.asapsports.com/show_interview.php?id=138752.

29. Brendan Quinn, "Muscle and Willpower: Moritz Wagner Lifts Michigan to Verge of National Championship," *The Athletic*, April 1, 2018, theathletic.com/296043/2018/04/01/muscle-and-willpower-moritz-wagner-lifts-michigan-to-verge-of-national-championship/.

30. Ibid.

31. Joel Anderson, "Moe Wagner's Michigan Career Really Is a Dream Come True," ESPN.com, April 1, 2018, www.espn.com/mens-college-basketball/story/_/id/22922995/ncaa-tournament-final-four-moe-wagner-michigan-wolverines-career-really-dream-come-true.

32. "NCAA Men's First Four: Dayton," ASAP Sports Transcripts, March 16, 2016, http://www.asapsports.com/show_interview.php?id=117603.

33. Steve Kornacki, "The Time Has Come for Moe to Go Pro," Mgoblue.com, April 14, 2018, mgoblue.com/news/2018/4/14/mens-basketball-kornacki-the-time-has-come-for-moe-to-go-pro.aspx.

34. "NCAA Men's 1st and 2nd Rounds: Brooklyn," ASAP Sports Transcripts, March 18, 2016, http://www.asapsports.com/show_interview.php?id=117858.

Chapter 9

1. "NCAA Men's Regional Semi-Finals and Finals: Los Angeles," ASAP Sports Transcripts, March 24, 2018, http://www.asapsports.com/show_interview.php?id=138853.

2. Steve Kornacki, "What's New with Michigan Men's Basketball," Mgoblue.com, October 3, 2016, www.mgoblue.com/news/2016/10/3/Kornacki_What_s_New_with_Michigan_Men_s_Basketball.aspx?path=mbball.

3. Mark Snyder, "'White collar' Michigan defense struggles in 85–69 loss to Illinois," *Detroit Free Press*, January 11, 2017, https://www.freep.com/story/sports/college/university-michigan/wolverines/2017/01/11/michigan-wolverines-illinois-fighting-illini/96476912/.

4. Nick Baumgardner, "Michigan dons blue collars, writes on the walls, finds a way to push back vs. Illinois," MLive.com, January 21, 2017, https://www.mlive.com/wolverines/2017/01/michigan_blue_collar.html.

5. "NCAA Men's 1st and 2nd Rounds: Indianapolis," ASAP Sports Transcripts, March 18, 2017, http://www.asapsports.com/show_interview.php?id=128334.

6. "NCAA Men's Regional Semi-Finals and Finals: Kansas City," ASAP Sports Transcripts, March 22, 2017, http://www.asapsports.com/show_interview.php?id=128513.

7. "Big Ten Conference Men's Basketball Championship," ASAP Sports Transcripts, March 10, 2017, http://www.asapsports.com/show_interview.php?id=127768.

8. "NCAA Men's 1st and 2nd Rounds: Indianapolis," ASAP Sports Transcripts, March 17, 2017, http://www.asapsports.com/show_interview.php?id=128229.

9. "Big Ten Conference Men's Basketball Championship," ASAP Sports Transcripts, March 12, 2017, http://www.asapsports.com/show_interview.php?id=127935.

10. Steve Kornacki, "Against All Odds, Wolverines Prevail in D.C.," Mgoblue.com, March 12, 2017, mgoblue.com/news/2017/3/13/kornacki_against_all_odds_wolverines_prevail_in_d_c_.aspx.

11. Russ Brown, "'Career Day' by Michigan's Wagner Leaves Louisville on the Outside Looking in at NCAA Tournament," KyForward.com, March 19, 2017, www.kyforward.com/career-day-by-michigans-wagner-leaves-louisville-on-the-outside-looking-in-at-ncaa-tournament/.

12. Ibid.

13. "NCAA Men's 1st and 2nd Rounds: Indianapolis," ASAP Sports Transcripts, March 19, 2017, http://www.asapsports.com/show_interview.php?id=128436.

14. Ibid.

15. "NCAA Men's Final Four," ASAP Sports Transcripts, April 1, 2018, http://www.asapsports.com/show_interview.php?id=139019.

16. "NCAA Men's Regional Semi-Finals and Finals: Kansas City," ASAP Sports Transcripts, March 23, 2017, http://www.asapsports.com/show_interview.php?id=128641.

17. Ibid.

18. Steve Kornacki, "Reflecting on a Special NCAA Tourney Run," Mgoblue.com, March 24, 2017, mgoblue.com/news/2017/3/24/Kornacki_Reflecting_on_a_Special_NCAA_Tourney_Run.aspx?path=mbball.

19. Ibid.

Chapter 10

1. Brendan Quinn, "It Sure Seems like Michigan Has a New Weapon in Charles Matthews," *The Athletic*, November 4, 2017, theathletic.com/146418/2017/11/04/it-sure-seems-like-michigan-has-a-new-weapon-in-charles-matthews/.

2. Steve Kornacki, "How Wilson Went from Suspect to NBA Draft Prospect," Mgoblue.com, June 21, 2017, mgoblue.com/news/2017/6/21/mens-basketball-kornacki-how-wilson-went-from-suspect-to-nba-draft-prospect.aspx?path=mbball.

3. Ibid.

4. Steve Kornacki, "Wagner Explains Decision to Remain at U-M," Mgoblue.com, March 24, 2017, mgoblue.com/news/2017/5/24/Kornacki_Wagner_Explains_Decision_to_Remain_at_U_M.aspx?path=mbball.

5. Tim Hackett, "Embraced by a Home Away from Home, Moritz Wagner Is Finally Ready for a New Challenge," SI.com, June 12, 2018, www.si.com/nba/2018/06/12/moritz-wagner-michigan-nba-draft-john-beilein-dirk-nowitzki.

6. Steve Kornacki, "The Time Has Come for Moe to Go Pro," Mgoblue.com, April 14, 2018, mgoblue.com/news/2018/4/14/mens-basketball-kornacki-the-time-has-come-for-moe-to-go-pro.aspx.

7. Brendan Quinn, "Moritz Wagner's Development Moves Front and Center for Michigan Basketball," MLive.com, May 30, 2017, www.mlive.com/wolverines/index.ssf/2017/05/moritz_wagners_development_mov.html.
8. "Michigan Adds Matthews, Wright-Jones to Roster," Mgoblue.com, July 1, 2016, https://mgoblue.com/news/2016/7/1/Michigan_Adds_Matthews_Wright_Jones_to_Roster.aspx?path=mbball.
9. Steve Kornacki, "Beilein Embraces Changes with Team, Staff," Mgoblue.com, August 7, 2017, mgoblue.com/news/2017/8/7/mens-basketball-kornacki-beilein-embraces-changes-with-team-staff.aspx?path=mbball.
10. Steve Kornacki, "How Yaklich Has Helped Turn Michigan Into a Formidable Defensive Team," Mgoblue.com, March 21, 2018, mgoblue.com/news/2018/3/21/mens-basketball-how-yaklich-has-helped-turn-michigan-into-a-formidable-defensive-team.aspx.
11. Nicole Auerbach, "Defense Always Came First for Luke Yaklich, and the Results are Showing at Michigan," *The Athletic*, March 30, 2018, theathletic.com/294094/2018/03/30/defense-always-came-first-for-luke-yaklich-and-the-results-are-showing-at-michigan/.
12. Matt Norlander, "How an ex-high school social studies teacher helped put Michigan in the Final Four," CBSsports.com, March 29, 2018, https://www.cbssports.com/college-basketball/news/how-an-ex-high-school-social-studies-teacher-helped-put-michigan-in-the-final-four/.
13. Nicole Auerbach, "Defense Always Came First for Luke Yaklich, and the Results are Showing at Michigan," *The Athletic*, March 30, 2018, theathletic.com/294094/2018/03/30/defense-always-came-first-for-luke-yaklich-and-the-results-are-showing-at-michigan/.
14. Brian Cook, "Unverified Voracity FIGHTS IN THE STREETS," Mgoblog.com, March 28, 2018, www.mgoblog.com/comment/4994503.
15. Steve Kornacki, "Beilein Embraces Changes with Team, Staff," Mgoblue.com, August 7, 2017, mgoblue.com/news/2017/8/7/mens-basketball-kornacki-beilein-embraces-changes-with-team-staff.aspx?path=mbball.
16. Steve Kornacki, "Beilein's More Evident Joy and Smile Make an Impression," Mgoblue.com, October 25, 2017, mgoblue.com/news/2017/10/25/mens-basketball-kornacki-beileins-more-evident-joy-and-smile-makes-an-impression.aspx?path=mbball.
17. Ibid.
18. Brendan Quinn, "A Team, a Teammate and Michigan Basketball's Mighty Assist," *The Athletic*, January 22, 2018, theathletic.com/218614/2018/01/22/a-team-a-teammate-and-michigan-basketballs-mighty-assist/.
19. Ryan Zuke, "Michigan Basketball's Newest Team Member Is 12, and He's Living the Dream," MLive.com, November 7, 2017, www.mlive.com/wolverines/index.ssf/2017/11/12-year-old_with_serious_illne.html.
20. "The Journey: Jude Stamper and Michigan," *Big Ten Network*, 2:44, February 16, 2018, https://www.btn2go.com/video/the-journey-jude-stamper-is-part-of-michigan-basketball.
21. Ibid.
22. Ibid.
23. Ibid.
24. "NCAA Men's Final Four," ASAP Sports Transcripts, April 1, 2018, http://www.asapsports.com/show_interview.php?id=139019.

Chapter 11

1. Brendan Quinn, "Jordan Poole and a Michigan team unlike any other," *The Athletic*, March 18, 2018, https://theathletic.com/278731/2018/03/18/jordan-poole-and-a-michigan-team-unlike-any-other/.
2. Brendan Quinn, "Michigan's Absurd and Exhilarating Journey Ends, but the Process Marches On," *The Athletic*, April 3, 2018, theathletic.com/297093/2018/04/03/michigans-absurd-and-exhilarating-journey-ends-but-the-process-marches-on/.
3. Brendan Quinn, "24 Hours inside Michigan Basketball: Behind the Scenes at Maui

Invitational," *The Athletic*, November 22, 2017, theathletic.com/162870/2017/11/22/24-hours-inside-michigan-basketball-behind-the-scenes-at-maui-invitational/.

4. "Maui Jim Maui Invitational," ASAP Sports Transcripts, November 22, 2017, http://www.asapsports.com/show_interview.php?id=136141.

5. Andrew Vailliencourt, "Michigan Basketball: Jordan Poole's Big Day Leads Michigan To Win Over IU," TheWolverine.com, December 2, 2017, https://michigan.rivals.com/news/michigan-basketball-jordan-poole-s-big-day-leads-michigan-to-win-over-iu.

6. Brendan Quinn, "You Don't Know Jordan Poole," *The Athletic*, March 22, 2018, theathletic.com/283370/2018/03/22/you-dont-know-jordan-poole/.

7. Brendan Quinn, "The (Unexpected) Story of Michigan's Freshman Class," *The Athletic*, December 3, 2017, theathletic.com/172903/2017/12/03/michigan-wolverines-freshman-class-jordan-poole-eli-brooks-isaiah-livers-john-beilein/.

8. Andrew Kahn, "Jaaron Simmons Could Be a Malcontent for Michigan, but Has Been the Opposite," MLive.com, February 16, 2018, www.mlive.com/wolverines/index.ssf/2018/02/jaaron_simmons_could_be_a_malc.html.

9. Brendan Quinn, "An Inside Look at Michigan's Complicated Point Guard Situation," *The Athletic*, November 10, 2017, theathletic.com/150250/2017/11/10/an-inside-look-at-michigans-complicated-point-guard-situation/.

10. Andrew Kahn, "Jaaron Simmons Could Be a Malcontent for Michigan, but Has Been the Opposite," MLive.com, February 16, 2018, www.mlive.com/wolverines/index.ssf/2018/02/jaaron_simmons_could_be_a_malc.html.

11. Ethan Wolfe, "Michigan erases 15-point deficit, earns 78–69 overtime win over Bruins," *The Michigan Daily*, December 9, 2017, https://www.michigandaily.com/section/mens-basketball/michigan-ucla-offense-defense.

12. Brendan Quinn, "Once a Starter, Now a Closer, Zavier Simpson Leads U-M at Winning Time," *The Athletic*, December 28, 2017, theathletic.com/195966/2017/12/28/once-a-starter-now-a-closer-zavier-simpson-leads-u-m-at-winning-time/.

13. Mark Calcagno, "Doubt Zavier Simpson? Prepare to Be Proven Wrong," *The Michigan Daily*, March 8, 2018, www.michigandaily.com/section/mens-basketball/doubt-zavier-simpson-prepare-be-proven-wrong.

14. Steve Kornacki, "Teske Finds 'Double-Double' Success Playing in 'Traffic,'" Mgoblue.com, December 16, 2017, mgoblue.com/news/2017/12/16/mens-basketball-kornacki-teske-finds-double-double-success-playing-in-traffic.aspx?path=mbball.

15. James Hawkins, "Extra work helps UM's Simpson pick up scoring pace," *The Detroit News*, December 20, 2017, https://www.detroitnews.com/story/sports/college/university-michigan/2017/12/20/extra-shooting-helps-ums-simpson-pick-scoring-pace/108777656/.

16. James Hawkins, "Matthews' 20-Point Outing for UM Comes with Heavy Heart," *The Detroit News*, December 17, 2017, www.detroitnews.com/story/sports/college/university-michigan/wolverines/2017/12/16/matthews-20-point-outing-um-comes-heavy-heart/108665726/.

17. Steve Kornacki, "Simpson Developing Into a Force, 'Chopping Wood' and Draining Treys," Mgoblue.com, January 10, 2018, www.mgoblue.com/news/2018/1/10/mens-basketball-simpson-developing-into-a-force-chopping-wood-and-draining-treys.aspx?path=mbball.

18. *Ibid.*

19. *Ibid.*

20. "Jordan Poole post Illinois," YouTube Video, 2:46, posted by "Chris Balas," January 6, 2018, https://www.youtube.com/watch?v=i0pIXsTOPLI.

Chapter 12

1. Max Bultman, "It's All Leveling out for Duncan Robinson," *The Athletic*, March 1, 2018, theathletic.com/258891/2018/03/01/its-all-leveling-out-for-duncan-robinson/.

2. *Ibid.*

3. *Ibid.*

4. "The Journey: Michigan All-Access At Michigan State," *Big Ten Network*, 4:43, January 22, 2018, www.btn2go.com/video/the-journey-michigan-all-access-at-michigan-state.
5. *Ibid*.
6. Bob Wojnowski, "Michigan's huge win changes (almost) everything," *The Detroit News*, January 13, 2018, https://www.detroitnews.com/story/sports/columnists/bob-wojnowski/2018/01/13/wojo-ums-rivalry-win-changes-almost-everything/109433676/.
7. Brendan Quinn, "Then Dawud Said to Dave…: A Favor for the Abdur-Rahkmans and the Friendship that Followed," *The Athletic*, February 21, 2018, theathletic.com/248010/2018/02/21/then-dawud-said-to-dave-a-favor-for-the-abdur-rahkmans-and-the-friendship-that-followed/.
8. Brendan Quinn, "The Peculiar Story of Michigan Recruit Muhammad-Ali Abdur-Rahkman, Dave Rooney and the Phone Call That Changed Everything," MLive.com, May 10, 2015, www.mlive.com/wolverines/index.ssf/2014/04/the_peculiar_story_of_muhammad.html.
9. Steve Kornacki, "Rudy T, Jalen, Maceo and 'The Judge' Connect with Wolverines," Mgoblue.com, January 21 2018, mgoblue.com/news/2018/1/21/mens-basketball-kornacki-rudy-t-jalen-maceo-and-the-judge-connect-with-wolverines.aspx?path=mbball.
10. *Ibid*.
11. *Ibid*.
12. "John Beilein talks loss at Purdue (2/2)," YouTube Video, 6:36, posted by "UMHoops Videos," January 25, 2018, https://www.youtube.com/watch?v=t4GdOntZskE.

Chapter 13

1. Nicole Auerbach, "Defense Always Came First for Luke Yaklich, and the Results are Showing at Michigan," *The Athletic*, March 30, 2018, theathletic.com/294094/2018/03/30/defense-always-came-first-for-luke-yaklich-and-the-results-are-showing-at-michigan/.
2. "Luke Yaklich Media Day," YouTube Video, 7:03, posted by "UM Hoops.com," October 25, 2017, https://www.youtube.com/watch?v=cnZDwfKW6zg.
3. Steve Kornacki, "How Staying 'Connected' Helps Wolverines Dominate on Defense," Mgoblue.com, March 2, 2018, https://mgoblue.com/news/2018/3/2/mens-basketball-how-staying-connected-helps-wolverines-dominate-on-defense.aspx.
4. Jeff Eisenberg, "How a Former High School History Teacher Became the Key to Michigan's Final Four Run," *Yahoo! Sports*, March 26, 2018, sports.yahoo.com/assistant-coach-humble-roots-became-key-michigans-final-four-run-175719995.html.
5. Steve Kornacki, "How Staying 'Connected' Helps Wolverines Dominate on Defense," Mgoblue.com, March 2, 2018, https://mgoblue.com/news/2018/3/2/mens-basketball-how-staying-connected-helps-wolverines-dominate-on-defense.aspx.
6. Brendan Quinn, "The Story of Zavier Simpson and the Defensive Dogs of Michigan," *The Athletic*, March 4, 2018, theathletic.com/260616/2018/03/03/the-story-of-zavier-simpson-and-the-defensive-dogs-of-michigan/.
7. *Ibid*.
8. "Men of March: John Beilein," *CBS Sports Network*, aired January 10, 2018.
9. Max Bultman, "'We Need You': Michigan's Players Issue the Call, and a Big Ten Title Follows," *The Athletic*, March 5, 2018, theathletic.com/261918/2018/03/05/we-need-you-michigans-players-issue-the-call-and-a-big-ten-title-follows/.
10. Steve Kornacki, "The Stories Behind Abdur-Rahkman's Heroics in Maryland Victory," Mgoblue.com, January 16, 2018, https://mgoblue.com/news/2018/1/16/mens-basketball-kornacki-the-stories-behind-abdur-rahkman-heroics-in-maryland-victory.aspx.
11. "Moritz Wagner talks win over Minnesota 2.3.18," YouTube Video, 9:10, posted by "UMHoops Videos," February 3rd, 2018, https://www.youtube.com/watch?time_continue=125&v=_q6evthHRHg.
12. Brendan Quinn, "What's up with Charles Matthews?" *The Athletic*, February 25, 2018, theathletic.com/252682/2018/02/25/whats-up-with-charles-matthews/.

13. "John beilein post Rutgers," YouTube Video, 14:51, posted by "Chris Balas," January 21, 2018, https://www.youtube.com/watch?v=G1USNIxip7I.
14. Zach Shaw, "Charles Matthews Winding Road Leads to Bliss in Los Angeles," *247sports*, March 26, 2018, 247sports.com/Article/Charles-Matthews-winding-road-leads-to-bliss-in-Los-Angeles-for-Michigan-basketball-in-the-NCAA-Tournament-116720209.
15. Brendan Quinn, "What You Don't See in Jaaron Simmons' Very Strange Journey," *The Athletic*, March 17, 2018, theathletic.com/277051/2018/03/16/what-you-dont-see-in-jaaron-simmons-very-strange-journey/.
16. Mark Calcagno, "In a Turmoil-Filled Year, Simmons Gets Ultimate Reward," *The Michigan Daily*, March 26, 2018, www.michigandaily.com/section/mens-basketball/turmoil-filled-year-simmons-gets-ultimate-reward.
17. Andrew Kahn, "Jaaron Simmons Could Be a Malcontent for Michigan, but Has Been the Opposite," MLive.com, February 16, 2018, www.mlive.com/wolverines/index.ssf/2018/02/jaaron_simmons_could_be_a_malc.html.
18. Brendan Quinn, "What You Don't See in Jaaron Simmons' Very Strange Journey," *The Athletic*, March 17, 2018, theathletic.com/277051/2018/03/16/what-you-dont-see-in-jaaron-simmons-very-strange-journey/.
19. Andrew Kahn, "Jaaron Simmons Could Be a Malcontent for Michigan, but Has Been the Opposite," MLive.com, February 16, 2018, www.mlive.com/wolverines/index.ssf/2018/02/jaaron_simmons_could_be_a_malc.html.
20. "John Beilein post Iowa," YouTube Video, 9:59, posted by "Chris Balas," February 14, 2018, https://www.youtube.com/watch?v=jrGUS7bcgtw.
21. Jeff Seidel, "Duncan Robinson's Defense Put to Test in Sweet 16," *Detroit Free Press*, March 22, 2018, www.freep.com/story/sports/columnists/jeff-seidel/2018/03/22/michigan-wolverines-basketball-duncan-robinson/447644002/.
22. Ibid.
23. "NCAA Men's Regional Semi-Finals and Finals: Los Angeles," ASAP Sports Transcripts, March 22, 2018, http://www.asapsports.com/show_interview.php?id=138721.

Chapter 14

1. "Miraculous: The Austin Hatch Story—ESPN," YouTube Video, 16:06, posted by "Dan Arruda," September 7, 2016, www.youtube.com/watch?v=AmKUpj97ZB8.
2. "Austin Hatch Perseveres." *CBS Sports*, 7:04, 2018, www.facebook.com/CBSSports/videos/austin-hatch-perseveres/10155767432576773/.
3. Max Marcovitch, "Austin Hatch among seniors honored in emotional day," *The Michigan Daily*, February 18, 2018, https://www.michigandaily.com/section/basketball/austin-hatch-senior-day.
4. Nick Baumgardner, "Austin Hatch, Michigan Basketball: The Duo That Blessed Each Other," *Detroit Free Press*, March 27, 2018, www.freep.com/story/sports/college/university-michigan/wolverines/2018/03/15/michigan-wolverines-basketball-austin-hatch/426619002/.
5. Steve Kornacki, "Austin Hatch: A Storybook Ending Achieved After Unimaginable Tragedy," Mgoblue.com, February 27, 2018, mgoblue.com/news/2018/2/27/mens-basketball-austin-hatch-a-storybook-ending-achieved-after-unimaginable-tragedy.aspx.
6. Brendan Quinn, "Austin Hatch, Age 23, Has a Story to Tell," *The Athletic*, March 28, 2018, theathletic.com/290094/2018/03/28/austin-hatch-age-23-has-a-story-to-tell/.
7. Nick Baumgardner, "Austin Hatch, Michigan Basketball: The Duo That Blessed Each Other," *Detroit Free Press*, March 27, 2018, www.freep.com/story/sports/college/university-michigan/wolverines/2018/03/15/michigan-wolverines-basketball-austin-hatch/426619002/.
8. "Miraculous: The Austin Hatch Story—ESPN," YouTube Video, 16:06, posted by "Dan Arruda," September 7, 2016, www.youtube.com/watch?v=AmKUpj97ZB8.
9. Kyle Rowland, "Story of Michigan's Austin Hatch Remains an All-Time Account of Perseverance," *The Toledo Blade*, March 21, 2018, www.toledoblade.com/College/2018/03/21/Austin-Hatch-story-remains-an-all-time-account-of-perseverance.html.

10. Brendan Quinn, "You Don't Know Jordan Poole," *The Athletic*, March 22, 2018, theathletic.com/283370/2018/03/22/you-dont-know-jordan-poole/.
11. "John Beilein talks win over Maryland," YouTube Video, 9:35, posted by "UMHoops Videos," February 24, 2018, https://www.youtube.com/watch?v=2_1b9ycqSxA.

Chapter 15

1. Steve Kornacki, "Matthews Steps Up in Many Ways to Help Lead Wolverines Past Iowa," Mgoblue.com, March 1, 2018, https://mgoblue.com/news/2018/3/1/mens-basketball-kornacki-matthews-steps-up-in-many-ways-to-help-lead-wolverines-past-iowa.aspx?path=mbball.
2. Steve Kornacki, "How Staying 'Connected' Helps Wolverines Dominate on Defense." Mgoblue.com, March 2, 2018, mgoblue.com/news/2018/3/2/mens-basketball-how-staying-connected-helps-wolverines-dominate-on-defense.aspx?path=mbball.
3. "Coach John Beilein—It's Worth It (Narrow Way Café & Shop)," YouTube Video, 20:00, posted by "David Merritt," January 21, 2019, https://www.youtube.com/watch?v=pHuFq Nil9Z0&t=2s.
4. "Big Ten Conference Men's Basketball Tournament," ASAP Sports Transcripts, March 2, 2018, http://www.asapsports.com/show_interview.php?id=137672.
5. "Big Ten Conference Men's Basketball Tournament," ASAP Sports Transcripts, March 3, 2018, http://www.asapsports.com/show_interview.php?id=137733.
6. "John Beilein before Selection Sunday," YouTube Video, 19:20, posted by "UMHoops Video," March 9, 2018, https://www.youtube.com/watch?v=wNs0ewdHlzE.
7. Brendan Quinn, "Jordan Poole and a Michigan Team Like No Other," *The Athletic*, March 18, 2018, https://theathletic.com/278731/2018/03/18/jordan-poole-and-a-michigan-team-unlike-any-other/.

Chapter 16

1. "John Beilein before Selection Sunday," YouTube Video, 19:20, posted by "UMHoops Video," March 9, 2018, https://www.youtube.com/watch?v=wNs0ewdHlzE.
2. Brendan Quinn, "What You Don't See in Jaaron Simmons' Very Strange Journey," *The Athletic*, March 16, 2018, https://theathletic.com/277051/2018/03/16/what-you-dont-see-in-jaaron-simmons-very-strange-journey/.
3. "NCAA Men's 1st and 2nd Rounds: Wichita," ASAP Sports Transcripts, March 16, 2018, http://www.asapsports.com/show_interview.php?id=138567.
4. Moe Wagner, "Thank You, Michigan," *The Players' Tribune*, April 14, 2018, https://www.theplayerstribune.com/en-us/articles/moe-wagner-thank-you-michigan.
5. "Duncan Robinson after Houston," YouTube Video, 2:44, posted by "UM Hoops.com," March 17, 2018, https://www.youtube.com/watch?v=3-WloSBaIlA.

Chapter 17

1. "NCAA Men's Regional Semi-Finals and Finals: Los Angeles," ASAP Sports Transcripts, March 22, 2018, http://www.asapsports.com/show_interview.php?id=138721.
2. "Beilein looks ahead to Sweet 16, reflects on Poole shot," YouTube Video, 15:40, posted by "Maizeandbluenews," March 21, 2018, https://www.youtube.com/watch?v=We1FjYekrUg.
3. Ben Baby, "Duel between A&M's T.J. Starks and Michigan's Zavier Simpson may determine Thursday's Sweet 16 matchup," DallasNews.com, March 21, 2018, https://sportsday.dallasnews.com/college-sports/collegesports/2018/03/21/duel-ams-tj-starks-michiganszavier-simpson-may-determine-thursdays-sweet-16-matchup.
4. Tim Bontemps, "'I Got Shivers down My Whole Body': Michigan Walk-on Hits the Shot of His Life," *The Washington Post*, March 23, 2018, www.washingtonpost.com/news/sports/wp/2018/03/23/meet-c-j-baird-the-walk-on-whose-shot-gave-michigan-an-ncaa-tournament-record/?utm_term=.4893e62cea30.

5. James Hawkins, "Michigan Scout Team's Unsung Work Playing Pivotal Role," *The Detroit News*, March 29, 2018, www.detroitnews.com/story/sports/college/university-michigan/wolverines/2018/03/28/michigan-scout-teams-unsung-work-playing-pivotal-role/33375949/.
6. "NCAA Men's Regional Semi-Finals and Finals: Los Angeles," ASAP Sports Transcripts, March 23, 2018, http://www.asapsports.com/show_interview.php?id=138752.
7. Zach Shaw, "Once more, Michigan's revamped defense saves the day," 247sports.com, March 25, 2018, https://247sports.com/college/michigan/Article/Once-more-Michigan-basketballs-revamped-defense-saves-the-day-as-Wolverines-make-Final-Four-116664660/.
8. Brendan Quinn, "The Story of Zavier Simpson and the Defensive Dogs of Michigan," *The Athletic*, March 4, 2018, theathletic.com/260616/2018/03/03/the-story-of-zavier-simpson-and-the-defensive-dogs-of-michigan/.
9. Brian Bennett, "Michigan's Road to the Final Four Paved with Good Intentions and Great Defense," *The Athletic*, March 25 2018, theathletic.com/287210/2018/03/25/michigans-road-to-the-final-four-paved-with-good-intentions-and-great-defense/.
10. Zach Shaw, "Charles Matthews' Winding Road Leads to Bliss in Los Angeles," 247sports.com, March 26, 2018, 247sports.com/Article/Charles-Matthews-winding-road-leads-to-bliss-in-Los-Angeles-for-Michigan-basketball-in-the-NCAA-Tournament-116720209.
11. "Moe Wagner after FSU," YouTube Video, 4:02, posted by "UM Hoops.com," March 24, 2018, https://www.youtube.com/watch?v=BgZVTWO5n2Y.
12. Andrew Kahn, "Changed by a Plane Crash, John Beilein Has a New Outlook," MLive.com, March 29, 2018, www.mlive.com/wolverines/index.ssf/2018/03/changed_by_a_plane_crash_john.html#incart_river_index.

Chapter 18

1. "NCAA Men's Regional Semi-Finals and Finals: Los Angeles," ASAP Sports Transcripts, March 24, 2018, http://www.asapsports.com/show_interview.php?id=138853.
2. "NCAA Men's Basketball Championship: Final Four," ASAP Sports Transcripts, March 30, 2018, http://www.asapsports.com/show_interview.php?id=138971.
3. "Web Exclusive: Inside Michigan Basketball—NCAA Semifinal," Mgoblue.com, 7:27, April 1, 2018, mgoblue.com/watch/?Archive=12216&sport=7&type=Archive.
4. Ibid.
5. Ibid.
6. Steve Kornacki, "Wagner Dominates, Motivates and Puts on a Final Four Show," Mgoblue.com, April 1, 2018, mgoblue.com/news/2018/4/1/mens-basketball-kornacki-wagner-dominates-motivates-and-puts-on-a-final-four-show.aspx?path=mbball.
7. "Isaiah Livers after Loyola," YouTube Video, 4:04, posted by "UM Hoops.com," March 31, 2018, https://www.youtube.com/watch?v=ZaTA3-0947A.
8. Steve Kornacki, "Wagner Dominates, Motivates and Puts on a Final Four Show," Mgoblue.com, April 1, 2018, mgoblue.com/news/2018/4/1/mens-basketball-kornacki-wagner-dominates-motivates-and-puts-on-a-final-four-show.aspx?path=mbball.
9. "NCAA Men's Basketball Championship: Final Four," ASAP Sports Transcripts, March 31, 2018, http://www.asapsports.com/show_interview.php?id=139012.
10. "Web Exclusive: Inside Michigan Basketball—NCAA Semifinal," Mgoblue.com, 7:27, April 1, 2018, mgoblue.com/watch/?Archive=12216&sport=7&type=Archive.

Chapter 19

1. "NCAA Men's Basketball Championship: Final Four," ASAP Sports Transcripts, April 1, 2018, http://www.asapsports.com/show_interview.php?id=139019.
2. "NCAA Men's Basketball Championship: Final Four," ASAP Sports Transcripts, April 2, 2018, http://www.asapsports.com/show_interview.php?id=139039.
3. Ibid.

4. "Web Exclusive: Inside Michigan Basketball—NCAA Championship Game," Mgoblue.com, 5:33, April 3, 2018, mgoblue.com/watch/?Archive=12231&sport=7&type=Archive.
5. "NCAA Men's Regional Semi-Finals and Finals: Los Angeles," ASAP Sports Transcripts, March 22, 2018, http://www.asapsports.com/show_interview.php?id=138721.
6. "Moritz Wagner after Villanova," YouTube Video, 2:30, posted by "UM Hoops.com," April 2, 2018, https://www.youtube.com/watch?v=OFKrMqHYpYo.
7. Steve Kornacki, "One Last 'Victors' from Emotion-Filled Postgame Locker Room," Mgoblue.com, April 3, 2018, mgoblue.com/news/2018/4/3/mens-basketball-one-last-victors-from-postgame-locker-room.aspx?path=mbball.
8. Ibid.
9. Ibid.
10. "John Beilein talks loss to Villanova," YouTube Video, 7:21, posted by "UM Hoops.com," April 2, 2018, https://www.youtube.com/watch?v=Ne6Zw_9eTr4.

Chapter 20

1. Moe Wagner, "Thank You, Michigan," *The Players' Tribune*, April 14, 2018, https://www.theplayerstribune.com/en-us/articles/moe-wagner-thank-you-michigan.
2. Mike Trudell, "Pelinka Reacts to L.A.'s 2018 Draft," NBA.com, June 21, 2018, https://www.nba.com/lakers/news/180621-pelinka-reacts-to-la-2018-draft.
3. "Moritz Wagner Talks About His Michigan Experience," Mgoblue.com, 3:44, April 17, 2018, https://mgoblue.com/watch/?Archive=12291&type=Archive.
4. Joe Beguiristain, "The Journey Begins For Duncan Robinson," NBA.com, July 11, 2018, https://www.nba.com/heat/newsrecap/journey-begins-duncan-robinson.
5. Andrew Kahn, "How Jaaron Simmons realized his dreams in just one season with Michigan basketball," MLive.com, April 16, 2018, https://www.mlive.com/wolverines/2018/04/how_jaaron_simmons_realized_hi.html.
6. Jeff Seidel, "'Reprogrammed' Charles Matthews helped put Michigan in Final Four," *Detroit Free Press*, March 27, 2018, https://www.freep.com/story/sports/columnists/jeff-seidel/2018/03/27/michigan-basketball-charles-matthews-transformation-final-four/459896002/.
7. Andy Katz, "John Beilein and Chris Mullin," *March Madness 365 with Andy Katz*, Podcast Audio, June 12, 2018, https://podcasts.apple.com/us/podcast/john-beilein-and-chris-mullin/id1325823631?i=1000413532754.
8. James Hawkins, "Zavier Simpson, dad going back to 'ground zero' to improve shooting," *The Detroit News*, May 11, 2018, https://www.detroitnews.com/story/sports/college/university-michigan/wolverines/2018/05/11/michigan-guard-zavier-simpson-seeks-improve-jump-shot/600968002/.
9. "Isaiah Livers at Michigan Media Day," YouTube Video, 6:31, posted by "UM Hoops.com," October 23, 2018, https://www.youtube.com/watch?v=48LDjuzi43E.
10. "John Beilein talks loss to Villanova," YouTube Video, 7:21, posted by "UM Hoops.com," April 2, 2018, https://www.youtube.com/watch?v=Ne6Zw_9eTr4.
11. "Saddi Washington at Michigan Media Day," YouTube Video, 4:39, posted by "UM Hoops.com," October 22, 2018, https://www.youtube.com/watch?v=IoAh1QEOS6s.
12. Andy Katz, "John Beilein and Chris Mullin," *March Madness 365 with Andy Katz*, Podcast Audio, June 12, 2018, https://podcasts.apple.com/us/podcast/john-beilein-and-chris-mullin/id1325823631?i=1000413532754.
13. "Ignas Brazdeikis at Michigan Media Day," YouTube Video, 7:34, posted by "UM Hoops.com," October 22, 2018, https://www.youtube.com/watch?v=weJaz8Ds11E.
14. Dan Murphy, "Can Ignas Brazdeikis help fuel Michigan's defensive revolution?" ESPN.com, January 23, 2019, http://www.espn.com/mens-college-basketball/story/_/id/25818940/can-ignas-brazdeikis-help-fuel-michigan-defensive-revolution.
15. Chris Balas, "David DeJulius Dominates, Stating His Case For Mr. Basketball," TheWolverine.com, January 15, 2018, https://michigan.rivals.com/news/david-dejulius-dominates-stating-his-case-for-mr-basketball-with-video-.

16. Cody Tucker, "East Lansing's Brandon Johns dreams of playing at Breslin … in maize and blue," *Lansing State Journal*, January 11, 2018, https://www.lansingstatejournal.com/story/sports/2018/01/11/brandon-johns-east-lansing-michigan-wolverines-basketball/1018347001/.

17. "NCAA Men's Regional Semi-Finals and Finals: Los Angeles," ASAP Sports Transcripts, March 23, 2018, http://www.asapsports.com/show_interview.php?id=138752.

18. "John Beilein talks heart surgery, first practice," YouTube Video, 24:45, posted by "UM Hoops.com," September 25, 2018, https://www.youtube.com/watch?v=A1QHRzaeHVE&t=256s.

19. "Beilein, Matthews and Simpson at Media Day | Michigan | Big Ten Basketball," YouTube Video, 10:36, posted by "Big Ten Network," October 11, 2018, https://www.youtube.com/watch?v=GOxo4KyMUfo.

20. "Zavier Simpson talks first practice," YouTube Video, 2:52, posted by "UM Hoops.com," September 25, 2018, https://www.youtube.com/watch?v=smaicHiF-IQ.

21. "Saddi Washington at Michigan Media Day," YouTube Video, 4:39, posted by "UM Hoops.com," October 22, 2018, https://www.youtube.com/watch?v=IoAh1QEOS6s.

22. Brendan Quinn, "At Michigan, looking at life without John Beilein," *The Athletic*, August 10, 2018, https://theathletic.com/466243/2018/08/10/at-michigan-looking-at-life-without-john-beilein/.

23. "Beilein, Matthews and Simpson at Media Day | Michigan | Big Ten Basketball," YouTube Video, 10:36, posted by "Big Ten Network," October 11, 2018, https://www.youtube.com/watch?v=GOxo4KyMUfo.

Chapter 21

1. James Hawkins, "UM's Brazdeikis makes most of 'shining moment,'" *The Detroit News*, November 15, 2018, https://www.detroitnews.com/story/sports/college/university-michigan/2018/11/15/michigans-ignas-brazdeikis-makes-most-shining-moment/2009725002/.

2. "Video: John Beilein, Zavier Simpson and Charles Matthews recap win at Villanova," Umhoops.com, November 14, 2018, https://umhoops.com/2018/11/14/video-john-beilein-zavier-simpson-charles-matthews-recap-win-villanova/.

Chapter 22

1. James Hawkins, "Michigan braces for North Carolina 'freight train,'" *The Detroit News*, November 27, 2018, https://www.detroitnews.com/story/sports/college/university-michigan/2018/11/27/michigan-braces-north-carolina-freight-train/2124315002/.

2. Shawn Windsor, "Michigan basketball looks like title contender after routing UNC," *Detroit Free Press*, November 29, 2018, https://www.freep.com/story/sports/columnists/shawn-windsor/2018/11/29/michigan-basketball-title-shot/2145344002/.

3. "Iggy Brazdeikis talks win over North Carolina," YouTube Video, 2:47, posted by "Maizeandbluenews," November 29, 2018, https://www.youtube.com/watch?v=0_hx76Ss-YY.

4. "UNC Michigan Coby White postgame interview," YouTube Video, 3:30, posted by "Tar Heel Illustrated," November 28, 2018, https://www.youtube.com/watch?v=fOW19BENmpY.

5. James Hawkins, "Michigan aims for the moon with out-of-this-world defense," *The Detroit News*, November 29, 2018, https://www.detroitnews.com/story/sports/college/university-michigan/2018/11/29/michigan-wolverines-dissatisfied-defensive-results-win-over-north-carolina-tar-heels/2148584002/.

6. Steve Kornacki, "'Big Nasty' Teske Evolving into Quite a Weapon for the Wolverines," Mgoblue.com, December 1, 2018, https://mgoblue.com/news/2018/12/1/mens-basketball-big-nasty-teske-evolving-into-quite-a-weapon-for-the-wolverines.aspx?path=mbball.

7. "Beilein post Norfolk State," YouTube Video, 11:12, posted by "Chris Balas," November 6, 2018, https://www.youtube.com/watch?v=2BWeLZHZb78.

8. "Livers Norfolk State," YouTube Video, 4:09, posted by "Chris Balas," November 6, 2018, https://www.youtube.com/watch?v=KZcqq7YVkPQ.

9. Steve Kornacki, "Improvement in Simpson, Teske the Essence of Coaching to Beilein," Mgoblue.com, January 13, 2019, https://mgoblue.com/news/2019/1/13/mens-basketball-improvement-in-simpson-teske-the-essence-of-coaching-to-beilein.aspx?path=mbball.

Chapter 23

1. "Ignas Brazdeikis at Michigan Media Day," YouTube Video, 8:41, posted by "UM Hoops.com," October 22, 2018, https://www.youtube.com/watch?v=jzLJaQVBFUg.
2. Dan Murphy, "Can Ignas Brazdeikis help fuel Michigan's defensive revolution?" ESPN.com, January 23, 2019, http://www.espn.com/mens-college-basketball/story/_/id/25818940/can-ignas-brazdeikis-help-fuel-michigan-defensive-revolution.
3. "Jordan Poole at Michigan Media Day," YouTube Video, 8:23, posted by "UM Hoops.com," October 22, 2018, https://www.youtube.com/watch?v=oIAVsuP1qyc.
4. Steve Kornacki, "Brazdeikis is Confident, Coachable and Ready to Contribute," Mgoblue.com, October 23, 2018, https://mgoblue.com/news/2018/10/23/mens-basketball-kornacki-brazdeikis-is-confident-coachable-and-ready-to-contribute.aspx?path=mbball.
5. "The Journey: Meet Ignas Brazdeikis," *Big Ten Network*, 4:42, January 15, 2019, https://www.btn2go.com/video/meet-ignas-brazdeikis—michigan—big-ten-basketball—the-journey.
6. "John Beilein previews Michigan vs. North Carolina," YouTube Video, 14:47, posted by "Isaiah Hole," November 27, 2018, https://www.youtube.com/watch?v=NBFOvfSY2mk.
7. Brendan Quinn, "Ignas Brazdeikis vs. the world," *The Athletic*, August 20, 2018, https://theathletic.com/480660/2018/08/20/ignas-brazdeikis-vs-the-world/.
8. "John Beilein previews Purdue," YouTube Video, 17:36, posted by "Isaiah Hole," November 30, 2018, https://www.youtube.com/watch?v=FQnsXGXHHNg.
9. "Ignas Brazdeikis post Northwestern," YouTube Video, 2:43, posted by "Chris Balas," December 4, 2018, https://www.youtube.com/watch?v=clTygbH2WWU.

Chapter 24

1. "The Journey: Zavier Simpson: Michigan's 'Captain Hook,'" *Big Ten Network*, 4:30, February 26, 2019, https://www.btn2go.com/video/zavier-simpson-michigans-captain-hook—b1g-basketball—the-journey.
2. "The Journey: The Transformation of Michigan Big Man Jon Teske," *Big Ten Network*, 8:03, February 26, 2019, https://www.btn2go.com/video/the-transformation-of-michigan-big-man-jon-teske—b1g-basketball—the-journey.
3. *Ibid.*
4. *Ibid.*
5. "POSTGAME: Frank Martin on Michigan—12/8/18," YouTube Video, 6:36, posted by "South Carolina Gamecocks," December 10, 2018, https://www.youtube.com/watch?v=A4AVAXu-hlM&t=138s.
6. "Brad Underwood—Michigan postgame 2019," YouTube Video, 17:49, posted by "Illini Report," January 10, 2019, https://www.youtube.com/watch?v=abZpFyi1h-I&t=438s.
7. Josh Henschke, "Michigan takes buzzer-beater in stride amid flawed victory," 247sports.com, January 22, 2019, https://247sports.com/college/michigan/Article/michigan-wolverines-basketball-john-beilein-charles-matthews-minnesota-128195250/.

Chapter 25

1. "John Beilein reacts to Michigan going 17–0 with win over Northwestern," YouTube Video, 13:19, posted by "Isaiah Hole," January 13, 2019, https://www.youtube.com/watch?v=eB8mM6XweM0.
2. Steve Kornacki, "Simpson's Impact Extends Well Beyond Triple-Double Stat Line,"

Mgoblue.com, January 30, 2019, https://mgoblue.com/news/2019/1/30/mens-basketball-kornacki-simpsons-impact-extends-well-beyond-triple-double-stat-line.aspx?path=mbball.

3. "Zavier Simpson talks first practice," YouTube Video, 2:52, posted by "UM Hoops. com," September 25, 2018, https://www.youtube.com/watch?v=smaicHiF-IQ.

4. "Isaiah Livers at Michigan Media Day," YouTube Video, 6:31, posted by "UM Hoops.com," October 23, 2018, https://www.youtube.com/watch?v=48LDjuzi43E&t=1s.

5. "John Beilein reacts to win over Indiana," YouTube Video, 15:21, posted by "Isaiah Hole," January 6, 2019, https://www.youtube.com/watch?v=D2yIkFATXKs.

6. "John Beilein talks 84–67 win over North Carolina," YouTube Video, 13:42, posted by "Maizeandbluenews," November 28, 2018, https://www.youtube.com/watch?v=8rB2Jq8kOKs.

Chapter 26

1. "Inside Michigan Basketball: Episode 9," Mgoblue.com, 20:01, February 10, 2019, https://mgoblue.com/watch/?Archive=16057&type=Archive.

2. Steve Kornacki, "Simpson's Impact Extends Well Beyond Triple-Double Stat Line," Mgoblue.com, January 30, 2019, https://mgoblue.com/news/2019/1/30/mens-basketball-kornacki-simpsons-impact-extends-well-beyond-triple-double-stat-line.aspx?path=mbball.

Chapter 27

1. "John Beilein previews Michigan's home matchup against Wisconsin," YouTube Video, 15:30, posted by "Isaiah Hole," February 8, 2019, https://www.youtube.com/watch?v=7EAm8w7ogRk&t=527s.

2. *Ibid.*

3. "John Beilein previews Penn State," YouTube Video, 6:17, posted by "Isaiah Hole," January 2, 2019, https://www.youtube.com/watch?v=eg8QqMBw_jU.

4. "Men of March: John Beilein," *CBS Sports Network*, aired January 10, 2018.

5. Ethan Sears, "John Beilein has been an assistant coach," *The Michigan Daily*, December 7, 2018, https://www.michigandaily.com/section/mens-basketball/john-beilein-assistant-coach.

6. Andrew Kahn, "How sports psychology transformed Michigan's free throw shooting," MLive.com, March 26, 2019, https://www.mlive.com/wolverines/2019/03/how-sports-psychology-transformed-michigans-free-throw-shooting.html.

7. "John Beilein postgame press conference after win over Wisconsin," YouTube Video, 13:04, posted by "Isaiah Hole," February 9, 2019, https://www.youtube.com/watch?v=dFoB8fOGuX8.

8. "John Beilein previews Penn State," YouTube Video, 17:47, posted by "Isaiah Hole," February 11, 2019, https://www.youtube.com/watch?v=e2bhLrI_wSc.

9. James Hawkins, "Michigan's problems 'clear as day' to Charles Matthews," *The Detroit News*, February 13, 2019, https://www.detroitnews.com/story/sports/college/university-michigan/2019/02/13/michigan-wolverines-problems-clear-day-charles-matthews/2858906002/.

10. "Beilein recaps win over Minnesota," YouTube Video, 8:37, posted by "Matt Jessen-Howard," February 21, 2019, https://www.youtube.com/watch?v=a6-XWDF32iY.

11. Ethan Sears, "Jon Teske and what it takes to stay on the floor," *The Michigan Daily*, February 22, 2019, https://www.michigandaily.com/section/mens-basketball/jon-teske-and-what-it-takes-stay-floor.

Chapter 28

1. "Big Ten Conference Men's Basketball Tournament," ASAP Sports Transcripts, March 16, 2019, http://www.asapsports.com/show_interview.php?id=147931.

2. Theo Mackie, "Castleton steps up with postseason looming," *The Michigan Daily*,

March 3, 2019, https://www.michigandaily.com/section/mens-basketball/castleton-steps-postseason-looming.
   3. Zach Shaw, "No love, no problem: Michigan's Brazdeikis fueled by fan hate," 247sports.com, March 4, 2019, https://247sports.com/college/michigan/Article/No-love-no-problem-Michigan-basketballs-Ignas-Brazdeikis-fueled-by-fan-hate-129704140/.

Chapter 29 (no notes)

Chapter 30

   1. Zach Shaw, "Out of second chances, Michigan hungry to put it all together," 247sports.com, March 21, 2019, https://247sports.com/Article/Out-of-second-chances-Michigan-basketball-hungry-to-put-it-all-together-in-the-NCAA-Tournament-130336627/.
   2. *Ibid.*
   3. "NCAA Men's 1st and 2nd Rounds: Des Moines," ASAP Sports Transcripts, March 21, 2019, http://www.asapsports.com/show_interview.php?id=148181.
   4. "NCAA Men's 1st and 2nd Rounds: Des Moines," ASAP Sports Transcripts, March 22, 2019, http://www.asapsports.com/show_interview.php?id=148239.
   5. Josh Henschke, "Charles Matthews' halftime speech inspires second half rally," 247sports.com, March 23, 2019, https://247sports.com/college/michigan/Article/michigan-wolverines-basketball-ncaa-tournament-2019-march-madness-charles-matthews-halftime-speech-florida-gators-130448361/.
   6. James Hawkins, "Livers gets his turn in the spotlight in Michigan's win over Florida," *The Detroit News*, March 24, 2019, https://www.detroitnews.com/story/sports/college/university-michigan/2019/03/24/livers-gets-his-turn-spotlight-michigan-wolverines-win-over-florida-gators/3256788002/.
   7. Andrew Kahn, "Deep NCAA Tournament runs now the norm at Michigan, thanks to John Beilein," MLive.com, March 26, 2019, https://www.mlive.com/wolverines/2019/03/deep-ncaa-tournament-runs-now-the-norm-at-michigan-thanks-to-john-beilein.html.
   8. "NCAA Men's 1st and 2nd Rounds: Des Moines," ASAP Sports Transcripts, March 23, 2019, http://www.asapsports.com/show_interview.php?id=148373.
   9. Nick Baumgardner, "Michigan basketball has found its swagger again. Look out, NCAA field," *Detroit Free Press*, March 24, 2019, https://www.freep.com/story/sports/college/university-michigan/wolverines/2019/03/24/michigan-basketball-ncaa-tournament/3259346002/.
   10. Andrew Kahn, "Hook shot, hook pass: Michigan's Zavier Simpson 'controlled the whole game' in Tournament win," MLive.com, March 22, 2019, https://www.mlive.com/wolverines/2019/03/hook-shot-hook-pass-michigans-zavier-simpson-controlled-the-whole-game-in-tournament-win.html.
   11. *Ibid.*

Chapter 31

   1. Andrew Kahn, "Michigan is going back to Cali: 'I'm just trying to get to some nice weather,'" MLive.com, March 26, 2019, https://www.mlive.com/wolverines/2019/03/michigan-is-going-back-to-cali-im-just-trying-to-get-to-some-nice-weather.html.
   2. Evan Daniels, "Graduate transfer Matt Mooney has high major options," 247sports.com, April 10, 2018, https://247sports.com/college/basketball/recruiting/Article/South-Dakota-graduate-transfer-Matt-Mooney-has-high-major-options-117200673/.
   3. Andrew Kahn, "'A bad day to have a bad day': Michigan 'helpless at times' vs. Texas Tech," MLive.com, April 1, 2019, https://www.mlive.com/wolverines/2019/03/a-bad-day-to-have-a-bad-day-michigan-helpless-at-times-vs-texas-tech.html.
   4. Steve Kornacki, "Wolverines Reflect on Tough Defeat, Promise Next Season Holds," Mgoblue.com, March 29, 2019, https://mgoblue.com/news/2019/3/29/mens-basketball-

kornacki-wolverines-reflect-on-tough-defeat-promise-next-season-holds.aspx?path= mbball.

5. Andrew Kahn, "The impossible task for Michigan basketball: replacing Charles Matthews, a 'model of leadership,'" MLive.com, April 3, 2019, https://www.mlive.com/wolverines/2019/04/the-impossible-task-for-michigan-basketball-replacing-charles-matthews-a-model-of-leadership.html.

6. Aria Gerson, "Michigan players developing mental strength through meditation, other methods," *The Michigan Daily*, October 24, 2018, https://www.michigandaily.com/section/mens-basketball/meditation-development-mental-game.

7. "NCAA Men's Regional Semi-Finals and Finals: Anaheim," ASAP Sports Transcripts, March 28, 2019, http://www.asapsports.com/show_interview.php?id=148614.

Chapter 32

1. Steve Kornacki, "How Love, Connectivity Have Been at the Core of These Wolverines," Mgoblog.com, March 27, 2019, https://mgoblue.com/news/2019/3/27/mens-basketball-how-love-connectivity-have-been-at-the-core-of-these-wolverines.aspx?path=mbball.

2. Bob Wojnowski, "Plenty of clues foretold John Beilein's exit at Michigan," *The Detroit News*, May 13, 2019, https://www.detroitnews.com/story/sports/columnists/bob-wojnowski/2019/05/13/wojo-like-not-john-beileins-turn-test-nba/1189826001/.

3. *Ibid.*

4. Matt Wenzel, "John Beilein didn't take long to decide on leaving for Cavs, opportunity 'too difficult to pass up,'" MLive.com, May 15, 2019, https://www.mlive.com/sports/2019/05/john-beilein-didnt-take-long-to-decide-on-leaving-for-cavs-opportunity-too-difficult-to-pass-up.html.

5. James Hawkins, "Former players: John Beilein made excellence the standard at Michigan," *The Detroit News*, May 14, 2019, https://www.detroitnews.com/story/sports/college/university-michigan/2019/05/14/former-players-beilein-made-excellence-standard-michigan/3666050002/.

Bibliography

Albom, Mitch. "Why'd John Beilein leave Michigan? There's a simple reason." *Detroit Free Press.* May 14, 2019. https://www.freep.com/story/sports/columnists/mitch-albom/2019/05/14/john-beilein-cleveland-cavaliers-michigan-basketball-mitch-albom/1189468001/.
Allen, Jeremy. "Read President Obama's full speech from his University of Michigan visit." Mlive.com. April 2, 2014. https://www.mlive.com/news/ann-arbor/2014/04/read_president_obamas_full_spe.html.
Anbender, Ace. "The All-Beilein Teams: Giants." Mgoblog.com. June 10, 2017. mgoblog.com/content/all-beilein-teams-giants.
Anderson, Joel. "Moe Wagner's Michigan Career Really Is a Dream Come True." ESPN.com. April 1, 2018. www.espn.com/mens-college-basketball/story/_/id/22922995/ncaa-tournament-final-four-moe-wagner-michigan-wolverines-career-really-dream-come-true.
Associated Press. "Beilein gets $1.3M per season from Michigan." ESPN.com. April 6, 2007. http://www.espn.com/mens-college-basketball/news/story?id=2825254.
Associated Press. "Michigan's John Beilein: Still coaching thanks to ability to adapt." ESPN.com. March 12, 2018. http://www.espn.com/mens-college-basketball/story/_/id/22738209/john-beilein-michigan-wolverines-cites-ability-adapt-key-longevity.
Auerbach, Nicole. "After Loss, Michigan Appreciates Past, Relishes Future." *USA Today.* April 9, 2013. www.usatoday.com/story/sports/ncaab/2013/04/09/championship-michigan-behind-the-scenes/2066245/.
Auerbach, Nicole. "Defense Always Came First for Luke Yaklich, and the Results are Showing at Michigan." *The Athletic.* March 30, 2018. theathletic.com/294094/2018/03/30/defense-always-came-first-for-luke-yaklich-and-the-results-are-showing-at-michigan/.
"Austin Hatch Perseveres." *CBS Sports*, 7:04. 2018. www.facebook.com/CBSSports/videos/austin-hatch-perseveres/10155767432576773/.
Baby, Ben. "Duel between A&M's T.J. Starks and Michigan's Zavier Simpson may determine Thursday's Sweet 16 matchup." DallasNews.com. March 21, 2018. https://sportsday.dallasnews.com/college-sports/collegesports/2018/03/21/duel-ams-tj-starks-michiganszavier-simpson-may-determine-thursdays-sweet-16-matchup.
Balas, Chris. "David DeJulius Dominates, Stating His Case For Mr. Basketball." TheWolverine.com. January 15, 2018. https://michigan.rivals.com/news/david-dejulius-dominates-stating-his-case-for-mr-basketball-with-video-.
Bartelstein, Josh. "We On: An Inside Look at Michigan's Final Four Run." Blog Into Book. 2015. Inside This Book, https://www.amazon.com/We-Inside-Michigan-Basketballs-Final-ebook/dp/B00EZCLA76.
Baumgardner, Nick. "Austin Hatch, Michigan Basketball: The Duo That Blessed Each Other."

Detroit Free Press. March 27, 2018. www.freep.com/story/sports/college/university-michigan/wolverines/2018/03/15/michigan-wolverines-basketball-austin-hatch/426619002/.

Baumgardner, Nick. "The John Beilein Episode." The Michigan Rant. Podcast Audio. June 4, 2018. https://player.fm/series/the-michigan-rant/the-michigan-rant-the-john-beilein-episode.

Baumgardner, Nick. "John Beilein's Two First Round Picks a Major Recruiting Chip, Big Moment for Michigan Basketball." MLive.com. June 28, 2013. www.mlive.com/wolverines/index.ssf/2013/06/column_john_beileins_two_first.html.

Baumgardner, Nick. "Michigan basketball has found its swagger again. Look out, NCAA field." *Detroit Free Press.* March 24, 2019. https://www.freep.com/story/sports/college/university-michigan/wolverines/2019/03/24/michigan-basketball-ncaa-tournament/3259346002/.

Baumgardner, Nick. "Michigan dons blue collars, writes on the walls, finds a way to push back vs. Illinois." MLive.com. January 21, 2017. https://www.mlive.com/wolverines/2017/01/michigan_blue_collar.html.

Baumgardner, Nick. "Michigan's Jaaron Simmons, Charles Matthews Learned System Together." *Detroit Free Press.* March 17, 2018. www.freep.com/story/sports/college/university-michigan/wolverines/2018/03/17/michigan-basketball-ncaa-tournament-charles-matthews-jaaron-simmons/433901002/.

Baumgardner, Nick. "Michigan's John Beilein Celebrates Program Benchmark with Family in 'Knock down, Drag out Party.'" MLive.com. March 27, 2013. www.mlive.com/wolverines/index.ssf/2013/03/michigans_john_beilein_celebra.html.

Baumgardner, Nick. "Michigan's Jordan Morgan Has His Redemption Moment—Twice—in Final Four Win over Syracuse." MLive.com. April 8, 2013. www.mlive.com/wolverines/index.ssf/2013/04/michigans_jordan_morgan_has_hi.html.

Baumgardner, Nick. "Michigan's NBA Prospects Seeking Advice from Draft Board, John Beilein Being 'Proactive' with Process." MLive.com. April 11, 2013. www.mlive.com/wolverines/index.ssf/2013/04/michigan_nba_prospects_seeking.html.

Baumgardner, Nick. "A Program Turning Point? Zack Novak Reflects on His Signature Moment in East Lansing." *The Ann Arbor News.* February 4, 2012. www.annarbor.com/sports/um-basketball/a-program-turning-point-zack-novak-remembers-his-signature-moment-in-east-lansing/.

Baumgardner, Nick. "Underdogs forever: Zack Novak, Stu Douglass at core of Michigan basketball resurgence." *The Ann Arbor News.* February 23, 2012. http://www.annarbor.com/sports/um-basketball/underdogs-forever-zack-novak-stu-douglass-at-core-of-michigan-basketball-resurgence/.

Beard, Rod. "Celtics' Brad Stevens lauds UM's John Beilein as 'one of the best.'" *The Detroit News.* June 5, 2018. https://www.detroitnews.com/story/sports/college/university-michigan/2018/06/05/boston-celtics-brad-stevens-john-beilein-one-best/674522002/.

Beard, Rod. "Michigan's Beilein Still Coaching up His Players." *The Detroit News.* February 10, 2015. www.detroitnews.com/story/sports/college/university-michigan/2015/02/09/michigans-beilein-still-coaching-players/23148519/.

Beguiristain, Joe. "The Journey Begins For Duncan Robinson." NBA.com. July 11, 2018. https://www.nba.com/heat/newsrecap/journey-begins-duncan-robinson.

"Beilein looks ahead to Sweet 16, reflects on Poole shot." YouTube Video, 15:40. Posted by "Maizeandbluenews," March 21, 2018. https://www.youtube.com/watch?v=We1FjYekrUg.

"Beilein, Matthews and Simpson at Media Day | Michigan | Big Ten Basketball." YouTube Video, 10:36. Posted by "Big Ten Network," October 11, 2018. https://www.youtube.com/watch?v=GOxo4KyMUfo.

"Beilein post Norfolk State." YouTube Video, 11:12. Posted by "Chris Balas," November 6, 2018. https://www.youtube.com/watch?v=2BWeLZHZb78.

"Beilein recaps win over Minnesota." YouTube Video, 8:37. Posted by "Matt Jessen-Howard," February 21, 2019. https://www.youtube.com/watch?v=a6-XWDF32iY.

Bennett, Brian. "Michigan's Road to the Final Four Paved with Good Intentions and Great

Defense." *The Athletic.* March 25, 2018. theathletic.com/287210/2018/03/25/michigans-road-to-the-final-four-paved-with-good-intentions-and-great-defense/.
"Big Ten Conference Men's Basketball Championship." ASAP Sports Transcripts, March 10, 2017. http://www.asapsports.com/show_interview.php?id=127768.
"Big Ten Conference Men's Basketball Championship." ASAP Sports Transcripts, March 12, 2017. http://www.asapsports.com/show_interview.php?id=127935.
"Big Ten Conference Men's Basketball Tournament." ASAP Sports Transcripts, March 2, 2018. http://www.asapsports.com/show_interview.php?id=137672.
"Big Ten Conference Men's Basketball Tournament." ASAP Sports Transcripts, March 3, 2018. http://www.asapsports.com/show_interview.php?id=137733.
"Big Ten Conference Men's Basketball Tournament." ASAP Sports Transcripts, March 16, 2019. http://www.asapsports.com/show_interview.php?id=147931.
"Big Ten Elite: 1989 Michigan Basketball." *Big Ten Network,* 45:01. Aired January 14, 2014. https://www.btn2go.com/video/big-ten-elite-1989-michigan-basketball.
"Big Ten Elite: 2013 Michigan Basketball." *Big Ten Network,* 50:11. Aired January 2015. www.btn2go.com/video/big-ten-elite-2013-michigan-basketball.
Bontemps, Tim. "'I Got Shivers down My Whole Body': Michigan Walk-on Hits the Shot of His Life." *The Washington Post.* March 23, 2018. www.washingtonpost.com/news/sports/wp/2018/03/23/meet-c-j-baird-the-walk-on-whose-shot-gave-michigan-an-ncaa-tournament-record/?utm_term=.4893e62cea30.
"Brad Underwood—Michigan postgame 2019." YouTube Video, 17:49. Posted by "Illini Report," January 10, 2019. https://www.youtube.com/watch?v=abZpFyi1h-I&t=438s.
Brown, Russ. "'Career Day' by Michigan's Wagner Leaves Louisville on the Outside Looking in at NCAA Tournament." KyForward.com. March 19, 2017. www.kyforward.com/career-day-by-michigans-wagner-leaves-louisville-on-the-outside-looking-in-at-ncaa-tournament/.
Bultman, Max. "It's All Leveling out for Duncan Robinson." *The Athletic.* March 1, 2018. theathletic.com/258891/2018/03/01/its-all-leveling-out-for-duncan-robinson/.
Bultman, Max. "'We Need You': Michigan's Players Issue the Call, and a Big Ten Title Follows." *The Athletic.* March 5, 2018. theathletic.com/261918/2018/03/05/we-need-you-michigans-players-issue-the-call-and-a-big-ten-title-follows/.
Calcagno, Mark. "Doubt Zavier Simpson? Prepare to Be Proven Wrong." *The Michigan Daily.* March 8, 2018. www.michigandaily.com/section/mens-basketball/doubt-zavier-simpson-prepare-be-proven-wrong.
Calcagno, Mark. "In a Turmoil-Filled Year, Simmons Gets Ultimate Reward." *The Michigan Daily.* March 26, 2018. www.michigandaily.com/section/mens-basketball/turmoil-filled-year-simmons-gets-ultimate-reward.
Carty, Jim. "The Un-Fab Two—A Tale of Two Hoosiers." *Ann Arbor Observer.* January 2012. annarborobserver.com/articles/the_un-fab_two.html#.W7eveWhKjid.
"Coach John Beilein—It's Worth It (Narrow Way Café & Shop)." YouTube Video, 20:00. Posted by "David Merritt," January 21, 2019. https://www.youtube.com/watch?v=pHuFqNil9Z0&t=2s.
Cook, Brian. "The Aneurysm of Leadership." Mgoblog.com. January 28, 2011. www.mgoblog.com/content/aneurysm-leadership.
Cook, Brian. "Unverified Voracity FIGHTS IN THE STREETS." Mgoblog.com. March 28, 2018. www.mgoblog.com/comment/4994503.
Cook, Everett. "The Architect: How University of Michigan's Jon Sanderson Builds Better Basketball Players." STACK. March 13, 2014. www.stack.com/a/jon-sanderson.
Daniels, Evan. "Graduate transfer Matt Mooney has high major options." 247sports.com. April 10, 2018. https://247sports.com/college/basketball/recruiting/Article/South-Dakota-graduate-transfer-Matt-Mooney-has-high-major-options-117200673/.
"Duncan Robinson after Houston." YouTube Video, 2:44. Posted by "UM Hoops.com," March 17, 2018. https://www.youtube.com/watch?v=3-WloSBaIlA.
Eisenberg, Jeff. "How a Former High School History Teacher Became the Key to Michigan's

Final Four Run." *Yahoo! Sports.* March 26, 2018. sports.yahoo.com/assistant-coach-humble-roots-became-key-michigans-final-four-run-175719995.html.

Fallis, Jeremy. "Mental Health Wellness Plays a Role in Beilein's Championship Success." *Athletes Connected.* March 7, 2018. athletesconnected.umich.edu/mental-health-wellness-plays-a-role-in-beileins-championship-success/.

Feldman, Daniel. "John Beilein's Refusal to Leave." *The Michigan Daily.* June 27, 2014. www.michigandaily.com/sports/daniel-feldman-john-beileins-refusal-leave.

Fox, David. "Michigan's Nik Stauskas, Texas' Isaiah Taylor earn weekly honors." *Athlon Sports.* January 27, 2014. https://athlonsports.com/college-basketball/michigans-nik-stauskas-texas-isaiah-taylor-earn-weekly-honors.

Gerson, Aria. "Michigan players developing mental strength through meditation, other methods." *The Michigan Daily.* October 24, 2018. https://www.michigandaily.com/section/mens-basketball/meditation-development-mental-game.

Hackett, Tim. "Embraced by a Home Away from Home, Moritz Wagner Is Finally Ready for a New Challenge." SI.com. June 12, 2018. www.si.com/nba/2018/06/12/moritz-wagner-michigan-nba-draft-john-beilein-dirk-nowitzki.

Hawkins, James. "Austin Hatch receives touching 'Senior Day' send-off." *The Detroit News.* February 18, 2018. https://www.detroitnews.com/story/sports/college/university-michigan/wolverines/2018/02/18/austin-hatch-receives-touching-senior-day-send/110587918/.

Hawkins, James. "Extra work helps UM's Simpson pick up scoring pace." *The Detroit News.* December 20, 2017. https://www.detroitnews.com/story/sports/college/university-michigan/2017/12/20/extra-shooting-helps-ums-simpson-pick-scoring-pace/108777656/.

Hawkins, James. "Former players: John Beilein made excellence the standard at Michigan." *The Detroit News.* May 14, 2019. https://www.detroitnews.com/story/sports/college/university-michigan/2019/05/14/former-players-beilein-made-excellence-standard-michigan/3666050002/.

Hawkins, James. "Livers gets his turn in the spotlight in Michigan's win over Florida." *The Detroit News.* March 24, 2019. https://www.detroitnews.com/story/sports/college/university-michigan/2019/03/24/livers-gets-his-turn-spotlight-michigan-wolverines-win-over-florida-gators/3256788002/.

Hawkins, James. "Matthews' 20-Point Outing for UM Comes with Heavy Heart." *The Detroit News.* December 17, 2017. www.detroitnews.com/story/sports/college/university-michigan/wolverines/2017/12/16/matthews-20-point-outing-um-comes-heavy-heart/108665726/.

Hawkins, James. "Michigan aims for the moon with out-of-this-world defense." *The Detroit News.* November 29, 2018. https://www.detroitnews.com/story/sports/college/university-michigan/2018/11/29/michigan-wolverines-dissatisfied-defensive-results-win-over-north-carolina-tar-heels/2148584002/.

Hawkins, James. "Michigan braces for North Carolina 'freight train.'" *The Detroit News.* November 27, 2018. https://www.detroitnews.com/story/sports/college/university-michigan/2018/11/27/michigan-braces-north-carolina-freight-train/2124315002/.

Hawkins, James. "Michigan Scout Team's Unsung Work Playing Pivotal Role." *The Detroit News.* March 29, 2018. www.detroitnews.com/story/sports/college/university-michigan/wolverines/2018/03/28/michigan-scout-teams-unsung-work-playing-pivotal-role/33375949/.

Hawkins, James. "Michigan's problems 'clear as day' to Charles Matthews." *The Detroit News.* February 13, 2019. https://www.detroitnews.com/story/sports/college/university-michigan/2019/02/13/michigan-wolverines-problems-clear-day-charles-matthews/2858906002/.

Hawkins, James. "UM's Brazdeikis makes most of 'shining moment.'" *The Detroit News.* November 15, 2018. https://www.detroitnews.com/story/sports/college/university-michigan/2018/11/15/michigans-ignas-brazdeikis-makes-most-shining-moment/2009725002/.

Hawkins, James. "Zavier Simpson, dad going back to 'ground zero' to improve shooting." *The Detroit News.* May 11, 2018. https://www.detroitnews.com/story/sports/college/university-michigan/wolverines/2018/05/11/michigan-guard-zavier-simpson-seeks-improve-jump-shot/600968002/.

Henschke, Josh. "Charles Matthews' halftime speech inspires second half rally." 247 sports.com. March 23, 2019. https://247sports.com/college/michigan/Article/michigan-wolverines-basketball-ncaa-tournament-2019-march-madness-charles-matthews-halftime-speech-florida-gators-130448361/.

Henschke, Josh. "Michigan takes buzzer-beater in stride amid flawed victory." 247sports.com. January 22, 2019. https://247sports.com/college/michigan/Article/michigan-wolverines-basketball-john-beilein-charles-matthews-minnesota-128195250/.

"Iggy Brazdeikis talks win over North Carolina." YouTube Video, 2:47. Posted by "Maizeandbluenews," November 29, 2018. https://www.youtube.com/watch?v=0_hx76Ss-YY.

"Ignas Brazdeikis at Michigan Media Day." YouTube Video, 7:34. Posted by "UM Hoops.com," October 22, 2018. https://www.youtube.com/watch?v=weJaz8Dsl1E.

"Ignas Brazdeikis post Northwestern." YouTube Video, 2:43. Posted by "Chris Balas," December 4, 2018. https://www.youtube.com/watch?v=clTygbH2WWU.

"Inside Michigan Basketball: Episode 9." Mgoblue.com, 20:01. February 10, 2019. https://mgoblue.com/watch/?Archive=16057&type=Archive.

"Isaiah Livers after Loyola." YouTube Video, 4:04. Posted by "UM Hoops.com," March 31, 2018. https://www.youtube.com/watch?v=ZaTA3-0947A.

"Isaiah Livers at Michigan Media Day." YouTube Video, 6:31. Posted by "UM Hoops.com," October 23, 2018. https://www.youtube.com/watch?v=48LDjuzi43E.

"John Beilein before Selection Sunday." YouTube Video, 19:20. Posted by "UMHoops Video," March 9, 2018. https://www.youtube.com/watch?v=wNs0ewdHlzE.

"John Beilein post Iowa." YouTube Video, 9:59. Posted by "Chris Balas," February 14, 2018. https://www.youtube.com/watch?v=jrGUS7bcgtw.

"John Beilein post Rutgers." YouTube Video, 14:51. Posted by "Chris Balas," January 21, 2018. https://www.youtube.com/watch?v=G1USNIxip7I.

"John Beilein postgame press conference after win over Wisconsin." YouTube Video, 13:04. Posted by "Isaiah Hole," February 9, 2019. https://www.youtube.com/watch?v=dFoB8fOGuX8.

"John Beilein previews Michigan vs. North Carolina." YouTube Video, 14:47. Posted by "Isaiah Hole," November 27, 2018. https://www.youtube.com/watch?v=NBFOvfSY2mk.

"John Beilein previews Michigan's home matchup against Wisconsin." YouTube Video, 15:30. Posted by "Isaiah Hole," February 8, 2019. https://www.youtube.com/watch?v=7EAm8w7ogRk&t=527s.

"John Beilein previews Penn State." YouTube Video, 6:17. Posted by "Isaiah Hole," January 2, 2019. https://www.youtube.com/watch?v=eg8QqMBw_jU.

"John Beilein previews Penn State." YouTube Video, 17:47. Posted by "Isaiah Hole," February 11, 2019. https://www.youtube.com/watch?v=e2bhLrI_wSc.

"John Beilein previews Purdue." YouTube Video, 17:36. Posted by "Isaiah Hole," November 30, 2018. https://www.youtube.com/watch?v=FQnsXGXHHNg.

"John Beilein reacts to Michigan going 17–0 with win over Northwestern." YouTube Video, 13:19. Posted by "Isaiah Hole," January 13, 2019. https://www.youtube.com/watch?v=eB8mM6XweM0.

"John Beilein reacts to win over Indiana." YouTube Video, 15:21. Posted by "Isaiah Hole," January 6, 2019. https://www.youtube.com/watch?v=D2yIkFATXKs.

"John Beilein talks 84–67 win over North Carolina." YouTube Video, 13:42. Posted by "Maizeandbluenews," November 28, 2018. https://www.youtube.com/watch?v=8rB2Jq8kOKs.

"John Beilein talks heart surgery, first practice." YouTube Video, 24:45. Posted by "UM Hoops.com," September 25, 2018. https://www.youtube.com/watch?v=A1QHRzaeHVE&t=256s.

"John Beilein talks loss at Purdue (2/2)." YouTube Video, 6:36. Posted by "UMHoops Videos," January 25, 2018. https://www.youtube.com/watch?v=t4GdOntZskE.

"John Beilein talks loss to Villanova." YouTube Video, 7:21. Posted by "UM Hoops.com," April 2, 2018. https://www.youtube.com/watch?v=Ne6Zw_9eTr4.

"John Beilein talks win over Maryland." YouTube Video, 9:35. Posted by "UMHoops Videos," February 24, 2018. https://www.youtube.com/watch?v=2_1b9ycqSxA.

"Jordan Poole at Michigan Media Day." YouTube Video, 8:23. Posted by "UM Hoops.com," October 22, 2018. https://www.youtube.com/watch?v=oIAVsuP1qyc.

"Jordan Poole post Illinois." YouTube Video, 2:46. Posted by "Chris Balas," January 6, 2018. https://www.youtube.com/watch?v=i0pIXsTOPLI.

"The Journey: Jude Stamper and Michigan." *Big Ten Network*, 2:44. February 16, 2018. https://www.btn2go.com/video/the-journey-jude-stamper-is-part-of-michigan-basketball.

"The Journey: Meet Ignas Brazdeikis." *Big Ten Network*, 4:42. January 15, 2019. https://www.btn2go.com/video/meet-ignas-brazdeikis—michigan—big-ten-basketball—the-journey.

"The Journey: Michigan All-Access At Michigan State." *Big Ten Network*, 4:43. January 22, 2018. www.btn2go.com/video/the-journey-michigan-all-access-at-michigan-state.

"The Journey: The Transformation of Michigan Big Man Jon Teske." *Big Ten Network*, 8:03. February 26, 2019. https://www.btn2go.com/video/the-transformation-of-michigan-big-man-jon-teske—b1g-basketball—the-journey.

"The Journey: Zavier Simpson: Michigan's 'Captain Hook.'" *Big Ten Network*, 4:30. February 26, 2019. https://www.btn2go.com/video/zavier-simpson-michigans-captain-hook—b1g-basketball—the-journey.

Kahn, Andrew. "'A bad day to have a bad day': Michigan 'helpless at times' vs. Texas Tech." MLive.com. April 1, 2019. https://www.mlive.com/wolverines/2019/03/a-bad-day-to-have-a-bad-day-michigan-helpless-at-times-vs-texas-tech.html.

Kahn, Andrew. "Changed by a Plane Crash, John Beilein Has a New Outlook." MLive.com. March 29, 2018. www.mlive.com/wolverines/index.ssf/2018/03/changed_by_a_plane_crash_john.html#in cart_river_index.

Kahn, Andrew. "Deep NCAA Tournament runs now the norm at Michigan, thanks to John Beilein." MLive.com. March 26, 2019. https://www.mlive.com/wolverines/2019/03/deep-ncaa-tournament-runs-now-the-norm-at-michigan-thanks-to-john-beilein.html.

Kahn, Andrew. "Hook shot, hook pass: Michigan's Zavier Simpson 'controlled the whole game' in Tournament win." MLive.com. March 22, 2019. https://www.mlive.com/wolverines/2019/03/hook-shot-hook-pass-michigans-zavier-simpson-controlled-the-whole-game-in-tournament-win.html.

Kahn, Andrew. "How Jaaron Simmons realized his dreams in just one season with Michigan basketball." MLive.com. April 16, 2018. https://www.mlive.com/wolverines/2018/04/how_jaaron_simmons_realized_hi.html.

Kahn, Andrew. "How sports psychology transformed Michigan's free throw shooting." MLive.com. March 26, 2019. https://www.mlive.com/wolverines/2019/03/how-sports-psychology-transformed-michigans-free-throw-shooting.html.

Kahn, Andrew. "The impossible task for Michigan basketball: replacing Charles Matthews, a 'model of leadership.'" MLive.com. April 3, 2019. https://www.mlive.com/wolverines/2019/04/the-impossible-task-for-michigan-basketball-replacing-charles-matthews-a-model-of-leadership.html.

Kahn, Andrew. "Jaaron Simmons Could Be a Malcontent for Michigan, but Has Been the Opposite." MLive.com. February 16, 2018. www.mlive.com/wolverines/index.ssf/2018/02/jaaron_simmons_could_be_a_malc.html.

Kahn, Andrew. "Michigan is going back to Cali: 'I'm just trying to get to some nice weather.'" MLive.com. March 26, 2019. https://www.mlive.com/wolverines/2019/03/michigan-is-going-back-to-cali-im-just-trying-to-get-to-some-nice-weather.html.

Katz, Andy. "John Beilein and Chris Mullin." *March Madness 365 with Andy Katz*. Podcast Audio. June 12, 2018, https://podcasts.apple.com/us/podcast/john-beilein-and-chris-mullin/id1325823631?i=1000413532754.

Keown, Tim. "Director's Cut." ESPN.com. March 5, 2013. http://www.espn.com/mens-college-basketball/story/_/id/9014486/michigan-wolverines-head-coach-john-beilein-never-too-prepared-espn-magazine.

Kornacki, Steve. "Against All Odds, Wolverines Prevail in D.C." Mgoblue.com. March 12, 2017. mgoblue.com/news/2017/3/13/kornacki_against_all_odds_wolverines_prevail_in_d_c_.a spx.

Kornacki, Steve. "Austin Hatch: A Storybook Ending Achieved After Unimaginable Tragedy." Mgoblue.com. February 27, 2018. mgoblue.com/news/2018/2/27/mens-basketball-austin-hatch-a-storybook-ending-achieved-after-unimaginable-tragedy.aspx.

Kornacki, Steve. "Beilein Embraces Changes with Team, Staff." Mgoblue.com. August 7, 2017. mgoblue.com/news/2017/8/7/mens-basketball-kornacki-beilein-embraces-changes-with-team-staff.aspx?path=mbball.

Kornacki, Steve. "Beilein's More Evident Joy and Smile Make an Impression." Mgoblue.com. October 25, 2017. mgoblue.com/news/2017/10/25/mens-basketball-kornacki-beileins-more-evident-joy-and-smile-makes-an-impression.aspx?path=mbball.

Kornacki, Steve. "'Big Nasty' Teske Evolving into Quite a Weapon for the Wolverines." Mgoblue.com. December 1, 2018. https://mgoblue.com/news/2018/12/1/mens-basketball-big-nasty-teske-evolving-into-quite-a-weapon-for-the-wolverines.aspx?path=mbball.

Kornacki, Steve. "Brazdeikis is Confident, Coachable and Ready to Contribute." Mgoblue.com. October 23, 2018. https://mgoblue.com/news/2018/10/23/mens-basketball-kornacki-brazdeikis-is-confident-coachable-and-ready-to-contribute.aspx?path=mbball.

Kornacki, Steve. "How Love, Connectivity Have Been at the Core of These Wolverines." Mgoblue.com. March 27, 2019. https://mgoblue.com/news/2019/3/27/mens-basketball-how-love-connectivity-have-been-at-the-core-of-these-wolverines.aspx?path=mbball.

Kornacki, Steve. "How Muhammad-Ali Abdur-Rahkman Got His Name and Got His Game." Mgoblue.com. March 16, 2018. mgoblue.com/news/2018/3/16/mens-basketball-kornacki-how-muhammad-ali-abdur-rahkman-got-his-name-and-got-his-game.aspx?path=mbball.

Kornacki, Steve. "How Staying 'Connected' Helps Wolverines Dominate on Defense." Mgoblue.com. March 2, 2018. mgoblue.com/news/2018/3/2/mens-basketball-how-staying-connected-helps-wolverines-dominate-on-defense.aspx?path=mbball.

Kornacki, Steve. "How Wilson Went from Suspect to NBA Draft Prospect." Mgoblue.com. June 21, 2017. mgoblue.com/news/2017/6/21/mens-basketball-kornacki-how-wilson-went-from-suspect-to-nba-draft-prospect.aspx?path=mbball.

Kornacki, Steve. "How Yaklich Has Helped Turn Michigan Into a Formidable Defensive Team." Mgoblue.com. March 21, 2018. mgoblue.com/news/2018/3/21/mens-basketball-how-yaklich-has-helped-turn-michigan-into-a-formidable-defensive-team.aspx.

Kornacki, Steve. "Improvement in Simpson, Teske the Essence of Coaching to Beilein." Mgoblue.com. January 13, 2019. https://mgoblue.com/news/2019/1/13/mens-basketball-improvement-in-simpson-teske-the-essence-of-coaching-to-beilein.aspx?path=mbball.

Kornacki, Steve. "Matthews Steps Up in Many Ways to Help Lead Wolverines Past Iowa." Mgoblue.com. March 1, 2018. https://mgoblue.com/news/2018/3/1/mens-basketball-kornacki-matthews-steps-up-in-many-ways-to-help-lead-wolverines-past-iowa.aspx?path=mbball.

Kornacki, Steve. "One Last 'Victors' from Emotion-Filled Postgame Locker Room." Mgoblue.com. April 3, 2018. mgoblue.com/news/2018/4/3/mens-basketball-one-last-victors-from-postgame-locker-room.aspx?path=mbball.

Kornacki, Steve. "Reflecting on a Special NCAA Tourney Run." Mgoblue.com. March 24, 2017. mgoblue.com/news/2017/3/24/Kornacki_Reflecting_on_a_Special_NCAA_Tourney_Ru n.aspx?path=mbball.

Kornacki, Steve. "Rudy T, Jalen, Maceo and 'The Judge' Connect with Wolverines." Mgoblue.com. January 21 2018. https://mgoblue.com/news/2018/1/21/mens-basketball-kornacki-rudy-t-jalen-maceo-and-the-judge-connect-with-wolverines.aspx?path=mbball.

Kornacki, Steve. "Simpson Developing Into a Force, 'Chopping Wood' and Draining Treys." Mgoblue.com. January 10, 2018. mgoblue.com/news/2018/1/10/mens-basketball-simpson-developing-into-a-force-chopping-wood-and-draining-treys.aspx?path=mbball.

Kornacki, Steve. "Simpson's Impact Extends Well Beyond Triple-Double Stat Line." Mgoblue.com. January 30, 2019. https://mgoblue.com/news/2019/1/30/mens-basketball-kornacki-simpsons-impact-extends-well-beyond-triple-double-stat-line.aspx?path=mbball.

Kornacki, Steve. "So Far, So Fast: How Beilein Took U-M from Obscurity to Title Game in Three Months." Mgoblue.com. April 1, 2018. https://mgoblue.com/news/2018/4/1/mens-basketball-so-far-so-fast-how-beilein-took-u-m-from-obscurity-to-title-game-in-three-months.aspx?path=mbball.

Kornacki, Steve. "The Stories Behind Abdur-Rahkman's Heroics in Maryland Victory." Mgoblue.com. January 16, 2018. https://mgoblue.com/news/2018/1/16/mens-basketball-kornacki-the-stories-behind-abdur-rahkman-heroics-in-maryland-victory.aspx.

Kornacki, Steve. "Teske Finds 'Double-Double' Success Playing in 'Traffic.'" Mgoblue.com. December 16, 2017. mgoblue.com/news/2017/12/16/mens-basketball-kornacki-teske-finds-double-double-success-playing-in-traffic.aspx?path=mbball.

Kornacki, Steve. "The Time Has Come for Moe to Go Pro." Mgoblue.com. April 14, 2018. mgoblue.com/news/2018/4/14/mens-basketball-kornacki-the-time-has-come-for-moe-to-go-pro.aspx.

Kornacki, Steve. "Wagner Dominates, Motivates and Puts on a Final Four Show." Mgoblue.com. April 1, 2018. mgoblue.com/news/2018/4/1/mens-basketball-kornacki-wagner-dominates-motivates-and-puts-on-a-final-four-show.aspx?path=mbball.

Kornacki, Steve. "Wagner Explains Decision to Remain at U-M." Mgoblue.com. March 24, 2017. mgoblue.com/news/2017/5/24/Kornacki_Wagner_Explains_Decision_to_Remain_at_U_ M.aspx?path=mbball.

Kornacki, Steve. "What's New with Michigan Men's Basketball." Mgoblue.com. October 3, 2016. mgoblue.com/news/2016/10/3/Kornacki_What_s_New_with_Michigan_Men_s_Basketb all.aspx?path=mbball.

Kornacki, Steve. "Wolverines Reflect on Tough Defeat, Promise Next Season Holds." Mgoblue.com. March 29, 2019. https://mgoblue.com/news/2019/3/29/mens-basketball-kornacki-wolverines-reflect-on-tough-defeat-promise-next-season-holds.aspx?path=mbball.

Layden, Tim. "The Transfer Story of Michigan's Duncan Robinson Is Not Your Average One." SI.com. March 29, 2018. www.si.com/college-basketball/2018/03/29/michigan-duncan-robinson-roots-williams-college-final-four.

Leung, Diamond. "John Beilein Explains Michigan's Five Core Values, Forming UPAID Acronym." MLive.com. August 17, 2013. www.mlive.com/wolverines/index.ssf/2013/08/john_beilein_explains_michigan.html.

"Livers Norfolk State." YouTube Video, 4:09. Posted by "Chris Balas," November 6, 2018. https://www.youtube.com/watch?v=KZcqq7YVkPQ.

"Luke Yaklich Media Day." YouTube Video, 7:03. Posted by "UM Hoops.com," October 25, 2017. https://www.youtube.com/watch?v=cnZDwfKW6zg.

Mackie, Theo. "Castleton steps up with postseason looming." *The Michigan Daily*. March 3, 2019. https://www.michigandaily.com/section/mens-basketball/castleton-steps-postseason-looming.

"MAN 5010 B 2.8 Every Role Matters in Teams." Vimeo Video, 2:04. Posted by "Massey Services," May 16, 2018. vimeo.com/270187962.

"MAN 5010 D 4.13 Instilling a Learning Mindset." Vimeo Video, 1:23. Posted by "Massey Services," July 29, 2018. vimeo.com/270200339.

Marcovitch, Max. "Austin Hatch among seniors honored in emotional day." *The Michigan Daily*. February 18, 2018. https://www.michigandaily.com/section/basketball/austin-hatch-senior-day.

Marcovitch, Max. "For Beilein, All That's Left Is a Title." *The Michigan Daily*. April 15, 2018. www.michigandaily.com/section/basketball/john-beilein-michigan-coach-legacy-culture.

"Maui Jim Maui Invitational." ASAP Sports Transcripts, November 22, 2017. http://www.asapsports.com/show_interview.php?id=136141.

"McGary, Robinson to Continue Collegiate Careers at Michigan." Mgoblue.com, April 18, 2013. https://mgoblue.com/news/2013/4/18/McGary_Robinson_to_Continue_Collegiate_Caree rs_at_Michigan.aspx?path=mbball.

"Men of March: John Beilein." *CBS Sports Network*, aired January 10, 2018.

"Michigan Adds Matthews, Wright-Jones to Roster." Mgoblue.com, July 1, 2016. https://mgoblue.com/news/2016/7/1/Michigan_Adds_Matthews_Wright_Jones_to_Roste r.aspx?path=mbball.

"Michigan head coach John Beilein addresses the media (6/26)." YouTube Video, 30:57. Posted by "Isaiah Hole," June 26, 2018. https://www.youtube.com/watch?v=kmaTaq_8R0E.

"Miraculous: The Austin Hatch Story—ESPN." YouTube Video, 16:06. Posted by "Dan Arruda." September 7, 2016, www.youtube.com/watch?v=AmKUpj97ZB8.

"Moe Wagner after FSU." YouTube Video, 4:02. Posted by "UM Hoops.com," March 24, 2018. https://www.youtube.com/watch?v=BgZVTWO5n2Y.

"Moritz Wagner after Villanova." YouTube Video, 2:30. Posted by "UM Hoops.com," April 2, 2018. https://www.youtube.com/watch?v=OFKrMqHYpYo.

"Moritz Wagner Talks About His Michigan Experience." Mgoblue.com, 3:44. April 17, 2018. https://mgoblue.com/watch/?Archive=12291&type=Archive.

"Moritz Wagner talks win over Minnesota 2.3.18." YouTube Video, 9:10. Posted by "UMHoops Videos," February 3rd, 2018. https://www.youtube.com/watch?time_continue=125&v=_q6evthHRHg.

Murphy, Dan. "Can Ignas Brazdeikis help fuel Michigan's defensive revolution?" ESPN.com. January 23, 2019. http://www.espn.com/mens-college-basketball/story/_/id/25818940/can-ignas-brazdeikis-help-fuel-michigan-defensive-revolution.

"NCAA Men's Basketball Championship: Final Four." ASAP Sports Transcripts, March 30, 2018. http://www.asapsports.com/show_interview.php?id=138971.

"NCAA Men's Basketball Championship: Final Four." ASAP Sports Transcripts, March 31, 2018. http://www.asapsports.com/show_interview.php?id=139012.

"NCAA Men's Basketball Championship: Final Four." ASAP Sports Transcripts, April 1, 2018. http://www.asapsports.com/show_interview.php?id=139019.

"NCAA Men's Basketball Championship: Final Four." ASAP Sports Transcripts, April 2, 2018. http://www.asapsports.com/show_interview.php?id=139039.

"NCAA Men's Final Four." ASAP Sports Transcripts, April 1, 2013. http://www.asapsports.com/show_interview.php?id=88137.

"NCAA Men's Final Four." ASAP Sports Transcripts, April 4, 2013. http://www.asapsports.com/show_interview.php?id=88182.

"NCAA Men's Final Four." ASAP Sports Transcripts, April 7, 2013. http://www.asapsports.com/show_interview.php?id=88266.

"NCAA Men's Final Four." ASAP Sports Transcripts, April 8, 2013. http://www.asapsports.com/show_interview.php?id=88297.

"NCAA Men's Final Four." ASAP Sports Transcripts, March 29, 2018. http://www.asapsports.com/show_interview.php?id=138938.

"NCAA Men's Final Four." ASAP Sports Transcripts, March 30, 2018. http://www.asapsports.com/show_interview.php?id=138971.

"NCAA Men's Final Four." ASAP Sports Transcripts, April 1, 2018. http://www.asapsports.com/show_interview.php?id=139019.

"NCAA Men's Final Four." ASAP Sports Transcripts, April 2, 2018. http://www.asapsports.com/show_interview.php?id=139039.

"NCAA Men's 1st and 2nd Rounds: Brooklyn." ASAP Sports Transcripts, March 18, 2016. http://www.asapsports.com/show_interview.php?id=117858.

"NCAA Men's 1st and 2nd Rounds: Des Moines." ASAP Sports Transcripts, March 21, 2019. http://www.asapsports.com/show_interview.php?id=148181.

"NCAA Men's 1st and 2nd Rounds: Des Moines." ASAP Sports Transcripts, March 22, 2019. http://www.asapsports.com/show_interview.php?id=148239.

"NCAA Men's 1st and 2nd Rounds: Des Moines." ASAP Sports Transcripts, March 23, 2019. http://www.asapsports.com/show_interview.php?id=148373.

"NCAA Men's 1st and 2nd Rounds: Indianapolis." ASAP Sports Transcripts, March 17, 2017. http://www.asapsports.com/show_interview.php?id=128229.

"NCAA Men's 1st and 2nd Rounds: Indianapolis." ASAP Sports Transcripts, March 18, 2017. http://www.asapsports.com/show_interview.php?id=128334.

"NCAA Men's 1st and 2nd Rounds: Indianapolis." ASAP Sports Transcripts, March 19, 2017. http://www.asapsports.com/show_interview.php?id=128436.

"NCAA Men's 1st and 2nd Rounds: Wichita." ASAP Sports Transcripts, March 15, 2018. http://www.asapsports.com/show_interview.php?id=138317.

"NCAA Men's 1st and 2nd Rounds: Wichita." ASAP Sports Transcripts, March 16, 2018. http://www.asapsports.com/show_interview.php?id=138367.

"NCAA Men's First Four: Dayton." ASAP Sports Transcripts, March 16, 2016. http://www.asapsports.com/show_interview.php?id=117603.

"NCAA Men's Regional Semi-Finals and Finals: Anaheim." ASAP Sports Transcripts, March 28, 2019. http://www.asapsports.com/show_interview.php?id=148614.

"NCAA Men's Regional Semi-Finals and Finals: Arlington." ASAP Sports Transcripts, March 29, 2013. http://www.asapsports.com/show_interview.php?id=88074.

"NCAA Men's Regional Semi-Finals and Finals: Indianapolis." ASAP Sports Transcripts, March 27, 2014. http://www.asapsports.com/show_interview.php?id=97626.

"NCAA Men's Regional Semi-Finals and Finals: Indianapolis." ASAP Sports Transcripts, March 29, 2014. http://www.asapsports.com/show_interview.php?id=97718.

"NCAA Men's Regional Semi-Finals and Finals: Kansas City." ASAP Sports Transcripts, March 22, 2017. http://www.asapsports.com/show_interview.php?id=128513.

"NCAA Men's Regional Semi-Finals and Finals: Kansas City." ASAP Sports Transcripts, March 23, 2017. http://www.asapsports.com/show_interview.php?id=128641.

"NCAA Men's Regional Semi-Finals and Finals: Los Angeles." ASAP Sports Transcripts, March 22, 2018. http://www.asapsports.com/show_interview.php?id=138721.

"NCAA Men's Regional Semi-Finals and Finals: Los Angeles." ASAP Sports Transcripts, March 23, 2018. http://www.asapsports.com/show_interview.php?id=138752.

"NCAA Men's Regional Semi-Finals and Finals: Los Angeles." ASAP Sports Transcripts, March 24, 2018. http://www.asapsports.com/show_interview.php?id=138853.

"NCAA Men's 2nd and 3rd Rounds: Auburn Hills." ASAP Sports Transcripts, March 22, 2013. http://www.asapsports.com/show_interview.php?id=87780.

"NCAA Men's 2nd and 3rd Rounds: Auburn Hills." ASAP Sports Transcripts, March 23, 2013. http://www.asapsports.com/show_interview.php?id=87871.

"NCAA Men's 2nd and 3rd Rounds: Milwaukee." ASAP Sports Transcripts, March 22, 2014. http://www.asapsports.com/show_interview.php?id=97458.

Niyo, John. "Beilein, Michigan take high road to Final Four." *The Detroit News*. March 25, 2018. https://www.detroitnews.com/story/sports/columnists/john-niyo/2018/03/25/niyo-beilein-um-take-high-road-final-four/33271509/.

Norlander, Matt. "How an ex-high school social studies teacher helped put Michigan in the Final Four." CBSsports.com. March 29, 2018. https://www.cbssports.com/college-basketball/news/how-an-ex-high-school-social-studies-teacher-helped-put-michigan-in-the-final-four/.

O'Donnell, B.R.J. "Coaching Players for Life." *The Atlantic*. August 21, 2017. www.theatlantic.com/business/archive/2017/08/beilein-mentoring/536994/.

O'Neil, Dana. "Austin Hatch Is an Uncommon Man." ESPN.com. February 9, 2015. www.espn.com/mens-college-basketball/story/_/id/12299896/michigan-wolverines-basketball-player-austin-hatch-survived-two-plane-crashes.

Parrish, Gary. "Is John Beilein the Best at Turning Lowly Recruits into Lottery Picks?" CBS Sports.com. April 6, 2017. www.cbssports.com/college-basketball/news/is-john-beilein-the-best-at-turning-lowly-recruits-into-lottery-picks/.

"POSTGAME: Frank Martin on Michigan—12/8/18." YouTube Video, 6:36. Posted by "South Carolina Gamecocks," December 10, 2018. https://www.youtube.com/watch?v=A4AVAXuhlM&t=138s.

Quinn, Brendan. "At Michigan, looking at life without John Beilein." *The Athletic*. August 10, 2018. https://theathletic.com/466243/2018/08/10/at-michigan-looking-at-life-without-john-beilein/.

Quinn, Brendan. "Austin Hatch, Age 23, Has a Story to Tell." *The Athletic*. March 28, 2018. theathletic.com/290094/2018/03/28/austin-hatch-age-23-has-a-story-to-tell/.

Quinn, Brendan. "Does John Beilein make sense for the Pistons? Do the Pistons make sense for John Beilein?" *The Athletic*. June 1, 2018. https://theathletic.com/377257/2018/06/01/does-john-beilein-make-sense-for-the-pistons-do-the-pistons-make-sense-for-john-beilein/.

Quinn, Brendan. "How John Beilein Snuck off to Germany to Meet Moritz Wagner and 'Look Him in the Eye.'" MLive.com. June 14, 2015. www.mlive.com/wolverines/index.ssf/2015/06/moritz_wagner_john_beilein.html.

Quinn, Brendan. "Ignas Brazdeikis vs. the world." *The Athletic*. August 20, 2018. https://theathletic.com/480660/2018/08/20/ignas-brazdeikis-vs-the-world/.

Quinn, Brendan. "An Inside Look at Michigan's Complicated Point Guard Situation." *The Athletic*. November 10, 2017. theathletic.com/150250/2017/11/10/an-inside-look-at-michigans-complicated-point-guard-situation/.

Quinn, Brendan. "It Sure Seems like Michigan Has a New Weapon in Charles Matthews." *The Athletic*. November 4, 2017. theathletic.com/146418/2017/11/04/it-sure-seems-like-michigan-has-a-new-weapon-in-charles-matthews/.

Quinn, Brendan. "Jordan Poole and a Michigan team unlike any other." *The Athletic*. March 18, 2018. https://theathletic.com/278731/2018/03/18/jordan-poole-and-a-michigan-team-unlike-any-other/.

Quinn, Brendan. "Michigan AD Warde Manuel says he never gave any thought to John Beilein's job security." MLive.com. March 18, 2017. https://www.mlive.com/wolverines/index.ssf/2017/03/michigan_ad_warde_manuel_says.html.

Quinn, Brendan. "Michigan's Absurd and Exhilarating Journey Ends, but the Process Marches On." *The Athletic*. April 3, 2018. theathletic.com/297093/2018/04/03/michigans-absurd-and-exhilarating-journey-ends-but-the-process-marches-on/.

Quinn, Brendan. "Moritz Wagner's Development Moves Front and Center for Michigan Basketball." MLive.com. May 30, 2017. www.mlive.com/wolverines/index.ssf/2017/05/moritz_wagners_development_mov.html.

Quinn, Brendan. "Muscle and Willpower: Moritz Wagner Lifts Michigan to Verge of National Championship." *The Athletic*. April 1, 2018. theathletic.com/296043/2018/04/01/muscle-and-willpower-moritz-wagner-lifts-michigan-to-verge-of-national-championship/.

Quinn, Brendan. "Old Faces, New Places: This Is Charles Matthews' Moment, Again." *The Athletic*. November 3, 2017. theathletic.com/143050/2017/11/03/old-faces-new-places-this-is-charles-matthews-moment-again/.

Quinn, Brendan. "Once a Starter, Now a Closer, Zavier Simpson Leads U-M at Winning Time." *The Athletic*. December 28, 2017. theathletic.com/195966/2017/12/28/once-a-starter-now-a-closer-zavier-simpson-leads-u-m-at-winning-time/.

Quinn, Brendan. "The Peculiar Story of Michigan Recruit Muhammad-Ali Abdur-Rahkman, Dave Rooney and the Phone Call That Changed Everything." MLive.com. May 10, 2015. www.mlive.com/wolverines/index.ssf/2014/04/the_peculiar_story_of_muhammad.html.

Quinn, Brendan. "The Story of Zavier Simpson and the Defensive Dogs of Michigan." *The Athletic*. March 4, 2018. theathletic.com/260616/2018/03/03/the-story-of-zavier-simpson-and-the-defensive-dogs-of-michigan/.

Quinn, Brendan. "A Team, a Teammate and Michigan Basketball's Mighty Assist." *The Athletic*. January 22, 2018. theathletic.com/218614/2018/01/22/a-team-a-teammate-and-michigan-basketballs-mighty-assist/.

Quinn, Brendan. "Then Dawud Said to Dave…: A Favor for the Abdur-Rahkmans and the Friendship that Followed." *The Athletic*. February 21, 2018. theathletic.com/248010/2018/02/21/then-dawud-said-to-dave-a-favor-for-the-abdur-rahkmans-and-the-friendship-that-followed/.

Quinn, Brendan. "This is John Beilein." MLive.com. November 12, 2014. https://www.mlive.com/john-beilein/.

Quinn, Brendan. "24 Hours inside Michigan Basketball: Behind the Scenes at Maui Invitational." *The Athletic*. November 22, 2017. theathletic.com/162870/2017/11/22/24-hours-inside-michigan-basketball-behind-the-scenes-at-maui-invitational/.

Quinn, Brendan. "The (Unexpected) Story of Michigan's Freshman Class." *The Athletic*. December 3, 2017. theathletic.com/172903/2017/12/03/michigan-wolverines-freshman-class-jordan-poole-eli-brooks-isaiah-livers-john-beilein/.

Quinn, Brendan. "What Slump? Duncan Robinson and the Psychology of Makes vs. Misses." *The Athletic*. January 9, 2018. theathletic.com/207087/2018/01/09/what-slump-duncan-robinson-and-the-psychology-of-makes-vs-misses/.

Quinn, Brendan. "What You Don't See in Jaaron Simmons' Very Strange Journey." *The Athletic*. March 17, 2018. theathletic.com/277051/2018/03/16/what-you-dont-see-in-jaaron-simmons-very-strange-journey/.

Quinn, Brendan. "What's up with Charles Matthews?" *The Athletic*. February 25, 2018. theathletic.com/252682/2018/02/25/whats-up-with-charles-matthews/.

Quinn, Brendan. "When Moe Wagner Met Michigan: How Chance, a Film Clip and an Email Changed Everything." MLive.com. March 16, 2017. mlive.com/wolverines/index.ssf/2017/03/when_moe_wagner_met_michigan_t.html.

Quinn, Brendan. "You Don't Know Jordan Poole." *The Athletic*. March 22, 2018. theathletic.com/283370/2018/03/22/you-dont-know-jordan-poole/.

Rothstein, Michael. "Novak, Douglass Lead Revival." ESPN.com. February 24, 2012. www.espn.com/colleges/michigan/basketball/story/_/id/7609316/zack-novak-stu-douglass-foundation-michigan-wolverines-revival.

Rowland, Kyle. "Story of Michigan's Austin Hatch Remains an All-Time Account of Perseverance." *The Toledo Blade*. March 21, 2018. www.toledoblade.com/College/2018/03/21/Austin-Hatch-story-remains-an-all-time-account-of-perseverance.html.

"Saddi Washington at Michigan Media Day." YouTube Video, 4:39. Posted by "UM Hoops.com," October 22, 2018. https://www.youtube.com/watch?v=IoAh1QEOS6s.

Sears, Ethan. "John Beilein has been an assistant coach." *The Michigan Daily*. December 7, 2018. https://www.michigandaily.com/section/mens-basketball/john-beilein-assistant-coach.

Sears, Ethan. "Jon Teske and what it takes to stay on the floor." *The Michigan Daily*. February 22, 2019. https://www.michigandaily.com/section/mens-basketball/jon-teske-and-what-it-takes-stay-floor.

Seidel, Jeff. "Duncan Robinson's Defense Put to Test in Sweet 16." *Detroit Free Press*. March 22, 2018. www.freep.com/story/sports/columnists/jeff-seidel/2018/03/22/michigan-wolverines-basketball-duncan-robinson/447644002/.

Seidel, Jeff. "'Reprogrammed' Charles Matthews helped put Michigan in Final Four." *Detroit Free Press*. March 27, 2018. https://www.freep.com/story/sports/columnists/jeff-seidel/2018/03/27/michigan-basketball-charles-matthews-transformation-final-four/459896002/.

Shaw, Zach. "Charles Matthews Winding Road Leads to Bliss in Los Angeles." 247sports.com. March 26, 2018. 247sports.com/Article/Charles-Matthews-winding-road-leads-to-bliss-in-Los-Angeles-for-Michigan-basketball-in-the-NCAA-Tournament-116720209.

Shaw, Zach. "No love, no problem: Michigan's Brazdeikis fueled by fan hate." 247sports.com. March 4, 2019. https://247sports.com/college/michigan/Article/No-love-no-problem-Michigan-basketballs-Ignas-Brazdeikis-fueled-by-fan-hate-129704140/.

Shaw, Zach. "Once more, Michigan's revamped defense saves the day." 247sports.com. March 25, 2018. https://247sports.com/college/michigan/Article/Once-more-Michigan-basketballs-revamped-defense-saves-the-day-as-Wolverines-make-Final-Four-116664660/.

Shaw, Zach. "Out of second chances, Michigan hungry to put it all together." 247sports.com. March 21, 2019. https://247sports.com/Article/Out-of-second-chances-Michigan-basketball-hungry-to-put-it-all-together-in-the-NCAA-Tournament-130336627/.

Snyder, Mark. "Michigan's Jon Sanderson, John Beilein Development Boosts NBA Interest." *Detroit Free Press*. March 21, 2017. www.freep.com/story/sports/college/university-michigan/wolverines/2017/03/21/michigan-wolverines-basketball-jon-sanderson-john-beilein-nba-draft/99426592/.

Snyder, Mark. "'White collar' Michigan defense struggles in 85–69 loss to Illinois." *Detroit Free Press*. January 11, 2017. https://www.freep.com/story/sports/college/university-michigan/wolverines/2017/01/11/michigan-wolverines-illinois-fighting-illini/96476912/.

Trudell, Mike. "Pelinka Reacts to L.A.'s 2018 Draft." NBA.com. June 21, 2018. https://www.nba.com/lakers/news/180621-pelinka-reacts-to-la-2018-draft.

Tucker, Cole. "East Lansing's Brandon Johns dreams of playing at Breslin … in maize and blue." *Lansing State Journal.* January 11, 2018. https://www.lansingstatejournal.com/story/sports/2018/01/11/brandon-johns-east-lansing-michigan-wolverines-basketball/1018347001/.

"UNC Michigan Coby White postgame interview." YouTube Video, 3:30. Posted by "Tar Heel Illustrated." November 28, 2018, https://www.youtube.com/watch?v=fOW19BENmpY.

Vailliencourt, Andrew. "Michigan Basketball: Jordan Poole's Big Day Leads Michigan To Win Over IU." TheWolverine.com. December 2, 2017. https://michigan.rivals.com/news/michigan-basketball-jordan-poole-s-big-day-leads-michigan-to-win-over-iu.

"Video: John Beilein, Zavier Simpson and Charles Matthews recap win at Villanova." Umhoops.com, November 14, 2018. https://umhoops.com/2018/11/14/video-john-beilein-zavier-simpson-charles-matthews-recap-win-villanova/.

Wagner, Moe. "Still Alive." *The Players' Tribune.* March 23, 2017. https://www.theplayerstribune.com/en-us/articles/moritz-wagner-michigan-basketball-airplane.

Wagner, Moe. "Thank You, Michigan." *The Players' Tribune.* April 14, 2018. https://www.theplayerstribune.com/en-us/articles/moe-wagner-thank-you-michigan.

"Web Exclusive: Inside Michigan Basketball—NCAA Championship Game." Mgoblue.com, 5:33. April 3, 2018. mgoblue.com/watch/?Archive=12231&sport=7&type=Archive.

"Web Exclusive: Inside Michigan Basketball—NCAA Semifinal." Mgoblue.com, 7:27. April 1, 2018. mgoblue.com/watch/?Archive=12216&sport=7&type=Archive.

Webb, Sam. "Former Michigan Assistant has Seen Major Changes in Beilein." 247sports.com. March 30, 2018. https://247sports.com/college/michigan/Article/John-Mahoney-assisted-John-Beilein-during-his-first-three-years-at-Michigan-and-has-noticed-his-former-boss-adapting-with-the-times-116856224/.

Webb, Sam. "Michigan B1G's Top Performing Bball Program; Recruits Noticing?" 247sports.com. May 25, 2018. 247sports.com/college/michigan/Article/Over-the-last-six-seasons-no-program-in-the-Big-Ten-can-match-Michigans-on-court-and-draft-success-118513723/.

Wenzel, Matt. "John Beilein didn't take long to decide on leaving for Cavs, opportunity 'too difficult to pass up.'" MLive.com. May 15, 2019. https://www.mlive.com/sports/2019/05/john-beilein-didnt-take-long-to-decide-on-leaving-for-cavs-opportunity-too-difficult-to-pass-up.html.

Wetzel, Dan. "Michigan's John Beilein a descendant of soldiers that inspired 'Saving Private Ryan.'" *Yahoo! Sports.* April 2, 2013. https://sports.yahoo.com/news/ncaab—michigan-s-john-beilein-a-descendant-of-soldiers-that-inspired—saving-private-ryan—205604686.html.

Whitesall, Amy. "Inside Athletics: On the Recruiting Trail." *Michigan Alumnus.* 2013. alumnus.alumni.umich.edu/inside-athletics-on-the-recruiting-trail/.

Windsor, Shawn. "Michigan basketball looks like title contender after routing UNC." *Detroit Free Press.* November 29, 2018. https://www.freep.com/story/sports/columnists/shawn-windsor/2018/11/29/michigan-basketball-title-shot/2145344002/.

Windsor, Shawn. "U-M's Beilein a teacher looking to learn new ideas." *Detroit Free Press.* October 3, 2015. https://www.freep.com/story/sports/college/university-michigan-wolverines/2015/10/03/michigan-wolverines-john-beilein-teacher/73270532/.

Wojnarowski, Adrian. "David Griffin." *The Woj Pod.* Podcast Audio. April 4, 2018. https://art19.com/shows/thewojpod/episodes/e4455054-9488-41ca-9a8e-fd209139cbba.

Wojnowski, Bob. "Michigan's huge win changes (almost) everything." *The Detroit News.* January 13, 2018. https://www.detroitnews.com/story/sports/columnists/bob-wojnowski/2018/01/13/wojo-ums-rivalry-win-changes-almost-everything/109433676/.

Wojnowski, Bob. "Plenty of clues foretold John Beilein's exit at Michigan." *The Detroit News.* May 13, 2019. https://www.detroitnews.com/story/sports/columnists/bob-wojnowski/2019/05/13/wojo-like-not-john-beileins-turn-test-nba/1189826001/.

Wolfe, Ethan. "Michigan erases 15-point deficit, earns 78–69 overtime win over Bruins." *The Michigan Daily*. December 9, 2017. https://www.michigandaily.com/section/mens-basketball/michigan-ucla-offense-defense.

"Zavier Simpson talks first practice." YouTube Video, 2:52. Posted by "UM Hoops.com," September 25, 2018. https://www.youtube.com/watch?v=smaicHiF-IQ.

Zuke, Ryan. "Michigan Basketball's Newest Team Member Is 12, and He's Living the Dream." MLive.com. November 7, 2017. www.mlive.com/wolverines/index.ssf/2017/11/12-year-old_with_serious_illne.html.

Index

Abdur-Rahkman, Dawud 50, 91, 109
Abdur-Rahkman, Muhammad Ali 7, 57, 63, 67, 79, 81–83, 88, 92, 95–97, 99, 102–105, 107–111, 113–115, 118–122, 125–126, 130–132, 135, 137, 141, 166, 175; recruitment 50; stoic demeanor 90–91, 95
Adams, Jamal 53
Adel, Deng 67
Akoh, Jamar 193
Albrecht, Spike 25–26, 32–33, 44, 59, 61
Alexander, Bacari 18, 60, 79, 83
Allen, KeVaughn 197
Allen, Ray 1
Altman, Dana 67
Altman, Koby 207
Amaker, Tommy 16
analytics 10–11, 62, 93, 173–174, 192, 203
Angelo State University 201
Angola, Braian 119
Anlauf, Brad 44
Arizona State University 14
The Athletic 3, 11, 70, 73, 77, 87

Baird, C.J. 118–120, 127, 203–204
Ball, Lonzo 81
Bamba, Mo 83
Barley, Darrell 17
Barnes, Rick 45
Barron, Patrick 120–122, 193, 198
Bartelstein, Josh 18–19, 32, 34
BartTorvik.com 3, 29, 111, 192, 204; win probability 33, 45
Basketball Strength and Conditioning: Above the Rim with Camp Sanderson 37
Bates-Diop, Keita 80, 100–101

Baumgardner, Nick 3, 11, 19, 29
Beard, Chris 201
Beilein, Art 6
Beilein, John: attending the draft 39, 49, 135; awards/milestones 9, 141, 172, 207, 210; building a program 17–19; ejection at Penn State 176; embracing adversity 38, 63, 65; end of season perspective 34, 69, 133; ethics and integrity 1–2, 8–9, 12, 209; evolution 11, 60, 74–75, 166–167, 173–175, 210; fundamentals 7, 10, 36, 112, 122; heart surgery 138–140; offensive system 9–11, 23, 136; preparation 31–32, 115–116, 177–178; as a teacher 7–9, 11, 74, 210; teaching shooting 24, 36–37, 173–174; upbringing 6–7; using date of birth to project 26, 35, 79–80; valuing relationships 73, 105; "we had subs" 29
Beilein, Josephine 6
Beilein, Patrick 7–8, 38
Bell, Jordan 68
Bielfeldt, Max 55
Big Ten Tournament 5–6, 21, 29, 43, 57–58, 63–65, 103–111, 187–191
Bird, Larry 127
Black, Leaky 147–148
Blackmon, James 51
Blanchard, LaVell 2
blowing kisses 42, 184
Boeheim, Jim 31
Bohannon, Jordan 104, 187
Booth, Phil 129, 142
Boston Celtics 205
Boston College 1–2
Brady, Tom 62

245

Brazdeikis, Ignas 140, 142–149, 159, 164, 166–167, 170–171, 178, 180–181, 187–191, 194–196, 199, 202–203; arrival 137–138; departure 205; friendship with Stauskas 137–138, 156, 184; maturity/background 138–139, 153–154; success on the road 142–144, 155–157, 183–184
Brazdeikis, Sigitas 153–154
Breslin Center 19, 42, 86–90, 179, 185–186
Bridges, Mikal 129, 131
Bridges, Miles 87–88, 94, 107, 179
Brockport State 8
Brooklyn Nets 61
Brooks, Eli 72, 77–78, 82–83, 96, 120, 142, 147, 156, 187, 196–197, 202
Brooks, Garrison 146–147
Brunson, Jalen 129–131
Brust, Ben 42, 163
Buntin, Bill 13
Burke, Trey 2, 20–22, 25, 28–34, 38–39, 47, 49, 56, 77, 102, 137, 145, 171, 194; the block 33, 171; the shot 29–30
Butler University 60, 73

Calipari, John 46
Campredon, Marc-Gregor 37, 68, 106, 109–110, 149, 151, 163, 170, 177, 189–190
Canisius College 8, 31, 208
Canton Charge 135
Carter, Ben 107
Castleton, Colin 138, 167, 182, 198, 202
CBS 81, 101, 105, 110, 198, 202
Central Michigan University 77
Chaminade University 77
Chatman, Kameron 57–58, 61, 83
Chicago 13, 52, 83, 95, 153, 156, 187–191
Clarke, Brandon 177
Clemson University 17
Cleveland Cavaliers 1, 135, 207–209
Cofer, Phil 120–121
Coffey, Amir 178
Cole, Abby 99, 136
College of the Holy Cross 141
Collins, Chris 72, 156
Cook, Brian 19, 74
Cook, Tyler 97
Coppin State University 54
core values 18–19, 22, 34, 69, 124–125, 128, 132–133, 140, 166–167
Corprew, Deshawn 202
Cosby-Roundtree, Dhamir 143
Cousy, Bob 1
Cowan, Anthony 90, 184

Crawford, Jamal 2
Crisler Center 13, 15, 20, 41, 43, 61–62, 81, 95, 99, 146–148, 164, 169–171, 182–183
culture 6, 18–19, 23, 28, 35, 94, 105, 122–123, 132–133, 140, 166–168, 207
Culver, Jarrett 201–203
Curry, Eric 164
Custer, Clayton 126

Dakich, Andrew 36
Dakich, Dan 8, 36
Davis, Austin 61, 118, 120, 137, 159
Davis, Devin 114–115
Davis, Seth 101
Dawkins, Aubrey 61
DeCuire, Travis 194
DeJulius, David 138, 167
Delaney, Jim 79
Detroit 5, 13, 18, 83, 138
Detroit Free Press 3, 11, 37
The Detroit News 3
Detroit Pistons 1, 5, 13, 136, 139, 208
development 2, 7, 20, 23–26, 35–38, 51, 61–62, 70–72, 84, 97–98, 122, 129, 134–140, 150–152, 174–175, 197, 207–210
Dieng, Gorgui 32
DiVincenzo, Dante 129–132
Donlon, Billy 11, 60–64, 72–73, 97, 140, 156
Donnal, Mark 5, 44, 55–56
Dorsey, Tyler 68
Douglass, Stu 17–22, 26, 43, 166, 179
Doyle, Ricky 55, 61
Driesell, Lefty 183
Duke University 2, 15, 17, 20, 26, 35, 40, 163, 185, 192
Durham, Al 159, 165

Eastern Michigan University 49
Edwards, Carsen 85, 148–149
Edwards, Vince 86, 92
Eisley, Howard 2
Ellerbe, Brian 16
Ennis, Dylan 68
Erie Community College 7–8, 50, 176
ESPN 16, 21, 148, 182, 185
European trips 18–19, 139–140
evaluation 2, 23–27, 35, 50–52, 55–56, 79–80
Evans, Jawun 65–66

The Fab Five 15–16, 28, 204
Falls, Timmy 194

Index

Faulds, Jaron 167
FBI Investigation 16, 67, 165, 208–209
Fernando, Bruno 178, 184
Final Four 15, 31–35, 121–133, 207
Finneran, Bill 143
Fisher, Steve 14–16
Florida State University 119–122, 124, 201
Frieder, Bill 14
Fuller, Bryan 21, 25, 30, 41, 43–44, 54, 127

Gansey, Mike 8, 208
Gard, Greg 163
Garland, Darius 209
Garza, Luka 172, 189
The George Washington University 144
Gillespie, Collin 142–143
Ginobli, Manu 155
Glass, Eric 135
Goins, Kenny 180, 186
Golden State Warriors 206
Gonzaga University 177, 201, 204
Gordon, Aaron 41
Gosz, Jim 80
Gray, Rob 113–115
Green, Devonte 159
Green, Draymond 19
Greer, Ryan 155
Griffin, Blake 17
Griffin, David 9, 11, 35
Groce, John 26, 56
growth mindset 2, 100, 138, 188

Haarns, Matt 149, 151
Haas, Isaac 63, 86, 92, 108, 110, 128, 151
Hancock, Luke 33–34
Hansen, Aiden 75
Happ, Ethan 64, 96, 164, 175, 177
Hardaway, Tim, Jr. 2, 7, 19–22, 25–26, 29–30, 38–39, 49, 72, 102, 145
Harden, Greg 62
Harlan, Kevin 197
Harris, Gary 42
Harris, Manny 17
Harrison, Aaron 46–47
Hatch, Austin 51–54, 99–100, 136, 207
Hatch, Stephen 52
Hawkins, James 3
Hayes, Kevarrius 195–196, 198
Haynes, DeAndre 73–74, 77, 79, 83, 85, 109, 122, 136, 174, 200
Hayward, Gordon 25
Hazzard, Rasheed 53
Herber, Johannes 17, 55

Hibbitts, Brent 58, 101
Higgins, Sean 15
Hill, Grant 15, 111, 127–128
Hinton, Jalyn 177
Holiday, Aaron 81–82
Holtmann, Chris 80, 100, 169, 171–172
Horford, Jon 26, 44, 46, 49
Howard, Desmond 62
Howard, Juwan 15–16, 209
Hudson, Jalen 195, 197–198
Huerter, Kevin 90
Hunter, Eric, Jr. 151
Hurley, Bobby 15

Illinois State University 73–74
Iowa State University 14, 40
Irvin, Zak 5, 40, 44, 56–57, 59, 61, 63–69, 94, 97
Iverson, Allen 1
Izzo, Tom 89, 107, 138, 179–180, 186, 191

Jackson, Jaren 87–88, 108, 179
Jackson, Ray 15
Jacksonville University 177
Jeter, Derek 90
Johns, Brandon 138, 160, 167
Johnson, Elijah 29
Johnson, Gus 89, 142
Johnson, Jaylen 67
Johnson, Keyontae 195
Johnson, Magic 134–135
Johnson, Vinnie 101
Jordan, Lavall 18, 60, 73

Kahn, Andrew 3
Kahraman, Yenal 55
Kalscheur, Gabe 164
Kennedy, Billy 119
Kenpom.com 3, 10–11, 42, 44, 60, 73, 102, 111, 157, 183, 204
Kent State University 74, 77, 195
Kimble, Keith 186
King, Jimmy 15
Kithier, Thomas 185, 190
Knight, Bob 36, 201
Koenig, Bronson 64
Kohl Center 42, 163–164
Kornacki, Steve 3, 50, 52
Koumadje, Christ 119
Kriener, Ryan 172
Krutwig, Cameron 125–127

Laettner, Christian 15
Langford, Josh 179

Langford, Romeo 158–160, 166
Larkin, Barry 31
Law, Vic 155–156
Leaf, T.J. 81
LeDee, Jaedon 171
Le Moyne College 8, 31, 129
Leonard, Kawhi 24
Levert, Caris 25–26, 33, 37, 40, 42, 44–45, 47, 49, 51, 56–57, 59, 61
Lindsey, Scottie 95
Little, Nassir 146–147
Livers, Isaiah 37, 72, 79, 84–85, 87, 90, 96, 101, 106, 115, 120, 125–126, 137–138, 142–143, 146, 151, 154, 160, 167, 171, 175, 178, 182, 185, 187–191, 196–197, 206
Locke, Noah 195–196
Longhorn Network 45
Los Angeles Lakers 134–135
Louisiana State University 77, 81, 84, 208
Loyer, Foster 138, 185
Loyola University Chicago 91, 124–128, 166

Madison Square Garden 1, 61, 103–111, 151, 205
Maker, Mike 51
Maker, Thon 153
Mann, Terrance 119
Manuel, Kendal 193
Manuel, Warde 12, 136
Marist College 51
Marquette University 61
Martin, Ed 16
Martin, Frank 161–162
Matthews, Charles 35, 61, 70, 72, 77–79, 85–86, 104–106, 112–114, 125–126, 130–131, 136, 142–149, 155, 170, 175, 178, 180, 182, 185, 187–188, 192–194, 203–206; coping with grandmother's death 81–84; game-winner vs. Minnesota 164; late-season slump 95, 101–102; leadership 140, 143–144, 176, 183, 196, 198–199; Most Outstanding Player at West Regional 118–122; shutdown defense 97, 158–160, 166, 178
Matthews, Charles (father) 183
Matthews, Nichole 183
Maui Invitational 20, 77–78, 82, 85
Maye, Luke 146
McConnell, Cole 44
McCormick, Tim 9, 38
McDonald's All-Americans 24, 46, 136, 146

McGary, Mitch 25–26, 30–32, 38–42, 48–49
McGee, Jaquan 73
McGregor, Conor 154
McIntosh, Bryant 95
McKillop, Bob 174
McMurry University 201
McQuaid, Matt 180–182, 189–191
McRae, Jordan 45
McRoberts, Zach 159
meditation 38, 153, 174–175, 205
Merritt, David 36
Meyer, Jeff 18, 73
Mgoblog.com 3, 74, 161
Mgoblue.com 3
Miami Heat 135, 209
Michigan Daily 3
Michigan State University 19–20, 28, 42–43, 62, 85, 87–90, 105–108, 138, 178–182, 184–186, 189–193, 196–197, 204
Miller, Archie 159, 165–166
Miller, Reggie 118
Miller, Sean 165, 208
Mills, Terry 14, 111
Milwaukee Bucks 70
Mincy, Jordan 195
Minnesota Timberwolves 49
Mitchell, Donovan 66–67
MLive.com 3
Mooney, Matt 201, 203
Moretti, Davide 201–203
Morgan, Jordan 18, 24–25, 29, 42–47, 49–50, 166, 209; drawing charges 32, 45–46; engineering degree 43, 46, 49
Morgan, Juwan 158–159
Morgan, Maverick 61, 63
Morris, Darius 18–20, 77
Morsell, Darryl 183
Morton, John 132
Mourning, Alonzo 1
Muller, Dan 73–74
Murphy, Jordan 163, 178, 190
Murray, Jamal 153

Nance, Larry, Jr. 209
Nantz, Jim 111, 127–128
Napier, Shabazz 72
Narrish, Bob 7
National Championship Game 15, 32–34, 129–133
National Transportation Safety Board 5
Nazareth College 8
NBA draft: decision-making process 38–39, 48–49, 70–71, 134–136, 204–206;

drafting of Michigan players 20, 39, 49, 70, 134–135, 205–206
NCAA Tournament 13–17, 20–21, 29–34, 44–47, 58–59, 65–69, 112–133, 192–206
Nembhard, Andrew 196–197
New Jersey Institute of Technology 49
New York Knicks 13, 39, 205
Newfane, NY 7
Nichols, Darris 195
Niland, Tommy, Jr. 8
Niland brothers 6–7
Norfolk State University 141
Northwestern University 49, 57, 72, 93, 95, 155–157, 162–163
Novak, Zack 17–22, 26, 166
Nowitzki, Dirk 89
Nunez, Adrian 138

Oakland University 60–61
Obama, Barack 49
Obiagu, Ike 119
Odiase, Norense 203
O'Donnell, Kevin 52
Oglesby, Terry 186
Oguine, Michael 193
Ohio State University 20–21, 28, 43, 71, 80–81, 83–84, 99–101, 169–172
Ohio University 21, 26, 72, 80, 99–101
Oklahoma City Thunder 49
Oklahoma State University 65–66, 85, 162
Olah, Alex 57
Olajuwon, Hakeem 127
Orangeville Prep 153–154
Orr, Johnny 13–14, 40, 172
Osman, Cedi 209
Oturu, Daniel 178, 200
Owens, Tariq 201, 203

Painter, Matt 108 109, 150
Pardon, Dererk 155
Parrish, Gary 36
Paschall, Eric 129, 131, 144, 154
Pelinka, Rob 134
Penn State University 28, 101, 158, 176, 195
Pitino, Richard 176, 188
Pitino, Rick 32, 66–67
Pittsnogle, Kevin 8, 17, 55
plane crash 5–6, 63–65, 69, 75
The Players' Tribune 115–116, 134
Poole, Anthony 182
Poole, Jordan 72, 85, 90, 102–103, 111, 113, 117–118, 120, 123, 125, 137, 140, 142–145, 147–150, 154–156, 170–171, 175–176, 185–189, 191, 193–197, 201–202, 204–206; buzzer beaters 112, 115–116; instant offense 78, 100–101, 126, 130, 159–160; late-season slump 166, 181–182; recruitment 79–80
Poole, Monet 79
Pridgett, Sayeed 194
Prout, Larry, Jr. 75
Providence College 144–145
Purdue University 6, 56, 58, 61, 63, 85–87, 92, 95–96, 108–110, 148–151, 176, 185–186, 188

Quinn, Brendan 3, 50, 55, 77, 182

Raftery, Bill 111, 127–128
recruiting 9, 23–26, 35, 50–51, 55, 79–80, 91, 129, 137–139, 183
Rice, Glen 14–15, 132
Robinson, Duncan 56–58, 64, 66, 68, 75–77, 79, 81, 84, 87–88, 91–92, 96, 99, 102–104, 107, 109, 113–114, 116, 118, 126–127, 132, 135, 137, 141, 166–167, 175; defensive improvement 93–94, 97–98, 101, 105, 121; recruitment 51
Robinson, Glenn, III 25–26, 29, 33, 38–39, 42, 44–46, 48, 72, 145
Robinson, Rumeal 1, 14–15
Rooney, Dave 50, 90–91
Rorie, Ahmaad 194
Rose, Jalen 15–16, 91
Rothstein, Michael 17
Russell, Cazzie 13, 22
Rutgers University 55, 76, 91–92, 172, 175
Ryan, Bo 173

Sacramento Kings 49
St. John's University 201
Samuels, Jermaine 143
San Diego State University 113
Sanderson, Jon 11, 37–38, 40, 51, 55, 65, 70, 107, 121, 123, 137–138, 154, 182, 198
Saving Private Ryan 6
Schembechler, Bo 14–15, 63, 111
Schlissel, Mark 9, 38
Seton Hall University 15, 132
Sexton, Collin 209
Shaw, Zach 4
Shulman, Dan 148
Simmons, Jaaron 36, 72, 77–78, 80, 96–97, 99, 112–113, 120, 135–136
Simpson, Lamont 186
Simpson, Quincey 83, 136–137, 160
Simpson, Zavier 6, 61, 71–72, 88–90, 95,

97, 99–100, 102, 104–110, 112–114, 117–118, 120–122, 125–126, 130–131, 136–137, 142–144, 146–150, 155–156, 175–176, 180–181, 185–191, 194–200, 202, 205–206; battling adversity 77–78, 82–85; defense and leadership 94, 105, 139–140, 151–152, 166–167, 205; hook shot 159–160, 183–184; synergy with Teske 160–163; triple-double 169–172
Sims, DeShawn 17
Sister Jean 124
Siva, Peyton 32–33
Skiles, Scott 89
Smart, Shaka 29, 83
Smith, Jalen 178
Smith, J.R. 101
Smith, Justin 159
Smith, Russ 32
Snow, Brian 35
Sonnenberg, Gary 73
South Dakota State University 29
Southerland, James 32
Southern Methodist University 56, 61
Spellman, Omari 129–131
Stamper, Courtney 75–76
Stamper, Jude 75–76, 91
Stanford University 42
Starks, T.J. 117
Stauskas, Nik 25–28, 30–31, 34, 37, 40–44, 46–49, 56, 102, 138, 156, 184; not just a shooter 27, 31, 40
Stevens, Brad 11, 209
Stokes, Jarnell 45
Strack, Dave 13
Sullinger, Jared 20–21
Swanigan, Caleb 63
Syracuse University 31–32, 45, 107, 117, 163
Szczerbiak, Wally 51

Tarczewski, Kaleb 41
TBS 118
Team IMPACT 75
Teske, Jon 61, 83–84, 88, 97, 102–104, 106, 112, 114, 120, 125, 137–138, 142, 144–145, 147–149, 155–156, 171–172, 175, 180–181, 183–186, 189, 191, 193–196, 202–203, 205–206; defending without fouling 177–178; synergy with Simpson 160–163; transformation 108, 110, 150–152, 205
Texas A&M University 9, 117–119
Texas Tech University 201–204
Thomas, Mary 81–83

Thompson, Klay 24
Tillman, Xavier 179–180, 186, 189–191
Tomjanovich, Rudy 13–14, 22, 24, 91
Triche, Brandon 32
Turgeon, Mark 90, 176, 183–184
247Sports.com 3

Umhoops.com 3, 164
Underwood, Brad 85, 162
Union Neuchatel 135
United States Air Force Academy 201
University of Alaska Anchorage 14
University of Arizona 41–42, 165, 208
University of Arkansas at Little Rock 201
University of California, Los Angeles 13, 17, 81–84
University of California, Riverside 78
University of Connecticut 47, 56, 72
University of Dayton 165
University of Detroit Mercy 60, 83–84
University of Florida 9, 31, 49, 194–199, 206
University of Houston 72, 113–116, 189, 206
University of Illinois 6, 15, 26, 43, 56, 61–63, 84–85, 160, 162, 175, 187
University of Indiana 14, 28–29, 42–43, 51, 57, 79–81, 158–160, 165–166
University of Iowa 84, 97, 103–104, 172, 187, 189
University of Kansas 29, 47, 183
University of Kentucky 35, 46–47, 61, 72, 102, 204
University of Louisville 32–34, 66–67, 71, 130
University of Maryland 90–91, 102, 115, 176–178, 183–184
University of Minnesota 6, 21, 64, 94–95, 163–164, 176–178, 188–190, 200
University of Montana 112–113, 193–194
University of Nebraska 91, 103–105, 182–183
University of North Carolina 15, 78–79, 81, 84, 117, 146–149, 153, 185
University of North Carolina at Charlotte 40, 58
University of North Florida 77
University of Notre Dame 58–59
University of Oklahoma 17
University of Oregon 67–69, 71, 97
University of Richmond 8, 208
University of Rochester 129
University of South Carolina 61, 161–162, 164

Index

University of South Dakota 201
University of Southern Mississippi 77
University of Tennessee 20, 45–46, 201
University of Tennessee at Chattanooga 146
University of Texas 10, 45–46, 81, 83, 146
University of Tulsa 58
University of Virginia 163, 204
University of Wisconsin 6, 42, 64, 95–97, 163–164, 172–173, 175

Van Gundy, Jeff 8
Vaught, Loy 14
Vecenie, Sam 206
Vergiels, Bobb 21
verticality 176–178
"The Victors" 8, 76, 82, 91, 133, 160, 197
Villanova University 129–133, 142–144, 153–154, 166
Virginia Commonwealth University 29–30, 78, 83
Virginia Tech 61
Vitale, Dick 148

Wade, Will 208
Wagner, Beate 110
Wagner, Moe 5–6, 37, 58, 62–63, 66–68, 75, 78–79, 81–86, 88–91, 95–96, 101, 103–111, 113–120, 122, 125–128, 130–132, 137, 141, 144, 154, 166, 179; junior year improvements 97, 134–135; recruitment 54–56; returning to school 70–71
Walton, Derrick 5, 40, 42, 44, 46–47, 51, 56–59, 61–69, 71, 74, 77, 80, 94, 135, 138, 167
Ward, Nick 55, 88–89, 106–108, 179, 189–190
Washington, Saadi 60–61, 90, 96, 113, 124–125, 132–133, 137, 139–140, 150–151, 207
Watson, Ibi 61, 79, 115, 118, 120, 122

Webb, Sam 4
Webber, Chris 15–16
Welsh, Thomas 81
Wesson, Andre 170–171
Wesson, Kaleb 169–171
West Virginia University 8–9, 31, 38, 51, 55, 195, 208
Western Michigan University 175
Wheeler, Jamari 176
Wheeling College 7
White, Coby 146–148
White, Mike 194–195, 199
Wichita State University 46
Wiggins, Aaron 184
Williams, Gary 183
Williams, Kenny 146
Williams, Roy 146
Williams College 51
Williamson, Zion 192
Wilson, D.J. 61, 63–64, 66–68, 70, 137, 160
Winston, Cassius 72, 89, 105–107, 179–182, 185–186, 189–191
Wofford College 44–45
Wojnarowski, Adrian 1, 35
Wooden, John 7, 13, 207; "Keys to Life" Award 207; Player of the Year Award 33, 38, 129
Woods, Keyshawn 170
Woodson, Charles 44
Wright, Jay 129, 142, 144

Xavier University 56

Yaklich, Luke 11, 78, 93–94, 97–98, 102–103, 121–122, 124–125, 128, 131, 134, 138, 150, 155, 161, 173, 176, 180, 192, 198; hiring process 73–74
Yost Field House 13, 171
Young, Kevin 30

Zeller, Cody 29
Zizic, Ante 209

www.ingramcontent.com/pod-product-compliance
Ingram Content Group UK Ltd.
Pitfield, Milton Keynes, MK11 3LW, UK
UKHW041936140426
5217IPUK00014B/507